Fishing in New South Wales

EXPLORE AUSTRALIA

Contents

How to Use This Book

The page illustrated shows a typical fishing area and explains the various features of text and maps

name of fishing area described

type of fishing – coastal or inland

region name

NEW SOUTH WALES

COASTAL FISHING PORT MACQUARIE REGION

type of fishing to be found in area

main fish caught in area

Port Macquarie

Type of fishing
beach, offshore, rock, wall

Target fish
bream, luderick, mulloway, rock blackfish

location map appears when there is more than one map for the area

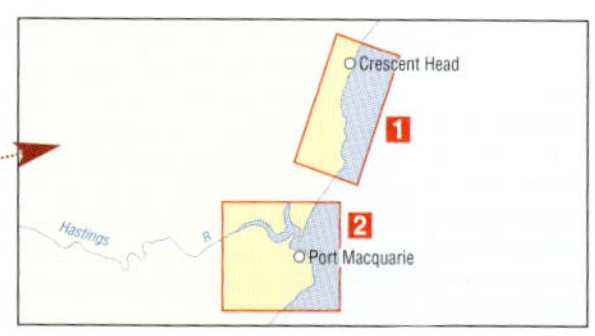

Fishing boats at Port Macquarie where the waters provide excellent fishing over autumn and winter

The excellent beach and rock fishing continues down this section of coast, and Port Macquarie – a historic town founded as a convict settlement – is one of New South Wales' most popular holiday resorts, offering a wonderful variety of fishing.

subheading generally relates to map titles in the case of more than one map for the area

CRESCENT HEAD TO QUEENS HEAD

The area from Racecourse Head to Queens Head is dotted with many safe rock fishing spots. Tailor from 1 to 3 kg are common, and rock blackfish are a regular catch in the washes. Bream, luderick, drummer and mulloway are around in good numbers. The best fishing is in autumn and winter.

Racecourse Head allows fishing into a gutter at the end of the beach for flathead and whiting, as well as rock blackfish and luderick behind the reef in rough waters. Similar conditions exist on **Racecourse Island**, which can be waded to at low tide. **Big Hill Point** has rugged rock formations above reefs and gutters. Two favourite bream and mulloway spots are **The Arch**, accessible at low tides, and **The Stairs**, reached by following a narrow path.

rock

The beach to the north of **Point Plomer** is sheltered in a southerly and is excellent for bream. The north side of the point is easy to fish for tailor, bream, luderick, rock blackfish, mulloway and groper. On the seaward side, fishing is for tailor off the point, and luderick and bream in the gutters. The beach on the southern side has good gutters for bream and whiting.

Barrys Bay is ideal for inshore fishing from a boat, and anglers can cast for the prime target fish caught here – Spanish mackerel, cobia and longtail tuna.

Neverfail is two rocky spurs surrounded by gutters, and is accessible in all but the biggest seas for luderick and rock blackfish close in, and bream, tailor and mulloway further out. **Queens Head** is the place for rock blackfish and luderick specialists.

PORT MACQUARIE

Of the ocean stretches near Port Macquarie, **North Beach** is just one area renowned for wonderful whiting catches on beach worm in summer, and tailor on pilchards, garfish or lures in winter.

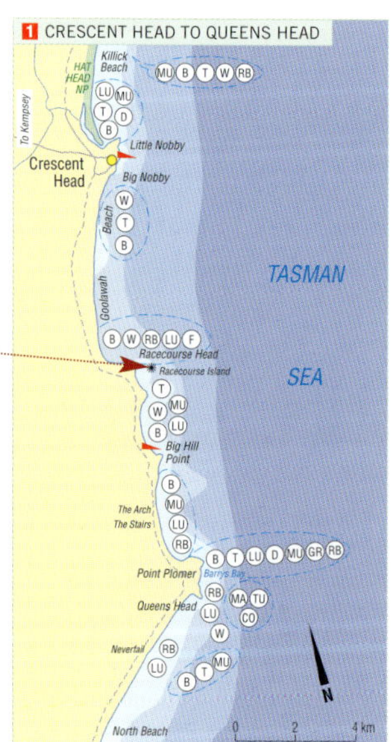

route destination

The **Hastings River** estuary provides great sport for whiting, flounder, flathead, bream and mulloway, and the weed-eating luderick, with some big tailor near the entrance in the winter.

Luderick are along the deeper banks and around the weed beds throughout the system. The best bait for them is either weed (available from local bait shops) or pink nippers, which are plentiful on the sandbanks.

The most popular fishing, however, is drifting for flathead and whiting along the

84

GUIDE TO LOCAL FISH

	Crescent Head to Queens Head	Port Macquarie
B bream	•	•
CO cobia	•	
DO dolphin fish		•
D drummer, silver	•	•
F flathead	•	•
FL flounder		•
GR groper	•	
KI kingfish, yellowtail		•
LU luderick	•	•
MA mackerel	•	
ML marlin		•
MO morwong		•
M mullet		•
MU mulloway	•	•
RB rock blackfish	•	•
SH shark		•
S snapper		•
T tailor	•	•
TU tuna	•	•
WH wahoo		•
W whiting	•	•

Guide to Local Fish lists species appearing on the maps; fish mentioned in the text but located off the maps are listed in the regional Guide to Local Fish

map corresponds to numbered area on location map

boat ramp

oyster lease

warning indicator

COASTAL FISHING PORT MACQUARIE REGION   NEW SOUTH WALES

cluster of fish, indicating species to be found within the area designated by dashed line

pier/jetty/wharf/breakwater

visitor information centre

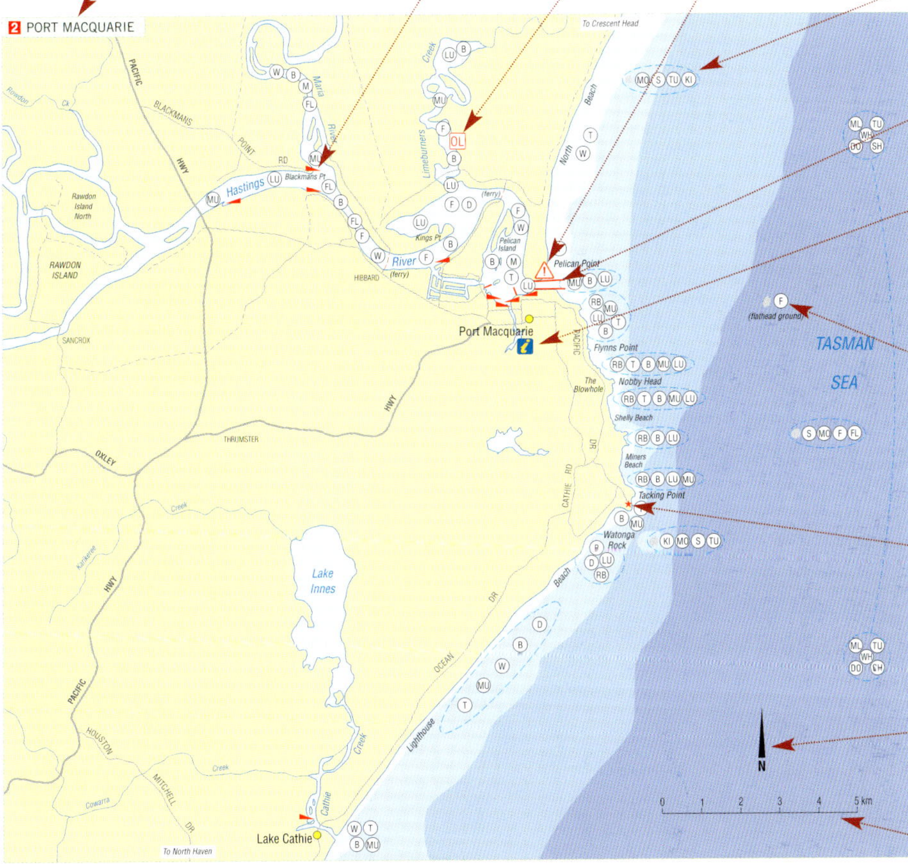

fish symbol, identified in Guide to Local Fish on adjoining page

lighthouse

north point

scale bar

channels and drop-offs, and over weed beds, with nippers or pilchards as bait. There are also bream, mulloway and mullet throughout the system.

Most of the mulloway are taken by fishing from the training walls at the entrance to the river with live mullet or luderick as bait, as they are the food the mulloway are naturally seeking in the area. These mulloway are big fish, requiring 20-kg line or more, with a beach rod and a big side cast or overhead reel to manage hooked fish in the tough terrain.

As the river swings north and then south inside the entrance, the water is mostly bream, flathead and whiting territory, with luderick along the banks. **Limeburners Creek** has oyster leases in the area close to its junction with the river. In the channels of the creek are big flathead, with bream in the upper reaches. In the Hastings River, the biggest mulloway are often found further upstream in deep water, past the confluence with the **Maria River**.

The rock and beach areas on the southern side of the town are convenient, offering tailor, rock blackfish, luderick, mulloway and bream. A good rock spot, though dangerous in big seas is **The Blowhole. Shelly Beach** offers excellent beach fishing.

Reefs north and south of Port Macquarie hold a good quotient of bottom and surface fish. Snapper is the prime target on the inshore reefs, taken by drifting baits down a berley stream. Straight in front of the town, from 5 to 7 km out, is a very big flathead ground. Off Shelly Beach, some 4 to 6 km, is a large area of rubble and reef attracting snapper, morwong, flathead and other reef fish.

Blue water game fishing off Port Macquarie is a growing sport, with the boats working out to areas 100 fathoms deep and more. Summer targets are marlin, wahoo, dolphin fish, yellowfin tuna and shark, and winter and early spring bring big catches of mako shark. Makos are known for their tremendous leaps from the water when hooked.

The entrance to Port Macquarie can be dangerous, particularly on a run-out tide when strong north winds are blowing. Boats can launch from Shelly Beach, or from Big Hill Point or Crescent Head for more northern offshore grounds.

85

maps are a guide only and show fishing information for the area but must not be used for marine navigation; such information is available from published hydrographic charts and visiting anglers should always check local information centres for danger spots and sand weather warnings

bold type indicates a fishing spot

HOW TO FISH

Estuary and Bay Fishing

Half of Australia's estimated four million anglers fish in estuaries and bays, because they offer easy access to a variety of fish in safety and comfort, and a range of locations and habitats. You can fish from the shore, or a small boat, and once you are aware of available fishing spots, best baits and local techniques, you should enjoy success.

Estuary and bay anglers fish from land, from land-based structures such as piers, wharves, jetties and bridges, or from boats. Estuaries exist in bays, inlets, lakes, lagoons and tidal rivers, wherever fresh water meets salt, resulting in brackish water. Many fish spend their entire lives in the estuary, but it is also a spawning ground, nursery and feeding area for fish from the open ocean or the lower reaches of freshwater rivers and streams.

WHEN TO FISH

Most fish inhabiting estuaries and bays feed at dawn and dusk; their behaviour is also strongly influenced by tides. For the angler, forward planning is important and should include: deciding on the species you are trying to catch, collecting bait, preparing berley, setting suitable tackle, and considering the effect that tide and time of day will have on where you fish.

Dawn and dusk feeders, such as bream, flathead, whiting, snapper and mulloway, will feed in the shallows in low light, but are inclined to seek safer depths during the day, especially in busy waterways. City anglers who cannot get away to fish during the day mid-week can use this dawn and dusk routine to advantage. Mullet, leatherjacket and luderick are less demanding about time of day, but still their behaviour is influenced by the tides.

Fish are habitual creatures with seasonal cycles of spawning and forage migrations, and certain habitat preferences. In temperate climes, for example, snapper, hairtail, luderick, mullet and bream move in and out of the sheltered waters of bays and estuaries according to season and locality. Generally, fishing is best during the warmer months, from September through to April, sometimes May. During winter many estuary dwellers move out of the estuaries to deeper offshore waters, returning in spring to spawn. In the tropics, species like barramundi, trevally, threadfin salmon and mangrove jack also move according to season and locality. However, the seasons in this region are predominantly the Wet and the Dry. During the Wet, which starts around November and lasts through to March or April, there are fish to be caught, but the Dry season is more conducive to fishing the northern estuaries.

WHERE TO FISH

Fish within estuaries and bays tend to base their lives around structures – whether artificial, like wharves, bridges, rock walls, oyster leases and buoys, or natural ones, like weed beds, gutters, channels, points and holes. Such places provide the fish with a reference point, with food and with relative safety. You will do much better fishing these areas than those that are featureless.

Sand or mudflats that are exposed at low tide are excellent areas to explore when the tide is rising. In southern estuaries, whiting, bream and flathead will search for food there, and trevally, shark and even barramundi will hunt through the shallows feeding on bait fish, attracted by the food sources on the flats. The best fishing occurs on flats that have a deep channel or gutter running alongside. A good flat will have around one metre or more of water over it at high tide.

In many bays and estuaries, you can fish quite effectively from shoreline features such as river banks, beaches and rocky points, or from structures such as piers or breakwalls. Such access becomes more difficult the further north you go; in the

A boat is usually necessary to fish Australia's northern estuaries

FISHING FETISHES

Knowing some basic rules about fish behaviour will help you to put your bait in the right place in the bay or estuary.

Fish face upstream or into the tidal flow in order to breathe more easily. This position also allows them to see their prey as they await the flow of food towards them.

Fish save energy by lurking just off the main current flow. Here they can hold position and grab food as it swirls past. They may also find shelter behind a rock or log, still close to the current.

Fish are attracted to structures such as rocks, logs, islands and trees, and to channels and shelving drop-offs, as they provide shelter.

Fish avoid shallow, clear water in daylight hours to protect themselves from the sun and animal predators – and anglers!

Fish use the tide to bring them food or allow them access to food-rich areas such as weed patches, encrusted pylons and yabby banks that are above water at low tide.

mangrove-lined estuaries of the far north, a boat is almost essential.

Piers – wharves, jetties, call them what you will – are usually more common in bays and lakes, but are also found in some rivers. In many estuarine rivers, however, breakwalls do much the same job, providing deepwater access for land-based angling. Bridges also are often good spots, provided that fishing is allowed from them.

Wherever you fish from the shore, you need to take into account your lack of mobility. Choose places where the fish have some reason to gather, or at least have to pass by. It also helps if you incorporate some form of berleying into your strategy, to attract passing fish or to encourage those already resident to feed.

The keys to successful land-based fishing are to be prepared, have the right tackle and bait for the species you are after, and work the tides so you are there at the same time as the fish.

BAIT

Fish tend to favour the food items commonly found in whatever habitat they are in, so when fishing in estuaries and bays, as elsewhere, locally available baits are often the best choice. To ease the pressure on bait stocks, especially near cities and towns, only gather as much bait as you need for immediate use.

A type of burrowing shrimp found in southern estuaries, variously called 'yabby',

Piers often provide deepwater access for land-based angling

BAY AND ESTUARY FISH

Fish	States
barracouta	Vic., Tas., SA, WA, Qld
barramundi	WA, NT, Qld
bream, black	NSW, Vic., Tas., SA, WA
bream, pikey	NT, Qld
bream, yellowfin	NSW, Vic., Qld
catfish, blue	NSW, Qld
catfish, eel-tailed	NSW, Vic., Qld
catfish, estuary	NSW, SA, WA
catfish, fork-tailed	WA, Qld
cod, estuary	WA, NT, Qld
elephant fish	NSW, Vic., Tas., SA
fingermark	NSW, Vic., Tas., Qld
flathead, dusky	NSW, Vic., Qld
flathead, sand	NSW, Vic., Tas., SA, WA
flounder, bay	NSW, Vic., Tas., SA, WA
garfish	NSW, Vic., Tas., SA, WA, Qld
garfish, northern	WA, NT, Qld
hairtail	NSW, WA, Qld
jack, mangrove	NSW, WA, NT, Qld
jewfish, black	WA, NT, Qld
kingfish, yellowtail	NSW, Vic., Tas., SA, WA, Qld
leatherjacket	NSW, Vic., Tas., SA, WA, Qld
ling, rock	NSW, Vic., Tas., SA, WA
luderick	NSW, Vic., Tas., Qld
mackerel, horse	NSW, Vic., SA, WA, Qld
mullet, flat-tail	NSW, Vic., SA, WA
mullet, sand	NSW, SA, WA, Qld
mullet, sea	All States and NT
mulloway	NSW, Vic., SA, WA, Qld
perch, estuary	NSW, Vic., Tas., SA
pike, long-finned	NSW, Vic., Tas., SA, WA
queenfish	WA, NT, Qld
salmon, Atlantic	Tas.
salmon, Australian	NSW, Vic., Tas., SA, WA
salmon, threadfin	WA, NT, Qld
snapper	NSW, Vic., SA, WA, Qld
snook	NSW, Vic., Tas., SA, WA
tailor	NSW, Vic., Tas., SA, WA, Qld
tarwhine	NSW, Vic., Tas., SA, WA, Qld
trevally, bigeye	NSW, WA, NT, Qld
trevally, giant	NSW, WA, NT, Qld
trevally, golden	WA, NT, Qld
trevally, gold-spotted	WA, NT, Qld
trevally, sand	Vic., Tas., SA, WA
trevally, silver	NSW, Vic., Tas., SA, WA, Qld
whiting, King George	NSW, Vic., Tas., SA, WA
whiting, sand	NSW, Vic., Tas., Qld
whiting, trumpeter	NSW, WA, NT, Qld
whiting, yellow-finned	SA, WA

'bass yabby' or 'pink nipper', lives in tidal sand flats and can be gathered with a suction pump. Similar 'green nippers' found in more northern regions can be 'puddled' by treading shallow weed beds and scooping them from the surface, or found under rocks and logs exposed by a falling tide. Bloodworms and squirt worms can be dug or pumped, using a bait pump, from exposed tidal flats. Prawns, shrimp, small fish and squid are good baits, as are cockles, oysters and mussels.

Other useful baits for estuary species include the various whitebaits, pilchards and bluebaits. They are best for flathead, though large flathead prefer tiny live mullet caught in a small bait trap. Baits of fresh striped tuna and squid are also effective and chicken gut is very popular for bream in Queensland.

You do not need bait for all species of fish. Many will attack lures, and tackle shops can often advise which lures work best on the fish in their locality.

WORKING THE TIDES

Estuary anglers must allow for the reversal every six hours of tidal flow, and alter their fishing spots accordingly. The most productive ends of reefs, structures, channels and gutters reverse with the tide. The sea entrance to an estuary is a good place to fish on a running tide, as fish passing from the estuary to the sea, or vice versa, must use this corridor.

As the tide falls, small fish, prawns and crabs leave the shelter of sand flats, weed areas and mangrove roots, and return to the channels, where the larger fish are waiting for them. A selected bait, cast into a channel at the right time, is likely to be grabbed by a fish expecting to feed. The main areas to fish at low tide are around structures, gutters and drop-offs, with the deepest holes carrying the best fish. Predatory fish such as flathead face the run of the tide, lurking around the edges of sandbars, gutters and channels waiting for smaller fish, prawns and food scraps to be drawn towards them.

At high tide the small fish, prawns and shellfish spread out, and the larger fish go after them and also the worms, crabs and other types of food that live around the flats and mangrove banks. This expands the range of fishing but makes it harder to pinpoint the spots where the fish are feeding. Structures, holes and gutters still exist and should remain the target.

Some fish break the rules and stay close to shelter behind structures and often close to overhanging banks or mangrove stands. Mangrove jack, for example, has to be sought in these sheltered spots.

Tides have less effect in the middle of an estuary or bay as the movement of water is not so strong.

Make sure you have a current tide chart for your area. The chart times relate to certain major points such as a port or headland. Work out the time variation of high and low tides between the places you normally fish and those named on the chart, and plan your trips around the tides.

One strategy is to gather bait at low tide and begin to fish along the channel edges and drop-offs as the tide rises and the water floods out of the channels. Equally, you could time your fishing to just before high tide, and fish the edges of the channels and drop-offs as the water recedes and the small creatures begin to be drawn back into the channels. In very shallow estuaries you must time your departure to avoid being left high and dry on a sandbank!

TARGET FISH

Nationally, the six most common estuary species are bream, flathead, mullet, mulloway, snapper and whiting. Others, such as barramundi, estuary perch, flounder, garfish, hairtail, mangrove jack, tailor and trevally, are important on a regional or seasonal basis.

Bream are likely to be found almost anywhere in an estuary or bay, but prefer areas offering a structure and shelter. The three main species are black bream, yellowfin bream and pikey bream. Unlike most other estuarine species, bream stay in the estuary over winter and, rather than migrating offshore, they move up the estuary to where fresh water meets salt and spawn there.

Flathead come in more than a dozen forms, but three commonly encountered species are sand flathead, a widespread inshore species; dusky flathead, the most common species in temperate estuaries kind; and tiger flathead, a heavily built version common in southern bays. In estuaries, flathead favour the edges of sandbanks, scattered patches of weed and any place where the current is deflected into eddies. In bays, they congregate where tidal flows meet, and offshore, they gather in depths around 40 m – wherever currents combine to form food lanes.

Mullet are one of the most widespread families of fish in Australia, one species or another appearing in the estuaries and bays of every state. Common types include: sea mullet, fantail (silver), yelloweye, flat-tail, tiger, diamond-scale, pop-eye and sand mullet (lano, tallegalane). Of these, the most easily line-caught types are the sand, yelloweye and tiger mullets. While others can be sometimes line-caught, they are more commonly netted by professionals.

Fishing from breakwalls is effective

Tuna and kingfish are the target at the Merimbula Wharf

Some of the **mulloway** (jewfish) found in bays and estuaries are residents, others are only occasional visitors. They frequent areas around bridges, points, holes and creek mouths, where they hunt or ambush their favoured foods of small fish, prawns or squid. Live or dead baits of these are effective, as are large minnow-style lures. Mulloway are found in estuaries at any time of the year, their whereabouts being dependent on the presence of prawns, squid and schools of pilchard, mullet and whitebait on which they feed.

Juvenile **snapper** live in temperate bays and estuaries along the east coast of New South Wales and Queensland, while adult fish spend much of their time around offshore reefs. Periodically, however, big fish

do move into sheltered waters, usually in spring and summer, and are reasonably easy to catch. In summer, numbers of large adults are also found in Port Phillip and Western Port, in Victoria, and Gulf St Vincent and Spencer Gulf in South Australia.

There are some eight common species of **whiting**; of these the best known are the trumpeter and sand whiting of the eastern seaboard (a trumpter species is also found in Western Australia), the yellow-finned whiting of Western Australia and South Australia, and the King George whiting, plentiful in South Australia and Victoria, but less abundant in New South Wales, Tasmania and Western Australia. Whiting are a warm weather fish and leave estuaries in winter.

Barramundi and **mangrove jack** often co-exist in mangrove-lined tidal creeks, frequenting the intersections of main and feeder streams, as well as rocky points on bays and inshore islands.

Garfish are a common catch in estuaries and bays and, if you do not mind the small

Mullet

Mullet, of which there are many species, are found in estuaries and bays Australia wide. The sea mullet is mainly estuarine, moving out to sea to spawn.

bones, are delicious food. They are even better as bait for larger fish. They can be berleyed up with bread or pollard and caught on tiny baits of uncooked prawn, fish flesh or bread dough. Use a light line attached to a slender float and small long-shanked hooks.

Leatherjacket are delicious to eat and easy to catch in good numbers once you have found their hiding places. These include deep water underneath jetties and alongside weed beds, and quiet corners of bays over mixed rock, weed and sand bottoms. Bait up with small baits on long-shanked hooks and periodically toss in a small handful of berley to keep them on the go.

Luderick mainly inhabit the east coast of New South Wales, Victoria and northern Tasmania. The adult fish are residents of the wash areas fronting ocean rocks. Luderick also spend much of their lives inside estuaries, bays and coastal lakes. Here, as juveniles up to about 30 cm, they stay and grow until ready for their run to the sea to spawn. After spawning migrations, some of them re-enter their home estuaries, others remain along the coastal shoreline or find new estuaries to call home. They take baits of green weed, sea-lettuce, squirt worms and pink nippers, and are usually best fished with a long flexible rod, light line and a float.

Tailor are common through New South Wales and southern Queensland, rare along the continent's southern coast, but in good numbers from the south to mid-coast of Western Australia. Known as the 'poor man's game fish', they are related to the bluefish of America, which grow to over 15 kg, but Australian tailor are usually under 2 kg. Most estuary tailor, known as 'choppers', are less than half that, but despite their size, they attack bait schools ferociously and will readily take either baits or lures.

Trevally frequent many estuaries, the silver variety being common in temperate zones, and species such as giant, golden, gold-spotted and bigeye usually found further north. Most trevally will take lures; all will take baits of small fish. Silvers will also take various worms, crustaceans and shellfish. Larger trevally are usually caught offshore.

Occasionally, but mainly in spring and summer, big, fast, ocean fish like **tuna** and **yellowtail kingfish** come into bays and large estuaries chasing schools of bait fish that are flushed in and out by warming waters and big tides. They can be a bit of a handful for beginners, being difficult to hook and even harder to land. Be aware that they exist, or you may wonder what kind of bream can rip 100 m of line off a reel – and then break free – all in a matter of seconds!

In the tropical north, estuaries can yield **pikey bream**, **barramundi**, **threadfin salmon**, **mangrove jack**, several types of **trevally**, **black jewfish (mulloway)**, **estuary cod** and **fingermark**. The list is longer, but these are the species you will most likely target and encounter. Lures are readily taken by all these species, but they also like to eat small live fish or large live prawns, so these make excellent baits. Because of the generally greater tidal range in the tropics, a tide chart is indispensable if you expect to catch anything worthwhile. Also the nature of tropical estuaries and creeks is such that you may find them easier to fish on the smaller neap tides than the much larger spring tides, which can scatter fish up into the mangrove forests where they become too hard to reach.

WORKING THE BAIT

Rather than casting your bait into the water and waiting passively for a bite, you will catch more fish if you have a more searching and aggressive approach.

Think about your casting spot: a shrimp sent towards a piece of sunken timber will be in a place where shrimps are numerous; a pilchard will look more normal 'swimming' along the edge of a gutter than lying inactive on the bottom.

Think about the way your bait will move. All marine creatures move; your bait should be lightly weighted so that it moves naturally in the currents of the water and at the depth appropriate for it. Sending a bomb weight to the deep will not attract many takers. Fish do not expect to see pieces of food, prawns or small fish coming towards them against the current. Your bait should look as if it is moving with the forces of the water.

Hold the rod so that you can feel the bite.

Rock and Beach Fishing

Land-based saltwater fishing offers anglers the opportunity to roam and seek out a special place, often in remote and beautiful surroundings, perhaps to have a private battle with wind, wave and water or to enjoy the camaraderie of other experts. The fishing can range from a gentle beach activity to the challenge of ocean-ravaged rocks and cliffs.

The vast ocean shoreline of Australia affords land-based anglers great opportunities. Rocky ledges and headlands all along the coast are interspersed with long stretches of beach, often away from population centres and providing a fishing paradise for anglers.

Most capital cities in Australia are within easy reach of ocean beaches, readily accessed by two-wheel-drive vehicles. Visiting anglers can have a rod in the water within an hour or two of leaving home, and be back in time to provide the catch of the day for the evening meal. This book directs you to the best spots to fish within easy reach of your capital city.

For the more intrepid angler there are beaches in remote parts of the country, particularly in the west, north and north-east of Australia. A four-wheel-drive will often be required to reach these places that are 'off the beaten track'.

Rock fishing should always be approached with care. Some of the rocky platforms that front deep ocean water are exciting places to fish, but also demand that anglers exercise good sense and caution. When fishing from rocks at sea level, most of the threat comes from the water itself. Large waves can mount the rocks and wash the unwary in, and natural growths of weed and algae can make surfaces extremely slippery underfoot.

The dangers of high-cliff fishing are obvious. There are also hidden traps, such as sandstone ledges that can be worn treacherously thin by erosion and weakened by saltwater absorption. You need to approach any climb-in spots with particular caution. There are injuries and fatalities each year among anglers who have been careless or inexperienced.

WHEN TO FISH

When fishing this 'edge of Australia', the tides come into play in a marked way. Low water can virtually obliterate holes and gutters on a beach, sending fish out to deeper water. On the rocks, low tide can create a stretch of broken rock between you and the water into which you want to cast. High tides can improve the fishing opportunities or wipe them out – it all depends on the terrain and the weather.

Channels and gutters form around wrecks providing productive fishing areas

By intelligently using tide charts and some knowledge of local terrain, you can prepare fishing plans that use the tides to best effect, and place you within safe and comfortable casting distance of fish that have been moved about by the changing water levels. An understanding of the feeding habits of your target species can help you focus your efforts on those times and places when the fish are likely to be in the greatest numbers.

The time of year is another important factor. The fishing from beach and rocks along the east coast of Australia is best from November to May. This period coincides with the warmer Pacific currents moving closer to shore, bringing with them the rich plankton, the bait fish and the larger fish that chase the bait schools. The further north you go the more extensive the fishing season becomes. The Great Barrier Reef protects the inshore waters and fish are present and active all year round, only being affected by the wet season.

The west coast is exposed to the big Indian Ocean swells. Here, pelagics such as

Time, tide, weather and terrain affect the success and safety of the rock angler

mackerel, tuna and shark can be taken all year round. The intense heat of summer can be very difficult for the angler north of Geraldton and Shark Bay, but plenty of fish are still present.

South from Perth, across the Bight to South Australia and into Victoria, the rock fishing is not as good, but there is excellent surf fishing in the cooler months for such species as tailor, Australian salmon, mulloway and gummy shark.

ROCK FISHING

Fish do not live in an environmental vacuum. They gather in places where it is easy, safe and productive to feed. These places relate to the underwater shape of the seabed. It is not always possible to see these bottom features clearly as the surging water off ocean rocks is often roiled and opaque.

Holes and gutters, and inshore reefs, which break the force of the surging water, attract and hold fish around the rocks. They allow fish to use eddies and back currents to keep their position near food. Rock crevices,

ROCK FISHING SAFETY

When you are rock fishing it is important to have a sure footing and to be constantly aware of your surroundings. A larger-than-normal wave can throw you off balance. Once you are off a ledge and in the sea, rescue can be difficult. It is wise to have an emergency procedure agreed between a fishing group so that equipment is at hand and there is no time lost if someone goes in.

Non-slip shoes and comfortable, waterproof clothing that is easy to remove if you go into the water, are part of the rock-hopper's gear.

Many high cliffs are of sandstone with overhangs that can be weakened by centuries of erosion and absorption of salt water. Never stand on thin ledges that overhang the cliff face, and be careful of wind gusts that could push you off balance.

If you are fishing close to the sea always keep an eye on the tide, waves and weather, as the pattern of waves can change quickly and a large wave can wash you into the water. Many victims were experienced anglers who had grown used to their location and become complacent about safety. If the safety rules are observed, cliff and rock fishing is basically a safe sport and a thrilling one.

ROCK AND BEACH FISH

Fish	States
barracouta	NSW, Vic., Tas., SA, WA
barracuda	WA, NT, Qld
barramundi	WA, NT, Qld
bonito	NSW, WA, Qld
bream, black	NSW, Vic., Tas., SA, WA, Qld
bream, pikey	WA, NT, Qld
bream, yellowfin	NSW, WA, Qld
cobia	NSW, WA, NT, Qld
cod, black	NSW
cod, coral	WA, NT, Qld
dart, swallowtail	NSW, Vic., SA, WA, Qld
drummer, silver	NSW, Vic., Tas., SA, WA
fingermark	WA, NT, Qld
flathead, dusky	NSW, Qld
flathead, sand	NSW, Vic., Tas., SA, WA, Qld
garfish	NSW, Vic., Tas., SA, WA, NT, Qld
groper	NSW, Tas., SA, WA, NT, Qld
gurnard	NSW, Vic., Tas., WA, Qld
jewfish, black	WA, NT, Qld
kingfish, yellowtail	NSW, Vic., Tas., SA, WA, Qld
ling	NSW, Vic., Tas., SA, WA
luderick	NSW, Vic., Tas., Qld
mackerel, grey	NSW, WA, NT, Qld
mackerel, school	NSW, WA, NT, Qld
mackerel, Spanish	NSW, WA, NT, Qld
mackerel, spotted	NSW, WA, NT, Qld
mullet, sea	NSW, Vic., Tas., SA, WA, NT, Qld
mullet, yelloweye	NSW, Vic., Tas., SA, WA
mulloway	NSW, Vic., SA, WA, Qld
parrotfish	NSW, Tas., WA, NT, Qld
pike, long-finned	NSW, Vic., Tas., SA, WA
queenfish	WA, NT, Qld
salmon, Australian	NSW, Vic., Tas., SA, WA
salmon, threadfin	WA, NT, Qld
shark, gummy	NSW, Vic., Tas., SA, WA
shark, school	NSW, Vic., Tas., SA, WA
shark, whaler	NSW, Vic., Tas., SA, WA, Qld
shark, white*	NSW, Vic., Tas., SA, WA
snapper	NSW, Vic., Tas., SA, WA, Qld
snook	NSW, Vic., Tas., SA, WA
sweep	NSW, Vic., Tas., SA, WA
tailor	NSW, Vic., Tas., SA, WA, Qld
trevally, bigeye	NSW, WA, NT, Qld
trevally, giant	NSW, WA, NT, Qld
trevally, golden	WA, NT, Qld
trevally, silver	NSW, Vic., Tas., SA, WA, Qld
tuna, mackerel	NSW, WA, NT, Qld
tuna, northern bluefin	NSW, WA, NT, Qld
tuna, southern bluefin	NSW, Vic., Tas., SA, WA
tuna, yellowfin	NSW, Vic., Tas., SA, WA, NT, Qld
whiting, King George	NSW, Vic., Tas., SA, WA
whiting, sand	NSW, Vic., Tas., Qld
whiting, trumpeter	NSW, Qld

*Denotes protected species

READING THE BEACH

The most important element in beach fishing is being able to 'read' the beach and understand the undersea formations that make fish gather in search of food. Waves on an ocean beach will scour channels and make holes, gutters, sandbars and spits, creating natural places for feeding and predation.

Surf anglers take time to study a beach at low tide to see the patterns of the exposed sands and reefs, and again at high tide to look for the feeding places indicated by changes in colour and the movement of the waves. Swelling, unbroken waves indicate deeper water, while those that curl over and break indicate shallows. Rips or run-outs create gutters, which are detectable by short, choppy waves and the movement of white water out to sea.

Channels are the main arterial roads of the undersea system. They are deep water formations parallel to the beach, often extending well past the shoreline. Gutters are the minor roads, which fish use to travel between channels, into holes or shallow waters near the beach. The banks of the channels are the drop-offs where the predators wait, out of the main wave action, for their food. Sandbars and flats are indicated by breaking waves and foaming water that spread across them, sweeping small fish and food items into the drop-off areas. Holes can be identified by darker green or blue water, and in the way the wave formation is interrupted.

Regulars always check their favourite beach to see the changes that time and weather have wrought since their last visit. In rough weather tonnes of sand can be moved around in a few hours. A high vantage point, polaroids and binoculars are good aids in reading the beach, as the best time for reconnaissance is when the sun is high and the scene is not distorted by shadows.

Tailor is one of the main targets for beach anglers

stands of kelp and weed, and the foamy blanket of white water provide places to hide from predators. Small fish, including yellowtail, garfish and sweep, tend to school quite close to the rocks, but usually at some depth. Larger foraging species, such as bream, blackfish, drummer and groper, skirt the rock face and work in close under the line of white water. More active fish, like snapper, yellowtail kingfish, tailor and Australian salmon, roam a little further out, calling in to the shoreline to make feeding raids or to get away from larger predators. The big surface fish of the summer months, such as longtail and yellowfin tuna, shark and even marlin, will also move in close to the rocks in season, but spend most of their time in clear open water, travelling from one patch of concentrated food to another. Mulloway (jewfish), on the other hand, tend to keep close to particular reefs, caves and gutters, usually venturing out on hunting sprees at first or last light, or during the hours of darkness.

Basically there are two types of rock fishing practised around Australia. The first could be called baitfishing for species for the table. In southern Australia these species include parrotfish, sweep and pike, and further north along the New South Wales coast, luderick, rock blackfish, drummer, groper and even snapper are the more common catches.

The other method of rock fishing practised is often referred to as land-based game fishing, and ranges from high-speed spinning for tuna to various live-bait fishing techniques for species such as tuna, yellowtail kingfish, mackerel, giant trevally and even marlin. The species just depends on where you are fishing – Quobba on the west coast or the Pulpit on the east coast.

Your tackle should be appropriate for the fish and the conditions. It is helpful if rods are around 3 m or more. Your line should be a little heavier than that used in sheltered waters, both to withstand the punishment of the terrain, and also to control the fish, which will often be larger than those found in estuaries.

There will be times when your rod and line will not be strong enough to land some fish and, in these instances, a gaff on a suitably long pole is a practical fishing tool. Anglers fishing from high cliffs are faced with unique problems in landing fish, and they may need to use a grapnel or flying gaff to secure their played-out fish and hoist it up.

BEACH FISHING

In the same way that fish are attracted to depth and rock areas, and feed most freely around such features, they are selective and at least partly predictable in their use of various seabed structures when they visit ocean beaches.

There are differences, however, between the productive fishing areas around rocks and those around beaches. Rocky terrain may include gradually shallowing bottom shapes, steeply rising bomboras or even cliff-like rock walls; whatever form it takes, it remains a more or less permanent feature of that locality. In the case of beaches, however, the

operative fish-attracting features are anything but permanent, often changing from week to week, or in heavy weather, being altered completely in a matter of hours.

This means that on any given day, it is likely you will have to check the beach before fishing it to see what changes have occurred. In periods of stable weather, or in seas that are somewhat sheltered, formations may persist for a long time, only being worn away gradually by water movement. On more exposed beaches (which often fish better), the changes can be sudden and dramatic, and the unobservant angler is likely to pay by catching few fish or none at all.

Australia's classic deep beaches extend from Fraser Island on the east coast, south to Victoria, across the Bight then north along the coast of Western Australia to Shark Bay. North of Fraser Island and Shark Bay, the beaches become much shallower.

Beaches are not natural habitats for fish, but are more like highways and feeding places through which the fish pass. In the tideline areas there is an abundance of marine life. There may be channels, gutters, drop-offs and banks close inshore as well as further out. The tideline and close-in areas are the likely spots for foraging fish such as whiting, luderick and bream, while the gutters and holes are popular places of concealment for predators such as mulloway, salmon, tailor and flathead.

Gutters inside offshore sandbanks are excellent for whiting and bream, as the wave action over the bank dislodges amounts of sand and the food within it to the foraging fish. Whiting will surf with a wave over a sandbank and into a gutter to seek this sort of food.

Tailor, bream, flathead and salmon are very common beach fish and tend to inhabit the midline between the inshore waters and the outer gutters. Mulloway favour the deeper channels and holes, and are mostly night feeders, while shark and stingray can be encountered at any time, but also have their peak activity at night.

Beach fishing tackle, suitable for tailor, Australian salmon, bream and whiting, usually consists of a 3 to 3.5-m rod, and a reel of your choice spooled with 4 to 8-kg line. If targeting larger fish, such as mulloway or gummy shark, or fishing close to the rocky corners at either end of a beach, you may need heavier tackle or at least a trace of heavier line for insurance. These rocky corners are often good for bream, tailor, flathead or whiting, but also sometimes provide bonuses, such as rock blackfish, trevally and snapper, if you can fish close enough to the rock shelves running into deeper water.

BAIT

In many cases, the best baits available will be lying buried beneath the sand you are standing on – baits such as beachworms, sand crabs, or the ubiquitous shellfish known in various locales as pipis, eugaries or cockles. Other excellent beach baits include bait fish, such as pilchards, whitebait and bluebait and strip baits of fish such as tuna, squid and mussels.

Often, if you arrive at low tide, or the last of the run-out, you can gather your bait from the beach before you start to fish. The intertidal area inhabited by these sand dwellers is then freshly exposed and they are still close to the surface.

Be aware of the vulnerability of the stocks of these intertidal creatures, and observe any bag limits or prohibitions that may apply to a particular area. Such regulations are not there just to inconvenience you; they are part of an overall management system to protect the resource – for your benefit and that of other anglers.

Watch the water when rock fishing at sea level

TARGET FISH

Around the southern perimeter of Australia, beach species include bream, whiting, flathead, tailor, Australian salmon and mulloway, as well as various rays, skates and shark. From the rocks, you can add groper, drummer, rock blackfish, luderick, snapper, yellowtail kingfish and mackerel, and occasional visitors such as trevally, sweetlip, cobia, sailfish, marlin and yellowfin tuna, as well as various other surface speedsters such as bonito and striped and mackerel tuna.

THE BITE

This is the most exciting or frustrating part of the day, depending on your skill and luck. Some fish seem to catch themselves, some get away from even the most expert strike. While fishing, hold your finger on the line so that you can feel any bites. Keep the line slack so that you give the fish a chance to move with the bait. Most fish take the bait with an intake of water and then expel the water. The fish that does this hooks itself unless it senses trouble (a tight line or a tug) and expels the lot.

Once you feel you have a fish, lift the rod tip smartly (but not wildly) or give a steady pull on a handline (to set the hook). If you are in whiting territory do not waste time, as they are one-hit feeders and need to be hooked instantly.

Offshore Fishing

Many boat anglers enjoy the adventure and variety of the ocean waters beyond the shore. Fishing around reefs and rocks, or over gravel beds, sand or mud; fishing the bottom with a heavy sinker and hooks on droppers; fishing with unweighted baits; drifting; trolling or fishing from an anchored position – all are options for the offshore angler.

Broadly, offshore fishing in Australia encompasses trolling for game and sportfish, bottom fishing with bait, jigging lures for reef-dwelling species or lure casting for sportfish around structures such as bomboras, reefs and washes. The size of the boat will depend on the seas likely to be encountered.

Most offshore fishing is done in proximity to land, near reefs, islands or the mainland shore itself. However, there is also good fishing to be had in more open water, where the influence of the structure of the seabed may not be so evident, but where the food-rich ocean currents play the major role in attracting offshore pelagic fish.

OFFSHORE SAFETY

Fishing in the open sea, no matter how close to shore, demands attention to boat equipment. You need to have life jackets for all on board, a reliable motor, flares for attracting attention, and enough anchor rope or chain and ground tackle to anchor in water up to 60 m deep. You should always inform a responsible person of your fishing plans.

Caution is imperative when fishing around reefs, bomboras and exposed rocks, as waves can rise up and break from an apparently flat sea, or surge suddenly and push boats around – at worst onto rocks or coral. It is wise to keep the engine running in potentially dangerous situations, so that the boat can be instantly manoeuvred should trouble threaten. In calm water it is sometimes possible to anchor to a bombora, and then drift your baits and berley back into the eddy area behind the structure.

READING THE WATER

Inshore, around shallow reefs, headlands and islands, it is easy to recognise areas where fish might be gathered, but out in open water, it is different. Fish will be spread over a wide area and their whereabouts must be gauged by guesswork and intuition. Atmospheric conditions, such as light levels, wind and barometric pressure, and factors such as the clarity, turbulence, temperature and oxygen content of the water – all have an influence on fish presence and behaviour, and all of these can affect the availability of food and the fish's willingness to bite. It is also important that you consider the prevailing conditions when deciding which baits and lures to use, and how to go about presenting them.

Islands can be viewed as enlarged structures, providing an ideal habitat for many fish species

The colour of the water indicates temperature changes: warm water appears to be bluish, and colder water has a greener tinge. However, just how warm or cold the water is depends on where you are. Off Bermagui (south coast of New South Wales), a water temperature of 21° Celsius might be considered warm, but off Townsville (north coast of Queensland) it would be regarded as a cold snap.

General light levels and the angle at which light falls on the water can also affect fish distribution and the willingness of fish to bite. Many species of fish prefer to feed under the cover of darkness, or at least at half light. Some fish that would not go anywhere near shallow water during the day, can be attracted by the half light of dawn or dusk, or the darkness of night to move into water barely deep enough to cover them, provided the pickings are rich enough to warrant the trouble. Others, in particular the pelagics like tuna and marlin, seem not to be affected by light.

The roughness of the sea not only determines your ability to venture offshore, it also affects general fish behaviour. A moderate degree of wind and wave action is beneficial to fishing, as the associated white water and wind chop allows fish to move about with reduced risk from predators.

Turbulence can also stimulate feeding, as there is often more to eat at such times. Wave action tears food loose from reefs and rock ledges. Prey species are driven by currents and wind into concentrations, providing an easily harvested food supply. Broken water also offers another prompt to fish activity: the ruptured surface film of the water allows higher than normal levels of oxygen from the atmosphere to be absorbed by the water. This boost in oxygen content both encourages and enables fish to maintain higher levels of sustained effort.

Fish that have a high metabolic rate feed almost constantly, and have a correspondingly high level of oxygen demand. Many surface-feeding species must roam extensively to find food; they burn up vast amounts of oxygen just

Game fishing often requires the use of a harness and heavy tackle

to survive. Such species include mackerel, yellowtail kingfish, marlin, tailor and especially those frenetic speed merchants, the tunas.

Other more sedentary species, such as snapper, bream or mulloway, have generally slower metabolic rates, and less continuous periods of activity. They often browse, rest or drift with the moving water, generally close to cover and always where they are most comfortable. But when the occasion demands, they can move like lightning, either to feed, to drive off intruders or to flee from danger.

A shift of some kind in the surrounding conditions usually triggers localised reef fish to exert themselves and feed vigorously. It might be a tide change, a flush of warm current, the onset of bumpy weather, a different moon phase or the sudden arrival of an attractive, easily harvested food supply.

GAME FISHING

Game fishing is a popular pastime and places such as Cairns, Port Stephens, Bermagui, Port Fairy and Rottnest Island are well-known locations, some with an international reputation.

Thirty years ago most game fishing in Australia was conducted from large professional charter boats catering for a select few devotees. Nowadays there is an even larger and thriving charter-boat industry in addition to thousands of anglers who fish offshore in private craft from around 4 to 20 m in length.

Large game fish are likely to be where there are warm, blue, ocean currents pushing southwards from the tropics. Other indicators are surface-feeding schools of intermediate predators, such as striped tuna or frigate mackerel. These gather where currents and wind concentrate dense schools of tiny bait fish, juvenile squid or other planktonic larvae, such as those of crabs or lobsters. In turn, big fish, such as yellowfin tuna, marlin or shark, move in to feed and these smaller predators then become the prey.

Feeding pods of fish are often signposted by wheeling flocks of sea birds, but you can also stumble across them by trolling along current lines. Generally, the more current

OFFSHORE FISH	
albacore	NSW, Vic., Tas., SA, WA
amberjack	NSW, Vic., Tas., SA, WA, Qld
barracouta	NSW, Vic., Tas., SA, WA
barracuda	WA, NT, Qld
bonito	NSW, WA, Qld
cobia	NSW, WA, NT, Qld
cod, coral	WA, NT, Qld
dart	NSW, Vic., SA, WA, Qld
dolphin fish	NSW, WA, NT, Qld
emperor, red	WA, NT, Qld
emperor, spangled	WA, NT, Qld
grenadier, blue	NSW, Vic., Tas., SA, WA
gurnard	NSW, Vic., Tas., WA, Qld
jewfish, Westralian	WA
Job-fish	WA, NT, Qld
john dory	NSW, Vic., Tas., SA, WA
kingfish, yellowtail	NSW, Vic., Tas., SA, WA, Qld
mackerel, grey	NSW, WA, NT, Qld
mackerel, school	NSW, WA, NT, Qld
mackerel, Spanish	NSW, Tas., WA, NT, Qld
mackerel, spotted	NSW, WA, NT, Qld
marlin, black	NSW, Vic., Tas., WA, NT, Qld
marlin, blue	NSW, Vic., Tas., WA, NT, Qld
marlin, striped	NSW, Vic., Tas., WA, NT, Qld
morwong	NSW, Vic., Tas., SA, WA, Qld
mulloway	NSW, Vic., SA, WA, Qld
nannygai	NSW, Vic., Tas., SA, Qld
perch, pearl	NSW, WA, Qld
perch, sea	WA, NT, Qld
queenfish	WA, NT, Qld
sailfish	WA, NT, Qld
salmon, Australian	NSW, Vic., Tas., SA, WA
samson fish	NSW, WA, Qld
shark, gummy	NSW, Vic., Tas., SA, WA
shark, school	NSW, Vic., Tas., SA, WA
shark, others	NSW, Vic., Tas., SA, WA, NT, Qld
snapper	NSW, Vic., Tas., SA, WA, Qld
snapper, saddletail	NSW, WA, NT, Qld
spearfish, shortbill	NSW, WA, Qld
sweep	NSW, Vic., Tas., SA, WA
sweetlip, grass	WA, NT, Qld
sweetlip, red-throated	NSW, WA, NT, Qld
swordfish, broadbill	NSW, Vic., Tas., SA, WA, Qld
teraglin	NSW, Vic., Qld
trevalla, blue-eye	NSW, Vic., Tas., SA
trevally, bigeye	NSW, WA, NT, Qld
trevally, giant	NSW, WA, NT, Qld
trout, coral	WA, NT, Qld
trumpeter, bastard	NSW, Vic., Tas., SA, WA
trumpeter, real bastard	Tas.
trumpeter, Tasmanian	NSW, Vic., Tas., SA, WA
tuna, longtail	NSW, WA, NT, Qld
tuna, mackerel	NSW, WA, NT, Qld
tuna, southern bluefin	NSW, Vic., Tas., SA, WA
tuna, striped	NSW, Vic., Tas., WA, Qld
tuna, yellowfin	NSW, Vic., Tas., SA, WA, NT, Qld
tuskfish	NSW, WA, NT, Qld
wahoo	NSW, WA, Qld
warehou	NSW, Vic., Tas., SA

Islands provide excellent fishing conditions

ISLAND FISHING

Islands provide particularly good fishing conditions, as they are really an enlarged version of a structure and thus provide the feeding, resting and ambushing areas that are part of the pattern of predator and victim. They can be rocks in the ocean, like Montague Island, off New South Wales, or have their own beaches, reefs, estuaries and bays, like Kangaroo Island, South Australia.

The bulk of the island creates a break in the ocean current, in the same way as a log in a river has the water eddying around it. This produces a pressure-free zone on the upcurrent side of the island where predators can wait for the concentrations of food swept in by the current. The washes, rocks and holes are natural feeding stations for predatory fish.

The best island fishing is usually on the rougher, upcurrent side and along the currents that sweep around an island. Headlands and reefs create secondary concentrations of fish, while the lee side still has potential, as fish will rest and wait off the current for food.

lines and the warmer and bluer the water, the better. When such oceanic streams converge, they create ideal conditions, attracting whole food chains into specific areas.

Game fishing methods include trolling lures, trolling dead 'skip' baits, trolling live baits, fishing live or dead baits from a drifting boat and at times (although rarely) fishing baits from an anchored boat. Trolling lures or bait is by far the most popular method. Fast trolling large dead scad or tuna off Cairns accounts for the huge black marlin caught in those waters.

Further south the preferred method for larger marlin and yellowfin tuna is to slow troll live striped tuna. Other areas have other methods depending on the fish targeted.

REEF FISHING

Not everyone who fishes offshore, however, will set their sights on game fish, nor do they need to. Many other species of offshore fish cost less to catch, provide plenty of fishing fun and supply good seafood for the family table into the bargain. Fish, such as emperor, snapper, yellowtail kingfish, cobia, mackerel, tailor and mulloway, inhabit inshore reefs, headland and island areas, and can be pursued with smaller boats and less sophisticated tackle.

In southern Australia, fishing for such species does not require travelling far out to sea as most reef dwellers are found within a couple of kilometres of shore. Further north in Queensland and the top half of Western Australia this situation changes due to the shallowness of the inshore waters, and a run of many kilometres may be required.

While fishing offshore reefs for a variety of species on the bottom, there is often an opportunity to pursue many sportfish that come past. Small mackerel tuna, snook, queenfish, trevally and barracouta are some of the sportfish found around offshore reefs.

USING BERLEY OFFSHORE

While you can not change the water temperature or the weather, much less control the moon, you can time your trips to take advantage of them. Similarly, even though seasonal movements of bait and injections of storm-washed foods are beyond your organisational ability, you can fake such events by the use of berley. Berley is used in all forms of offshore fishing including game and sportfishing as well as fishing over a reef for bottom dwellers. Sending down a cloud of easily-gathered food among a bunch of sleepy fish can change their attitude dramatically.

Offshore berley can be made from pieces of fish flesh and various fish oils, either used alone, or mixed together and extended with some kind of cereal product,

Yellowtail kingfish

This species, also known as yellowtail and kingfish, is found in southern Australian waters, from southern Queensland around to Shark Bay in Western Australia. Smaller specimens are caught from December to February but larger fish are best targeted in October and November.

such as bread, laying mash or stock-food pellets. It can be dispensed in various ways: through a berley bucket or berley bomb, or simply tossed over the side, a little at a time.

One technique used in game fishing for such species as yellowfin tuna is called 'cubing'. Small cubes of fresh tuna, 2 x 2 cm in size, are dropped into the ocean current from a drifting game boat. This sets up a long 'freeway' of enticing tid-bits, which after a couple of hours will stretch for a couple of kilometres. Tuna coming across the trail will simply follow it to the back of the boat, where the waiting angler is ready with live bait or a hook impaled cube. More conventional berleying techniques over reefs also produce results when the fish are not on the bite.

The key with berley is to use the right type and just enough to get the job done. A little, in a constant stream, is better than a big slug of it, then nothing. This is especially important offshore, where currents can take the berley away from you, and the fish with it. Remember: do not feed the fish! Berley should only stimulate them.

LOCATING THE CATCH

Regardless of the style of offshore fishing you pursue, it is important to fish in the right place, where all the hungry fish are congregated. Finding hungry fish in all that water relies on knowing the kinds of places fish frequent and how those places can be located.

A depth sounder can be a big advantage offshore and not only to tell the angler the depth of the water. Good sounders can easily pinpoint offshore reefs in 20 m of water and often locate fish over that structure as well. Used in conjunction with hydrographic charts, sounders enable anglers to return to the same location, particularly when out of sight of identifiable landmarks.

Having found your fish, all that is required is to determine the best rig and approach. While the 'right' tackle and baits remain fairly constant for certain species, the way you rig and go about presenting them will vary according to location and conditions. You do not need a rod and rig for every fish in the ocean, but you do need to take into account that fish differ in size, aggression and eating habits, and have a range of tackle on board to be adequately prepared. With much offshore fishing one needs a fair bit of lead to get down to the bottom.

At the simple end of things, you could get away with a set of light and heavy handlines, but by rod fishing you give yourself added versatility, being able to cast, troll, drift or bottom fish with a variety of baits or lures, or fish in a number of places for a range of species, from those that are small and slow to big fast deepwater game fish.

Saltwater fly casting for tuna in the Gulf of Carpentaria

HANDLING

If you plan to return your catch to the water, handle it as little as possible because the slime coating of the fish protects it from disease. If you are intending to eat your catch, your first task is to kill the fish immediately, either by a sharp blow with a blunt instrument (the heel of your knife or a small hammer) between or above the eyes, a knife-stab in the same spot, or by breaking the bridge across the throat and bending the head back. The last process helps to bleed the fish, which improves the final eating quality of some species.

It is advisable to have an old towel to hold a landed fish, and a pair of pliers to remove the hook. This is a tricky process, as some fish such as flathead have protective spines and spurs that can inflict a wound. Many tropical fish, such as stonefish, red rock cod, butterfly cod and fortescue, have poisonous spines that can cause severe illness.

You should immediately remove the gut and the gills of the fish, but leave the scales on to keep the flesh moist. Gutting is simply done by making a shallow cut from the throat to the anus and scooping out the entrails with your knife. Run the knife along each side of the backbone to remove any remaining pockets of blood. Don't cut into the gut. The fish should be washed to remove external slime and placed on ice; within 5 to 15 minutes of capture in the tropics, where fish flesh degenerates rapidly.

At the end of the day you must complete the job of cleaning the fish and preparing it for the table. You need a scaling tool, a strong working knife and a fine, sharp scaling knife. Once you have scaled the fish the easiest way to fillet it is to cut the fish behind the head down to the backbone and then flatten the knife and cut along the bone towards the tail with a sawing motion, taking the fillet and the skin at the same time. Next you can remove the skin by making a cut at the tail and, while holding the skin with one hand, cut along the skin with a flattened knife. (See Cooking Your Catch.) Many fish have oily skins that affect the taste of the flesh.

Finally, wash and dry the fillet thoroughly and, if refrigeration is not at hand, roll it in plastic to keep it airtight. In Australia's hot climate it is mandatory to keep fish refrigerated or on ice at all times.

Inland Fishing

To many, fly fishing is the pinnacle of fishing, the consummate battle between a skilled and patient angler and a noble opponent. But fly fishing is just one of the wide variety of freshwater fishing experiences available in Australia, each with its own excitement, fascination and keen devotees.

Australia is one of the driest continents on earth and the majority of its land mass is classed as desert. At first glance, it would seem that Australia is not well placed to provide a worthwhile freshwater fishery. After all, rain is needed for rivers and lakes – the habitat for freshwater fish.

Fortunately, while much of the Australian inland is very dry and virtually devoid of permanent waterways, the greater part of the coastal fringe enjoys good rainfall, and a resultant abundance of rivers and lakes. Even better, most of Australia's population lives on this fringe, giving them easy access to these same waterways, and some great freshwater fishing!

While there is no denying that inland waterways are beset by their share of environmental problems, a relatively small population (and a growing sense of environmental responsibility) means they have escaped the devastation that has claimed so many freshwater fisheries on other parts of the globe. Most inland waters remain public property and Australian anglers generally enjoy a right of access to rivers and lakes that would be the envy of those in many parts of the world, where huge fees can be paid for the 'privilege' of fishing in privately owned waters.

Most fresh water can be fished for the price of a licence. From the premier trout fisheries of Tasmania, to the giant barramundi of northern Australia, there is something for every angling taste. And whether your preference is for fly fishing, lure casting or baitfishing, there is sure to be a fishery not far away to indulge your sport.

BAITFISHING

At its most basic, baitfishing is the simplest and most widely known form of freshwater fishing. Even non-anglers are familiar with the concept of sitting beside a river holding a rod rigged with a sinker and a hook baited with a worm! Nowadays, baitfishing can be quite complex. For example, bait drifting – the casting and retrieving of virtually unweighted baits – requires perfectly tuned equipment and a good knowledge of natural baits.

Fly fishing is the art of casting almost weightless artificial lures called flies

Another form of baitfishing called coarse angling has all but developed into a distinct sport on its own, although the dividing line between it and conventional baitfishing is somewhat blurred. Coarse angling uses berley extensively: quantities of bread crumbs and similar mixtures to lure fish into the area the angler is fishing. Originally developed in the United Kingdom and Europe to fish for 'coarse' or non-game fish such as carp and tench, it is now very popular in Australia, where the techniques work on a wide range of species – even 'game' fish like trout. Many coarse anglers employ highly specialised equipment such as long and very sensitive rods and finely tuned floats, and choose from an array of surprisingly small hooks. Baits are also quite different to those normally used by regular bait fishers, and include maggots (gents), corn kernels and dough.

Despite the complexities of bait drifting and coarse angling, basic baitfishing remains a great technique for the casual angler, beginners and children. There is a delightful simplicity in a rod and threadline reel. Rigged with 3-kg line and either a small sinker or a float about half to one metre above a hook baited with a common bait like worms or shrimp, it remains a cheap, easy and quite effective method for catching many species. Redfin, eel, golden and silver perch, river blackfish, catfish, trout and sooty grunter are some fish that fall to basic baitfishing.

Of course learning about where to go, what type of water to fish, targeting a particular species, and the best way to present the right bait will all help improve your catch. Fish cannot hear your yelling and screaming but they will be scared away by splashing, heavy vibrations and lots of movement on the bank such as waving arms especially if covered in bright clothes. Most successful anglers have learned that finesse, using light gear and carefully approaching the water helps success. Watch an accomplished angler at work and you will soon discover that the notion of fishing being based on luck is a myth!

LURE CASTING AND TROLLING LURES

Lure casting involves casting and retrieving lures: artificial creations made from metal, wood or plastic that either mimic bait fish and other fish food, or simply 'trigger' an attack response in fish. Trolling works on the same principle, only the lure is towed behind a moving boat. Lure casting and trolling work best on active predators including barramundi, sooty grunter, redfin, golden perch, Australian bass, trout and Murray cod.

Like baitfishing, lure casting and trolling have become increasingly sophisticated in recent years. There are now endless varieties of lures on the market, including models that dive to great depth or wriggle along the surface. There are also spinners that have a flashing revolving blade, and even lures that contain a rattle to attract fish by vibrations. These days, anglers can purchase a range of Australian-made lures that are designed to appeal particularly to native species such as Murray cod, barramundi and bass.

Lure fishing can be as simple as trolling a wobbler behind a moving boat, or as complex as casting just the right lure to just the right location, and retrieving it at just the right speed and depth. Once again, experienced anglers target a particular fish species, and use gear that is not unnecessarily heavy.

FLY FISHING

Fly fishing is the art of casting almost weightless artificial lures called flies, which are made from materials such as fur and feather or modern substitutes. Because these flies have so little weight, conventional casting does not work. Instead, fly fishers use comparatively heavy lines (usually plastic wrapped around a braided core) and long flexible rods. The fly line is cast back and forth in the air until sufficient line speed is built up to enable the fly to be presented to the desired target.

The fly line is too thick to attach a hook, so a leader (a length of tapered fishing line) is linked to the end of the fly line, and to this is tied the fly itself. It takes practice to learn the timing and technique required to keep the fly line airborne and then deliver the final cast and present the fly. It is this element that has given rise to much of the mystique that surrounds fly fishing. Actually, a few days of informed practice is usually enough to cast well enough to begin catching fish, and some 'naturals' pick up fly casting in a few hours. It is worth noting

Baitfishing for species such as Murray cod and golden perch in the Condamine River, Queensland

FRESHWATER FISH

Species	States
barramundi	WA, NT, Qld
Bass, Australian	NSW, Vic., Qld
blackfish, river	NSW, Vic., Tas., SA
bream, black	NSW, Vic., Tas., SA, WA
bream, bony	NSW, Vic., SA, WA, NT, Qld
carp, European	NSW, Vic., SA
catfish, eel-tailed	NSW, Vic., WA, Qld
catfish, fork-tailed	WA, NT, Qld
cod, eastern	NSW
cod, Mary River	Qld
cod, Murray	NSW, Vic., SA, Qld
eel, long-finned	NSW, Vic., Tas., Qld
eel, short-finned	NSW, Vic., Tas., Qld
fish, archer	WA, NT, Qld
garfish, northern	WA, NT, Qld
goldfish	NSW, Vic., SA, Qld
grayling, Australian	NSW*, Vic.*, Tas.*
grunter, leathery	Qld
grunter, sooty	WA, NT, Qld
herring, freshwater	All States (Vic.*)
jack, mangrove	WA, NT, Qld
long tom, freshwater	Qld
mullet, freshwater	NSW, Qld
perch, estuary	NSW, Vic., Tas.
perch, golden	NSW, Vic., SA, Qld
perch, jungle	Qld
perch, Macquarie	NSW*, Vic.
perch, silver	NSW, Vic., SA, Qld
redfin	NSW, Vic., Tas., SA, WA
roach	NSW, Vic., WA, NT, Qld
salmon, Atlantic	NSW, Vic., Tas., SA, WA
salmon, Chinook	NSW, Vic., Tas., SA
saratoga, northern	NT, Qld
saratoga, southern	Qld
sawfish	NSW, WA, NT, Qld
tench	Vic., Tas., SA
trout, brook	NSW, Vic., Tas.
trout, brown	NSW, Vic., Tas., SA, WA
trout, rainbow	NSW, Vic., Tas., SA, WA

*Species totally protected in this state

that baitfishing and lure casting, in addition to being productive in their own right, can provide a good grounding for anglers wishing to take up fly fishing.

Until recently, freshwater fly fishing was regarded as the sole domain of the trout angler. While trout are still the number one target of fly fishers, more anglers are discovering that nearly every fish that swims can be caught on the fly. Fly fishing for trout will always remain especially popular because trout respond so well to the technique. Trout frequently feed on small insects like mayflies or caddis that may be only fingernail size, floating on the surface. When 'rising' to such tiny, buoyant insects, trout are all but uncatchable to anyone but fly fishers using dry (floating) artificial flies – lure casters and bait fishers are driven mad at such times!

Wet (sinking) flies can be used for trout and many other species. The huge diversity of wet fly patterns available means that just about every form of aquatic life is realistically copied. It is the clever use of wet flies that has led to a recent boom in fly fishing for species such as Murray cod and golden perch. Unlike dry flies, which are usually left to drift naturally on lake or stream, wet flies are normally retrieved to impart a swimming motion that matches that of the organism being imitated.

READING THE WATER

Despite all the other skills needed, the most important ingredient in freshwater fishing is reading the water: knowing where to lay that cast or run that bait or lure.

The habits of fish, either in fresh water or salt water, are predictable and this helps you to know where to seek them in rivers and lakes. They tend to position themselves near the main current flow, but not in it, and face into the current so that they can snatch up any morsels drifting with the current.

The biggest fish in any given area will take up the prized positions, in shelter but with the first chance at oncoming food. In rivers and streams they will be in the deeper, slower flowing sections – the pools or holes – and usually close to rapids or shallower sections that are washing food into the pools. The path of floating leaves or debris shows the natural places where the current is floating insects and other food.

In the heat of summer most fish, trout particularly, tend to go into the deeper water. The depth of pools can usually be gauged by the banks of rivers and lakes. A steeply sloping bank usually indicates deeper water. Fish like cover and protection, and some, such as Australian bass, estuary perch, Murray cod and barramundi, prefer the protection of underwater timber and overhanging branches. In apparently featureless water the smallest log may provide the hiding place for a fish.

Normanby River, Cape York: Northern Australia is renowned for its diversity of freshwater species

Whether using wet or dry flies, fly fishers sometimes utilise an interesting technique called polaroiding. Polarised sunglasses remove much of the glare and reflection from the water surface, enabling much clearer vision beneath it. If light conditions and water clarity are favourable, fly fishers wearing polaroids can locate their target fish, and present their fly to the right spot. Polaroiding is particularly effective for trout anglers, but is gaining popularity among those chasing other species, such as golden perch. Although it sounds simple, polaroiding takes practice to perfect – most fish are well camouflaged, and skilled fly fishers often rely on little more than an unusual movement or the flash of a white mouth to locate their quarry.

Fly fishing is arguably the most complex style of freshwater fishing, particularly where trout are concerned, but it is also a lot of fun!

SOUTH-EASTERN AUSTRALIA

New South Wales, Victoria and Tasmania have abundant freshwater fishing on offer. The Great Dividing Range, which arcs south then west through New South Wales and Victoria, is the source of every significant river in these states. It is in and around these hills and mountains, in cool, clean water, that the trout, the most sought-after freshwater sportfish, is found. Trout are often erroneously described as 'alpine' fish, but in fact they are confined to very elevated habitat only in northern New South Wales. Further south they are found at lower elevations. In Victoria, trout thrive in many waters at or near sea level, and a long way from true mountain country. Across Bass Strait, Tasmania has arguably the cream of Australian trout fishing. This large island has proved an ideal habitat for trout, and most freshwater lakes and streams (and many estuaries) hold good numbers.

In all three states, trout are the only significant angling species in the true alpine country, but as the elevation decreases, trout begin to share their habitat with other angling species. Redfin co-exist with trout in many lakes and rivers, and extend beyond this range to inhabit many of the slower, warmer waters of the inland. Because of their abundance, redfin are a popular angling species, but they can dominate some waters because of their prolific breeding habits and voracious appetites. Also caught from immediately outside the alpine country through to the edge of the warm inland waters are two sought-after native fish: Macquarie perch and river blackfish. Macquarie perch is the rarer of the two, and does best in Victoria (it is protected in New South Wales). The totally protected trout cod is rarer again, and should always be carefully returned to the water alive if caught.

Three superb warm-water natives, Murray cod, golden perch and silver perch, are making a strong comeback in many inland waters in Victoria and New South Wales, particularly those that flow west into the Murray–Darling system. Modern breeding programs and efforts to improve habitat mean that these fish are once more a viable angling option in south-eastern Australia. They are also making a comeback into several impoundments that previously held only trout and redfin. Lakes such as Burrinjuck, Hume and Eildon now offer a blend of cool and warm-water species.

The coastal streams of New South Wales contain another top native sportfish, the Australian bass. As one moves into coastal Victoria, these fish are replaced by a less well-known relative, the estuary perch. Bass, in particular, have returned to sportfishing prominence in recent years, thanks in part to a major scientific breakthrough that has enabled large-scale hatchery breeding, and the stocking of artificial lakes.

Of the four south-eastern states, South Australia is the poorest for freshwater fishing, simply because so much of it is desert country devoid of permanent lakes and rivers. However, the Murray River does offer fishing for golden perch, silver perch, Murray cod and redfin, and smaller streams around Adelaide contain some trout stocks, especially after a succession of wet years.

As well as the species already mentioned, anglers in south-eastern freshwater areas may also encounter eel and tench, and that most destructive invader, the European carp. Carp are considered to be responsible for damaging the habitat of many south-eastern waters, and every care should be taken to ensure they do not spread beyond their present range. Any carp caught should be killed immediately.

WESTERN AUSTRALIA

The largest state provides an enormous variety of freshwater fishing commensurate with its range of freshwater environments. The south-western corner has a temperate climate similar to Victoria and southern New South Wales. Not surprisingly, this area is the home of the west's trout fishery. Though not as successful as in the eastern states, trout have done quite well in a number of rivers and lakes, and some very big trout are caught each year.

Redfin are very successful in the south-west, and frequently overlap with trout. Native angling species of significance are rare in the area, although the locals enjoy catching a delicious crustacean called marron.

From just north of Perth through to the start of the Kimberley, freshwater fishing is limited. The country is very dry and there are few permanent waterways. Small natives provide the only freshwater fishing.

There is an abrupt change for the better once the remote tropics of the Kimberley are reached. Heavy monsoonal rains over summer feed a number of major rivers, and many permanent and semi-permanent lagoons. These waters are home to numerous tropical species, the most famous of which is the barramundi, one of Australia's premier sportfish. As well as barramundi, freshwater anglers may encounter species as diverse as long tom, giant catfish and various species of perch.

Underwater timber provides protection for native species

NORTHERN AUSTRALIA

The Top End of the Northern Territory, Queensland's Cape York Peninsula and the Gulf Country that separates the two, provide a continuation of the excellent tropical freshwater fishing found in the Kimberley. Barramundi continues to be the most prized sportfish, with species like sooty grunter and saratoga also popular. But the list of potential angling species is endless, as this area has perhaps the greatest diversity of fish in the country. Much of the tropical north is very difficult to access due to the lack of roads and, by southern standards, freshwater areas are relatively free from fishing pressure.

Moving south from Cape York Peninsula, Queensland freshwater fishing changes. Barramundi becomes less common, and ambitious stocking programs for impoundments have improved freshwater fishing significantly. Lake Tinaroo on the Atherton Tableland is showing great promise for landlocked barramundi, and consistently produces enormous sooty grunter. Further south, stocking with other species like golden perch, bass and saratoga is proving successful.

The Darling River feeder streams west of the Great Divide provide native fish like those found further down the system, with golden perch especially abundant. Catfish are found in eastern-flowing streams, with jungle perch in some tropical mountain streams in the north, and Mary River cod in the Maryborough area. South of the Noosa River, Australian bass can be caught in the coastal rivers where the habitat is suitable.

THE INLAND

Beyond the coastal rivers and the Murray–Darling system lies the dry inner core of Australia, containing rare small pockets of water inhabited by tiny, hardy fish that have no angling appeal. In a few places with slightly higher rainfall, mountain gorges or the termination of distant catchments provide larger waterholes where tough natives such as golden perch survive. The quality of the fishing most of the time would not be enough to warrant the long, difficult journey.

LANDING THE FISH

Do not try to reel the fish in and land it. The reel is not for dragging fish, but for taking up the slack or playing out line while you fight the fish and eventually bring it in.

A fish is never caught until it is in the boat or on the wharf. A last flurry of energy at any time close to retrieval may well dislodge a hook that is not fully set.

Jetty anglers are at peril of losing the fish if the pier platform is a long way above the water. It is best if the fish is exhausted so that it remains passive at the critical point when it leaves the water and its full weight comes onto the line as you bring it in. It is likely to make a last run under the jetty, so you have to be prepared to play out line and begin the process of bringing it back to the point of retrieval.

Fish should not be lifted from the water on a line if it can be avoided. For boat anglers a net or a short gaff (a large hook connected to a piece of cane) can be employed to secure the fish. On a jetty a long gaff, flying gaff or grapnel can be used.

If you use a gaff, align the hook with the side of the fish and insert it into the flesh, bringing it in at an angle that easily penetrates the protective scales. Aim for the bulkiest part of the fish but avoid touching the belly.

If your fish is too small, a species that you would prefer to release or one more than you need for the day, slip it back into the water as gently as possible. There are usually pier steps that will get you closer to the water level for this.

Remember that our fisheries are a precious resource. The only reason for killing a fish is for bait, for the table or if it is a pest species.

Rods and Reels

The perfect fishing outfit will be chosen for a certain style of fishing while retaining some versatility. The rod will be neither too heavy nor too light for the line and vice versa, and the reel and terminal tackle will complement both. Overall, a good outfit will feel comfortable and balanced in the hand. Your angling abilities should be enhanced by the gear you choose, not diminished.

A wide variety of fishing styles has created a staggering array of equipment, each designed for a particular purpose. Before you buy, you will need to work out your fishing preferences. It is best to know something about all the components of a fishing outfit and then find the particular combinations to suit your needs.

RODS

There are hundreds of different types of fishing rods available. Twenty years ago, multipurpose rods were common; today, rods are made of space-age materials and usually designed for specific uses. Some rods can be used for two or three applications. For example a double-handed, pistol-grip rod can be used for lure casting for barramundi, bait fishing for snapper and drifting for flathead. When selecting a rod, its length, action and power should be considered.

Rods can be broadly classified as light, medium and heavy, but within these categories there is also a variety of types usually made for particular reels.

Long, heavier rods are used for beach fishing

LIGHT RODS

Light rods are the most common type, as they are generally used in the popular pursuits of freshwater and estuary angling. Among the light rods are single-handed spinning rods, single-handed plugs and fly rods. They should have a whippy tip that will easily cast lightweight lures and sinkers, and should have a solid feel at the base.

Generally, the shortest rods are for baitcaster reels, which are designed for accurate lure or light bait casting. These rods usually have a pistol grip for controlled casting. Single-handed light rods are used to cast light baits and lures.

MEDIUM RODS

Medium rods include double-handed plugs, double-handed spinning rods and boat rods. A medium rod, measuring between 2.5 and 3.3 m, is very versatile and can be used for either heavier estuary and bay fishing, or for beach and rock work. It can give a longer cast when necessary, but retain enough sensitivity for accuracy. It should have a tip responsive enough to cast a bait or lure as little as 50 g in weight. These rods are often used with threadline and sidecast reels. Rods in this category will easily cast distances between 50 and 80 m due to their length and power, if matched with appropriate line diameter.

HEAVY RODS

Rock and surf threadlines, overhead and sidecast threadlines, game rods and jig rods are examples of heavy rods. A heavy, long outfit is used for beach, rock and jetty casting. Measuring between 2.8 and 3.8 m, it needs good weight in the lower half and a tip rigid enough to throw a rig weighing up to 100 g, with a line up to 20-kg breaking strain. They are used mainly with sidecast and overhead reels.

ROD TALK

The way the rod curves when it is under load is called its action. The way it narrows from its butt to its tip is called its taper. The most common rods have a medium taper and medium action, bending down to about two-thirds of the rod under pressure and being easier to cast for the less expert angler.

Rods that taper gradually from butt to tip are called slow taper rods and have a parabolic action, with the entire rod bending as the load pressure increases. They are favoured by fly and luderick anglers as they cast more gently and accurately, and exert minimum pressure on a hooked fish.

Fast action rods taper quickly at the top from a thick butt. Under pressure, the top third of the rod bends while the butt is not affected. They are popular with boat anglers for trolling, jigging, spinning and lure casting; and with rock and beach anglers. They deliver a long, fast cast. Light fast-taper rods are used in light-line spinning.

REELS

Just as there is no such thing as an all-purpose rod, there is no all-purpose reel. Nobody would put a huge reel on a light rod or vice versa; matching a rod and reel is very important. Your selection has to be based on your perceived needs and personal preference. This is an important choice and advice from a reputable retailer or experienced angler should be considered. The rod, when placed on one hand just ahead of the reel, should be at the point of balance, neither tip-heavy nor butt-heavy.

THREADLINES

These reels are more accurately described as fixed-spool reels and are mounted underneath the rod. They are versatile and easy to use, and excellent for general fishing. Threadlines suit

SOME TACKLE COMBINATIONS

Rod	Reel	Line	Casting weight	Swivel size	Hook size
1.5–2.2	baitcast	1.3 kg	6–30 g	16–10	12–1/0
	threadline	3–5 kg	10–50 g	2–8	6–5/0
1.7–2.8	threadline	4–8 kg	20–70 g	10–8	4–4/0
	sidecast	6–10 kg	30–80 g	0–6	4–6/0
2.5–3.7	sidecast	6–15 kg	50–120 g	6–4	1–8/0
	overhead	8–20 kg	70–150 g	6–4	2/0–10/0

Spinning rods with threadline reels

Designed to cast all types of artificial lures, spinning rods need to be as light as possible for angler comfort during hours of repetitive casting and retrieving. A medium-action rod is best for general spinning. Anglers concentrating on fishing surface lures require a stiffer tip-actioned rod. Light threadline reels are ideal for spinning with the lightest of lures and cast more efficiently than baitcaster/overhead reels. The long butt section on the third model makes the rod more suitable for trolling in fresh water or estuaries, and is useful for longer casts in salt water.

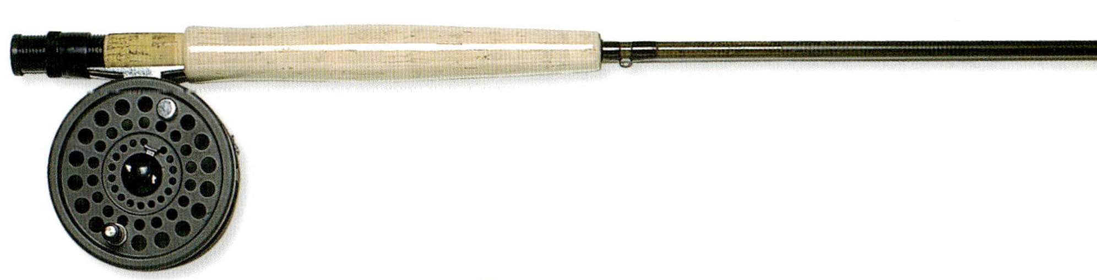

Fly rod and reel

Designed specifically for casting a fly line as far as possible, fly rods bend with a gradual curve to deliver the fly line smoothly. It is vital to match reel and line with the rod. Fly rods are from 1.8 to 3.3 m long. A simple centre-pin reel is used with a drag to prevent line over-run when casting. Fly reels are often drilled to lessen the weight and to provide ventilation for the line to dry.

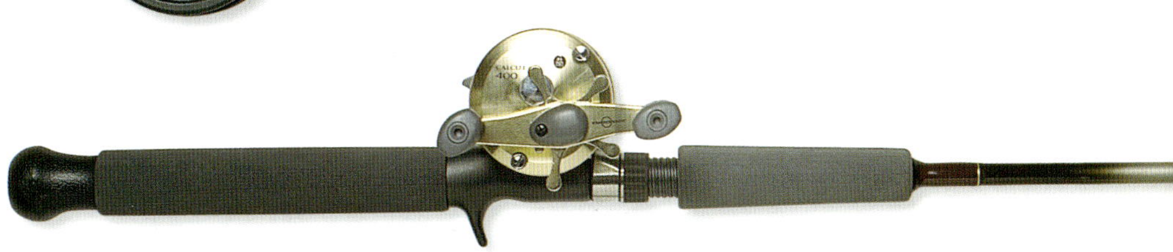

Double-handed pistol grip rod with baitcaster reel

These rods are used for casting lures accurately for medium to heavy-weight fish such as barramundi and Murray cod. Matching reels are medium to heavy-weight baitcasters.

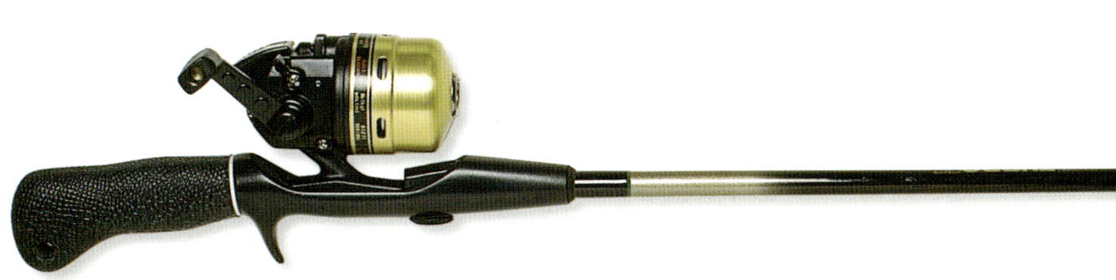

Single-handed pistol grip rod and closed-face reel

Used for estuary and light freshwater angling for fish such as Australian bass and bream. Suitable reels for use with this type of rod are small baitcasters, or closed-face reels.

Young anglers quickly learn the fundamentals of fishing

fishing with lures or bait, and can handle most freshwater, estuary and some beach and rock fishing; they work best with an 8-kg breaking strength line or less. When cast, line must travel across the edge of the spool, and thin line offers less resistance.

Since their spools are relatively small, using thick line on threadlines means you cannot fit much line on the reel. Heavy line will not help you get the best out of such gear; it will simply inhibit the reel's casting ability and reduce the amount of line you have to play out.

Offshore rods are designed to handle maximum stress. A rod bucket is a useful support

OVERHEAD REELS

So called because they are mounted on top of, or 'over', the rod, these come in a range of sizes from small baitcasters, through medium-sized surf or jig reels, to heavy-duty trolling reels. Baitcasters can cast lures over short distances with great accuracy, while surf or jig reels suit beach, rock or boat spinning, bottom fishing, jigging or light tackle live-baiting. Game fishing or trolling reels are the big models in this group and are used to capture the large pelagics such as tuna and marlin.

One type of overhead will not suit all fishing jobs. For example, you would not chase large game fish on a baitcaster, or try to cast any distance with a large, heavy-spooled game reel. You might be able to use a baitcaster or a mid-sized, good quality jig reel, for both a bit of light tackle fishing and maybe some ambitious fishing for a few heavyweights (provided you have the skill and some luck).

SIDECAST REELS

The sidecast reel is an Australian innovation made by the Brisbane-based Alvey reel company. Sidecasts are popular with beach and rock anglers, and also many boat anglers. The reel has some advantages over both threadlines and overheads. To cast, the spool is rotated 90°, allowing the line to flow off the reel almost unimpeded. Unlike an overhead, there is no spool inertia to overcome, so light casting weights can be easily flicked out. Their main advantage is that unweighted baits, which so often attract big fish, can be fished on line that is heavy enough to keep hooked whoppers under control.

MAINTENANCE

Rods and reels should be separated when not in use and stored out of the weather. After each outing they should be washed with warm fresh water and dried, and the moving parts of the reels oiled regularly. If you do not feel competent to repair a faulty mechanism, take it to a tackle shop. You might also want the shop to strip, clean and oil your reel every year or so.

The mechanical advantage of a sidecast's direct drive and large spool diameter enables you to wind line in against considerable pressure. Small fish can be brought in quickly, and hefty fish can be battled and beaten, then winched from the water.

CLOSED-FACE REELS

Sometimes called 'pushbutton' or 'spincast' reels, these small reels sit on top of the rod like a baitcaster, have a fixed spool like a threadline, but differ in that the spool is enclosed behind a front cover, which has a hole in the middle through which the line can pass.

Closed-face reels can be used with either lures or bait, and are very simple to operate, but since they have very limited line capacity, they are only suitable for freshwater and light saltwater use.

HANDCASTER

The simplest system of all is the handline or handcaster. Handlines can be as simple as line on a cylinder of cork, and these are commonly available in tackle shops. A plastic ring with a curved spooling lip is more generally favoured, as the larger diameter of the ring allows line to be more easily wound in. To cast, you can strip a couple of metres of line from the lip and throw your tackle out, holding the lipped side of the ring towards the casting area. The line will play out over the lip and any slack can easily be wound back.

Rods and reels need to be compatible with line sizes, casting weights and rigs in use, and all should suit the fish and the terrain.

DRAGS ON REELS

Most reels have drag systems of various kinds which prevent a hooked fish from running effortlessly. The drag system requires a running fish to haul the line from the reel, thus (theoretically!) preventing the fish from making line-breaking jolts or pulls against immovable resistance. The drag also tires the fish and allows it to be 'played'. The drag setting should be well below the line strength, say at 4 kg for a 10-kg line.

Leger rod with threadline reel

Leger rods are most commonly used for advanced baitfishing techniques in fresh water and estuaries. They usually have a solid glass nibble tip for the last 30 cm of the rod. Threadline reels are a popular reel type for use with leger rods.

Float rod with threadline reel

Float rods around 3.7 to 4 m in length are used mostly for freshwater bait fishing. Longer rods, between 4.3 and 4.6 m, are better when fishing salt water and for species such as luderick. Threadline reels work best with these rods: in fresh water, with lines between 1 and 3 kg; in salt water, with lines between 3 and 6 kg.

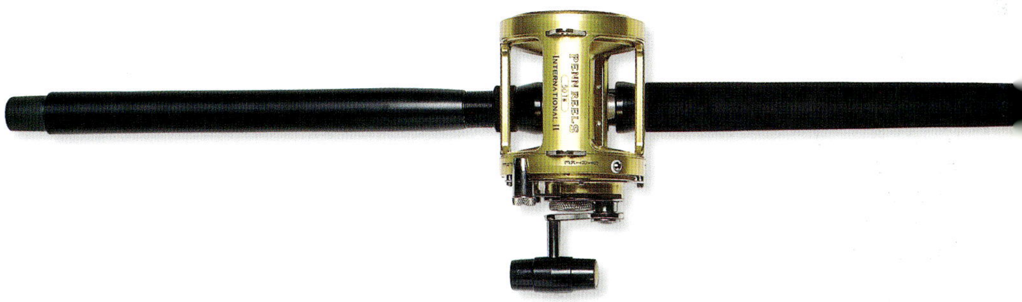

Game and sportfishing rods with overhead reels

These rods are designed to handle maximum stress and to apply maximum leverage for powerful game fish. Usually 1.6 to 2 m long, they are highly specialised, single-purpose rods. Game fishing reels are large overhead reels used for bluewater fishing where strength, enormous line capacity, heavy-duty braking and an efficient, heat dissipating drag system are necessary.

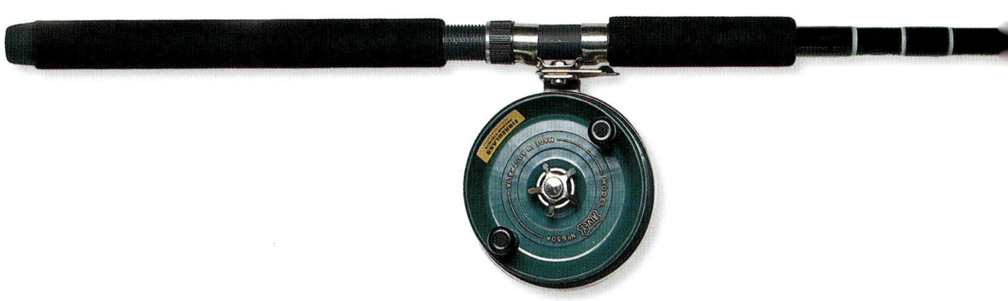

Sidecast rod with Alvey reel

These rods most commonly range in length between 3.5 to 4 m. Sidecast rods with a slow taper are needed for soft baits and float rigs. Fast tapered rods are required for big baits and big fish. They are popular with beach, rock and boat anglers. A sidecast reel is often used with this rod because of the way it allows line to flow off the reel, although practice is necessary to avoid line twist and tangles.

Surf rod with threadline reel

Surf rods are usually heavier and longer to assist casting over long distances. This particular reel is designed for heavy duty spinning in either salt or fresh water.

Hooks, Lines and Sinkers

Hooks and sinkers are part of a host of items that are described as terminal tackle. Despite their simple functions, their design is often complex and there are innumerable variations available, each designed for a particular purpose. Work out your fishing preferences, then find the particular combinations to suit your needs. The golden rule is to keep it simple.

HOOKS

Hooks used for fishing range from size 14 to size 1 in the smaller sizes, the larger number designating the smaller hook. Larger hooks range upwards from size 1/0 to 20/0. Specialized hooks, some much smaller than size 14, are used for tying very small flies.

A detailed discourse on hook patterns or designs is not appropriate here as is clearly indicated by the fact that leading hook manufacturer, Mustad of Norway, currently has the capacity to produce some 25,000 different hook patterns.

Dedicated anglers seeking large, or trophy-size fish, usually sharpen their hooks. However, the recent introduction of hardened steel, pre-sharpened hooks, which are usually marketed as chemically sharpened hooks, has made the sharpening stone redundant by anglers using them.

The point on chemically sharpened hooks is created by a brew of corrosive chemicals that is applied to hooks to get rid of irregularities and produce a smooth needle-point that maximises penetrating power. It is more like polishing than sharpening, although by improving the penetration power of the point it can accurately be said to sharpen the hook.

The recent introduction of small, light-gauge 'circle' hooks has also benefited anglers because of their superior holding capacity over 'J' pattern hooks. However, care needs to be taken when baiting circles so that the gap between point and shank is not obscured.

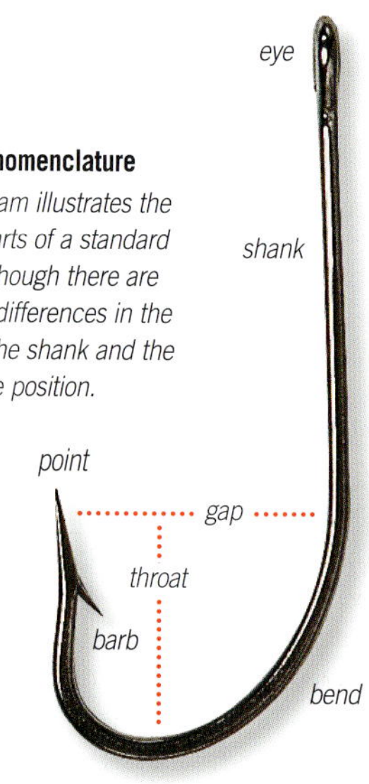

Hook nomenclature

This diagram illustrates the various parts of a standard hook, although there are obviously differences in the length of the shank and the eye position.

Sliced-shanks

These can be suicides or other styles; what makes them special is that there are barbs formed in the shank. These help bait presentation by holding the bait up and preventing it sliding down and bunching unnaturally in the bend of the hook.

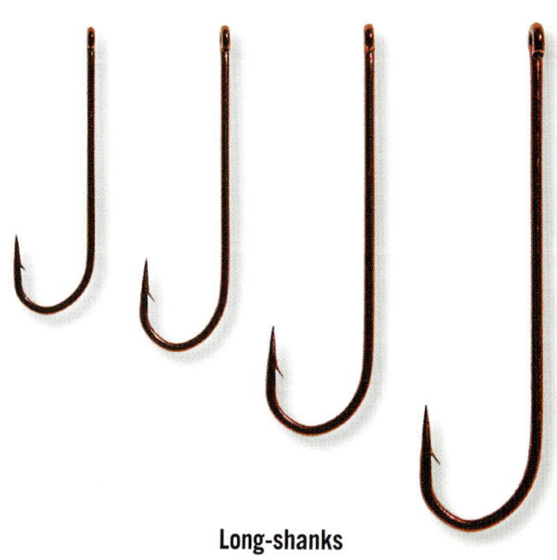

Long-shanks

These suit fish with teeth that can bite through line. Fish such as leatherjacket need sizes 12 to 8, and flathead, sizes 2/0 to 5/0. They can also be used to catch small bait fish.

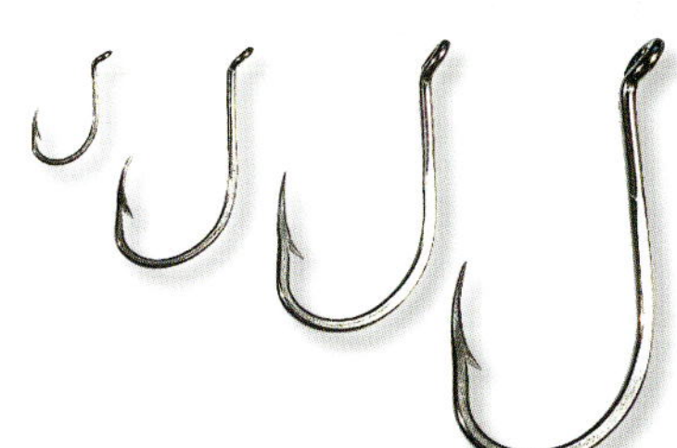

Suicides

These are recurved or 'beak' hooks with a turned up eye and fairly short shank. Sizes 2 to 10 are for carrying trout baits like mudeyes, shrimp and earthworms; for bream, sizes 1 to 2/0 carry baits like prawns, fish strips and pipis; and for snapper, mulloway and yellowtail kingfish, use sizes 3/0 to 6/0.

Forged hooks

This hook has a flattened shank, which helps resist damage by the fish's jaws. Forged hooks generally suit heavy rather than light tackle. This hook type works well for groper, drummer, rock blackfish, snapper and mulloway; or open water speedsters like mackerel, trevally, yellowtail kingfish, tuna and marlin.

O'Shaughnessy hooks

These stainless steel, multi-purpose hooks can be used anytime and anywhere, in fresh or salt water. They are most commonly used in salt water for snapper, Australian salmon and flathead.

Treble hooks

Treble hooks are designed for use on lures and need to be replaced, along with the split rings holding them, regularly. Any suggestion that a treble hook gives the angler three times the chance of hooking a fish is simply wrong.

LINES

Nylon monofilament fishing lines have dominated the fishing line market for more than fifty years in all sizes and can usually be joined or rigged, using just a few basic knots.

The chief disadvantage of nylon monofilament is its elasticity. This becomes a problem when there is lot of line out, for example when playing a very large fish, or when fishing on the bottom in very deep water.

Woven dacron lines with minimal stretch are available but are more expensive than monofilament. Dedicated game-fishermen who use dacron lines readily attest to the advantages of reduced elasticity which permits large game fish like marlin to be subdued more quickly, an especially important consideration if the fish is to be released.

Polyethylene gelspun fishing lines are much stronger than other fishing lines of comparable diameter. This coupled with their low stretch and high sensitivity makes them ideal for bottom fishing in deep water. However, careful attention needs to be made when tying knots or unexpected separations may occur.

Specialised lines, like those used for fly-fishing, and dedicated leader materials, are separate subjects and require a more detailed description than space allows for here.

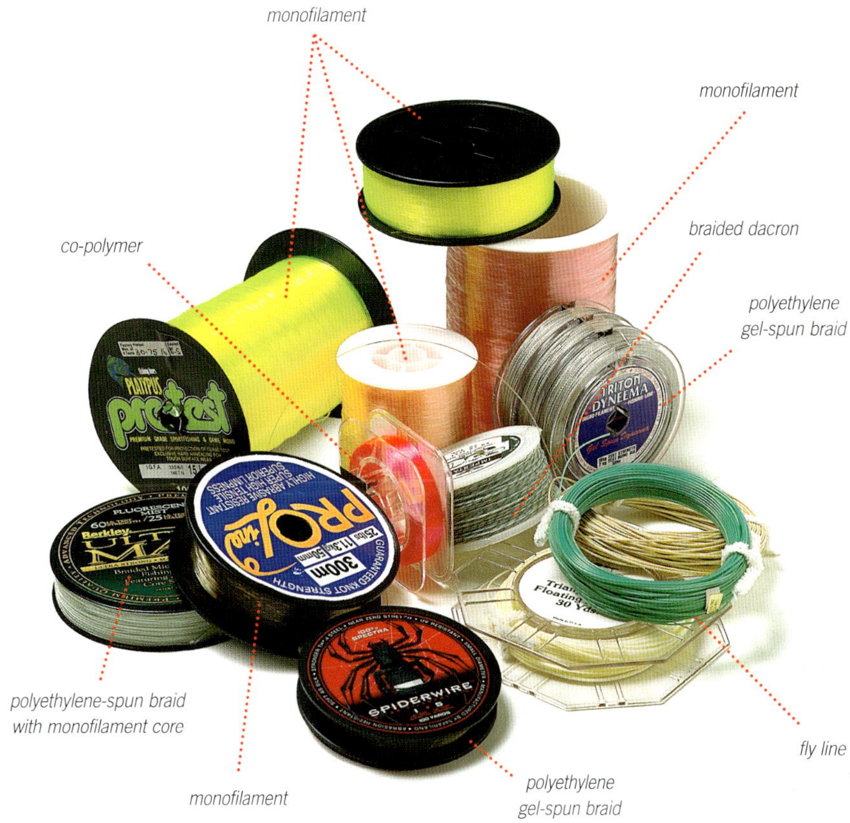

SINKERS

Sinkers come in a wide range of weights and designs. Some have a ring or eye at one end so that they can be tied to the end of the line. These are called fixed sinkers. Others have a hole through the centre through which the line is threaded so they slide along the line. These are called running sinkers.

Split shot are small lead spheres which are split half way through so that they may be clamped onto the line, often to provide additional weight to ballast a float, or to sink a buoyant bait. With these factors in mind, choosing a sinker of the correct design is fairly easy.

Choosing the correct type and weight of sinker is a matter of judgement which comes with experience, but the use of a sinker which is either too heavy or too light, is soon indicated by difficulty in casting or holding bottom.

Several dozen barrel sinkers are sometimes threaded onto hand-lines used for trolling. They are then crimped at close intervals along the line so that the bait or lure is presented some distance below the surface of the water.

A general range of all-purpose sinkers for use in saltwater and freshwater situations; beans (top left and bottom); barrels (left); balls (top right and mid right); bug (centre)

Star sinkers, used for surf fishing. These come in a large range of sizes

Bomb or teardrop sinkers used for saltwater fishing; the largest ones in surf, rock or boat situations, the smaller variety with either heavy or light tackle in heavy or light saltwater situations

Snapper lead sinkers for use in conjunction with deepsea rigs. Popular with anglers fishing places where there is a big tidal flow and a large sinker is required to hold the bait near the seabed

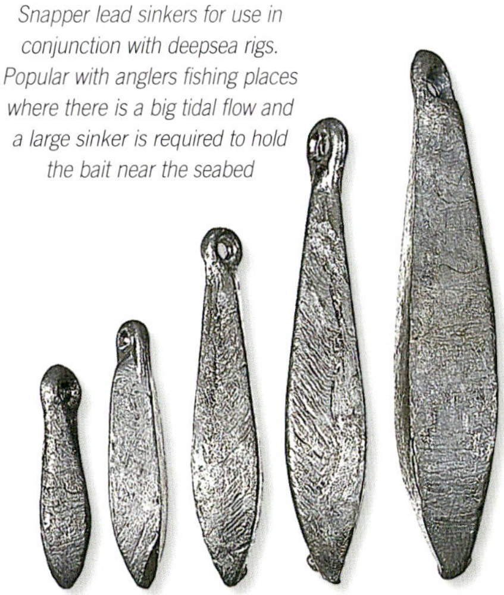

FLOATS

The primary function of a float is to suspend bait at a predetermined depth. When the depth at which the bait is to be presented is modest, say not more than 1.5 metres, a fixed float is used.

When the depth is greater than that allowed by a fixed float, then a running float, which is free to slide along the line between two stoppers, is used.

A running float enables the angler to cast out with the float resting on the bottom stopper. However, when the rig hits the water, the bait sinks, drawing line through the float until the top stopper comes to rest at the top of the float.

A variation of the running float is the bubble float, which is rigged in tandem with a second smaller float as a bottom stopper. The bubble itself is partially filled with water to make it heavy enough to cast out. When a fish takes the bait, only the small float submerges, the line being free to pass through the larger bubble float without resistance.

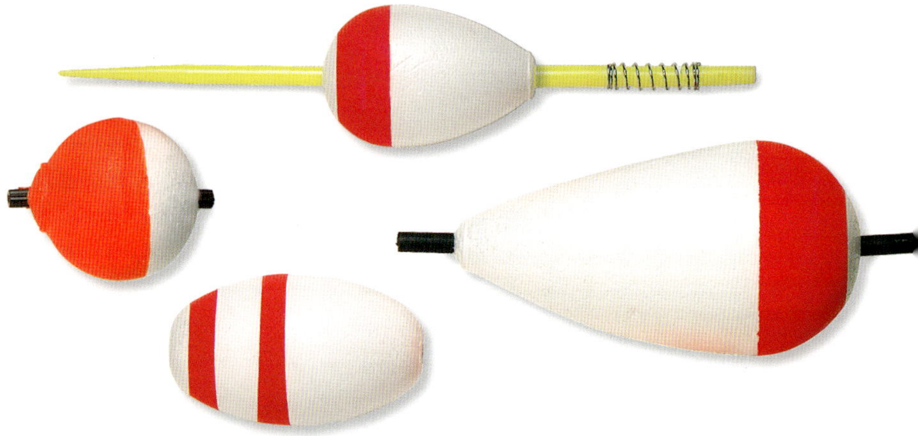

Polystyrene floats

These torpedo-shaped floats are particularly suited to live baiting off the rocks. Designed for heavier baits, the larger pear-shaped versions work well in rough seas when fishing for tailor, drummer or snapper.

Bubble floats

Bubble floats, usually made of plastic, are designed to be partially filled with water to assist casting. They are mainly used for baitfishing in fresh water. Some are coloured or luminous to aid visibility.

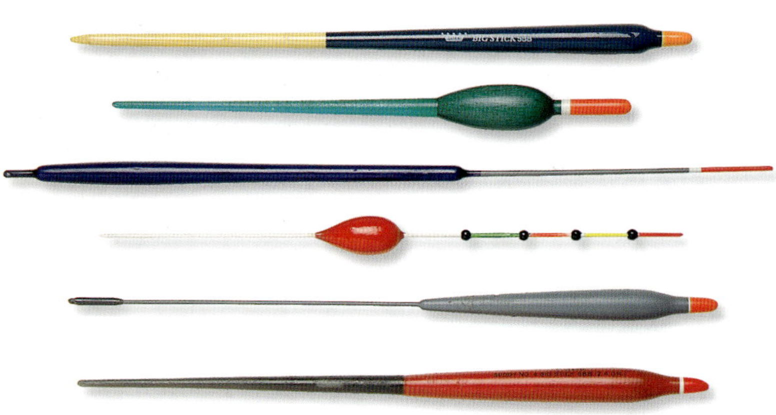

Coarse angling: Stick floats

These floats are used mainly in moving fresh water such as rivers and creeks. The line is usually attached to the top and the bottom with the aid of a small plastic grommet. Split shot is used to weigh them so that 80 to 90 per cent is submerged.

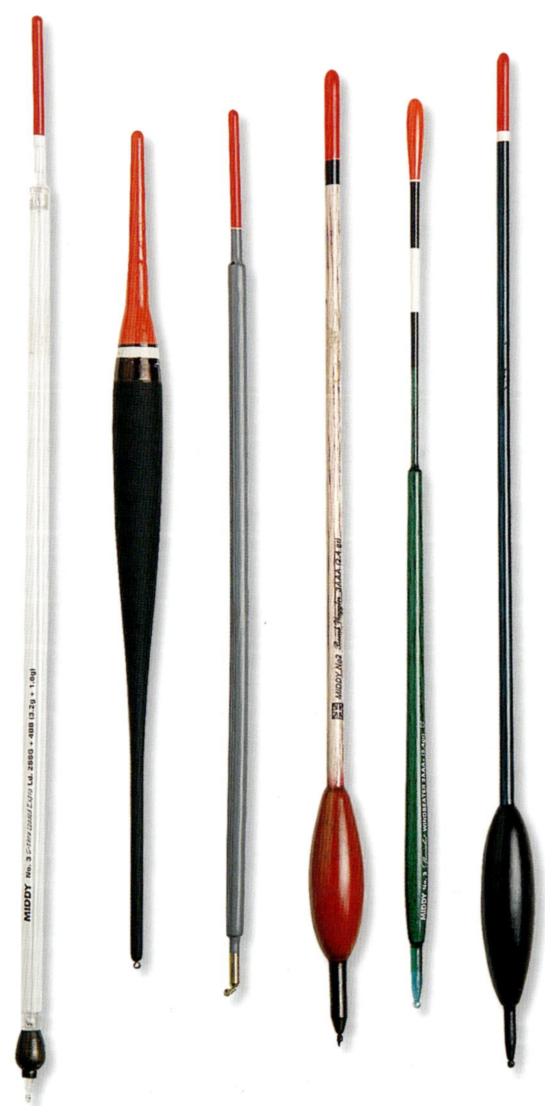

Coarse angling: Waggler floats

These are used in fresh still waters such as lakes and impoundments. The line is attached to the bottom of the float only, via a ring. The line is pinned either side with split shot, weighted so only the tip shows above the water. This prevents fast drifting in high winds.

SWIVELS AND RINGS

The primary objectives of swivels are to eliminate line twist and provide a point to which the line may be tied.

Unfortunately, even the best swivels do not eliminate line twist completely, and their efficiency is further reduced as the size of the swivel increases in comparison to the line being used.

Swivels sometimes incorporate additional features like a third eyelet, as in the case of a cross-line swivel, or a wire snap-lock to enable the easy attachment of a pre-rigged leader.

Game fishers often use ball-bearing snap-lock swivels. These are designed for heavy fishing applications where the amount of pressure likely to be applied through the line could pull a normal snap swivel free. Snaps are suitable for quick changing ready-made terminal rigs or lures when trolling or spinning.

Swivel sizes are categorized like hooks with the smallest swivels beginning at number 14 and increasing in size to number 1, then 1/0, 2/0 etc.

Black barrel swivels of various sizes, used to keep the twist out of the line, as a link or join, and as a sinker stop.

Black ball bearing swivels. Larger sizes are used in heavy saltwater and game fishing and the smaller sizes for light to medium saltwater fishing.

Brass swivels. The larger variety incorporate a barrel with safety snap; the smaller ones have an interlock snap. Snap swivels are used in conjunction with bladed lures.

Black snap swivels, used in conjunction with minnow lures or bladed lures. Swivels allow the lures to move around without the line twisting.

Brass barrel swivels and three-way crossline swivels. The latter are multi-purpose, allowing for various attachments to the rig. Use in salt and fresh water depending on size.

Black ball bearing snap-lock swivel, which can be used in conjunction with traces and lures. The black colour is preferable to the brass in some situations for camouflage reasons.

TRACES AND LEADERS

The terms trace and leader are interchangeable, but in common usage, the term leader usually refers to an extended length or separate length of heavier line on which a lure or hook is rigged as is the practice when game fishing.

The term trace usually refers to a separate, often quite short length of line to which a hook is tied. When sharks, or other fish with sharp teeth are sought, then a wire trace or leader may be used to reduce the chance of being bitten off.

Wire is also incorporated in some commercially prepared terminal rigs for bottom fishing. These are also constructed with wire snap-locks at their extremities, so hooks and sinkers may be easily attached. These rigs make no concession to timid fish, but will take the occasional fish when they are abundant and 'on the bite'.

In some situations, the leader on which the hook is tied is lighter than the main line. The best example is in freshwater fly-fishing where the fly, which is really a 'dressed' hook, is tied to the fine end of a tapered leader.

Nylon trace encompasses any heavier than normal main line traces. Often used for snapper, barramundi, tuna and marlin.

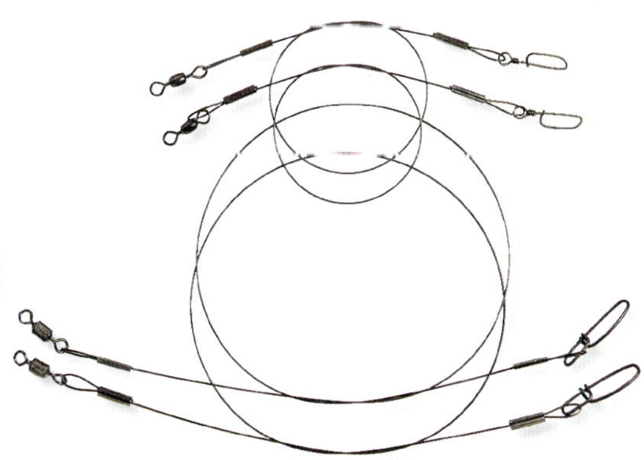

Nylon-coated pre-rigged wire trace, available in various lengths and breaking strains, is most often used in conjunction with lures. At times used with bait but only recommended if fish are aggressive and traces are required.

Pre-rigged traces. Popular wire traces rigged paternoster style can be purchased. They are suitable for surf to deepsea bottom fishing. Not recommended if fish are timid.

Lures and Flies

At one time, lures and flies were carefully fashioned to imitate as closely as possible the prey of the target fish. Today, many lures and flies are unrecognisable as prey; some even come in fluorescent colours. But they are 'real' to the target fish, which can be duped into taking a lure or a fly providing it looks appealing, behaves correctly and is presented in the right place at the right time in the right way.

LURES

There are thousands of different types of lures made. There are floating lures, sinking lures, huge half-metre-long lures for marlin and tiny micro jigs for trout. There are lures for trolling, casting, jigging, flipping, pitching and just about any other style of fishing one can imagine.

Whatever the type, the principle remains the same: a lure is used in the hope that it represents the prey of the target fish such that it will fool the fish into making a strike. Thus it is critical that the lure matches in some way the natural food of the fish. A lure need not be an exact resemblance of the prey in appearance; as long as it represents particular features of the prey such as movement and colour, it will be successful.

The main groups of lures are minnows, surface lures, soft plastics, skirted trolling lures, spinner blade lures, spoons and slices, Tassie lures and jigs. Of these, the minnow group is one of the most popular styles of lures that are available.

Spinner blade lures

One of the best styles of lure for trout is the basic spinner. These spinners are designed to be cast and retrieved, but are rarely trolled as they can produce excessive line twist.

Soft plastics

Classic soft plastic fishing involves slow jigging or jerking of the lure over the bottom structure. As the hook is embedded in the soft plastic itself, the lure is virtually snag proof. Soft plastics work well on native fish such as Murray cod, golden perch and impoundment bass.

Jigs

Jigs, despite the variety of shapes and sizes, are all designed to be worked or jigged vertically. Small marabou jigs are excellent for trout in rivers, but remember to free drift and not retrieve them. Larger and heavier bucktail jigs account for dozens of fish species in salt water from snapper to many other reef dwellers.

FLIES

The term artificial flies describes a huge range of fish deceiving creations, primarily constructed with fur and feathers, or artificial substitutes. Most are so light they are unable to be cast; they must be presented using a fly line where the weight of the line takes the fly to the fish.

The different types of flies are often categorised by whether the fly floats or sinks, and by the type of food imitated. Dry flies float on the water surface; wet flies are designed to fish below the surface.

Flies are most popular for trout fishing in fresh water, but many other species including Australian bass, Murray cod, barramundi, tuna, flathead and bream will take a fly.

Saltwater fly fishing has become popular. Most saltwater flies are wet, and are usually larger than freshwater flies.

Red Humpy *Kelly's Hopper* *Gum Beetle* *Red Tag*

Freshwater dry flies: Terrestrial

This group represents terrestrial insects, ranging from tiny midges to large beetles, that fall onto the water surface.

Barry Lodge's Emerger *Blue Dun* *Black Spinner* *Elk Hair Caddis*

Freshwater dry flies: Aquatic

These represent insects that live underwater during their nymphal stage and then hatch on or return to, the water surface as airborne insects, such as mayfly, caddis and damselflies.

Skirted trolling lures

These lures are used almost exclusively as trolling lures and almost always in salt water. They are trolled fast behind a boat in offshore fishing grounds for pelagic fish such as tuna, marlin or sailfish.

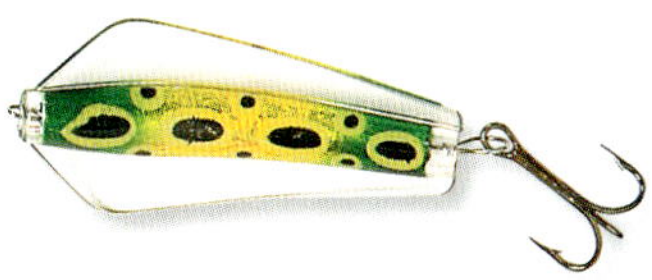
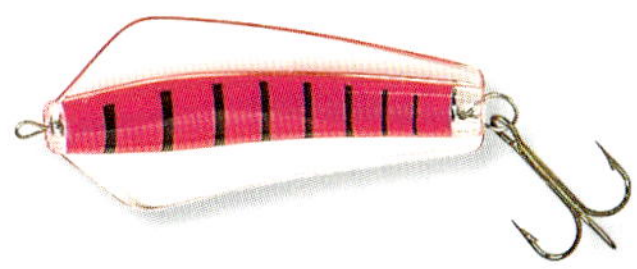

Tassie lures

The Tassie lure is an Australian invention that combines a minnow profile with an enticing action all of its own. They are primarily designed to be trolled in fresh water for trout and are easily one of the most effective designs for this type of fishing. They account for many fish taken in salt water as well, but are yet to gain widespread acceptance by saltwater anglers.

Spoons and slices

These are primarily designed to be cast and retrieved at a range of retrieve speeds. The more slim the profile, the faster the retrieve; the larger and wider the profile, the slower the retrieve. These lures can catch almost any fish that swims in salt or fresh water.

Minnows

This group is designed to resemble and behave like prey that will entice a strike from a larger predator. There are a variety of general types: floating divers, sinking divers, floating deep divers and neutral buoyancy lures. Minnow lures will catch many species of fish in both salt and fresh water, and they can either be cast or trolled behind a boat.

Surface lures

Surface lures are designed mainly to be cast and retrieved, and are rarely trolled behind a boat. They float on or near the surface and make a considerable disturbance on the surface when retrieved. This disturbance often attracts predator fish to the surface to smash the lure, sometimes in a spectacular fashion.

Bead-head Nymph

Damselfly Nymph

Brown Nymph

Freshwater wet flies: Nymphs

These patterns are particularly successful with trout. They represent the aquatic nymphal stage of some freshwater insects including mudeyes (dragonfly nymphs) and caddis.

Mrs Simpson

Craigs Nightime

Tom Jones

Freshwater wet flies: General

These represent aquatic animals such as bait fish (like galaxias), tadpoles, water beetles and shrimp.

Weed Wizard

Green Lizard

Deep Pink Thing

Red Marabou

G. D. Deceiver

Saltwater flies

Wet flies: These are used in salt water for fish ranging from barramundi to flathead, and bream to marlin. Wet flies usually represent such prey as bait fish and cephalopods. Poppers: These are dry flies used in both salt and fresh water. They are designed to stimulate a fish's propensity to strike a food source on the surface; for example, a Deer Hair Muddler for trout, a big polystyrene popper for marlin or sailfish.

Knots and Rigs

Practical knots are essential for successful angling and it is absolutely necessary to have a series of knots at your disposal to cater for the various rigging situations required for the different styles of fishing.

KNOTS

The full blood knot is probably the strongest to use for tying a hook, ring, or swivel to nylon monofilament. Limitations are only experienced when the line or leader is too heavy, or stiff, to permit the knot to be pulled tight.

The perfection loop is used for tying lure to leader because it does not impede the action of the lure. It is also useful for attaching fly to leader or tippet because it lays straight and does not cock to one side.

The double blood knot is useful for joining nylon monofilament lines of the same or similar size. Limitations are experienced when attempting to join lines of markedly different sizes.

RIGS

The basic rig is the Paternoster rig – one that is useful offshore, in bays and estuaries, and occasionally in fresh water. To make this rig correctly, you must learn the simple techniques of tying a tagless dropper loop and a blood bight loop, then all you do is put them together.

Another useful rig is the running sinker rig, which may be constructed in a number of ways using rings, swivels and even patented 'easy' running devices. These rigs are very suitable for estuary and freshwater fishing.

Perfection Loop

Attaching a lure to a heavy monofilament leader is the main use of the perfection loop.

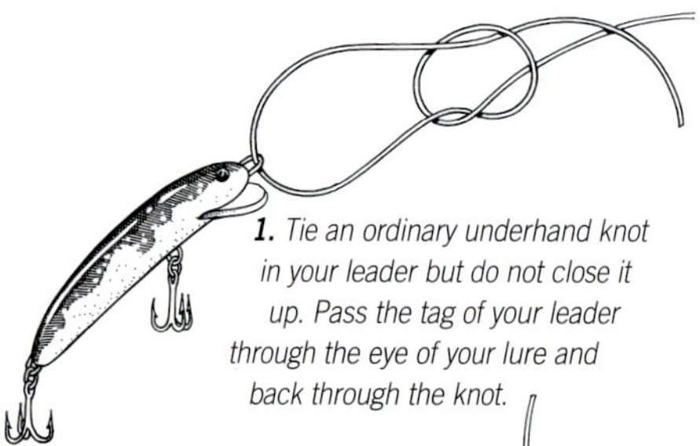

***1.** Tie an ordinary underhand knot in your leader but do not close it up. Pass the tag of your leader through the eye of your lure and back through the knot.*

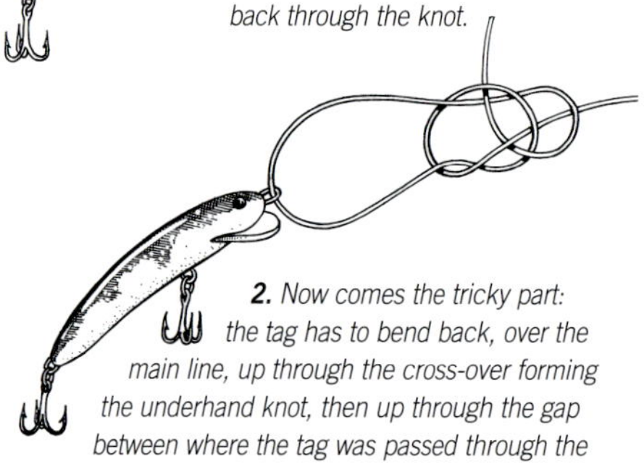

***2.** Now comes the tricky part: the tag has to bend back, over the main line, up through the cross-over forming the underhand knot, then up through the gap between where the tag was passed through the knot in step 1.*

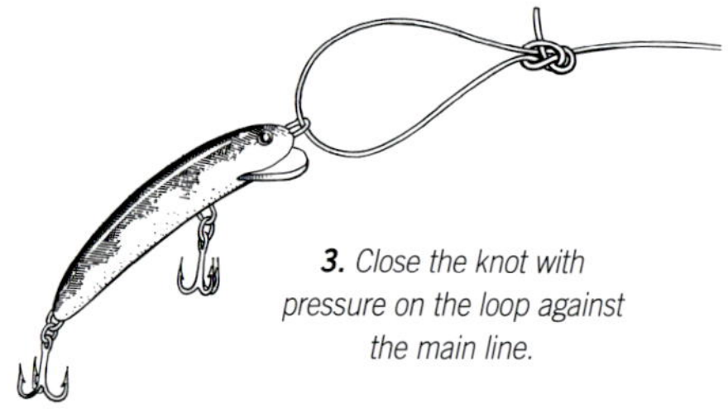

***3.** Close the knot with pressure on the loop against the main line.*

FULL BLOOD KNOT

If bay and estuary anglers were limited to using one knot, the full blood knot would be a good choice. At its best in lines from 3 to 30 kg, this knot is easy to tie and retains around 80 per cent of the line's strength.

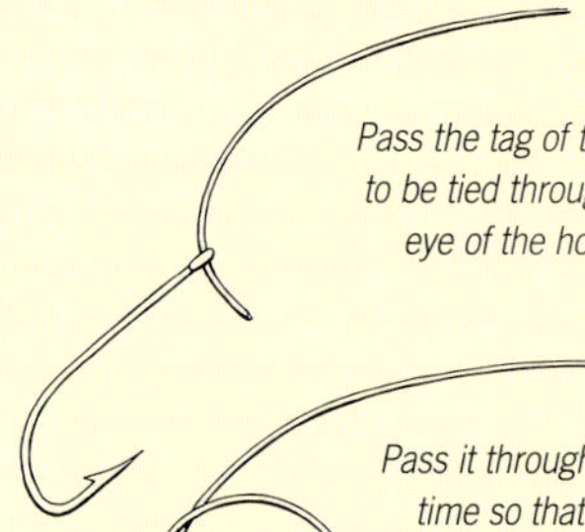

Pass the tag of the line to be tied through the eye of the hook.

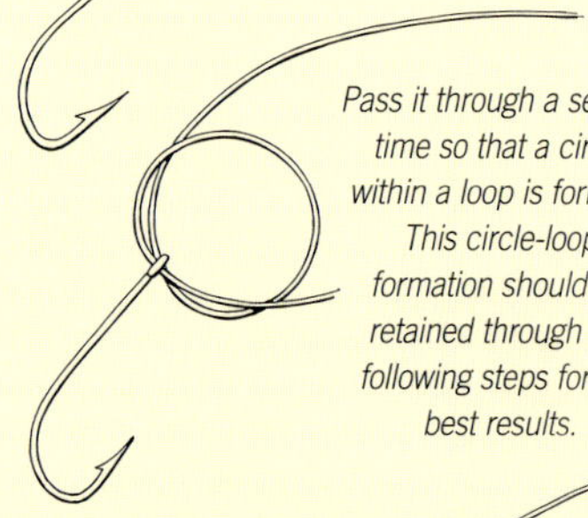

Pass it through a second time so that a circle within a loop is formed. This circle-loop formation should be retained through the following steps for the best results.

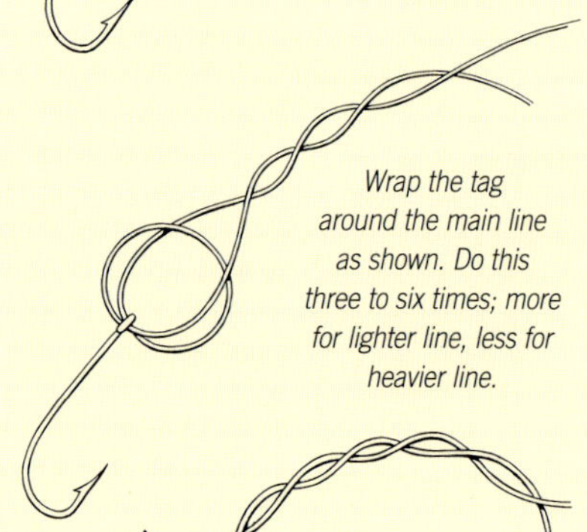

Wrap the tag around the main line as shown. Do this three to six times; more for lighter line, less for heavier line.

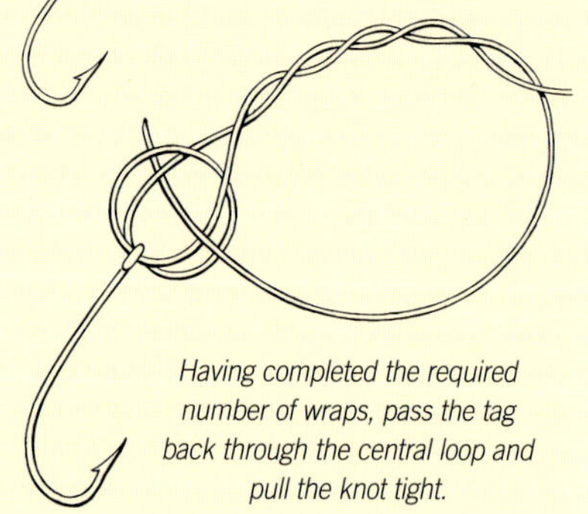

Having completed the required number of wraps, pass the tag back through the central loop and pull the knot tight.

Double Blood Knot

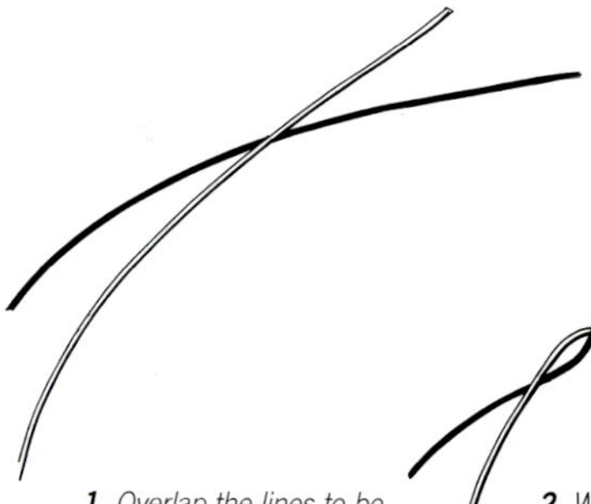

***1.** Overlap the lines to be joined by a generous margin.*

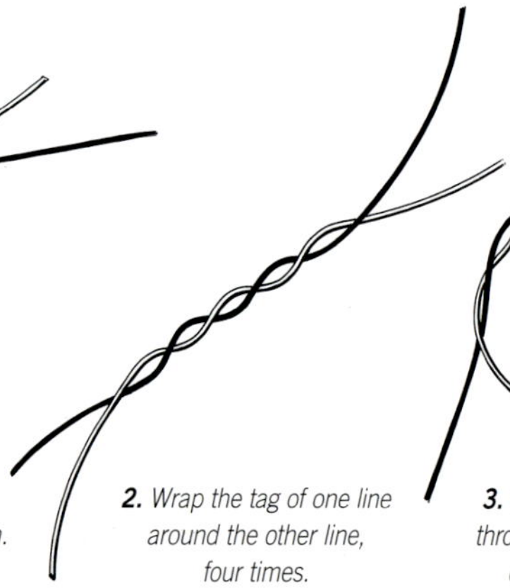

***2.** Wrap the tag of one line around the other line, four times.*

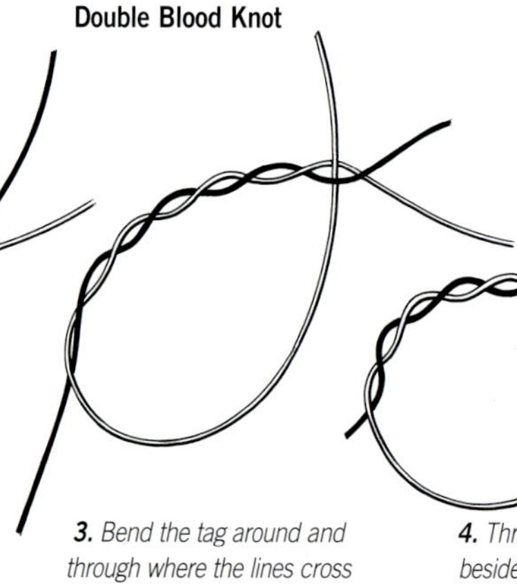

***3.** Bend the tag around and through where the lines cross over. Then commence wrapping with the opposite tag.*

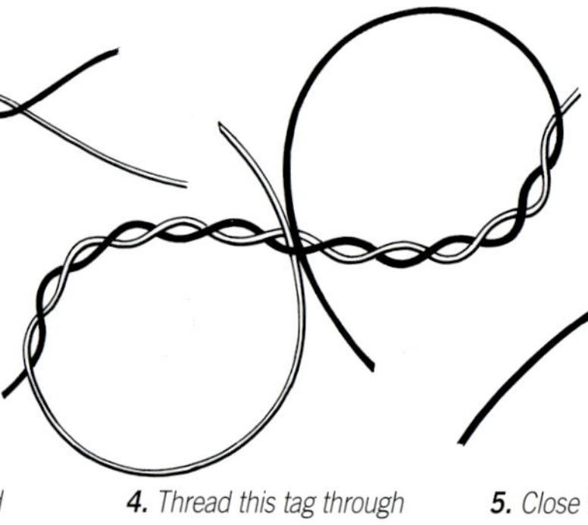

***4.** Thread this tag through beside the other, but from the opposite direction.*

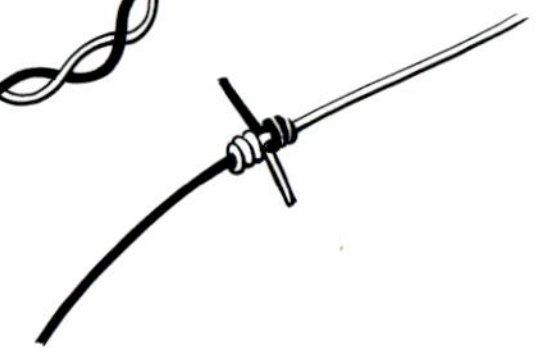

***5.** Close the knot with firm pressure on the lines on each side of the knot then trim the tags.*

Paternoster rig

To put together the rig, first tie a tagless dropper loop. This can be tied anywhere along the line enabling the angler to use multiple droppers. To attach the sinker and the dropper line to the hook, tie a blood bight loop.

Tagless Dropper Loop

This method allows the angler to tie a loop that will not slip anywhere along the line.

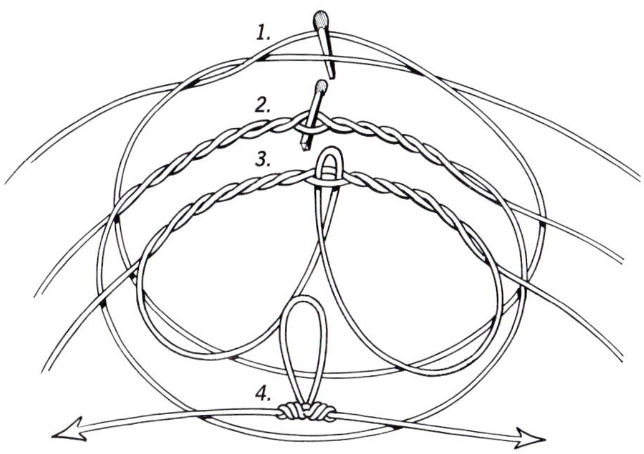

1. *Make a loop in your line and insert a match or something similar to one side of the crossover.*

2. *Rotate the match through three or four complete turns.*

3. *Remove the match and insert the loop through the same wrap from where you removed the match.*

4. *Close the knot with pressure on each side of the loop.*

Blood Bight Loop

This is a loop for attaching droppers or snoods to a dropper loop in the main line.

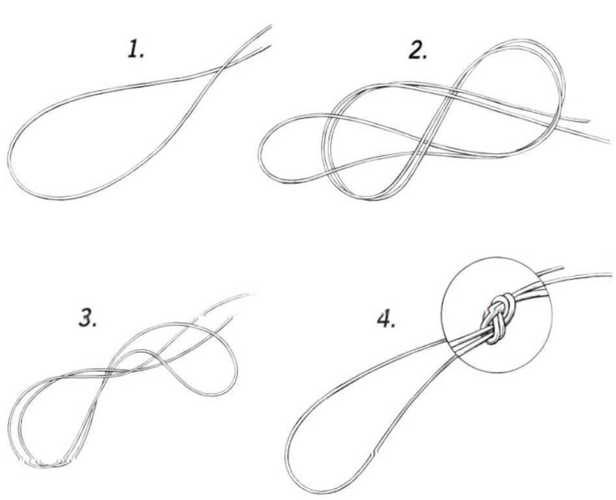

1. *Make a loop in the opposite end of the dropper to the hook.*

2. *Bend the loop back on itself to form a second loop.*

3. *Thread the first loop through the second so that you have a figure-of-eight configuration.*

4. *Pull the knot up and trim the tag. The inset shows the appearance of the knot.*

Making a Paternoster rig

Join the two loops together by interlocking.

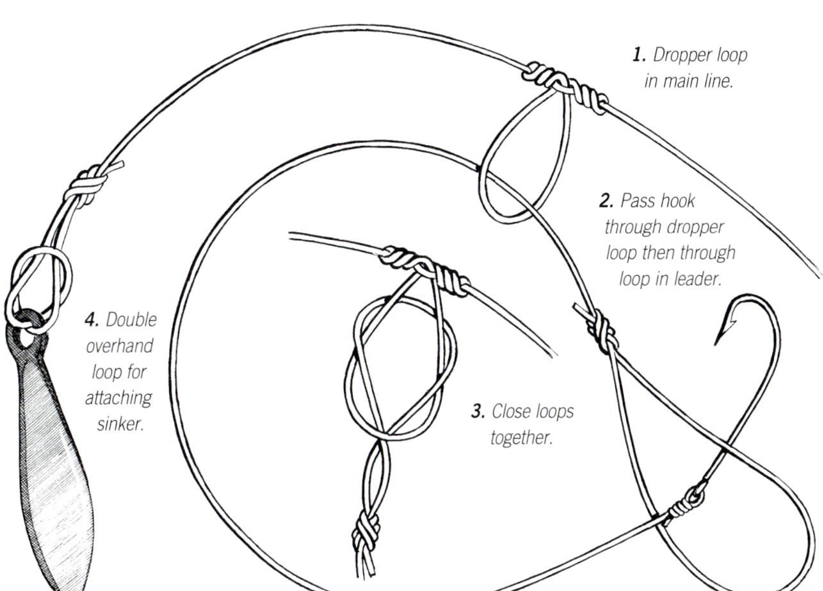

1. *Dropper loop in main line.*

2. *Pass hook through dropper loop then through loop in leader.*

3. *Close loops together.*

4. *Double overhand loop for attaching sinker.*

Running Sinker rig

The purpose of a running sinker rig is to allow the line to run freely through the sinker when a fish picks up and then pulls on the bait. Sinkers used for this rig should have a hole through them, the larger the better.

Shown is a running sinker rig in its simplest form with a small ball sinker threaded onto the line and running all the way down to the hook. This rig works well but has no provision for a heavier leader. As well, only very small sinkers can be used to avoid damage to the bait when casting out.

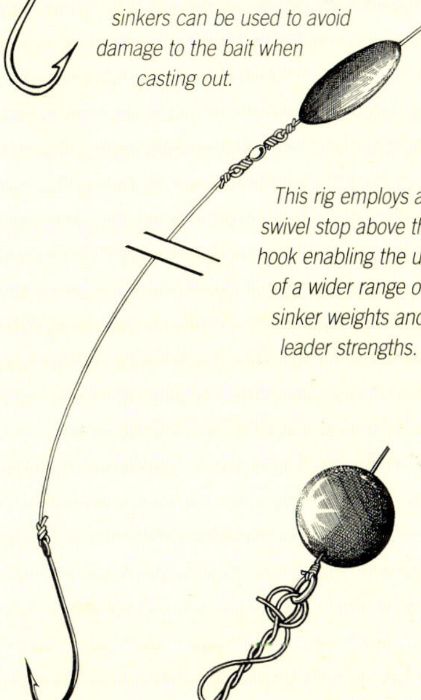

This rig employs a swivel stop above the hook enabling the use of a wider range of sinker weights and leader strengths.

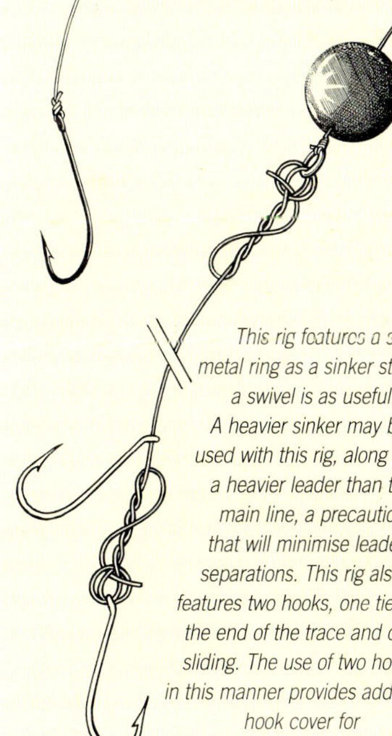

This rig features a solid metal ring as a sinker stop but a swivel is as useful. A heavier sinker may be used with this rig, along with a heavier leader than the main line, a precaution that will minimise leader separations. This rig also features two hooks, one tied to the end of the trace and one sliding. The use of two hooks in this manner provides additional hook cover for larger baits.

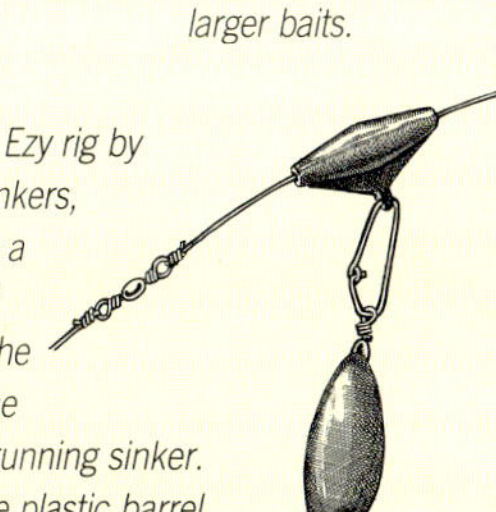

Shown is the Ezy rig by Symmetric Sinkers, which features a plastic barrel threaded onto the line in the same manner as a running sinker. The clip on the plastic barrel permits heavier or lighter sinkers to be used as the tidal stream increases or slows. The bomb style sinker is most suited for use with the Ezy rig.

All About Bait

Fish will respond best to a bait that is presented as naturally and attractively as possible. It should be a bait that offers no reason for the fish to become suspicious or alarmed and, preferably, one that is a naturally occurring food item in the habitat of the target fish.

SALTWATER BAITS

A fussy fish, and there are many of these, will often baulk at something that seems unnatural in the water, is unfamiliar or stale. A well presented bait freshly procurred from the bait grounds where one is fishing works almost every time.

A fish's attraction to bait is partly visual, but mostly has to do with taste, smell and touch. For this reason, contaminants such as sun cream, insect repellent and some kinds of food, such as bananas, onion and oranges, can turn fish off. Even some human odours, such as pheromones exuded from the skin and pores, can have a detrimental effect. There is a good reason to use masking substances such as various fish attractant solutions, or simply 'washing' your hands with bait, much like you would with soap.

Fresh and live baits work best because they secrete various chemical signals that stimulate fish to feed. These natural chemicals are, however, labile; that is, they become dispersed and destroyed on contact with air and water. Dead or cut baits lose their attraction very rapidly, while live baits continue to exude chemical strike triggers for a short time but, as fatigue and stress mount, the production of these attractants slows down. This is why you can often get a result by pulling in a bait that has lain untouched for some time and replacing it with a fresh one.

The key to baitfishing is to realise that you are talking about food. Fish food, it is true, but food nonetheless, and to understand the importance of top grade bait, look no further than your own preference for fresh and attractively presented food.

Anchovies
Good estuary bait. Use for snapper, tailor and other estuary-type species.

Squid *(bottley squid shown here)*
A good general purpose bait for snapper, flathead and whiting.

Mussels
A good bait for whiting and bream. The shell and remains can be used as berley.

Whitebait
A popular bait fish that attracts a wide range of estuary species.

Beachworm
Use for bream, luderick and whiting.

Pilchards or mulies
One of Australia's most widely used bait fish.

Prawns
Use for estuary and bay fishing.

Pippis
One of the better all-round baits. Target fish are whiting, bream and Australian salmon.

POPULAR SALTWATER BAITS

Description	Location	Method of catching	Buying	Storage	Target fish
Bait fish (whole dead or live garfish, pilchards, hardyheads, whitebait, slimy mackerel, poddy mullet, fish strips, cubes, slabs)	Estuaries over sand flats and weed beds or in deep water near wharves; close to ocean rocks.	Line fishing, scoop netting, trapping.	Fresh or frozen from most bait outlets.	Keep alive for a day or overnight in broad, shallow container, open to the air. Refrigerate dead fish overnight; salt or freeze for longer periods.	Dead: drift or cast whole fish or pieces for flathead, large bream, tailor, snapper, mulloway, barramundi, tuna, mackerel; rig and troll large whole fish for pelagics. Live: drift or troll for tuna, mackerel, shark, john dory, flathead, barramundi.
Beachworms	Intertidal area of shelving ocean beaches.	Entice to surface with 'stink' bait of dead fish; look for 'V' wake as wave recedes, grab with fingers or worming pliers.	Available live, frozen and preserved from bait outlets.	Roll live worms in dry sand for temporary storage; keep cool in covered shallow dish overnight.	Bream, flathead, whiting, luderick, Australian salmon, mulloway, dart, javelin fish.
Crabs (whole, live or dead; or dead, cut into pieces)	Intertidal shoreline of estuary mud and sand flats; rocks on coastal shoreline.	By hand.	Difficult to buy.	Keep live overnight in 8 cm of water in bucket with aerator. Dead crabs do not keep well.	Bream in estuaries, groper and big bream from ocean rocks.
Cunjevoi (cunje)	Intertidal zone of ocean rocks and rocky shoreline of open bays.	Cut casing with strong knife and remove flesh of animal.	Some bait outlets.	Freeze in sealed containers or use same day; keep cool and damp.	Bream, drummer, groper.
Estuarine worms (bloodworms, squirt worms, tube worms blubber worms)	Saltwater creeks, tidal mud and sand flats, exposed weedbeds.	Dig blood and tube worms; pump or pressurise squirt worms; dig tube worms and blubber worms.	Preserved and live bloodworms available from bait outlets.	Live worms best used immediately; refrigerate preserved worms.	Bream, flathead, whiting, Australian salmon, luderick, mulloway, javelin fish.
Green nippers (green shrimp, mud shrimp, pistol prawn, snapping shrimp)	Intertidal mudflats and seagrass beds; under logs, rocks and debris exposed by falling tide	Pump as for pink nippers; tread shallows over weed beds until shrimp float to top of muddy water; turn over debris.	Rarely available for sale.	Overnight in bucket of clean aerated sea water.	All estuary species and some inshore species.
Green weed	Estuary shorelines, quiet bays especially; some ocean or bay rock platforms.	Rake or by hand.	Bait outlets. Wrap in paper, not plastic	Foam Esky, or wrapped in newspaper and kept cool in fridge.	Luderick in estuaries and from ocean rocks; also rock blackfish.
Mussels	Wharf and bridge pylons, oyster rack timbers.	Hand pick or use mussel rake to remove from beds.	Bait outlets, fish shops.	Keep live for 2 to 3 days in sealed container in fridge; freeze as dead baits.	Most estuary species, especially whiting when slit into thin strips.
Pink nippers (bass yabbies, yabbies, ghost shrimp)	Intertidal estuary sand and mudflats.	Pump from sand by placing yabby pump over holes.	Sold live from some bait outlets.	Overnight in bucket of clean aerated sea water.	All estuary species and some inshore species.
Pippis (eugaries, wongs, Goolwa cockles in SA)	Intertidal zone of surf beaches.	Hand-dig under raised mounds, or look for twin siphon holes and 'V' wake as wave recedes.	Most bait outlets.	Keep live for 2 to 3 days in sealed container in fridge; freeze as dead baits.	Bream, flathead, whiting, tailor, garfish, mullet, Australian salmon.
Prawns	Estuaries and coastal lakes.	As for shrimp; or with lights and scoop, or drag nets at night when no moon.	Bait outlets.	Live: in wet weed and hessian or in aerated bucket. Dead: on ice for 1 to 2 days, or freeze for longer.	All estuary fish, and also inshore species. Peeled prawns good offshore for morwong and snapper.
Sea cabbage (cabbage, sea lettuce)	Intertidal zone of ocean rocks.	Pick by hand.	Rarely available for sale.	As for green weed.	As for green weed.
Shrimp	Weed beds, tidal creeks.	Push prawn scoop through weed beds, or disturb with garden rake and scoop up escaping shrimp.	Difficult to buy, but seasonally available in some localities.	Live: in wet weed and hessian or in aerated bucket. Dead: on ice for 1 to 2 days, or freeze for longer.	All estuary fish.
Squid (calamari, flying squid)	Offshore or bays near rocks or jetties.	Yo Zuri squid jig or baited squid jig.	From bait outlets.	Freeze or refrigerate.	Whole squid for pelagics; strips for estuary species.

FRESHWATER BAITS

As with saltwater baits, the best freshwater baits are those that are gathered fresh from the area where you are fishing. They should be presented live if practical and as naturally as possible.

A very interesting side of baitfishing emerges when angling in fresh water that runs down into estuarine rivers and lakes. Here, marine baits, such as prawns and shrimp, can be taken by bass from one spot and bream from another only metres downstream.

In some Victorian lakes, saltwater whitebait have been used with success on land-locked salmon and, in various large New South Wales water storages, trout have fallen to cooked saltwater prawns. The counterpoint is that bream have been seen smashing live cicadas from the surface, just like a bass. There are some universal baits that 'travel' well, and they will work just about anywhere. This does not, however, invalidate the principle of selecting baits that the fish might expect to see in their habitat.

The traditional trout fishing ploy of examining the stomach contents of captured fish is wonderfully enlightening, once you wash and sift through the contents to identify what it is that the fish have been eating. Such examinations will often reveal that much of the diet of freshwater fish is insects and, because it is so difficult to mount all but the largest of insects on a hook, one can see why artificial fly fishing came into being.

Large insects, like grasshoppers, mudeyes, beetles, cicadas, and various larvae of moths, beetles and so on, are all prime candidates for freshwater baits. So are small foragers, such as galaxias, gudgeons and many others. Crustaceans are important too. Various forms of shrimp and yabbies work on everything from barramundi to trout. Worms and grubs – the quintessential bait of small children and truant executives alike – are dynamite on a range of freshwater fish. There are even various shellfish found inside captured fish, but these present rigging difficulties which mean they are seldom used.

As with saltwater baitfishing, bait selection, rigging and methods of presentation are of paramount importance. The same rules apply: show the fish something it likes to eat and expects to see, and put it where it can be eaten without risk to the fish.

When baitfishing in either fresh or salt water, care should be taken to prevent the escape of live baits not taken from the same water you are fishing. Leftover live baits should be returned to the water from whence they came.

Maggots
Used for a range of freshwater fishing particularly for smaller species. Especially popular when coarse fishing for trout, redfin and tench.

Earthworms
A popular bait that attracts most freshwater species including trout, redfin, silver perch and eel.

Mudeyes
These larvae of dragonflies are one of the most effective trout baits. Sometimes expensive, or difficult to find, especially during winter.

Glassies
Inhabit salt water but best for freshwater fishing, especially when chinook salmon and rainbow trout are the targets.

Mussels
A good bait for whiting and bream. The shell and remains can be used as berley.

Meal worms
Used mainly for trout.

Yabbies
A good all-round bait. Excellent for native species including Murray cod.

Shrimp
A multi-purpose bait, good for trout and native species, and the northern estuary dwellers such as barramundi and sooty grunter.

POPULAR FRESHWATER BAITS

Description	*Location*	*Method of catching*	*Buying*	*Storage*	*Target fish*
Crickets (black and sand, or 'mole')	Black crickets in paddocks under cow dung, rotting vegetation; mole crickets buried in riverside sand banks.	Turn over mulch and dung for black crickets; dig for mole crickets or gather them whenever they swarm on hot summer nights.	Rarely available.	Push gently down into old sock, which lets them breathe but traps them until required.	Australian bass, perch, trout, cod, redfin.
Grasshoppers	Any grassy area, usually the sunny side of hills.	Catch by hand (best early morning, before dew evaporates, as grasshoppers cannot fly until wings are dry).	Not generally available.	Push gently down into old sock, which lets them breathe but traps them until required.	Australian bass, perch, trout, cod, redfin.
Grubs (bardi grubs, witchetty grubs)	Burrows or holes around gum trees, river banks and river flats.	Either dig or use bardi cable.	Most bait outlets.	Containers of cool damp earth or canvas boxes that allow grubs to breathe.	Trout, Murray cod, perch, catfish; bream and whiting in estuaries.
'Kitchen' baits (sweet corn, potato, bread, dough)	Home kitchen or grocery store.	Kitchen scraps.	Supermarket.	As for normal food storage.	European carp, freshwater mullet, sometimes trout.
Maggots (blowfly larvae, gentles)	Home grown.	Hang pieces of meat outside to attract blowflies.	Good bait outlets.	Keep cool to delay pupation.	Trout and other freshwater species; popular with coarse anglers.
Mudeyes (larvae of common dragonfly)	Small, weedy farm dams; lake shores at night.	Fine mesh net dragged through likely habitat, or scooping insects and plucking them from reed stems, etc., as they migrate to shore during hatches.	Good bait outlets.	Keep refrigerated, or in cool damp environment.	Trout, redfin, perch, Australian bass, cod.
Mussels	Mud bottom of large rivers, particularly in cooler climates.	Collect from river bottom.	Not generally available.	Keep alive for 2 to 3 days in sealed container in refrigerator, or freeze as dead baits for longer periods.	Catfish, eels, European carp; bream in estuarine areas.
Shrimp	Weed beds in dams, creeks and rivers.	Scoop net; shrimp trap, baited with soap or luncheon meat.	Not widely available.	Cool damp bag or canvas box; cover loosely with freshly cut weed, use as soon as possible.	Perch, Australian bass, cod, trout, redfin, barramundi, saratoga, catfish, sooty grunter.
Whole dead baitfish (gambusia, galaxias, glassies, gudgeons, bony bream, marine whitebait)	Small dams, creeks, ponds, backwaters, edges of lakes and rivers (except marine baitfish).	Fish traps; scoop netting; berley; and in case of bony bream, tiny baited hooks.	Can be bought frozen, chilled or preserved from bait outlets.	Refrigerate or freeze in sealed plastic packs, or preserve in salt.	Trout, Australian bass, perch, barramundi (fresh best), cod.
Worms (earthworms, tiger worms, scrub worms)	Under rotting vegetation in home gardens or gullies below dairies. Scrub worms from well-watered rock and sand slopes, or under leaf litter.	Lift mulch, rocks and logs, or dig.	Most bait outlets.	Containers filled with cool damp earth and mulch, or dampened canvas boxes that allow the baits to breathe.	Redfin, trout, Australian bass, cod, perch, catfish and European carp; bream and whiting in estuarine areas.
Yabbies (crayfish)	Mud banks of large rivers and dams, rock piles and edges of weed beds.	Piece of meat on string in farm dams (scoop up as feelers break the surface); spotlight at night in sandy lake shallows.	Good bait outlets.	Damp, cool aerated bag or canvas box.	Big trout, Australian bass, perch, barramundi, saratoga, redfin, catfish, sooty grunter.

Fishing Safely

Fishing is one of the safer sports. Rock anglers are the most vulnerable; their keenness can lead them to make foolhardy decisions. When accidents happen they can usually be traced to foolishness or inexperience.

THE WEATHER

Weather has a lot of bearing on water safety, so whether you are fishing from a boat or from land, be aware of the weather forecast and watch for changes.

Wind is the single greatest threat to fishing safety. Offshore winds (blowing from land to sea) can occur any time but are most common in winter. They blow up quickly and often violently, and pose most threat to boats, especially those with mechanical problems, inadequate horsepower or marginal sea ability. A disabled boat can be blown kilometres out to sea.

Cool changes, too, can come through with a rush, usually from the south. They can whip up seas in a matter of minutes, threatening boat anglers or rock hoppers. Onshore winds also affect rock and boat anglers, but tend to give more notice in that they often blow gently from daybreak and strengthen as the day progresses. However, any wind that increases force perceptibly needs to be treated with respect. Boat anglers should quit early and run home in reasonable conditions, rather than wait until the squall hits and have to battle their way back.

Watch weather reports on television each night, phone your local boating weather information service before you go out, and keep an eye on the sky during the day yourself. Indications of developing low pressure cells and associated winds show up on weather maps as a lot of lines (isobars) compressed together. Recorded phone weather information is usually a few hours old by the time you hear it, so bear in mind that a system that is a couple of hundred kilometres away at night might be just about to hit next morning. Look for dense cloud banks developing on the horizon, or seabirds flying low and fast – and all in the same direction – both of which are natural signs nearly always heralding that strong winds are to follow.

ROCK FISHING

When fishing the rocks, especially in an unfamiliar place, keep the following in mind.

- On arrival always first work out where you might be able to swim to and climb out, should you fall or be washed in. If there is the slightest risk of going in and you have any doubt about your ability to get safely back out again, do not fish that spot. There are plenty of fish in less dangerous places.
- Be aware of swell sizes and the way changing weather or tide levels can affect particular locations. Many spots are sheltered from one direction but exposed to another. Pick your spots to suit the weather.
- Watch the sea for at least twenty minutes to assess the safety of the platform, before you venture down to sea level.
- Look for hazard signs such as wet rock surfaces or substantial growths of weed. These areas are sure to be covered with water at times and can be slippery.
- Use suitable footwear: on weedy rocks, wear rock plates or at least studded plastic sandals. Sneakers are fine on dry rock, but can be dangerous on slime. Leather-soled shoes are suicidal.
- Never fish the rocks alone.

Bar crossing can be particularly hazardous for boat anglers

BOATING

Safety in boats means not placing yourself or your boat in situations beyond your control. Bigger boats are more stable than smaller ones, but the safety of both depends on responsible and accomplished boating ability. You need to maintain the boat's balance by sensible loading, avoid water too rough for the boat to handle, and have the safety gear required by law, for whatever environment you are fishing – including lifejackets for everyone on board, especially children.

Many rivers are tranquil, and aside from possible collisions you should encounter few risks. Punts and tiny craft suitable for placid water should not be used in rough conditions or where fast currents exist. Spend enough time in calm water to become familiar with your boat's capabilities before venturing into open and rough water. Ease yourself gradually into more demanding conditions over several outings; don't just trust to luck and tackle the big stuff right away.

Shallow waters such as bays, estuaries and large lakes can become extremely choppy in windy conditions, and a small boat can get into difficulties very quickly. Beyond

POSITION FINDERS

Most offshore boats are equipped with depth sounders; some are also equipped with a global positioning satellite (GPS) navigation system. Basically this is a receiver that allows you to lock onto several satellites that are constantly orbiting the earth, and obtain a 'fix' of your position quickly and precisely. Hand-held models are available.

A GPS receiver also has the advantage of enabling you to locate a fishing spot, once you have 'fixed' its position, or once its co-ordinates are known. Further information is available from your supplier.

Ensure junior anglers wear lifejackets at all times

HOOK REMOVAL

While the most common fishing accident is a cut or graze, the next is the one that the angler most fears: being impaled by a fish hook. If such a misfortune occurs, and the barb is protruding, you can cut it off and withdraw the hook easily. If the barb is embedded in the flesh, seek medical attention if possible; if not, put a line around the throat of the hook and, when downward pressure is placed on the shank, pull the hook straight out. The downward pressure brings the barb out through the hole already in the flesh, enlarging it somewhat, but not making a ragged tear. If two people can perform this service for the sufferer, so much the better. The one pulling on the cord should not be kind, but get the hook out in one swift pull. Once the hook has been removed, follow standard first-aid procedures.

sheltered waters, the open ocean beckons many anglers but the risks are greater. Offshore boating demands a larger boat, more experience and a greater level of preparedness to cope with the risks involved.

The entrances between estuaries and the ocean can be particularly hazardous places for boat anglers. These entrances, called bars, are where tidal flows, offshore weather and the shallowing sea floor combine to create steep breaking seas and dangerous currents. They are most dangerous when a strong outgoing tide runs against an onshore wind.

Anglers in boats under 4 m should not contemplate bar crossings in anything but the calmest of conditions. Since conditions can quickly change, boats of 5 or 6 m are a more realistic minimum offshore size. Even large boats can get into trouble if their skippers plan poorly and return to port to face a run-out tide and onshore wind. Storms increase the hazards, of course.

Open boats will expose their occupants to the elements more than boats with cabins or at least covers of some sort. But one of the greatest safety aids is being able to see where you are going and covers that obscure vision are not safe at all. Your boat engine should be regularly serviced, and a backup engine is sensible too – either as a smaller auxiliary or a twin engine set-up. A marine radio is an essential safety item, enabling you to radio for help in a variety of situations.

To gain the best idea you can of the water you are fishing, start with Admiralty charts of the area, supplemented by fishing information on various locality maps. These will help you avoid known hazards and increase your fishing success as well. Always tell someone where you are going and what time you expect to be back, and if you change your mind, tell them again. Staying out later or coming in early without signing off can have a lot of people worried for nothing.

Alcohol and boats do not mix any better than alcohol and cars. Alcohol will cloud your judgement, impair your ability to control the boat and slow down your response to emergencies. Save your hard drinking for dry land; water or soft drinks are the way to go while in charge of a boat.

CLOTHING

Carry adequate clothing. Temperatures can drop quickly overnight or even in the middle of the day if there is a sudden change of weather. Being caught in a rainstorm and chilled by wind can lead to hypothermia.

Extra clothing can be stowed in the boat until required and even land-based anglers can roll up a lightweight rain jacket, or keep a jumper on hand for emergencies.

Minimise the discomfort of sunburn and the risk of skin cancer with suitable clothing, a hat and a 15+ sunscreen. Carry an insect repellent too as many good fishing areas attract insects such as mosquitoes.

FIRST AID

Anyone going fishing needs some first aid training and a basic first-aid kit. When an accident happens, it is likely you will be some distance away from help. First-aid kits should include band-aids, wound dressings, antiseptic, a clean surgical blade or scissors, and a pressure bandage.

Caring for the Environment

Recreational fishing is great fun – lots of fresh air, beautiful scenery, peace and quiet, and with a bit of luck a fish or two! It certainly seems like a sport with a low impact on the environment, and responsible angling can be just that. A solitary angler fishing off a jetty or wandering a river bank may not seem capable of doing any significant harm, but multiply that impact by the millions of Australians who fish every year and the story is quite different.

Everybody who ventures out with a rod and line should remember one important fact: Australia's fisheries are very much a finite resource.

A big school of tailor off a beach, a rock platform covered with shellfish, or a heavy 'rise' on a trout lake may each give the illusion of endless abundance, but an illusion is all it is. Australia's fisheries are slowly but surely shrinking, and they were never particularly rich in the first place. Scientists state that Australian coastal waters have always been less fertile than waters found in many other parts of the globe. The relative lack of inland rivers and lakes has also limited the productivity of the freshwater fisheries.

Since European settlement, three dangers have steadily encroached on Australia's fragile fisheries: habitat depletion, pollution and fishing pressure. While ruthless industries, urban sprawl or commercial anglers might be blamed for the decline, the sad fact is that the humble recreational angler has done, and continues to do, a share of the damage. Harsh words, but the good news is that with a bit of care and a sense of responsibility, fishing can be virtually harmless to the environment. The following information shows how anglers can enjoy fishing without damaging the fishery.

OBEY FISHING REGULATIONS

Recreational fishing should never be seen as a 'free-for-all'. Regulations prescribing bag and size limits, closed seasons, closed waters and protected species are there for a reason. Many fish are vulnerable, especially at spawning (breeding) time, and fish populations can be, and have been, decimated by greedy or ignorant anglers. Other species are slow to breed, or have had their habitat so reduced that they cannot rebuild large populations.

Some fish that are especially vulnerable to over-fishing include Australian bass, Murray cod, gummy and school shark, southern bluefin tuna and snapper. Others, like trout cod and Australian grayling, are now so rare they are totally protected. Even seemingly abundant species, such as trout, bream and whiting, are vulnerable in some locations.

Regulations also apply to the equipment you may use – the number of rods and hooks, and (where permitted at all) the size and shape of nets. Fortunately, the use of destructive set-lines and set-nets is largely illegal now, and offenders risk heavy penalties in many parts of Australia.

It is the responsibility of all anglers to know the regulations pertaining to the waters they choose to fish. Many shellfish and crustaceans are also the subject of regulations. Take the wrong species, or too many, and you may be breaking the law. The regulations outlined in this book are intended as a guide only; contact your nearest State fisheries office or consult the guide issued with your fishing licence for up-to-date information.

An abalone inspector looks out for poachers. Avoid breaking the law – know the regulations

LIMIT YOUR CATCH

Throughout Australia, a welcome trend has appeared over the last decade or two: anglers are starting to release fish, even where no limits apply or bag limits have not been met. Many anglers now realise that most legal limits are extremely generous. Australia lags far behind many western nations, where limits of just one or two fish per angler per day are now commonplace. While a few pest species like carp need heavy culling by anglers, for the vast majority of species there is a growing realisation that overloaded bags of fish are a loss Australian waters – fresh or salt – can no longer withstand. Keeping a couple of fish for dinner is usually okay, but otherwise, fish should be carefully released.

Line-caught fish can usually be released with a high chance of survival if the following recommendations are observed.

- Handle the fish as gently and as little as possible, with wet hands.
- Keep it out of the water for a minimal time. If the hook is too deep to easily wriggle free, cut it off with clippers as close to the hook eye as possible.

LITTER

Discarded bottles, cans and wrappers are an eyesore in otherwise beautiful fishing environments. Six-pack rings and discarded fishing line are killers – fish and numerous aquatic animals become tangled in these and die by the thousands each year.

POLLUTION

Anglers are most likely to risk polluting waters when boating or camping. The obvious threat from boats is oil and petrol leaks, and spills, so motors, tanks and lines should be checked regularly. Campers can inadvertently pollute lakes and streams by the use of soaps and detergents, which even in small quantities can upset the chemical balance of the waters. The safest solution is to do the dishes and any washing in basins or buckets back at camp. Incidentally, if camp site toilets are not available, burying human waste 50 m or more from waterways will help avoid possible contamination. Of course, driving off-road vehicles and motorbikes for any distance along stream beds is physically and chemically damaging. Crossing a stream via the shortest practical route is the

When gathering bait, only take as much as you need for immediate use

only acceptable method, and if a bridge is available nearby, use it.

Finally, berleying is beginning to cause concern as coarse fishing becomes more popular. While not likely to pose too many problems in the ocean, berleying on confined inland waters may have a negative impact on the environment if large quantities are used. For this reason, berleying is illegal on some inland waters. It is totally prohibited on Tasmanian inland waters.

NOXIOUS SPECIES AND DISEASE

Noxious fish such as European carp have done tremendous damage to Australia's inland fisheries. With few natural enemies, incredible breeding abilities and destructive feeding habits, they are the 'aquatic rabbit' of inland waters. Ironically, it was the illegal release of these fish for angling that caused the problem. While carp have grabbed the spotlight, numerous other fish, even natives, can cause great damage if introduced into the wrong aquatic environments. Not only does the translocation of the fish themselves carry risks, there is also a danger of spreading fish diseases in the process.

Anglers most commonly distribute undesirable fish species in two ways: inadvertently through the careless use of live bait, or deliberately through illegal stocking. Both can have equally devastating consequences. Great care should be taken to prevent the escape of any live baits not taken from the same water you are fishing. Under no circumstances should carp, redfin, gambusia or aquarium fish ever be used as live bait. Note that using live bait is prohibited in some waters. Needless to say, stocking of any species of fish is usually illegal without the approval of State fisheries departments.

GATHERING BAIT

As well as the environmental risks of using live fish baits outlined above, anglers should be aware of the damage that gathering other baits can cause. Concentrated digging for the humble earthworm has caused substantial damage on several inland waterways. Similar damage on a smaller scale can result from anglers turning over logs and rocks when bait collecting. On the subject of bait collecting, it should be noted that frogs are now a prohibited bait in some areas.

All the above dos and don'ts might seem to suggest that anglers are an uncaring lot where the environment is concerned, but usually the reverse is true. Most have a vested interest in ensuring the environment is well cared for – after all, a healthy environment equals more fish to catch!

All over the country, anglers are not only acting with environmental responsibility, they are also taking positive steps to actually mend the damage done by others in years gone by. Many angling clubs in particular are doing plenty of good work to rehabilitate the waterways, with restocking programs, streamside revegetation schemes, and the lobbying of governments for better care of fisheries and other activities. If you are not content with merely avoiding damage to the environment, call your local club and see what projects they are involved in – you may get an opportunity to help your local fisheries, and directly improve your fishing in the process.

WHERE TO FISH

Reebok

Contents

Introduction

New South Wales is a big fishing state, with its offshore, coastal and inland waters diverse enough to provide wonderful fishing across a whole range of styles. Rock and beach fishing is more heavily practised here than in other states, and there are some superb locations to attract the highly skilled devotees to this branch of the sport. Trout and native streams are the most extensive in the country.

There are reefs offshore for the 'outside' boat anglers, and big game in the oceanic currents that come within the range of the experienced and well-equipped sports anglers.

The lower reaches of the big rivers of the north, and the superb estuarine lakes of the south, can be explored for Australia's best known table fish – flathead, whiting and bream.

Inland, there are plentiful supplies of natives like golden perch in the warmer waters. Trout abound in the cooler lakes and rivers from the New England tablelands right down south to the famous Snowy Mountains' fisheries. The long, slow-flowing rivers in the west of the state provide a more relaxed style of freshwater fishing. Holiday makers here will find fishing just one of the attractions.

Rock fishing in Port Jackson

PROTECTED MARINE AREAS

Australia's oceans are home to some of the world's most unique marine features and creatures. Due to this the commonwealth and state governments have created marine, coastal or aquatic protected areas (also known as zones, parks, reserves or sanctuaries) to protect some areas of our coastline from human impacts. The degree to which you can fish within these zones differs within and between each state. In some areas you can't fish at all, whereas in others there are selected areas in which certain species or fishing methods are restricted. These areas are constantly changing in size and scope and so the sites, locations and restrictions listed here could change in the near future. We have not listed the exact locations of the restricted areas; it is up to you as a responsible angler to find out accurate locations and information on full restrictions from the relevant government authority, just as you do for licences. This list provides the names of protected areas, with brief details of fishing restrictions. The maps featured in this guide do not show all sites listed here, so remember to use this table in conjunction with the maps and also to get information from the fisheries or conservation departments to ensure you have the most accurate information on restrictions before you cast off.

Site	*Location*	*Restrictions*
Elizabeth and Middleton Reefs Marine National Nature Reserve	Located in the Tasman Sea, some 600 kilometres east of Coffs Harbour, northern New South Wales.	No commercial fishing. Recreational pelagic fishing allowed more than 500 metres from reef edge. Recreational demersal hand lining (fishing using sinkers) allowed more than 2 kilometres from reef edge.
Lord Howe Island Marine Park	Lord Howe Island is located in the South West Pacific Ocean at 31' 33" S 159' 05" E, approximately 700 kilometres north-east of Sydney.	No commercial fishing. Recreational pelagic fishing allowed more than 500 metres from reef edge. Recreational demersal hand lining (fishing using sinkers) allowed more than 2 kilometres from reef edge. No fishing or collecting allowed in the sanctuary zone. Line fishing, spearfishing and hand gathering are all permitted within a habitat protection zone.
Solitary Islands Marine Reserve	Located in the Tasman Sea, east of Coffs Harbour in northern New South Wales.	No commercial fishing. Recreational pelagic fishing allowed more than 500 metres from reef edge. Recreational demersal hand lining (fishing using sinkers) allowed more than 2 kilometres from reef edge.
Booderee National Park	3 hours drive south of Sydney, at Jervis Bay Marine Park.	Spearfishing prohibited, no live bait other than some fish or squids may be collected. Many plants and animals are protected. Jet skis, towing or persons behind boats, boom riding, anchoring on seagrass communities are prohibited.
Solitary Islands Marine Park	Stretches along 75 kilometres of coastline north from Coffs Harbour.	No fishing or collecting allowed in the sanctuary zone. Line fishing, spearfishing and hand gathering are all permitted within a habitat protection zone.
Jervis Bay Marine Park	170 kilometres south of Sydney, 25 kilometres south-east of Nowra.	No fishing or collecting allowed in the sanctuary zone. Line fishing, spearfishing and hand gathering are all permitted within a habitat protection zone.
Cape Byron Marine Park	Extends from Brunswick Heads in the north to Lennox Head in the south.	No fishing or collecting allowed in the sanctuary zone. Line fishing, spearfishing and hand gathering are all permitted within a habitat protection zone.
Long Reef Aquatic Reserve	On Sydney's northern beaches, from Collaroy rock baths south to Long Reef Surf Lifesaving Club, and from mean high water out 100 metres from mean low water.	You can line fish for finfish only. The collection or disturbance of marine life or habitat is prohibited, including collecting shellfish, pumping for worms, spearfishing and collecting dead or empty shells.
North Harbour Aquatic Reserve	The boundaries are formed by a line between the headlands at North Head and Grotto Point and a line joining Little Manly Point, Manly Point, and Forty Baskets Beach.	You can line fish for finfish only. The collection or disturbance of marine life or habitat is prohibited, including collecting shellfish, pumping for worms, spearfishing and collecting dead or empty shells.
Batemans Marine Park	Includes the coastal and estuarine waters from the northern end of Murramarang Beach to Wallaga Lake.	Fishing restrictions for this park were not finalised at the time of printing. Contact NSW Marine Parks Authority, tel. (02) 4476 0845, for details as they become available

Site	*Location*	*Restrictions*
Towra Point Aquatic Reserve	16 kilometres south of Sydney on the southern shore of Botany Bay.	Fishing and the collection of marine vegetation is prohibited within the sanctuary zone of the reserve. Within the refuge zone people can take fish with hook and line.
Shiprock Aquatic Reserve	2 hectare site, in the headland between Burraneer and Dolans Bay, at Port Hacking.	All fishing and the collection, disturbance or destruction of marine animals or plants is prohibited.
Bushrangers Bay Aquatic Reserve	Located at the eastern end of Bass Point, approximately 4 kilometres south of Shellharbour on the NSW south coast.	All fishing and the collection, disturbance or destruction of marine animal or plants is prohibited.
Cook Island Aquatic Reserve	600 metres offshore from Fingal Head and 4 kilometres south-east of Tweed Heads in northern New South Wales.	Fishing by all methods is prohibited for all waters from the mean high water mark to a boundary defined by five marker buoys. Fishing by setlines is prohibited within the whole aquatic reserve.
Fly Point–Halifax Park Aquatic Reserve	Off Port Stephens, between Fly Point and Nelson Head and extends seaward from the mean high water mark out to 500 metres.	Fishing is only permitted by hook and line from the two jetties within the reserve at Little Beach and from the beach between these two jetties. Fishing is strictly prohibited in the rest of the reserve.
Port Stephens–Great Lakes Marine Park	Extends from Cape Hawke Surf Life Saving Club near Foster to Birubi Beach Surf Life Saving Club at the northern end of Stockton Beach.	Baitfishing in some areas will be prohibited. Contact the NSW Marine Parks Authority, tel. (02) 4916 3970, for details on the full restrictions as they become available.
Barrenjoey Head Aquatic Reserve	Includes the entire rocky platform around Barrenjoey Head – from the northern end of Station Beach to the northern end of Palm Beach – and extends 100 metres seaward from mean low water.	It is prohibited to collect cunjevoi and all invertebrates, including abalone.
Narrabeen Head Aquatic Reserve	Includes the whole foreshore from the south end of Turimetta Beach to the rock baths at Narrabeen Head, and extends 100 metres from mean low water.	It is prohibited to collect cunjevoi and all invertebrates, including abalone.
Cabbage Tree Bay Aquatic Reserve	Includes the whole foreshore of the bay from Manly Surf Life Saving Club to the northern end of Shelly Beach Headland, and includes the whole of Cabbage Tree Bay.	Fishing or collecting of marine organisms is prohibited.
Cape Banks Aquatic Reserve	Includes the whole foreshore from the bridge at Cape Banks to the Endeavour Light at Henry Head, and extends 100 metres seaward from mean low water.	It is prohibited to collect cunjevoi and all invertebrates, including abalone.
Bronte–Coogee Aquatic Reserve	Includes the whole foreshore from the southern end of Bronte Beach to the rock baths at Coogee Beach – 4000 metres of coastline – and extends 100 metres seaward from mean low water.	It is prohibited to spearfish or to take groper by any method from the northern end of Clovelly to the southern end of Gordons Bay. It is prohibited to collect cunjevoi and all invertebrates, including abalone.
Boat Harbour Aquatic Reserve	Includes the southern part of the Kurnell Peninsula, incorporating the whole of Merries Reef and extending east to three green 'Waterboard' vents at Potter Point. The seaward boundary extends 100 metres from mean low water.	It is prohibited to collect cunjevoi and all invertebrates, including abalone.
Bouddi National Park Marine Extension	Covers about 300 hectares between Gerrin Point and Third Point.	Fishing by all methods prohibited (including spearfishing and collecting worms, nippers, shellfish and crustaceans).

For more information contact NSW Fisheries on 1300 550 474 or www.fisheries.nsw.gov.au

Coastal Fishing

The estuaries and shores, rocks, beaches, outcrops and offshore reefs along the coast provide varied fishing. The Sydney Region is Australia's busiest fishing area. Explore the Newcastle Region's inland waterways, the rivers of the Grafton Region, and the rock ledges, beaches, estuaries and offshore and inshore spots around Wollongong. Bermagui is legendary for its game fishing.

State regulations

To fish anywhere in New South Wales, whether in fresh or saltwater, you must have a recreational fishing licence, unless you are exempt on grounds of age, aboriginality or are the holder of a specific Government exemption. There are several Aquatic Reserves within New South Wales and within these, various fishing restrictions apply. For further details, to purchase a licence or check whether you qualify for any current exemption, contact NSW Fisheries on 1300 550 474, or visit their website at www.fisheries.nsw.gov.au

Protected species

Some fish are totally protected in New South Wales. If you catch one it must be carefully returned to the water. Protected marine species include: giant Queensland groper, estuary cod, black rock cod (or saddletail rock cod), eastern blue devil fish, elegant wrasse, grey nurse shark, Herbsts nurse shark, the great white shark, Ballina angelfish, weedy sea dragon (or common sea dragon).

Boating rules

Any person who drives a mechanically propelled recreational vessel on New South Wales waters at 10 knots or more must be licensed. Most categories of recreational vessels in New South Wales must also be registered and carry a Hull Identification Number (HIN) also known as Boatcode. For information regarding licensing, registration and Boatcode, contact NSW Maritime on 131 256 or visit their website at www.maritime.nsw.gov.au

WHERE TO FISH

Along the coast

SYDNEY REGION ● 46

This is Australia's busiest fishing area, with superb rock and beach spots all along the coast. There is good fishing in Broken Bay, the Hawkesbury, Sydney Harbour, Botany Bay, the Georges River and Port Hacking.

GRAFTON REGION ● 66

The big rivers, such as the Tweed, Brunswick, Richmond, Sandon and Wooli, fish well and there are fine rock spots, beaches and offshore reefs. The Solitary Islands mark the transition point between temperate and tropical waters.

PORT MACQUARIE REGION ● 78

This region provides great coastal fishing with arguably the best rock areas in the state. There is also fine estuary fishing and wonderful wharves and walls for shore-based anglers.

NEWCASTLE REGION ● 90

The major features of this area are the big coastal waterways – Lake Macquarie, Myall Lakes, Port Stephens and Tuggerah Lake.

WOLLONGONG REGION ● 102

Royal National Park to Wollongong has rock ledges and quiet beaches. Fishing inshore and offshore from Kiama to Gerroa is excellent as is estuary fishing in the Shoalhaven and offshore fishing at the Sir Joseph Young Banks.

BERMAGUI REGION ● 114

The far south coast is a legendary place for its game fishing grounds. It also offers rocks, beaches, estuaries and good inshore grounds. The Tathra wharf is famous and Eden and Merimbula are very busy, especially during school holidays.

Weather

Weather forecasts can be obtained by ringing the Weather Bureau on (02) 9296 1555 or 1900 955 361 for recorded information. To receive weather reports via fax, put your machine on receive and dial 1902 935 220 for coastal waters forecasts and reports. Weather forecasts are also available at: www.bom.gov.au/weather/nsw

GUIDE TO LOCAL FISH

AC	albacore	LJ	leatherjacket	SM	samson fish
AJ	amberjack	LU	luderick	GS	shark, school
BC	barracouta	MA	mackerel, slimy	S	snapper
BA	bass, Australian	MA	mackerel, Spanish	SW	sweep
B	bream, black	MA	mackerel, spotted	T	tailor
B	bream, yellowfin	MJ	mangrove jack	TR	trevally, others
CO	cobia	ML	marlin, black	TR	trevally, giant
DA	dart	ML	marlin, blue	TR	trevally, golden
DO	dolphin fish	ML	marlin, striped	TR	trevally, silver
D	drummer, silver	MO	morwong, jackass	TP	trumpeter
F	flathead, dusky	MO	morwong, red	TU	tuna, bigeye
F	flathead, sand	MO	morwong, rubberlip	TU	tuna, frigate mackerel
F	flathead, tiger	M	mullet, sand	TU	tuna, mackerel
F	flathead, others	M	mullet, sea or bully	TU	tuna, longtail
FL	flounder	MU	mulloway	TU	tuna, southern bluefin
G	garfish	NG	nannygai	TU	tuna, striped
GR	groper	EP	perch, estuary	TU	tuna, yellowfin
GU	gurnard	PP	perch, pearl	WH	wahoo
HT	hairtail	PI	pike, long-finned	W	whiting, King George
DR	john dory	RB	rock blackfish	W	whiting, sand
KI	kingfish, yellowtail	SA	salmon, Australian	W	whiting, trumpeter

Bag and size limits apply. Consult NSW Fisheries on (02) 9527 8411, or the 'Saltwater Fishing Guide' for details.

Tailor, salmon and kingfish are the main target fish from the Merimbula Wharf

FISHING TIP

Ever wonder why so many boats seem to congregate around channel beacons and old pilings? The answer is simple: old pilings have collected all manner of vegetation and crustacean life over the years and the natural build up creates a vertical reef that provides cover and food. Small fish come to feed on even smaller marine animals, and wherever you find small fish you are sure to find bigger fish. Species such as yellowtail kingfish, john dory, Australian salmon and bonito are some of the fish that find channel beacons and piers attractive.

FURTHER INFORMATION

Fishing *For fishing regulations, contact NSW Fisheries at 202 Nicholson Pde, Cronulla, tel. (02) 9527 8411, any of its regional offices or check the website, www.fisheries.nsw.gov.au. There is a general Fisheries information line on tel. 1300 369 365. Obtain Fisheries publications from its offices, bait and tackle shops or its website.*

Boating *NSW Maritime is at James Craig Rd, Rozelle, tel. (02) 9563 8511. It produces a variety of boating maps and guides and videos on waterways regulations and boat safety. Available from Maritime offices and some marine supply shops. Also check its website, www.maritime.nsw.gov.au.*

Sydney Region

Despite the mass of population around Sydney, the fishing is mainly in clean waterways. Sydney Harbour and Botany Bay, while severely affected by crowds and industry, nevertheless maintain reasonable fish stocks.

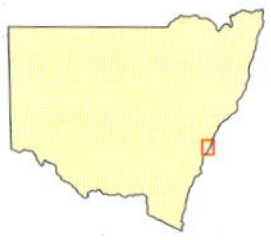

The Hawkesbury is a magnificent, safe waterway for varied fishing. Sydney Harbour is best fished at dawn and dusk. It is then very good for boat and shore fishing as the wash of thousands of craft is not churning up the water.

The northern coastline has rock and beach fishing, and the coast from South Head to Botany Bay and then on to the Kurnell Peninsula is a mecca for rock anglers. Georges River and Port Hacking are relatively quiet southern estuaries, especially popular with boat anglers.

Boat ramp tips

- Before launching your boat, have the bungs in, all ropes, lights, and tie-downs off and the bow-lead attached
- To help you back the trailer straight, attach a high, clearly-seen stick to one or both rear corners of the boat
- When you park the car and trailer, pull the winch cable down to the rear of the trailer and position the hook where you can reach it when retrieving the boat later

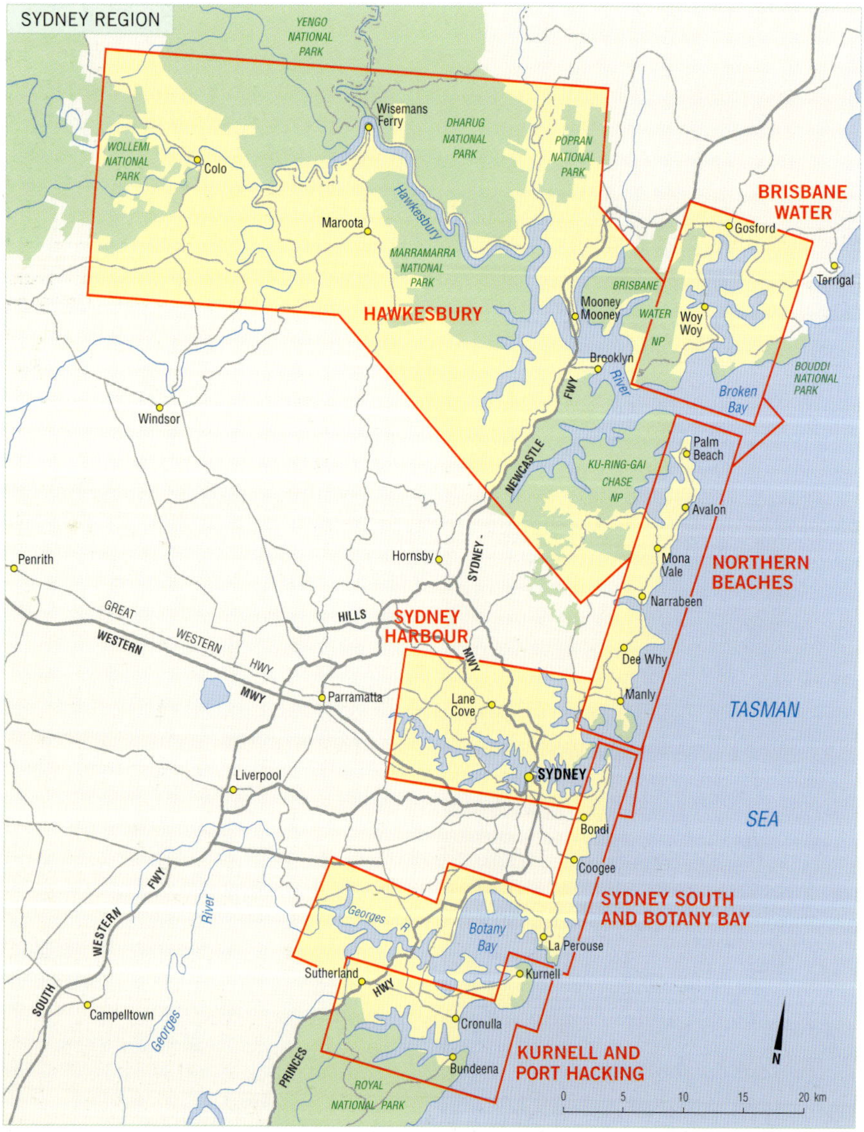

WHERE TO FISH

Sydney Region

BRISBANE WATER • 48

This waterway, with its sandbanks, weed beds, channels and oyster leases, offers a variety of fishing. The best area is the southern section, especially in autumn and summer. Whiting, flathead, flounder, mulloway, bream and garfish are the targets. There are plenty of good land-based spots.

HAWKESBURY • 50

The clear waters of the Hawkesbury are ideal for trouble-free fishing. Try for whiting, bream, luderick, mulloway and flathead. Pittwater has fine drifting runs and Cowan Creek provides a highlight with hairtail in winter. Mangrove Creek is a tranquil paradise. Bass are available further up the Hawkesbury.

NORTHERN BEACHES • 54

There is a great diversity of ocean fishing from rocks, headlands and beaches in this area. Whiting, flathead, bream and other estuary fish can be caught at the eastern end of Narrabeen Lakes. Fish from either a boat or land.

SYDNEY HARBOUR • 56

Australia's busiest waterway is still very productive. There are plenty of wharves and rocky points in Port Jackson for shore-based anglers, and hot spots for boat anglers like the Sow and Pigs reef and the Wedding Cakes (shipping markers). Fishing at dawn and dusk is best in these busy waters. Middle Harbour is sheltered and more tranquil.

SYDNEY SOUTH AND BOTANY BAY • 62

The coast from Sydney to Botany Bay is a great place for rock anglers. There are towering sandstone cliffs with rock spots at many levels, and fine trolling grounds and close-in reefs. Botany Bay and the Georges River have good shore and boat fishing, and the breakwalls in Botany Bay are very popular with land-based anglers.

KURNELL AND PORT HACKING • 64

Although access is somewhat restricted, there are classic rock spots on the Kurnell Peninsula, and good surf fishing from the beaches around Cronulla. The weed areas in Port Hacking provide typical estuary fishing, and there are great boating facilities.

Typical winter run bream from the north coast

Baitfishing tips

- Fresh bait is best – whatever type of bait you use, always try to ensure that it is as fresh as possible
- Ensure that all hooks are sharp, clean and securely attached with appropriate knots
- Always wash your hands over the side after handling fuel, insect repellants or sunscreen
- Rig baits so they appear as natural and enticing as possible
- Try not to let baits slump down into the bend of the hook so they don't block the hook point

GUIDE TO LOCAL FISH

bass, Australian
bonito
bream
drummer, silver
flathead
flounder
garfish
groper
hairtail
john dory
kingfish, yellowtail
leatherjacket
luderick
mackerel
mullet
mulloway
perch, estuary
rock blackfish
salmon, Australian
shark
snapper
tailor
tarwhine
teraglin
trevally
tuna
whiting

Weather

Do not venture out in low pressure systems unless you have a large, well-equipped boat as conditions can get rough, and always keep an eye out for signs of a change in the weather. Best times for fishing are early morning and late afternoon unless you are going offshore in a boat of 5 m or more. You can check weather details with the Weather Bureau on tel. (02) 9296 1555, or the local Coast Guard or Coastal Patrol.

Boating

Be aware of boating hazards like the Sow and Pigs reef, just inside South Head; the cardinal markers that warn of dangerous areas; and all wash zones and speed limits. For offshore fishing, be aware of the East Australian current running south and present all year. During the summer months it can run at up to 4 knots. If you are fishing in areas like Long Reef or north of Pittwater, speak to a local first and ensure your boat has all the necessary safety equipment. In some areas, the fish are contaminated by pollution and should not be eaten. Look out for warning signs and return these fish to the water. For further information, contact the NSW Maritime offices.

FURTHER INFORMATION

Fishing and boating *New South Wales Fisheries has two offices in the Sydney Metropolitan area, Northern Beaches at 12 Shirley Rd, Wollstonecraft, tel. (02) 9439 3148 and Sydney South Metropolitan at 1 Water St, Sans Souci, tel. (02) 9529 6021. NSW Maritime issues publications with information for boaters and has a number of offices in the Sydney area. Head office is at James Craig Rd, Rozelle, Sydney, tel. (02) 9563 8511. Others are at: 5/18 Third Ave, Blacktown, tel. (02) 9831 7200; 131 Donnison St, Gosford, tel. (02) 4323 7171; 4 Bridge Rd, Hornsby, tel. (02) 9477 6600; and 207 Kent St, Sydney, tel. (02) 9241 6307. The Royal Volunteer Coastal Patrol has radio bases at Botany Bay, Sydney Harbour and Mosman, tel. (02) 9960 3311; the Hawkesbury, tel. (02) 9985 9012; and Broken Bay, tel. (02) 9999 3554. The Coast Guard's main base in Sydney is at South Head, tel. (02) 9337 5033.*

Tourist centres *Tourism Hawkesbury, Ham Common, Bicentenary Park, Richmond Rd, Clarendon, tel. (02) 4578 0233; Sydney Harbour Foreshore Authority, tel. (02) 9240 8500; Rotary Park, Terrigal Dr, Terrigal, tel. (02) 4385 4430; Wharf Forecourt, East Esplanade, Manly, tel. (02) 9976 1430; Sydney Visitor Centre, cnr Argyle and Playfair sts, The Rocks, tel. (02) 9240 8788; Peninsula Chamber of Commerce, Railway St, Umina, tel. (02) 4344 4930.*

Davidson's oyster farm gives a rustic charm to the banks of the Hawkesbury; waters around oyster leases invariably offer good fishing in the Sydney Region

Brisbane Water

Lure casting for bream can be as successful as bait fishing, especially near the oyster leases at Gosford

Type of fishing
beach, estuary
Target fish
bream, flathead, luderick, whiting

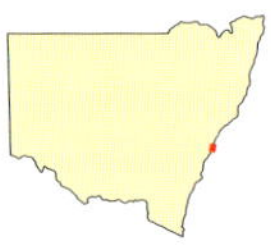

Brisbane Water is an estuary system within a system as it feeds into the northern side of Broken Bay and runs some 6 km up to Gosford, through a labyrinth of fascinating fishing waters. There are sandbanks, weed beds, channels and oyster leases, providing varied types of fishing.

It is productive and safe water, well supplied with launching ramps, mostly in Gosford and Woy Woy, the main population centres. Hire boats, tackle and bait are abundantly available. Live baits can be gathered from sandbanks and from bays and shallows close to shore.

The Rip Ridge area is a narrow part of the waterway and has perhaps the strongest tidal flow on the whole New South Wales coast. Boat anglers should be wary of this area, and when they cross the bar at Wagstaff Point, near the entrance to Broken Bay.

Summer and autumn are the best fishing times, with the waters yielding whiting, flathead, flounder, mulloway, tailor, luderick, young snapper and garfish. The tidal areas are best fished at the top or bottom of the tide.

There is good fishing outside the Brisbane Water entrance, with garfish and whiting off **Lobster Beach**, and luderick outside **Wagstaff Point** on a run-out tide.

On the other side of the entrance, **Ocean Beach** can be fished for mulloway in January and February, and bream and whiting from June to September, but only at night as the surfers are in charge during the day. The sandbar at the end of the beach is good for flathead and whiting.

Favoured land spots inside the estuary are Wagstaff Jetty, Hardys Bay Jetty, The Rip Bridge, St Huberts Island Bridge, and Woy Woy public wharves.

The most popular approach in this estuary system is to fish out of a small craft. The bottom half of the estuary, up to Lintern Channel, at the top of **Rileys Island**, provides the best fishing. Luderick and bream can be caught in the channel off Wagstaff Point. From Kourung Gourung Point, across Hardys Bay and into The Rip, the target species are whiting, flathead and bream. Right under The Rip Bridge are bream, mulloway and sharks, but the area can only be fished at slack tide.

The area west of Rileys Island and into Lintern Channel is very productive, with good quantities of bream, whiting and flathead. It is a night area for bream. Around the corner, in **Cockle Channel** and at **Empire Bay**, there is drifting for flathead and bream.

About half-way across Lintern Channel from the **Woy Woy ramp** is a mulloway hole. The edges of the oyster leases are good bream spots at night, and also home to luderick, which go for the weed around the oyster poles and frames. The best bream baits are chicken gut, live mullet and yellowtail. Blue pilchards are the best bait shop offerings.

The top of Brisbane Water does not fish so well as there are few features to attract fish. Flathead and bream are fished inshore, or in **Narara Creek**, which runs into the system near Gosford.

Land-based angling from jetties and piers on Brisbane Water is almost as popular as boat fishing

GUIDE TO LOCAL FISH

(B)	bream
(F)	flathead
(FL)	flounder
(G)	garfish
(LJ)	leatherjacket
(LU)	luderick
(M)	mullet
(MU)	mulloway
(SH)	shark
(S)	snapper
(T)	tailor
(W)	whiting

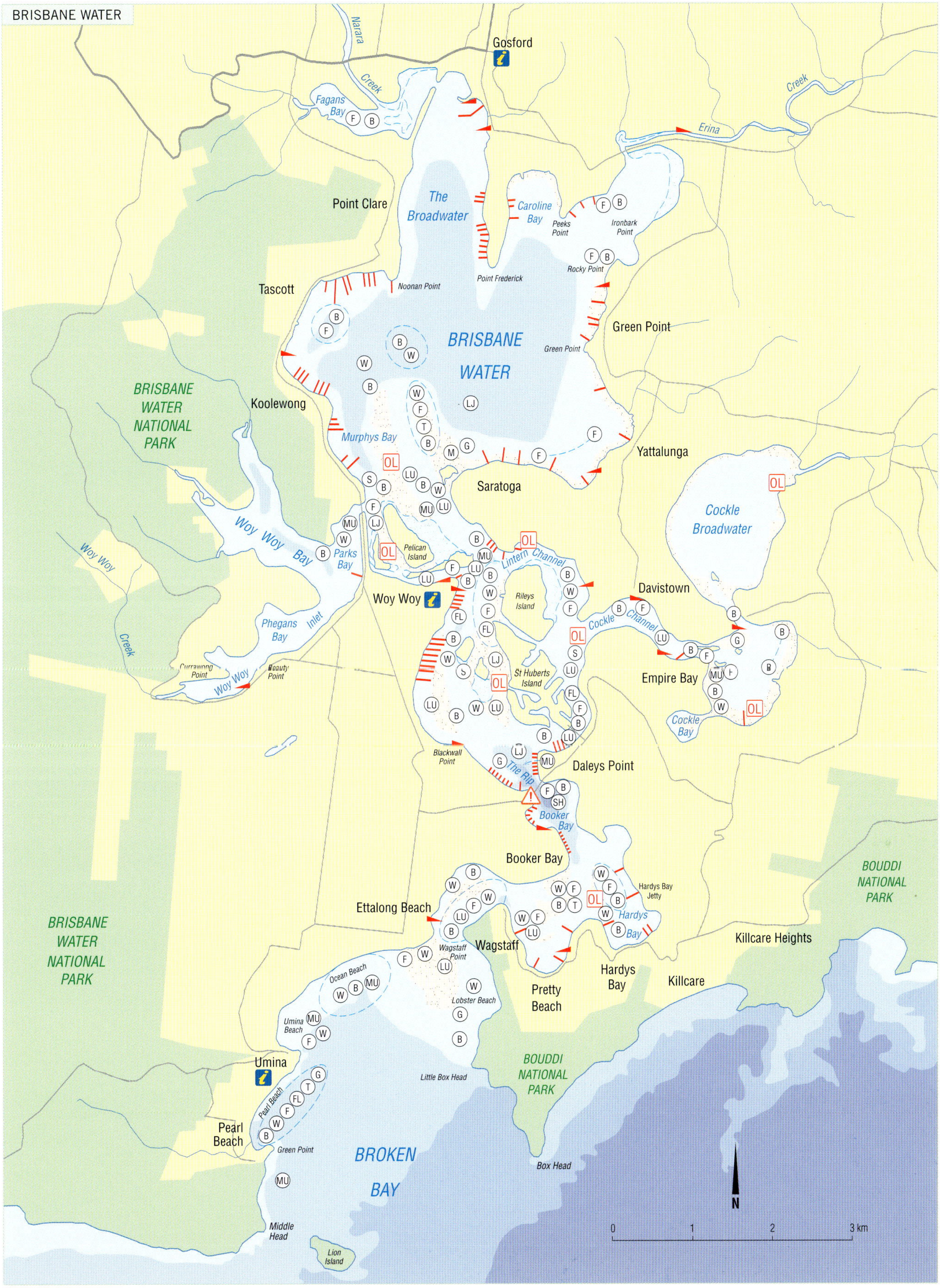
BRISBANE WATER
Gosford
Narara Creek
Fagans Bay
Erina Creek
Point Clare
The Broadwater
Caroline Bay
Peeks Point
Ironbark Point
Rocky Point
Point Frederick
Noonan Point
Tascott
BRISBANE WATER
Green Point
Green Point
BRISBANE WATER NATIONAL PARK
Koolewong
Murphys Bay
Yattalunga
Saratoga
Cockle Broadwater
Woy Woy Bay
Parks Bay
Pelican Island
Lintern Channel
Woy Woy Creek
Woy Woy
Rileys Island
Davistown
Cockle Channel
Phegans Bay
Inlet
Empire Bay
Currawong Point
Woy Woy
Beauty Point
St Huberts Island
Cockle Bay
Blackwall Point
The Rip
Daleys Point
Booker Bay
Booker Bay
Hardys Bay Jetty
Hardys Bay
BOUDDI NATIONAL PARK
Ettalong Beach
Wagstaff
Wagstaff Point
Killcare Heights
BRISBANE WATER NATIONAL PARK
Ocean Beach
Lobster Beach
Pretty Beach
Hardys Bay
Killcare
Umina Beach
Umina
Little Box Head
BOUDDI NATIONAL PARK
Pearl Beach
Pearl Beach
Green Point
BROKEN BAY
Box Head
N
0
1
2
3 km
Middle Head
Lion Island

Hawkesbury

Type of fishing
bay, estuary, river
Target fish
bass, bream, estuary perch, flathead, hairtail, mulloway, whiting

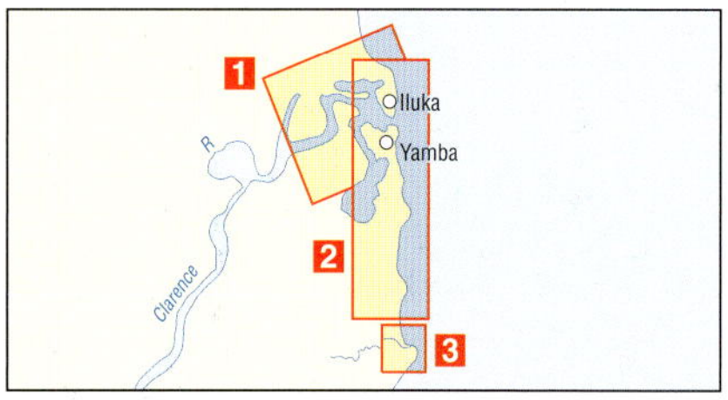

The Hawkesbury flows through Sydney's western suburbs as the Nepean River, becomes the Hawkesbury at Windsor, and then turns into a broadwater, with many waterways branching off into wooded valleys. Eventually it flows past Brisbane Water and Pittwater to enter the sea at Broken Bay. Its clean and clear waters are ideal for trouble-free fishing and there are many access points, boat ramps and facilities. Houseboats for hire provide the most comfortable fishing platforms.

GUIDE TO LOCAL FISH

B	bream
D	drummer, silver
F	flathead
FL	flounder
GR	groper
HT	hairtail
DR	john dory
KI	kingfish, yellowtail
LJ	leatherjacket
LU	luderick
MA	mackerel
MU	mulloway
SA	salmon, Australian
S	snapper
T	tailor
TR	trevally
W	whiting

LOWER HAWKESBURY

Pittwater is a clear waterway, so is best fished with fine line and lightly weighted baits. At the entrance to Pittwater, near **Barrenjoey Head**, groper and drummer can be taken on the full tide. The best places for luderick are at the top reaches of Pittwater, near **Scotland Island**. Off the jetties at Scotland Island there is a chance of yellowtail kingfish, and snapper and black bream near **Longnose Point** around dawn and dusk. But the best way of fishing Pittwater is to drift in the middle reaches, not too far from shore.

The Lower Hawkesbury has the influence of sea and tides. Around **Flint and Steel Bay**, just west of the entrance to Pittwater, there are many places to moor and seek black bream, juvenile snapper, flathead and mulloway, all on the ebb tide, although school mulloway are prevalent in many areas.

Cowan Creek, a drowned river valley, is a beautiful place, surrounded by the bush of the Ku-ring-gai Chase National Park. Fish for hairtail with blue pilchards or live yellowtail and with a wire trace to resist their razor sharp teeth. On a crisp winter night, there are few better experiences than watching the phosphorescent flashes of hooked hairtail in the clear depths. Fish a suspended or slow-sinking bait until you find how deep the school is congregating, then fish at that depth, experimenting when the bite slackens off. The best spots are **Waratah Bay**, **Jerusalem Bay**, **Yeomans Bay** and **Akuna Bay**. The arms of the Cowan Creek system usually end in sandy bays – good for flathead and whiting – while the rocky shores are haunts for bream, leatherjacket, luderick and mulloway. Winter anglers also find john dory a good catch.

There are luderick haunts at **Soldiers Point**, **West Head**, **Refuge Bay** and **Gunyah Point**. Close to **Juno Point** is a good spot for mulloway on the rising tide. Mooring from **Eleanor Bluffs** to **Green Point** on a high tide is productive for bream, flathead and mulloway, as it is on the other side of the river, off **Little Wobby Beach** and around **Dangar Island**.

Behind Dangar Island, the fishing is best on the ebb tide. There are also some superb bream grounds, particularly off **Cow Rock**, just past Peats Ferry Bridge; at **The Vines**, on the north shore from Milson Island; around the ***Parramatta* wreck**; at **Graces Shore**; and at **Bar Point**.

Berowra Creek is similar in style to Cowan Creek, but it is shallower and generally yields fewer fish. The only road access is from the Berowra Waters ferry.

Coba Point, at the Berowra Creek mouth, has mulloway, flathead and bream to be fished at the top of the tide. Further down the inlet, Calabash Bay and Joe Crafts Creek offer the same fare.

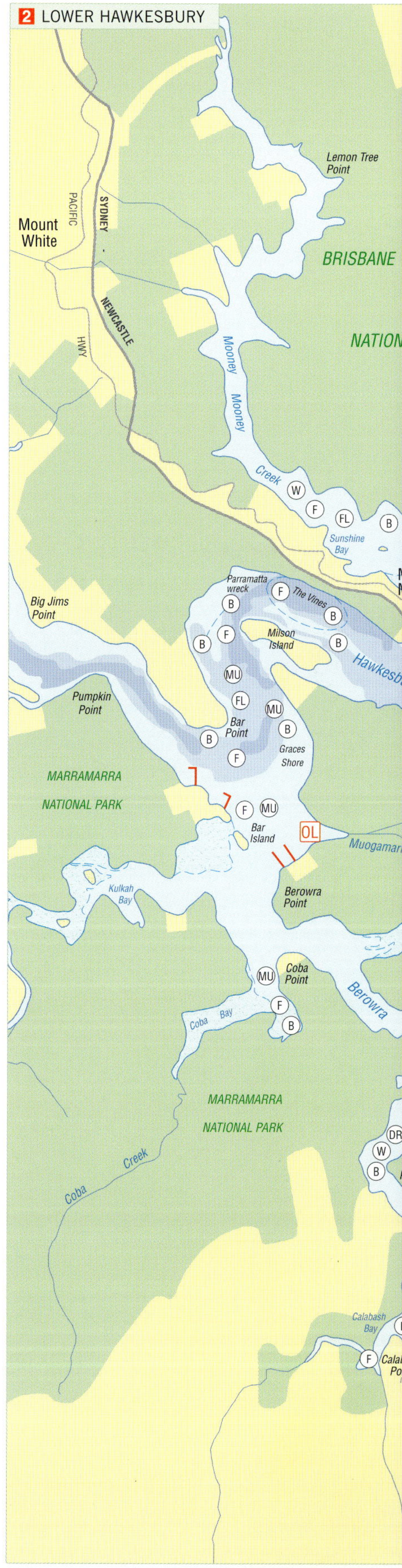

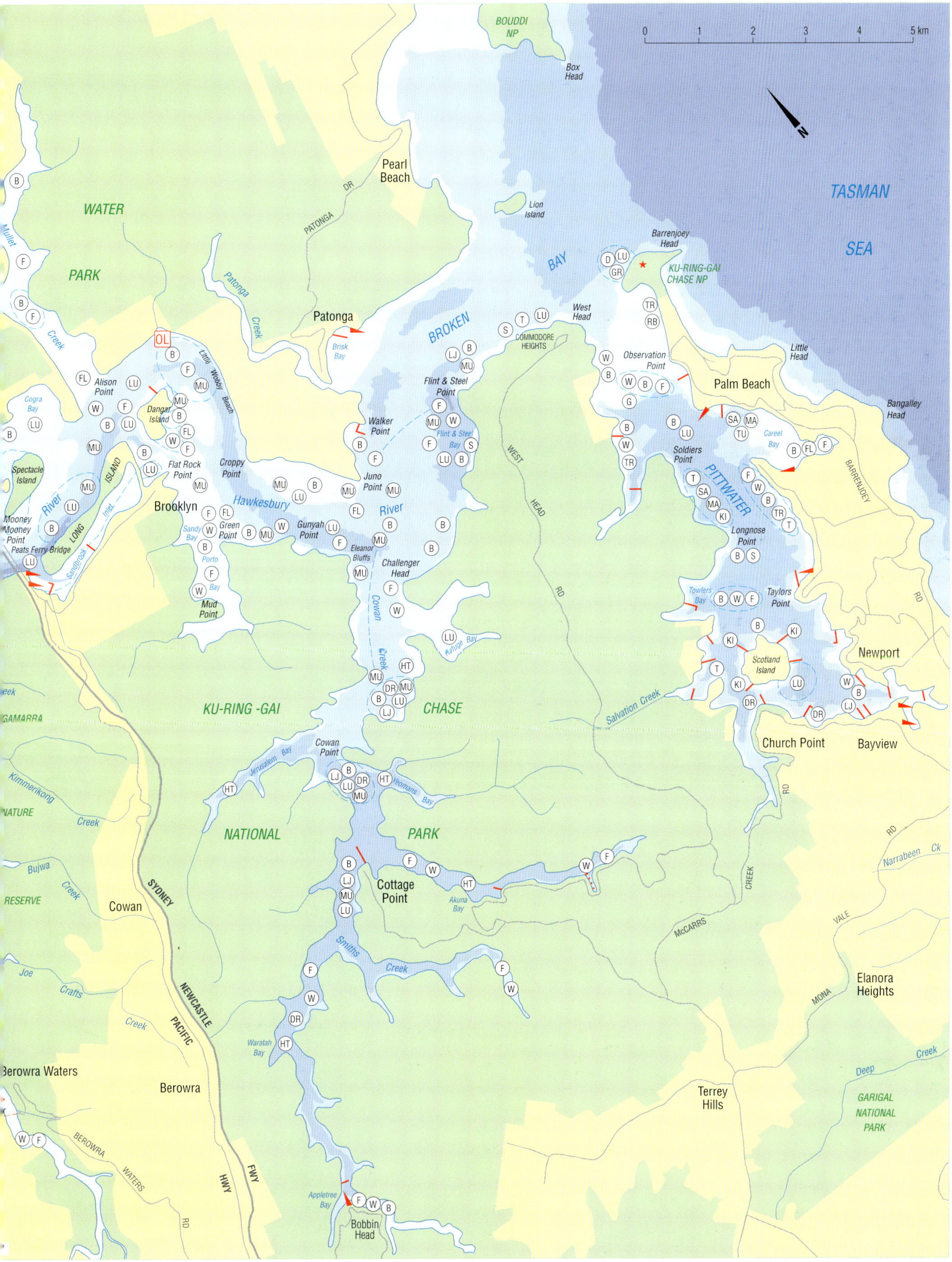
BOUDDI NP
Box Head
0 1 2 3 4 5 km
N
TASMAN SEA
Pearl Beach
Lion Island
Barrenjoey Head
KU-RING-GAI CHASE NP
BROKEN BAY
WATER PARK
Mullet Creek
Patonga Creek
PATONGA DR
Patonga
Brisk Bay
West Head
COMMODORE HEIGHTS
Observation Point
Palm Beach
Little Head
Bangalley Head
Little Wobby Beach
Alison Point
Cogra Bay
Dangar Island
Walker Point
Flint & Steel Point
Flint & Steel Bay
Spectacle Island
Flat Rock Point
Croppy Point
Juno Point
Hawkesbury River
LONG ISLAND
Sandbrook Inlet
Mooney Mooney Point
Peats Ferry Bridge
Brooklyn
Sandy Bay
Green Point
Gunyah Point
Eleanor Bluffs
Challenger Head
Porto Bay
Mud Point
Cowan Creek
Refuge Bay
WEST HEAD RD
Soldiers Point
Careel Bay
BARRENJOEY RD
PITTWATER
Longnose Point
Towlers Bay
Taylors Point
Scotland Island
Newport
Church Point
Bayview
Salvation Creek
KU-RING-GAI CHASE NATIONAL PARK
Cowan Point
Jerusalem Bay
Yeomans Bay
Kimmerikong Creek
NATURE RESERVE
Bujwa Creek
Cottage Point
Akuna Bay
Cowan
SYDNEY NEWCASTLE FWY
PACIFIC HWY
Smiths Creek
Joe Crafts Creek
Waratah Bay
Berowra Waters
Berowra
BEROWRA WATERS RD
Appletree Bay
Bobbin Head
McCARRS CREEK RD
VALE RD
Narrabeen Ck
MONA
Elanora Heights
Deep Creek
Terrey Hills
GARIGAL NATIONAL PARK

Anglers launch a boat in the early morning on the Hawkesbury River near Wisemans Ferry

UPPER HAWKESBURY

The fishing resources of the picturesque Upper Hawkesbury keep pace with the productive richness of the river flats. The best fishing time is spring, and the best way to fish is by boat, although there are plenty of spots for land-based fishing from the roads that run on either side of the river, downstream from **Wisemans Ferry**. The target fish in this waterway are bass and estuary perch.

There is productive drifting for flathead near **Spencer**, while school mulloway, bream, and the odd luderick are around the oyster lease at **Triangle Island. Spencer Wharf** and the nearby pontoon landing is a good mulloway spot, particularly with live yellowtail bait at dusk and night.

Mangrove Creek has bream, flathead and mulloway, and an abundance of mud crabs. The entrances to **Tarbay Gully** and **Scotchmans Creek** are similar. Bream are off the mud bank at the beach of **Neverfail Island**, and flathead, bream and mulloway are in midstream. You will find these fish again upriver at the **Popran Creek** entrance and at the **Wisemans Ferry** road bridge.

GUIDE TO LOCAL FISH

BA	bass, Australian
B	bream
F	flathead
LU	luderick
M	mullet
MU	mulloway
EP	perch, estuary

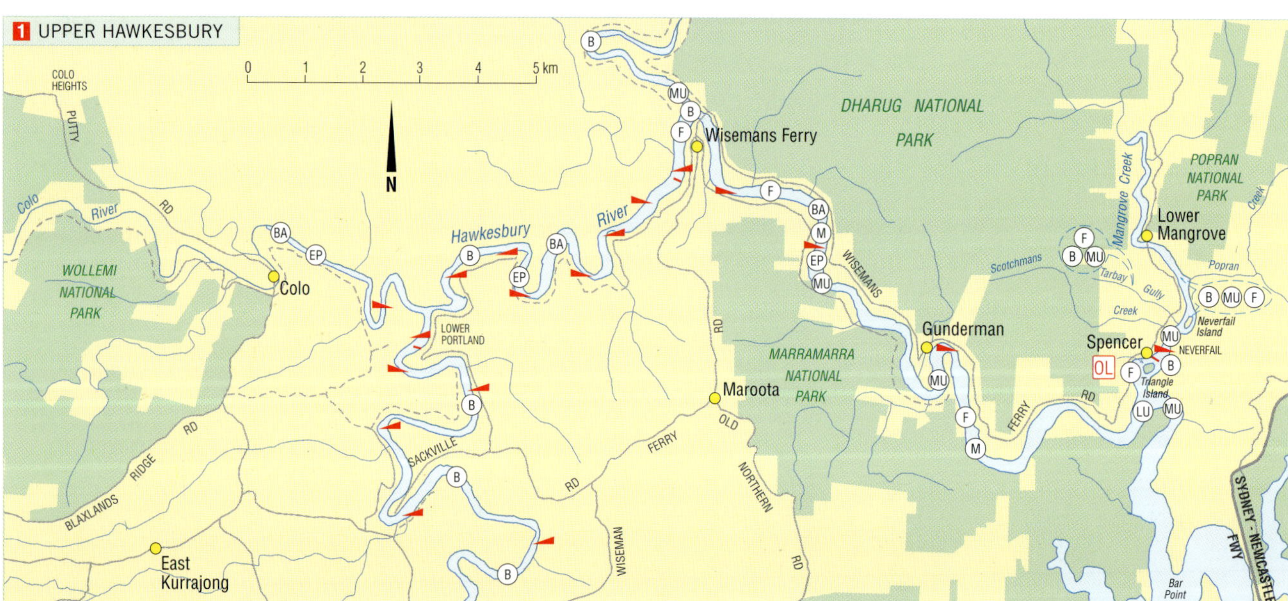

Jurassic jewfish*

What's 140 km long, flanked by visible rock strata over 160 million years old, is known to carry over 7 million megalitres of water in a single year and lies within two hours drive of any part of Greater Sydney?

Give up? The answer is the Hawkesbury River – a huge complex of mother flow and feeder streams, flung casually across the Sydney flood plain like a great gnarled geological tree. If its trunk is in the Pacific Ocean near Broken Bay, its limbs and branches reach deep into the heartland of the south and west. Here, its waters rise in places as diverse and far-flung as Goulburn, Katoomba, and the Colo wilderness.

The upper extremities of the river are near the crossing known as Yarramundi, where the Grose River runs in from the eastern slopes of the Blackheath–Katoomba Rim. Above Yarramundi, the river is known as the Nepean, and is a purely freshwater system. The fresh water continues down for some distance into the Hawkesbury itself, however – for about another 40 km, to Sackville Reach. But even then, there is still a good hundred kilometres of main saltwater river and nearly five times that again in tributaries for estuarine anglers to enjoy.

Estimates of the number of anglers who visit the Hawkesbury annually approach the one million mark, but it is still possible to find your own quiet corner to chase bass, flathead, bream, whiting, tailor, leatherjacket, luderick, or that mystical target species of all serious river anglers, the large and elusive mulloway. If the Hawkesbury is famous for one species above all the other fish available throughout its length, it is for its large and plentiful jewfish.

Each of the bends and stretches of the Hawkesbury is famed for one kind of fish or another: Sentry Box and Haycock reaches, Spencer and its environs, all produce fish. Creeks, such as Mangrove, Berowra, Cowan and Coal and Candle are all known treasure troves. The points, too, are famed, and worthy of it. Examples include Prickly, Green, Cottage, Juno and Flint and Steel points. There are hundreds of bays – try Illawong, Yeomans, and Jerusalem bays, not to mention massive and productive waters within Broken Bay and Pittwater.

Nowhere else in Sydney, and in few places within New South Wales, could you find such a rich and varied estuarine system as the Hawkesbury. What is more, that it survives after two centuries of environmental abuse and sometimes rapacious fishing is something of a miracle.

But when you consider that the Permian outcrops of rock on the river's western escarpments have peered down over the ebb and flow of dinosaurs, indigenous peoples, white settlers, agriculture, commerce and urbanisation, you sort of get the feeling that the Hawkesbury is in it for the long haul.

Fishing through the chill of a foggy winter's night, and seeing the sun come up through the mist and labyrinth of riverside gorges, you do get a different perspective on how much beauty, richness and grandeur can be summed up in that one simple word 'estuary'.

Even though there's room for debate about whether the Hawkesbury will survive us – or we it – sitting in a gently rocking boat and taking in the magic glow of a sunfired cliff as the bush comes to life around you, it's easier to think if we do change our ways enough, maybe we'll both be around for some time to come.

– Peter Horrobin

** Throughout this book jewfish are referred to as mulloway.*

Northern Beaches

Type of fishing
beach, estuary, rock

Target fish
bream, flathead, luderick, tailor, whiting

The coastal area north of Sydney offers a wide variety of fishing. There are plenty of good spots from the beaches and off the rocky headlands from Palm Beach down to North Head. Just inland, at Narrabeen Lakes, there is a change of pace with estuary fishing on offer.

There is a huge variety of ocean fishing from the rocks, headlands and beaches north of Sydney. Luderick hunters have ample rocky washes to work around, with rock blackfish and bream also available, and tailor in winter. From the rocks you can fish with live bait for yellowtail kingfish, tuna and salmon, with whiting, bream and small tailor available from the beaches. Many beaches are popular with surfers and fishing is best done at dawn and dusk, but anglers can usually find an end of a beach to themselves. Some of the most favoured beach spots are **Palm Beach**, a reliable summer whiting and flathead beach; **Bilgola and Bungan beaches** (both yielding bait); off **Narrabeen** and **Collaroy** for whiting, tailor, bream, flathead and mulloway; and **Dee Why Beach**.

Popular rock spots include under the lighthouse at **Barrenjoey Head**, Little Head at **Whale Beach**, the Hole in the Wall at **Avalon**, the rocks north of **Bilgola Head**, the flat outcrops south of **Bilgola**, the rocks south of **Newport** near Little Reef, the **Warriewood Ledges** at Turimetta Head and the headlands at the entrance to **Narrabeen Lakes**.

The rocky headlands between Mona Vale and North Head carry a lot of fishing traffic. **Long Reef Point** is an Aquatic Reserve and restrictions apply. All other headlands offer less restricted fishing for luderick, drummer, rock blackfish, bream and snapper fishing, and spinning for tailor. Care must be taken on a rising sea as these headlands are dangerous, but not quite to the extent of Suicide Point at **Turimetta Head** and the **Mona Vale Headland**.

There are many other spots, each with their devotees. If you are fishing a place for the first time, it pays to let the locals take up their customary stands and to allow yourself to blend quietly into the scene. It is also important to look after these busy locations, leaving them clean for the next people who happen along.

Safety comes first on the rocks. To that end take a few minutes to study the waves before venturing down.

Dee Why Beach still fishes well: the rule is to be up with the joggers and fish an incoming tide at dawn

Estuary entrances are always good surf fishing areas; the southern spit at North Narrabeen is popular due to its easy access and the availability of bait in the intertidal zone

NARRABEEN LAKES

The only estuary within the busy north Sydney metropolitan region, **Narrabeen Lakes** has plenty of fishing opportunities. At the eastern end, whiting, flathead and bream can be taken, with bait in the form of nippers pumped on the sand flats around the **Ocean Street Bridge**. Luderick are generally found around the edges of the weed beds and are most active on the run-out tide.

The **Pittwater Road Bridge** area carries flathead, tailor and luderick, and there is good fishing for whiting and bream around the eastern side of the islands, on either side of the bridge, with luderick in the northern channel. Around the corner from the Picnic Reserve on the point is a stretch known as **Dark Hole**, where the bream are prolific. The sandbar at **Pipeclay Point** is an ideal platform for prawners between October and February, with whiting over the weed beds, and flathead and bream lurking in the drop-offs. Bream and mullet are close to the opposite shore.

The western end of the lakes opens out into drifting grounds for very big flathead, with whiting, flounder and mullet also plentiful. Live poddy mullet are a great attraction to the flathead, which can be up to 5 kg, and mullet gut is good for the bream. Mullet can also be caught at the creek entrances and in Deep Creek, while you may find an estuary perch further up the creek.

GUIDE TO LOCAL FISH

	Northern Beaches	Narrabeen Lakes
(BT) bonito	•	
(B) bream	•	•
(D) drummer, silver	•	
(F) flathead	•	•
(FL) flounder	•	•
(G) garfish	•	
(GR) groper	•	
(KI) kingfish, yellowtail	•	
(LJ) leatherjacket	•	
(LU) luderick	•	•
(M) mullet		•
(MU) mulloway	•	
(EP) perch, estuary		•
(RB) rock blackfish	•	
(SA) salmon, Australian	•	
(S) snapper	•	
(T) tailor	•	•
(TR) trevally	•	
(TU) tuna	•	
(W) whiting	•	•

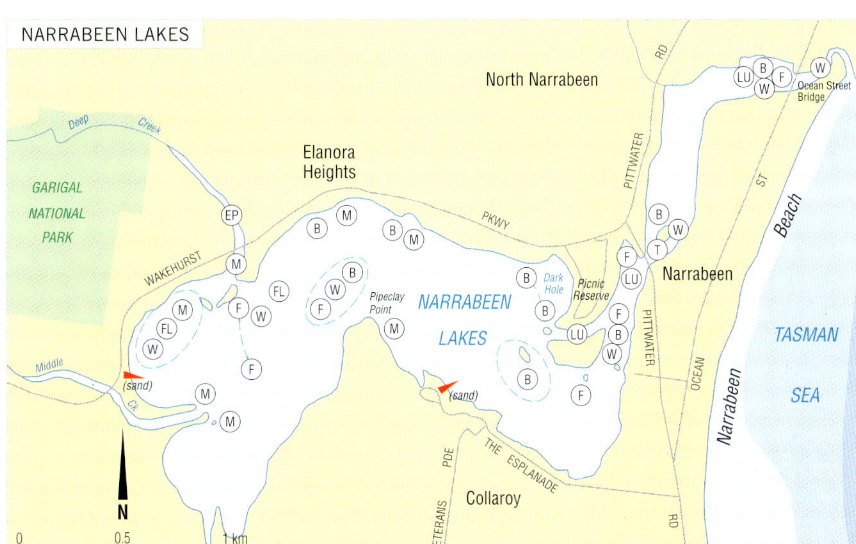

Sydney Harbour

Type of fishing
beach, harbour, rock

Target fish
bream, flathead, leatherjacket, luderick, tailor, trevally, whiting

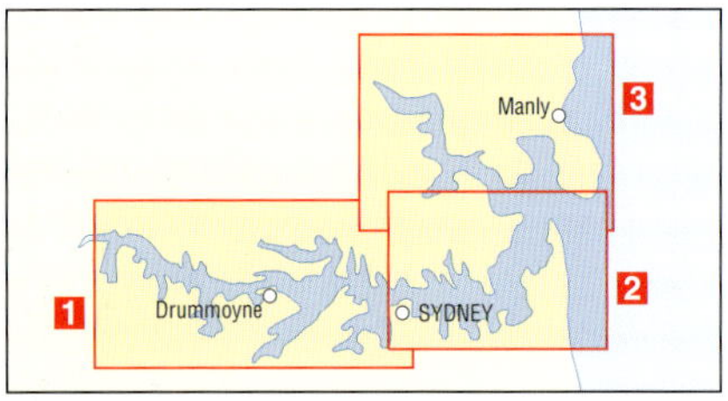

Sydney Harbour can be neatly divided into three major areas. Middle Harbour is comparatively unspoilt by industry or shipping and is the cleanest Sydney Harbour arm. Port Jackson is the busiest Australian waterway and one of the most heavily fished sections of water, while the upper harbour, west of the bridge, is overlooked by the city and bound by the grimy structures of industry. It does not look too enticing, but once you discover the points of access and action it is a huge and productive fishery.

MIDDLE HARBOUR

Middle Harbour is more sheltered than the harbour proper, and a delightful place to fish, particularly for the big population of bream that abounds within its waters. This is where shore-based anglers come into their own as there are many pleasant and accessible spots from which to cast a line. Look for rocks, pylons, wharves, rocky outcrops and other features that attract the fish. You will need to be here early or late, as the fish take off for the deeper water in the middle of the day.

The ideal gear is a 2-m rod with a light tip for casting and a solid butt for lifting; a 2-kg line with a heavier shock trace; little or no weight; and a number 1 or 1/0 hook, which is needle sharp. Baits include local black crabs, mussels, clams and worms. The water you are fishing should be berleyed.

Inner **North Head** is a favoured place for close-in fishing, with mulloway, tailor, yellowtail kingfish and bream the targets. The North Harbour area, from Quarantine Beach to Dobroyd Head, contains the **North Harbour Aquatic Reserve**, where restrictions apply – consult NSW Fisheries for details. **Manly Point** and **Forty Baskets Beach** offer good fishing, with bream, john dory, leatherjacket and luderick on the agenda. Boat drifting from **Quarantine Beach** can yield good catches of flathead, flounder, bream and trevally. **Manly Wharf** is a good bait catching ground, with john dory a possibility in winter using live yellowtail for bait. Out in the swell of the

GUIDE TO LOCAL FISH

B	bream
F	flathead
FL	flounder
G	garfish
DR	john dory
KI	kingfish, yellowtail
LJ	leatherjacket
LU	luderick
M	mullet
MU	mulloway
S	snapper
T	tailor
TR	trevally
W	whiting

All migratory fish visiting Middle Harbour must pass under Spit Bridge

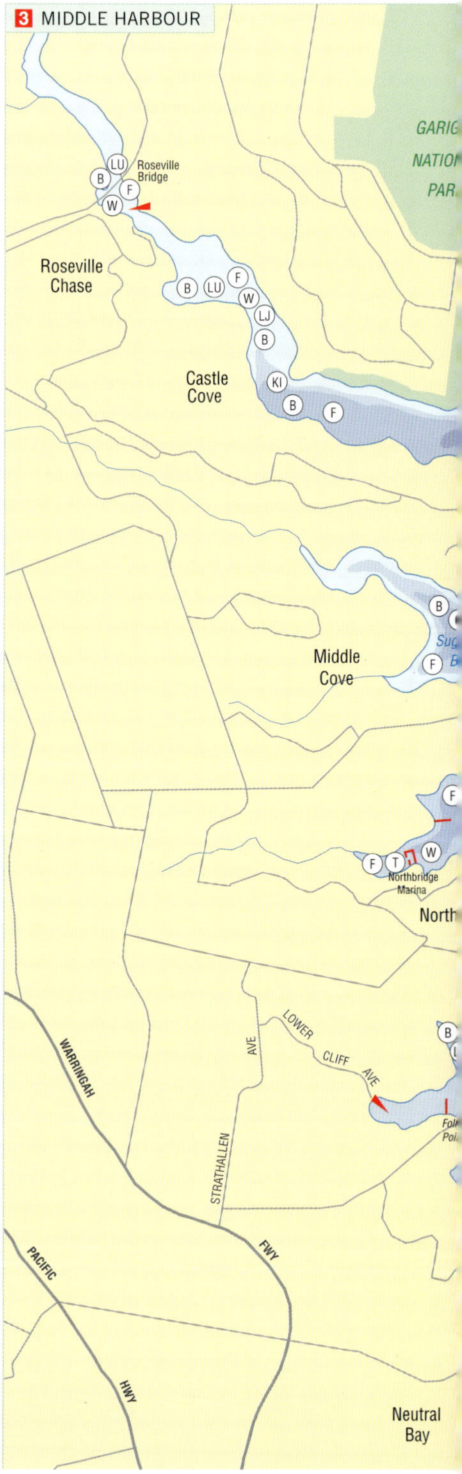

Dobroyd Head area, near the bombora markers, is a good boat spot for bream, snapper, trevally and tailor, but only when the seas are calm. Similarly, rock fishing for bream or luderick should only be tried on the calmest days. Anywhere off **Grotto Point** is equally good for bream and mulloway.

Top spots in Middle Harbour are in **Pearl Bay**, at **Beauty Point** and **Quakers Hat**, in **Willoughby Bay**, at **Folly Point**, around the wreck in **Salt Pan Creek**, at **Fig Tree Point**, **Northbridge Marina**, and the reserve adjoining the **Roseville Bridge**.

All migratory fish that visit the area must pass under **Spit Bridge**, so anglers do well to fish around the bridge or moor close to it. The deep holes at **Bluff Head** are mulloway haunts. Further into the harbour, **Sailors**, **Sugarloaf and Bantry bays** are good drifting areas for whiting, bream and flathead.

Middle Harbour is also home to mulloway around the rocks and holes, and to luderick, flathead, whiting, flounder and tailor, with yellowtail kingfish in the more ocean-influenced Spit area. There are plenty of yellowtail, mullet and garfish to provide the live bait needed for mulloway and kingfish, as well as being targets in their own right.

Rose Bay is a popular boat harbour for big game craft

PORT JACKSON

Fishing is particularly difficult on weekends in Port Jackson, so it is important to be up early before the boat traffic churns the waters to a froth. The land-based anglers, who take up a lot of space on wharves and rocky points, are mainly rigged for bream, fishing in shallow water at dawn and dusk, and casting into the deep during the day, usually with bloodworm or fresh prawn baits. Other targets are tailor, leatherjacket, luderick, flathead and trevally. Whiting can

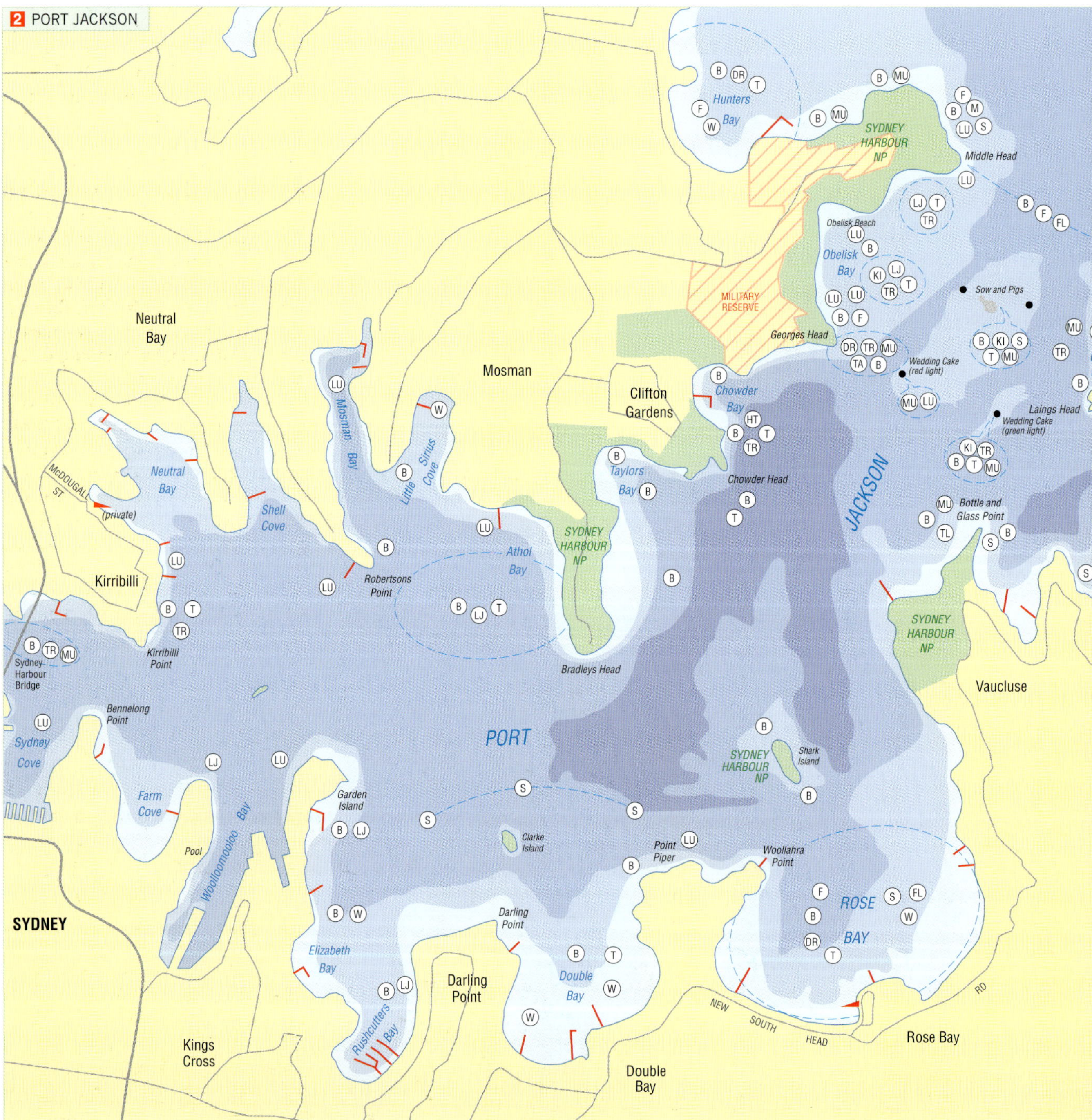

be sought in bays like **Camp Cove**, **Rose Bay**, **Double Bay** and **Little Sirius Cove** on the northern shore.

Rose Bay is merely one of the bays harbouring big game craft that fish for pelagic species offshore. Inside South Head, boat anglers can get out to some very hot places, notably the Sow and Pigs reef off Obelisk Beach and the Wedding Cakes structures that mark the shipping lane into Sydney. When fishing these and other channel markers, you are obliged and advised to stay out of the channel, or you risk being run down. The best fishing practice is to anchor away from the channel and run your bait down to the markers, where the fish tend to congregate. In a strong southerly the dawn to dusk rules are overturned, and in these weather conditions the fish tend to bite all day. However, it is also a time for boating caution.

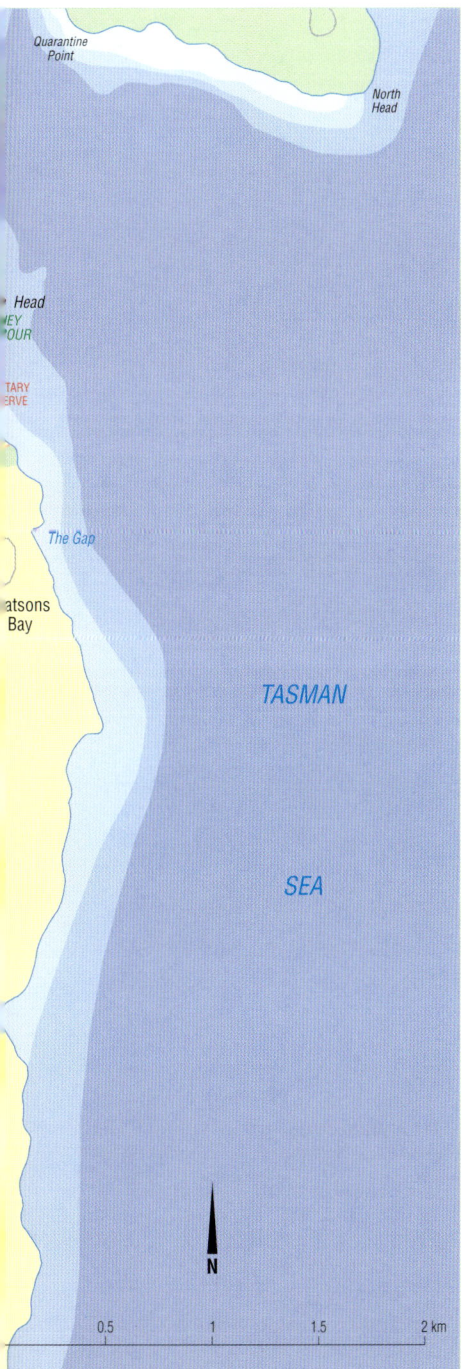

The drift from outside **South Head** to the inside of **Middle Head** is rewarding for bream, flathead and flounder on worm baits, while just off South Head, fishing an inward tide in summer and anchoring firmly on the rough bottom, you may harvest yellowtail kingfish and mulloway, along with bream.

The inside of South Head is great fishing water for land or boat anglers. Bream and luderick can be fished from the rocks at **Lady Beach**, bream off the rocks at **Camp Cove**, and trevally and mulloway offshore. You can also find bream and snapper off the rocks at **Bottle and Glass Point**, with bream, mulloway and teraglin nearby.

GUIDE TO LOCAL FISH

Ⓑ	bream
Ⓕ	flathead
FL	flounder
HT	hairtail
DR	john dory
KI	kingfish, yellowtail
LJ	leatherjacket
LU	luderick
Ⓜ	mullet
MU	mulloway
Ⓢ	snapper
Ⓣ	tailor
TA	tarwhine
TL	teraglin
TR	trevally
Ⓦ	whiting

The **Green Light Wedding Cake**, offshore from Bottle and Glass Point, is a great spot for yellowtail kingfish, bream, trevally, mulloway and tailor. There are bream at **Shark Island**; flathead, whiting, flounder, john dory and tailor drifting at **Rose Bay**; luderick and bream at **Point Piper**; and year-round boat and shore angling for bream across the harbour at **Taylors Bay** and **Chowder Head**. Hairtail are attracted to a deep hole to the north-east of **Chowder Head**, and bream, tarwhine and mulloway are at **Georges Head**. Here you should moor according to the wind. Luderick are at the northern end of **Obelisk Beach**, with a good bream hole 60 m out.

Offshore from Georges Head is the famous **Sow and Pigs reef**, well known for tailor catches in winter, and bream, yellowtail kingfish and mulloway all year. On a run-in tide moor on the north side and fish towards the reef, vice versa on an outgoing tide. You can also drift the area and troll around it, according to your fancy. Nearby is the **Red Light Wedding Cake**, with mulloway and luderick.

There are good rocks for luderick fishing between Georges Head and Middle Head (again take care with the weather), and more luderick at the end of the beach running to Georges Head. Bream and flathead are noted inhabitants of the drop-off out from Middle Head. Moor and fish with berley, or drift with the right wind and tide. Continue on to the wharf just east of **Hunters Bay** for good bream and mulloway grounds.

Fishing on the harbour below the Royal Botanic Gardens

WEST OF THE BRIDGE

In comparison with the lower reaches of Sydney Harbour, the upper harbour area has the advantage of fewer pleasure craft disturbing the waters on weekends. Wharves, jetties, parklands and rocky points are there for the shore-based angler, with whiting and flathead on the sandy-bottomed regions, and bream, luderick and leatherjacket amid the rocks and rubble.

Some of the best shore-based locations are **Dawes Point** and **McMahons Point**, just west of the bridge, where long casts may find bream, trevally and school mulloway; **Luna Park** for luderick; opposite at **Walsh Bay** for luderick, bream and leatherjacket around the pylons, and bream around the boats; **Pyrmont wharves** where tailor and leatherjacket can be caught; **Balls Head** on the northern side of the harbour for leatherjacket and luderick; the seawall at **Clarkes Point Reserve** for bream, luderick and leatherjacket; around to **Kellys Bush Reserve**, a good place for bream at night; opposite at the **Dawn Fraser Pool** for trevally; and then around to the **Wolseley Street Wharf** for bream, trevally, tailor and leatherjacket; **Old Gladesville Bridge** at Five Dock Point, for bream and leatherjacket; **Abbotsford Wharf** for mullet, leatherjacket and bream; and **Cabarita Point** for bream and leatherjacket.

Hen and Chicken Bay and **Half Moon Bay** on the southern side, and **Tarban Creek** on the northern shore are all excellent locations for prawning and crabbing, and the shallow, weedy sand flats attract bream, whiting and flathead.

Boat anglers, either drifting or anchoring out from the rocky shores, will find variety and action. Those after bream should anchor and berley heavily, then use light tackle and lightly weighted baits. Luderick can be taken, especially using the favoured Parramatta River weed baits, some 4 to 5 m under floats, and berleying with a chopped weed and sand mixture. Drifters for bream, trevally, whiting, flathead and school

GUIDE TO LOCAL FISH

B	bream
F	flathead
LJ	leatherjacket
LU	luderick
M	mullet
MU	mulloway
S	snapper
T	tailor
TR	trevally
W	whiting

The Parramatta River, starting at the Gladesville Bridge, produces good schools of fish

mulloway should bait up with prawn or bloodworm. Top areas are between **Goat Island** and **Balmain**, drifting for tailor; west of Goat Island for trevally, bream and tailor; **Balls Head** light beacon for big mulloway, trevally and tailor; **Greenwich Sailing Club** for bream from boat or shore; between **Cockatoo and Spectacle islands**, drifting for bream and trevally; **Pulpit Point**, either moored for bream, trevally and school mulloway, or drifting to **Wrights Point** for flathead and whiting; **Gladesville Bridge**, drifting for bream, flathead, trevally and tailor; the **Blackwall Point** mussel bed for school mulloway, bream and trevally on the run-out tide; and up into the **Lane Cove River**, drifting for school mulloway, bream, tailor and flathead.

Jetties around Five Dock and Gladesville often see young anglers casting for the estuary dwellers

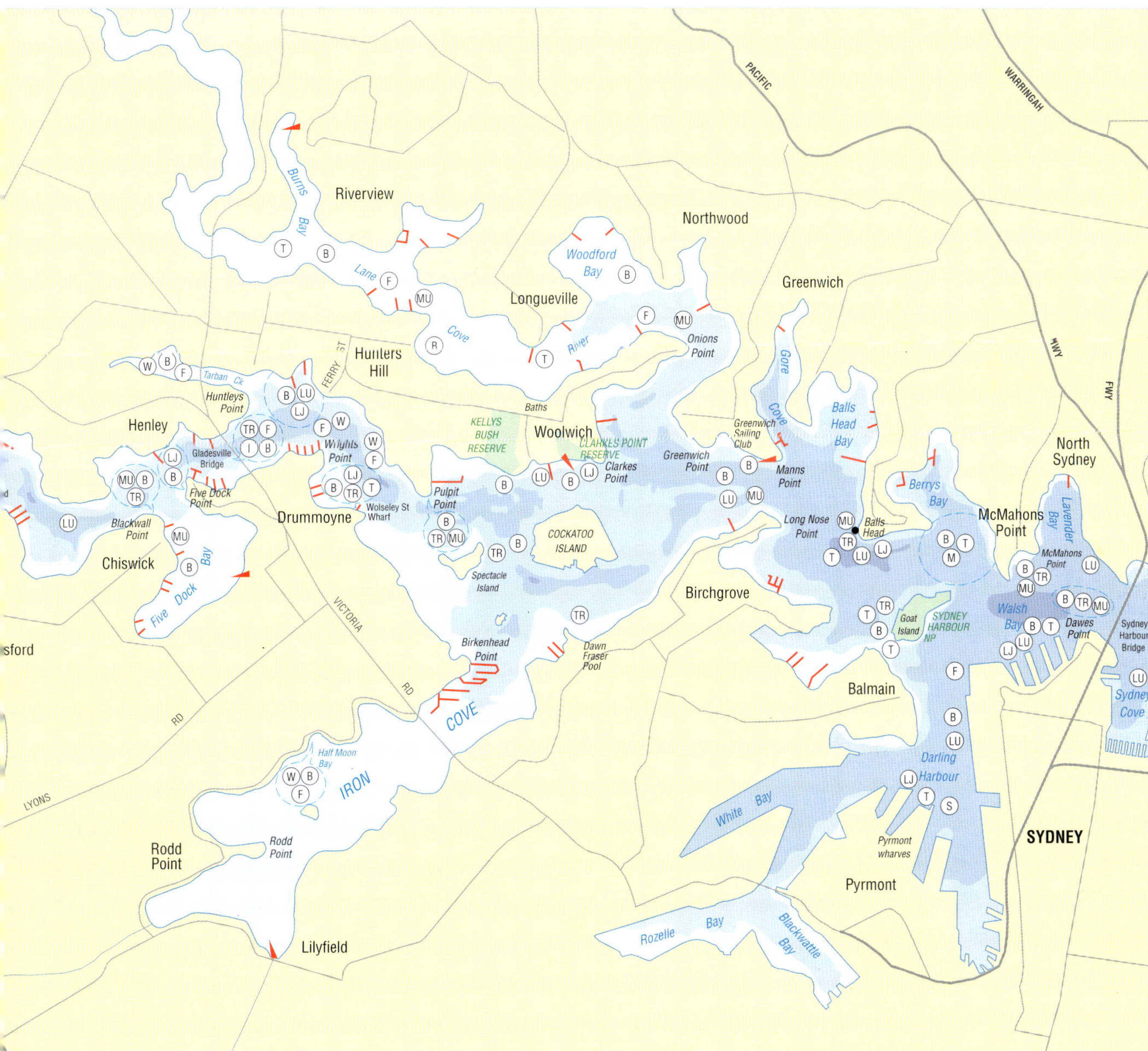

Sydney South and Botany Bay

Type of fishing
bay, beach, estuary, rock
Target fish
bream, flathead, luderick, rock blackfish, whiting

The coastline from Sydney to Botany has everything for the rock angler, with its towering sandstone cliffs containing rocky platforms at various levels, including many that are pounded by the sea at high tides. Botany Bay itself is surrounded by the airport, industry and suburbia. It is heavily fished and ever threatened by pollution and dredging, but it is still a reasonable fishing water.

SOUTHERN BEACHES

This area is a place for local knowledge about safety. Many fishing locations are easily accessible, while others may involve climbing ropes and ladders. The uninitiated should begin with safe and easily reached locations. Luderick, bream and rock blackfish inhabit the rocky washes, with tailor, Australian salmon, snapper and trevally also possible.

Mulloway and yellowtail kingfish can be caught outside **South Head** using live yellowtail for bait. South Head's best place in calmer seas is **Elephant Rock**. The targets are bream, rock blackfish, luderick and tailor. From **The Gap** to **Rosa Gully** is all high cliffs, but there is a steel ladder down to Rosa Gully. However, the spots are only good in calm weather. Again try for rock blackfish, luderick, bream and tailor.

Ben Buckler, the northern point of Bondi Beach, provides a wide variety of fishing – rock blackfish, luderick, bream, tailor, salmon – while it is mainly bream and rock blackfish at **Mackenzies Point**. One of the best spots is **Shark Point**, which can provide catches of luderick, bream, rock blackfish, Australian salmon, tailor and groper, with the occasional yellowtail kingfish for lure casters. In

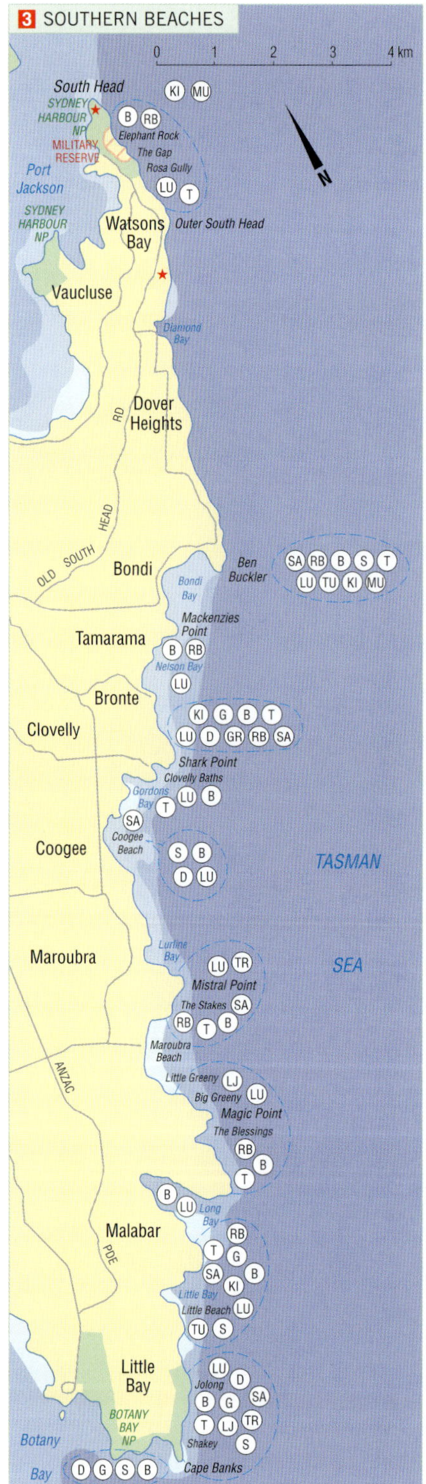

rough weather there is still a good chance of luderick on the rocks near **Clovelly Baths**. Well protected from the ocean swell, **Coogee Beach** is the best beach fishing location along this stretch.

The Stakes at the northern end of **Maroubra Beach** is great for luderick and rock blackfish, and in the winter there is excellent fishing with live bait for tailor, Australian salmon, trevally and bream. There are three good ledges further south (**Little Greeny**, **Big Greeny** and **The Blessings**), all excellent for luderick and rock blackfish.

South to **Cape Banks** is excellent rock fishing territory, particularly for luderick specialists, although bream, Australian salmon and tailor are also caught. This is a particularly dangerous area, and iron stakes have been driven into the rocks to provide a hold if a wave washes over. Rock plates are advised for shoes. Some of the well-known spots include Donkeys and Julieann (access north from Little Beach); The Gutter, Doctors Rocks, The Trap and The Pinnacle (south from Little Beach); and **Jolong** and **Shakey**, which are on the Cape.

BOTANY BAY

Botany Bay was once outstanding, but its future for fishing is in the balance. There are some very busy parts of the bay, with anglers, sailors, workboats and ships all taking up space, so it pays to be alert and to check your position.

A popular land-based spot is the **Cooks River** breakwall, where bream, luderick, flathead, tailor and the occasional mulloway are available. Other good land locations are **Bare Island**, the retaining wall at **Molineaux Point**, **Brighton Wharf**, **Lady Robinsons Beach**, **Ramsgate Baths** and **Dolls Point**. Generally Botany Bay is best fished at the start of a run-in tide, but the **Towra Point** area is best on the run-out.

Fishing the rocks outside South Head can be dangerous but often rewarding

GUIDE TO LOCAL FISH

	Southern Beaches	Botany Bay	Georges River
Ⓑ bream	●	●	●
Ⓓ drummer, silver	●	●	
Ⓕ flathead		●	●
(FL) flounder			●
Ⓖ garfish	●		
(GR) groper	●	●	
(HT) hairtail		●	
(KI) kingfish, yellowtail	●	●	
(LJ) leatherjacket	●		●
(LU) luderick	●	●	●
(MU) mulloway	●	●	●
(RB) rock blackfish	●		
(SA) salmon, Australian	●		
Ⓢ snapper	●	●	
Ⓣ tailor	●	●	
(TR) trevally	●	●	
(TU) tuna	●		
Ⓦ whiting		●	●

Sunrise over Botany Bay and the best time to catch fish from one of the many piers on the western side of the bay

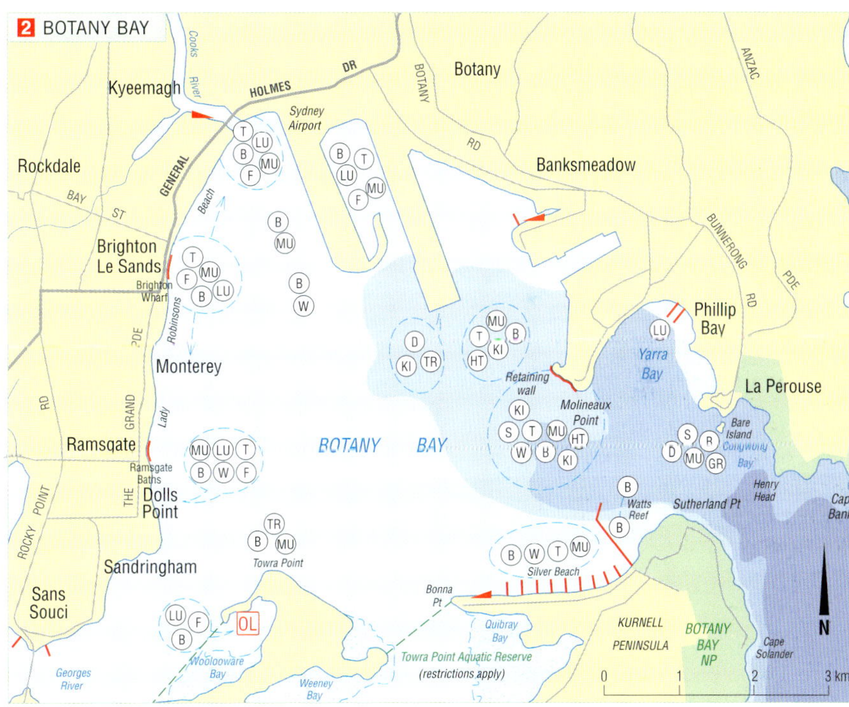

Inshore fishing all around the bay is mainly for bream, whiting, tailor and mulloway, and drifting for flathead is a popular exercise. One of the best inshore spots is 200 to 300 m out from **Silver Beach**.

Out into the bay, the end of the new airport runway is a yellowtail kingfish haunt; off **Molineaux Point**, there is deep water for mulloway, hairtail, snapper, yellowtail kingfish, tailor, whiting and bream; and **Watts Reef**, off Kurnell Peninsula, is a renowned big bream spot at night. The Aquatic Reserve at Towra Point has restrictions applying. To the south-west, in **Woolooware Bay**, the weed beds around the oyster leases attract bream, flathead and luderick.

GEORGES RIVER

Georges River has a lot to offer. Just inside the entrance is a good flathead drifting area, while its lower reaches have popular stands from either shore for bream, luderick and flathead. The **Captain Cook Bridge** area is fished for bream, again from either shore, and there are some noted mulloway holes between here and the **Georges River Bridge**. Bream, flathead and whiting can be caught all along the river, with bloodworms the best bait. Luderick are plentiful further upstream, particularly around the mouth of the **Woronora River**, but berley and a run-out tide are essential. **Jewfish Bay** and **Jewfish Point** have mulloway residing in some deepwater areas.

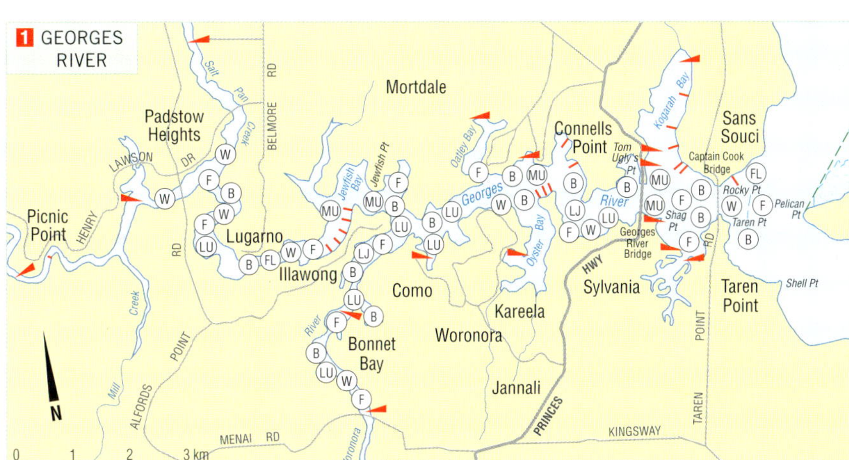

Kurnell and Port Hacking

Type of fishing
bay, beach, estuary, rock

Target fish
bream, flathead, luderick, mulloway, tailor, whiting

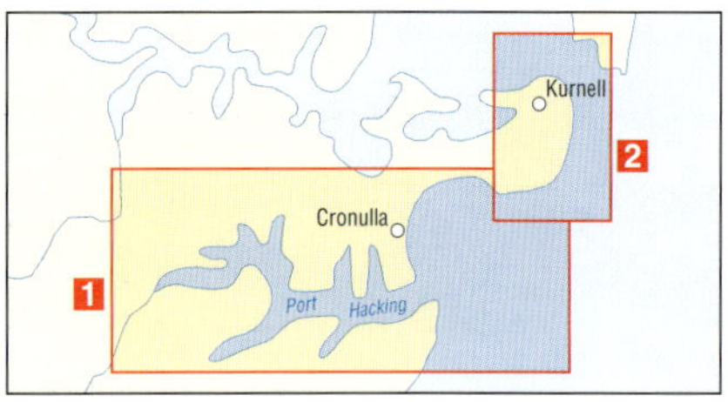

Access to the rocky Kurnell Peninsula is limited by the security of the nearby refinery and the national park, but the park gates open at about 7 a.m. The fishing produces luderick, rock blackfish, bream, trevally, Australian salmon, tailor and groper, but care must be taken on the often dangerous rock ledges. The beaches in the Cronulla area create a long stretch for surf fishing. Port Hacking has estuary fishing, with weed areas, sandbanks and channels.

KURNELL PENINSULA

Cape Solander Drive leads to great fishing nearby at **Inscription Point**, where there are comparatively safe rock ledges from which to seek luderick and rock blackfish. Others facing the sea are dangerous, even in reasonably calm weather. From Sir Joseph Banks Drive, roads branch off towards the coast – one towards the **Tabbigai** area, and another south to **Potter Point**. Again a weather watch is essential, but this is great rock blackfish, luderick and bream water. Potter Point is heavy with luderick, but it is one of the most dangerous places in the area. It is better to move around the corner to **Boat Harbour** to try for bream, whiting and tailor.

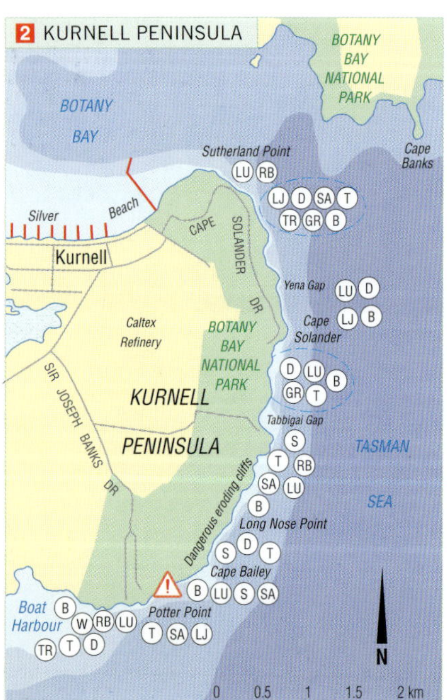

GUIDE TO LOCAL FISH

	Kurnell Peninsula	Cronulla and Port Hacking
(B) bream	●	●
(D) drummer, silver	●	●
(F) flathead		●
(FL) flounder		●
(GR) groper	●	
(DR) john dory		●
(KI) kingfish, yellowtail		●
(LJ) leatherjacket	●	●
(LU) luderick	●	●
(M) mullet		●
(MU) mulloway		●
(RB) rock blackfish	●	
(SA) salmon, Australian	●	●
(S) snapper	●	●
(T) tailor	●	●
(TR) trevally	●	●
(W) whiting	●	●

CRONULLA AND PORT HACKING

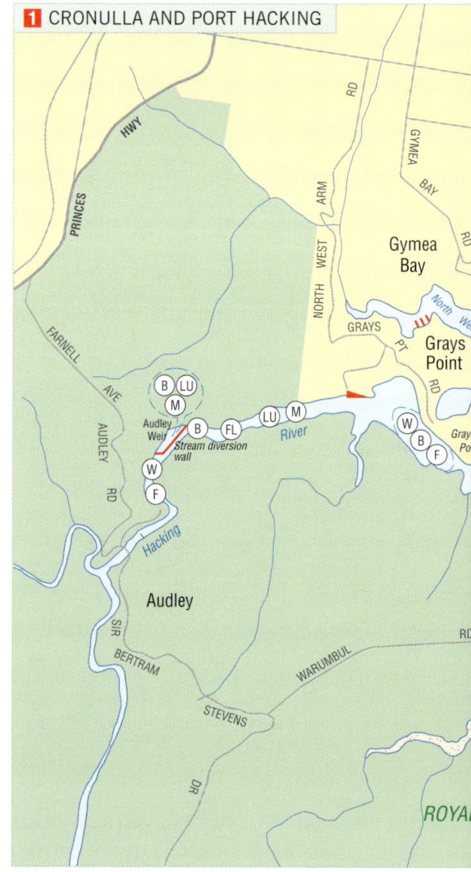

Outside Port Hacking, tailor, flathead, whiting and bream are the predominant fish at the **Cronulla beaches**, with the chance of mulloway in the deeper gutters at night. Fishing on a high tide in the evenings provides good catches of bream on the rocks south of **Sandshoes Beach** towards the entrance to Port Hacking.

Port Hacking is essentially a boating water as there are few accessible land-based fishing points on the rocky shores. Low tide, when the fish retreat from the flats to the channels, is the best time to fish, but at high tide, fishing inshore will also bring

The dramatic sea cliffs and rock platforms at Cape Solander should be approached with caution

good yields. There is an Aquatic Reserve at Shiprock, near Little Turriel Point, where fishing restrictions apply.

The best all-round spot is at the **Ballast Heap**, on the western point of Fishermans Bay, where the sand flat runs into Maianbar. The fishery also includes visitors like snapper, mulloway, trevally, tailor, yellowtail kingfish and john dory.

Some of the other good places in Port Hacking are **Hungry Point** for luderick; **Gunnamatta Bay** for shore-based catches of flathead, bream and trevally in winter; **Bonnievale Spit** for snapper on an outgoing tide; **Dolans Bay Wharf** for bream and flathead, and bait of yellowtail and mullet; **South West Arm**, for mulloway and yellowtail kingfish as well as flathead and bream; and **Lilli Pilli Baths** for bream, trevally, yellowtail kingfish, tailor and school mulloway.

The ideal baits for Port Hacking are pink nippers and squirt worms, which can be gathered on the sand flats at Maianbar. It is illegal to remove shellfish, just as any kind of fish trap or net is illegal in Port Hacking.

In the **Hacking River**, Grays Point is a great whiting, flathead and bream spot. At the stream diversion wall and **Audley Weir**, the river yields bream, luderick and mullet.

Mulloway or jewfish fall to beach, rock and offshore anglers as well as estuary fishers

Grafton Region

Big rivers weave through the beautiful northern coastal country of New South Wales, providing a major focus for fishing in the towns. Flathead, whiting and bream are in these waters, but mulloway and more tropical species may surprise. Bass and estuary perch are further upriver.

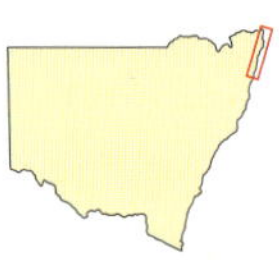

The facilities, climate and an abundance of fish make this region a popular resort all year round. A variety of rock and beach fishing is all along the coast, and there are some rewarding platforms for angling. There is also great game fishing in the area, with wahoo, mackerel and tuna, in particular, caught offshore from Cape Byron, east of Byron Bay. Further south, between Wooli and Coffs Harbour, several reefs can be fished for cobia and Spanish mackerel. For estuary anglers, flathead and bream are the targets at the Evans River entrance, with bream, tailor and mulloway available in the Clarence River estuary, between Iluka and Yamba. The Clarence River above Grafton is one of the best bass rivers in New South Wales.

At Yamba, looking up the tremendously productive Clarence River

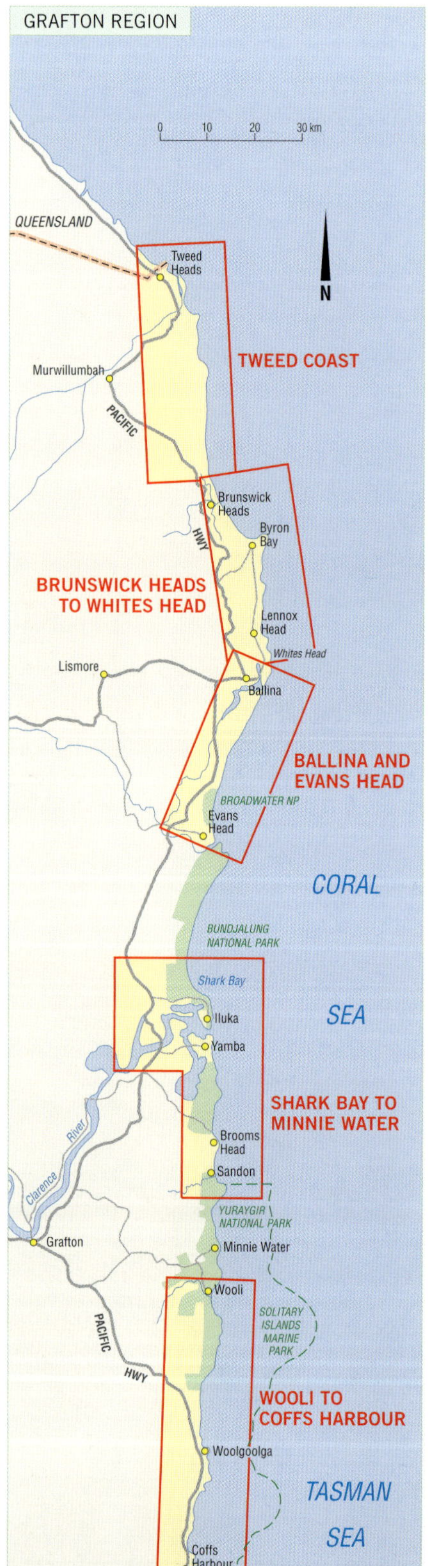

WHERE TO FISH

Grafton Region

TWEED COAST ● 68

This is a good area for river fishing, with whiting, flathead and bream the target fish. Breakwall and bridge fishing are options for mulloway and mangrove jack. There is a great variety of rock fishing, with Fingal Head the best spot. Beaches and offshore reefs are also possible locations.

BRUNSWICK HEADS TO WHITES HEAD ● 70

Brunswick Heads has long and productive surf beaches, and great wall and boat fishing in and around the Brunswick River. Cape Byron has good rock fishing, and is a vantage point for the gutters at Suffolk Park Beach. Lennox Head is also a top rock spot. There is great game fishing offshore at the Julian Rocks Aquatic Reserve.

BALLINA AND EVANS HEAD ● 72

The big Richmond River is a superb and varied fishing area, and Ballina has both rock and breakwall fishing for land anglers. The beach fishing offshore is excellent. The Evans River is a productive area for estuary fishing, with more rock and beach fishing outside the heads.

SHARK BAY TO MINNIE WATER ● 74

The Clarence River is ideal for estuary anglers, with many land-based spots at the entrance. The Yamba–Iluka coastline has excellent rock and beach spots, and the Sandon River–Minnie Water area is a great fishing hideaway.

WOOLI TO COFFS HARBOUR ● 76

This part of the coast has a delightful combination of estuaries, beaches, headlands, rock platforms and offshore islands.

Rock blackfish

The distribution of rock blackfish is along the entire New South Wales coast and into southern Queensland. They should not be confused with luderick (also known as blackfish). They are excellent fighting fish, sometimes called 'pigs' as well as 'black drummer'.

GUIDE TO LOCAL FISH

amberjack
bass, Australian
bream, yellowfin
bream, black
cobia
dart
dolphin fish
drummer, silver
flathead
flounder
garfish
groper
kingfish, yellowtail
luderick
mackerel, Spanish
mackerel, spotted
mackerel, slimy
mangrove jack
marlin, black
marlin, blue
marlin, striped
mullet
mulloway
perch, estuary
perch, pearl
pike, yellow-finned sea
rock blackfish
samson fish
snapper
tailor
tarwhine
teraglin
trevally, giant
trevally, golden
trevally, silver
tuna, mackerel
tuna, longtail
tuna, striped
tuna, yellowfin
wahoo
whiting, sand
whiting, trumpeter

FISHING TIP

Northern New South Wales can offer surprisingly good snapper fishing in winter, usually out over deeper offshore reefs. Tackle needs to be scaled down as the fish are shyer in the clear cold water, and braided line helps here, offering increased breaking strength for greatly reduced line diameter and low stretch to help feel tentative bites. After heavy southerly weather, winter snapper move inshore, to feast on cuttlefish, or to prey on dense shoals of baitfish pushed inshore by the rough seas. At such times, big schools of migrating tailor also sometimes attack these inshore bait schools and snapper can be found underneath this carnage.

The Clarence River at Iluka: a recent move by prawn trawlers here to fit fish exclusion devices to their nets should see greater survival of juveniles such as mulloway

Weather

North-easterlies are the prevailing winds in this region in early summer, and can reach 15 to 20 knots. From July to September west winds can be very rough, and southerlies are prevalent in winter. Always watch for sudden changes, especially when the 'Southerly Buster' comes in during the afternoon, or when crossing the bars at Ballina, Brunswick Heads, Evans Head and Tweed Heads. For up-to-date weather information, contact the Weather Bureau on (02) 9296 1555 or the local Coast Guard or Coastal Patrol.

Boating

Offshore, there are washes and rocks around South Solitary Island (part of a marine reserve, off Emerald Beach and just north of Coffs Harbour) and three large surface-level bomboras, which are not easily visible and should be checked from charts. For specific conditions in particular areas, check with the NSW Maritime officer or the local Coastal Patrol.

FURTHER INFORMATION

Fishing and boating *NSW Fisheries has offices at 5 Regatta Ave, Ballina, tel. (02) 6686 2018; Coffs Harbour Jetty, Coffs Harbour, tel. (02) 6652 3997; 18A River St, Maclean, tel. (02) 6645 0500; and 10/12 Greenway Dr, Tweed Heads, tel. (07) 5523 1822. NSW Maritime has offices at 2/16 Isles Dr, Coffs Harbour Jetty, Coffs Harbour, tel. (02) 6651 3400; Tweed City Arcade, 69 Wharf St, Tweed Heads, tel. (07) 5536 1001; and Shop 6, Ballina Boulevard, 70 River St, Ballina, tel. (02) 6680 8417. The Coast Guard's main bases are at Ballina, tel. (02) 6680 8417 and Iluka, tel. (02) 6646 6311. The Coastal Patrol has bases at Byron Bay, tel. (02) 6685 5474 and at Coffs Harbour, tel. (02) 6652 3155.*

Tourist centres *Cnr River St and Las Balsa Plaza, Ballina, tel. (02) 6686 3484; 80 Jonson St, Byron Bay, tel. (02) 6680 8558; cnr Elizabeth and Mclean sts, Coffs Harbour, tel. (02) 6652 1522; The Professionals Real Estate, 9 Oak St, Evans Head, tel. (02) 6682 4611; Lower Clarence Visitors Centre, Ferry Park, Pacific Hwy, Maclean, tel. (02) 6645 4121; World Heritage Rainforest Centre, cnr Pacific Hwy and Alma St, Murwillumbah, tel. (02) 6672 1340; 4 Wharf St, Tweed Heads, tel. (07) 5536 4244.*

Tweed Coast

Type of fishing
beach, offshore, river, rock, wall
Target fish
bream, flathead, mulloway, whiting

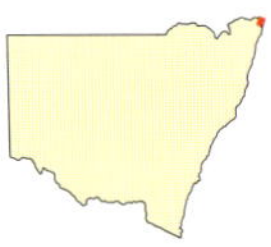

There is a wonderful variety of rock and beach fishing all along the coast from Tweed Heads to Brunswick Heads, and the huge Tweed River system is one of the most attractive and well-serviced fishing areas in New South Wales.

TWEED COAST

Fingal Beach, on the south side of the wall, is a good start for beach anglers as it has a long gutter for about a third of its length, yielding tailor, bream and sometimes mulloway. Fingal Head is the best rock spot in the area, but the Giants Causeway must be carefully negotiated. Big bream, tailor and mulloway are the general reward, but pelagics are also attracted to this rich food source.

The washes around Marys Rock on the north side of **Cook Island** carry yellowtail kingfish and tailor, while mulloway, wahoo and marlin are on the lee side in summer. North-east of Cook is **Fidos Reef**. It can be quite dangerous in heavy weather, but provides a bonanza of snapper, yellowtail kingfish, Spanish mackerel, cobia and other pelagics. **Nine Mile Reef**, a further 8 km east, is an underwater cliff that reaches to within 6 m of the surface, again dangerous in heavy weather. It attracts dolphin fish, wahoo, tuna, yellowtail kingfish and marlin in the summer.

Dreamtime Beach, at Wommin Bay, and **Kingscliff Beach** are subject to changing gutters, but may reward with whiting, bream and dart. The Kingscliff bar at the mouth of Cudgen Creek can provide people in boats with an alternative access to the ocean when the dangerous Tweed Heads bar is subject to south-easterlies. In calm conditions there is good fishing for tailor, mulloway and bream on the rocks below the Kingscliff south wall, at the mouth of the creek.

Bogangar Beach has good gutters. The southern end is known for quality whiting, and Towners Hole and Spencers Hole are popular for big mulloway and tailor. Norries Head has good rock spots for tailor and bream, but they can be very dangerous.

There are rock platforms near **Hastings Point** that fish well for tailor or snapper. The most comfortable of them is Flat Rock, just off the southern point of Cudgera Creek. Pottsville, Mooball and Wooyung beaches will have tailor, bream, whiting and mulloway if there are good sand formations in place. The Black Rocks, several kilometres offshore between Pottsville and Wooyung, is a good spot for bream, tailor and mulloway, with whiting in the gutters on either side.

A reef about 2 km offshore from New Brighton has snapper, yellowtail kingfish, school tailor in winter, and spotted and Spanish mackerel in abundance in summer.

GUIDE TO LOCAL FISH

	Tweed Coast	Tweed River
(B) bream	•	•
(CO) cobia	•	
(DA) dart	•	
(F) flathead		•
(KI) kingfish, yellowtail	•	
(LU) luderick		•
(MA) mackerel	•	
(MJ) mangrove jack		•
(ML) marlin	•	
(MU) mulloway	•	•
(PP) perch, pearl	•	
(S) snapper	•	
(T) tailor	•	•
(TL) teraglin	•	
(TR) trevally		•
(TU) tuna	•	
(WH) wahoo	•	
(W) whiting	•	•

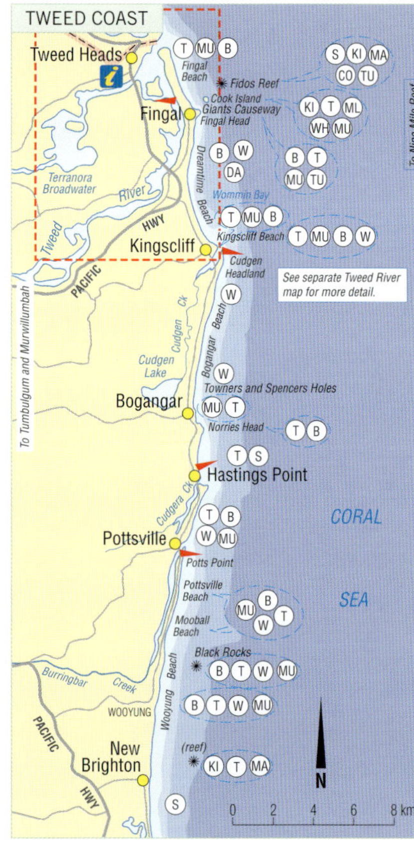

Tweed Heads entrance with Fingal Beach in the background – a good start for the visiting land-based angler as there are bream, tailor and often mulloway to be caught here

TWEED RIVER

The broad reaches of the **Lower Tweed** provide all-round action, starting with the breakwalls and headlands around the entrance, which are renowned for luderick, and for tailor in the autumn and winter. Mulloway are in this area when the tailor are schooling and during the poddy mullet run in spring.

Whiting and bream are the main targets in the river. Flathead are also often present, as are big mulloway from October to March, particularly around the **Blue Hole** at the head of Ukerebagh Island, the **Boyds Bay and Barneys Point bridges**, **Tonys Island** and **Lillies Island**. The bridges are also good for jigging with feathered lures, with trevally the target, while the wooded edges of Barneys Point are haunts for mangrove jack. In the summer months, whiting and bream are more likely to be caught after rain or at dawn or dusk. Flathead, however, will be in holes and drop-offs close to the water's edge as the tide recedes.

Bream in the Tweed appear to prefer strips of fish flesh, especially tailor, rather than the prawns fancied in waters around Brisbane. Nippers can also be pumped from sand and mudflats along the edges of the waterways, and will be grabbed by the flathead.

The Tweed has good fishing all the way to Murwillumbah, some 30 km from Tweed Heads, and beyond. **Chinderah**, opposite the caravan park, is a good spot for whiting, and luderick around the banks. North of **Dodds Island** is a reef where bream and mulloway are present, and the shallow sandy stretch up to **Stotts Island** is whiting territory. The river has to be carefully navigated as there are shallow areas, particularly between Tumbulgum (just upstream from Stotts Island) and Murwillumbah, and you have to look out for waterskiers by day and dredges by night. The southern side of the river is generally deeper. Whiting, flathead and mulloway are the targets in this busy area.

Mulloway

Colloquially known as jewfish, the mulloway is a popular game and table fish throughout the southern regions of Australia. It is often confused with teraglin or northern mulloway.

The waters of the upper Tweed near Murwillumbah, navigable by boat although there are shallow areas

Brunswick Heads to Whites Head

Type of fishing
beach, estuary, offshore, river, rock
Target fish
bream, flathead, mulloway, tailor, whiting

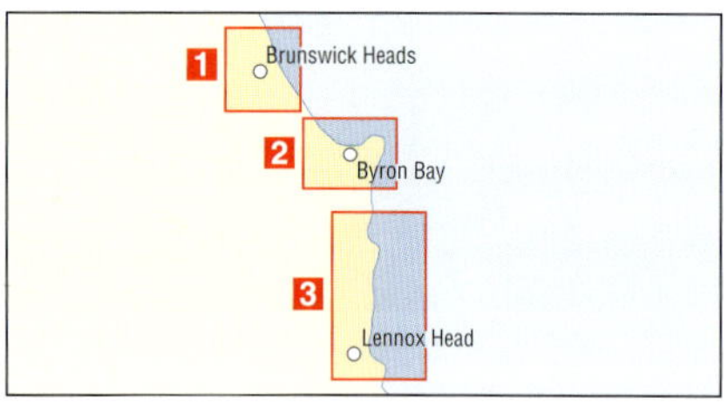

The fishing is reliable at Brunswick Heads, either in the Brunswick River or around its entrance. Byron Bay's popularity as a surfing area can be limiting to fishing on the long surf beaches that stretch out on either side of the town. There is good offshore fishing along the coast.

The oyster beds in the Brunswick River harbour good populations of bream that live and feed in and around the leases

BRUNSWICK HEADS

The main targets in the **Brunswick River** and nearby beaches are tailor, bream, whiting and mulloway, with flathead, whiting and bream in the estuary. The estuary breaks into Marshalls and Simpsons creeks, known as the north and south arms, which are shallow and require knowledge of the channels.

A particularly good land-based angling place for bream, flathead, luderick and school mulloway is the **Spur Wall**, at the inland entrance of the south arm. Bream and luderick are the main quarries further west at the **Memorial Wall**, and bream make for the boat harbour, just west of the wall, when the prawn trawlers arrive with their catch. Further into the estuary, whiting, flathead and bream continue to abound. Oyster leases provide good fishing areas.

Land anglers also do well on the breakwalls at the river entrance. The seaward side of the **North Wall** is good for tailor and mulloway, with bream, whiting and luderick on the sheltered side. Bream, tailor and mulloway are around both sides of the **South Wall**, with some flathead on the river side. **Seagull Rocks** offer whiting, bream, tailor and luderick in the rocky washes, while the 10-km long **South Beach** has good formations for whiting, tailor and bream. Boat anglers should be aware that the bar is dangerous.

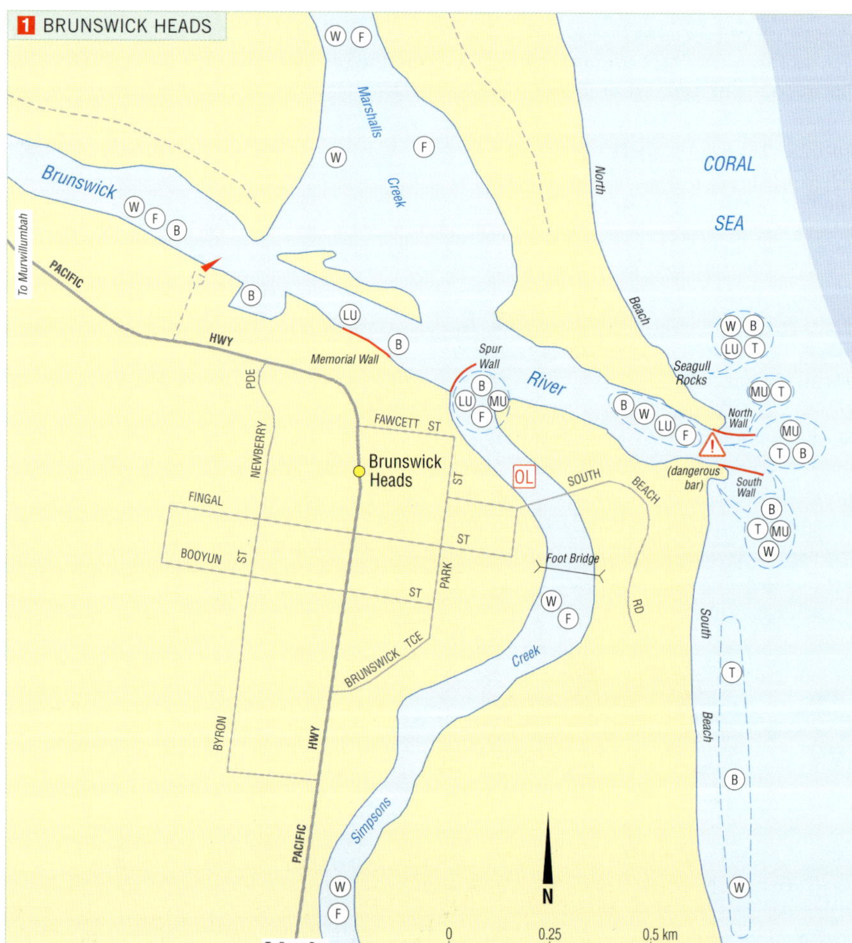

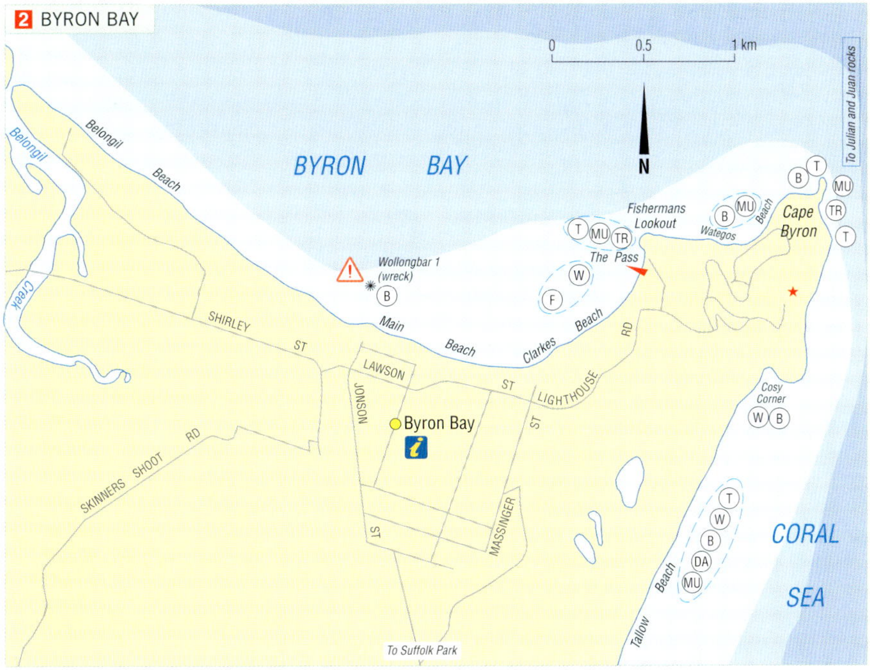

GUIDE TO LOCAL FISH

	Brunswick Heads	Byron Bay	Tallow Beach to Whites Head
(B) bream		●	●
(DA) dart		●	●
(D) drummer, silver			●
(F) flathead	●	●	
(LU) luderick	●		●
(MA) mackerel			●
(MU) mulloway	●	●	●
(RB) rock blackfish			●
(S) snapper	●		●
(T) tailor	●	●	●
(TR) trevally		●	
(TU) tuna			●
(W) whiting	●	●	●

BYRON BAY

Some 40 m offshore from Main Beach lies the wreck of the *Wollongbar 1*, which can be a good bream spot in rough weather. However, people in boats anchor at their peril, as the waves here are unpredictable. The main swimming areas in Byron Bay, **Clarkes Beach** and **Wategos Beach**, are seldom fished by day, but the former has flathead, and big whiting in the autumn, while the rocks around Wategos can be good for bream and mulloway in poor weather. **The Pass** at the Cape Byron end of Clarkes Beach offers the only boat-launching facility, and four-wheel drives are recommended. You will need to be fit and determined to get down to the rocks on the seaward side of the rugged cape, but the rewards of tailor and mulloway are sometimes enhanced by summer visits of tropical trevally, a rare happening in New South Wales.

Offshore there are two rocky outcrops about 4 km north-east of the cape, known as **Julian and Juan rocks**. These are brilliant game fishing locations for wahoo, mackerel, tuna, snapper, bream, mulloway, teraglin, pearl perch and trevally, but as the area is a marine reserve, only one line and one hook per angler are allowed.

TALLOW BEACH TO WHITES HEAD

The **Tallow Beach and Suffolk Park area** has gutters with tailor, whiting, dart, bream and mulloway sometimes present, while further south **Broken Head** is good for bream, tailor, mulloway, rock blackfish and drummer.

Seven Mile Beach requires a vehicle permit, but provides a ready source of bait with worms, pippis and crabs for the bream, whiting and mulloway in the gutters and holes. The area in front of the surf club is recommended. **Lennox Head** is a great place for tailor and big bream, and **The Point** has big tailor, but is virtually unfishable by day because of surfers. **The Ledge**, on the southern side of Lennox Head, requires a stiff climb to the high platform, but good rock anglers will enjoy the tailor, mulloway, luderick and passing pelagics, along with snapper after a heavy blow. **Shag Rock** has tailor and rock blackfish. The **Iron Peg** is a narrow finger of rock over deep water. This is a dangerous spot in any weather, but can yield an abundance of fish. **Skennars Head** is for the fit and experienced, as it requires a rope descent.

Tallow Beach provides good surf fishing for bream, whiting, tailor and sometimes even dart

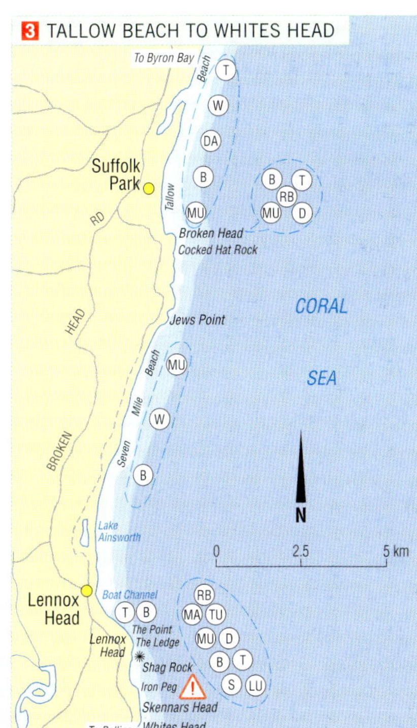

Ballina and Evans Head

Type of fishing
beach, estuary, river, rock, wall
Target fish
bream, flathead, luderick, mulloway, tailor

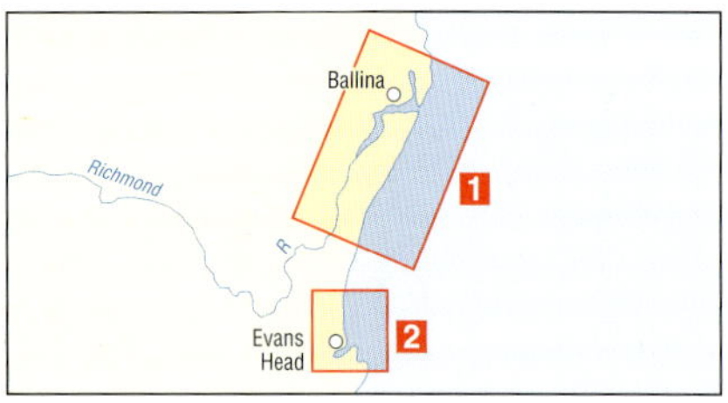

Ballina is a great place for fishing with good rock, breakwall and beach angling around the town, highly productive fishing and prawning in the Richmond River, and some excellent offshore spots. Evans Head is one of the best snapper ports in New South Wales, with quality mulloway, teraglin and diminishing pearl perch to be found.

BALLINA

Outside and north of Ballina, the action starts at **Sharps Beach**, with a good hole at the northern end of the beach for bream and school mulloway. At the southern end, **Flat Rock** headland has some rocky gutters on the northern side, attracting bream, luderick, rock blackfish, trevally and tailor.

South of Flat Rock, **Angels Beach** has productive holes and gutters for whiting, flathead and mulloway, with **Pontoon Rocks** in the middle of the beach making a good platform for bream, tailor and mulloway. Further south, **Black Head** is also a popular spot, with mulloway, bream and whiting close in, and mackerel and marlin possibilities in summer. **Ballina Head** and the beaches on either side have bream, whiting and mulloway as their main targets.

Around the walls of the **Richmond River** there are bream, mulloway and tailor, with the occasional mackerel and bluefin tuna coming close in summer. The North Wall fishes well on the outside for bream, tailor and mulloway, and on the inside for bream sheltering from a north-easterly. Low tide is best. The end of the South Wall is great for mulloway and bream.

Just inside the entrance is the landlocked but tidal **Shaws Bay**, which carries very big tailor, mangrove jack, bream and luderick. It is best at dusk with a floating prawn bait. The mangrove-lined **North Creek** requires knowledge of the channels and shallows, but is terrific for big flathead, whiting, bream and occasionally mangrove jack. The **Missingham Bridge** over the creek entrance is a fine place to try for luderick, bream, whiting and flathead, while the **Porpoise Wall** has bream and luderick

GUIDE TO LOCAL FISH

	Ballina	Evans Head
(B) bream	•	•
(D) drummer, silver		•
(F) flathead	•	•
(LU) luderick	•	•
(MA) mackerel	•	•
(MJ) mangrove jack	•	•
(ML) marlin	•	
(MU) mulloway	•	•
(RB) rock blackfish	•	•
(S) snapper	•	
(T) tailor	•	•
(TR) trevally	•	
(TU) tuna	•	•
(W) whiting	•	•

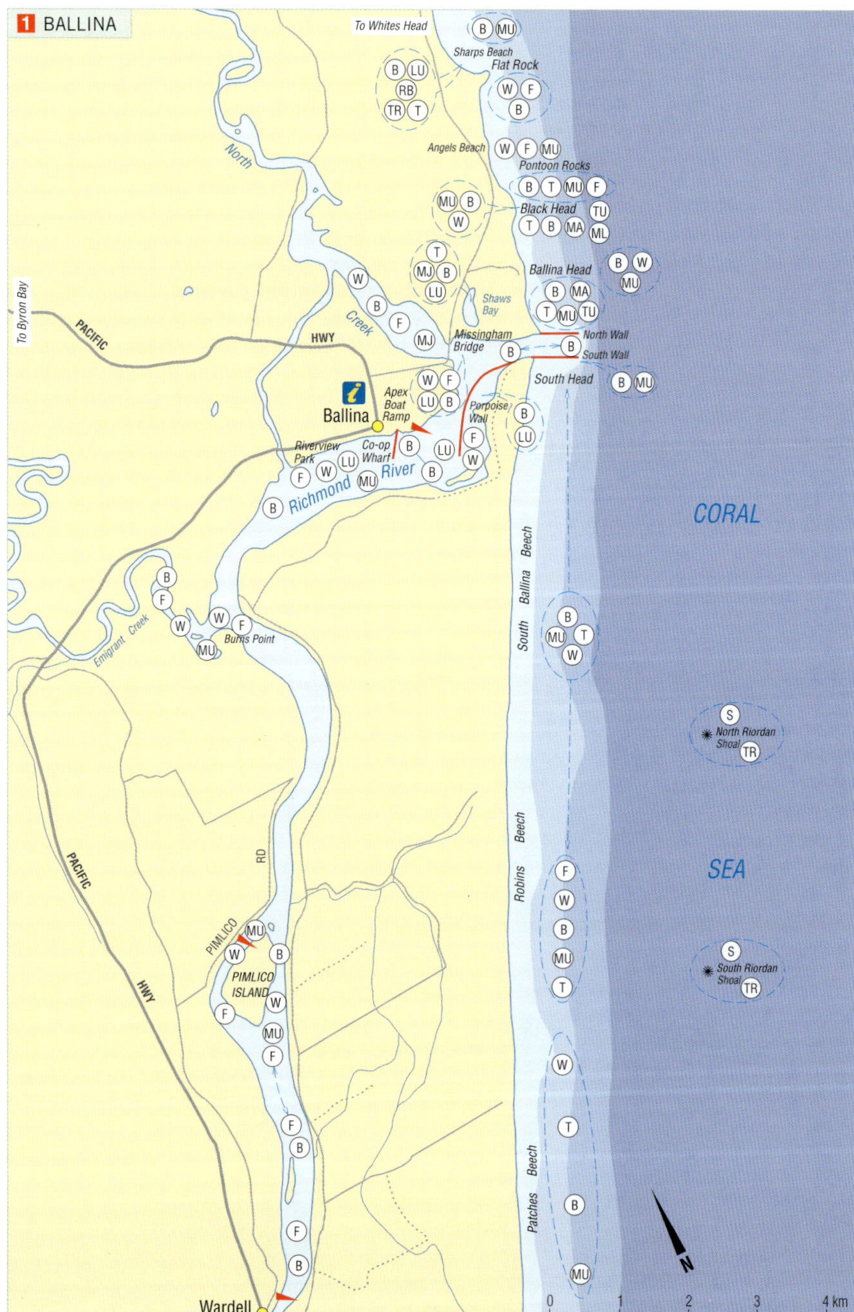

on the channel side and flathead and whiting in the shallows on the other side.

Just out from the Apex boat ramp on the north shore is a bream hole that attracts a lot of boats seeking the fish that abound there in winter. The hole is best fished around sunset.

The river continues to be one of Australia's finest areas for bream, whiting, school mulloway and flathead, all the way down to **Pimlico Island**. Some of the best places are the **Co-op Wharf**, **Riverview Park**, **Burns Point** and **Emigrant Creek**. Further upriver, bream can be caught around the structures, while drifting for big flathead continues all the way to Wardell.

The 20-km long beach on the south side of the Richmond River entrance has four-wheel drive access for those with permits from the Ballina Shire Council; worms and pippis for the taking; and gutters carrying whiting, tailor, bream and mulloway. For boat anglers, the **North and South Riordan shoals** are about 2.5 km off the beach and 3 km apart. They are hard to find, but the snapper and trevally are abundant.

The Richmond River at Ballina, permanently open to the ocean, provides a port for many professional boats

EVANS HEAD

Airforce Beach at **Evans Head** often has a hole in front of the surf club, which is best fished at dawn and dusk for bream and whiting. The **North Wall** fishes very well after rain, with bream, whiting, tailor and mulloway on the seaward side, luderick and bream inside. Nearby, the **Little Wall** is renowned for autumn and winter bream. The **South Wall** is also worth trying for bream, whiting, tailor and flathead. There are some hot spots in the deep lower estuary and the boat ramp and bridge area, with flathead as the main target, while the boat harbour attracts big bream when the prawn fleet arrives in the morning. The beach on the seaward side of the bridge is a good fishing spot, and also a great bait spot for yabbies.

A little further upstream, whiting and flathead are caught off the sand flats around the island, and the flats here are also crawling with yabbies. Inland from the island the stream narrows, and the old iron floodgates (which have given the area its name, Iron Gates) are a great place for bream. A little further along, a bay in the river has a good mulloway hole and is also a reliable spot for mangrove jack, bream and flathead.

There are many good rock places around the headland on the southern side of the river. South-east of Little Beach is **Half Tide Inlet**, where mulloway and bream are the main targets. **Joggly Point** can only be reached by walking or four-wheel drive and is a dangerous place in a swell, but on a good day it can be fished for mulloway, bream, tailor, drummer and luderick. Bream is the main target from the sandy bottom beneath a series of rocks called the **Piano Rocks**. The **Red Hill headland** is for walkers only, but can have mulloway, bream, tailor and rock blackfish.

Chinamans Beach and **New Zealand Beach**, both good for bream, tailor and whiting, are split by some rocks, which are best fished in rough conditions for bream and tailor. **Snapper Rock** has a low ledge on its seaward side, to be avoided in a swell, but in good weather try for bream, luderick, rock blackfish, mulloway and pelagics such as mackerel and longtail tuna. An exposed bombora called **Chaos** can be seen to the south-east and is known for its big Spanish mackerel and yellowtail kingfish.

Shark Bay to Minnie Water

Type of fishing
beach, estuary, offshore, river, rock, wall
Target fish
bream, flathead, mulloway, tailor, whiting

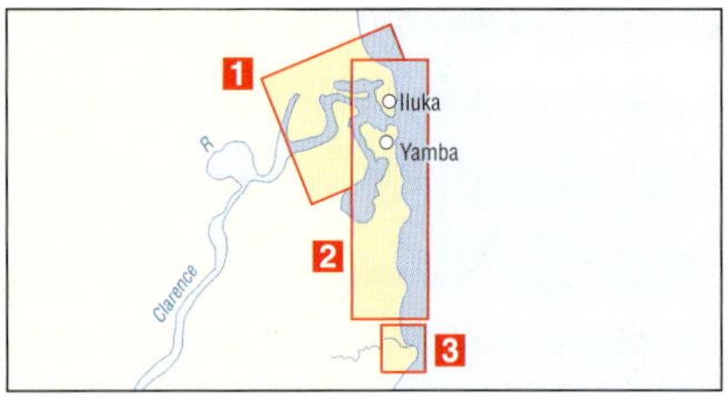

There is good outside fishing in the Yamba–Iluka area, with plenty of rock and beach spots. The Clarence River is a mecca for anglers in New South Wales, and further south, the village of Minnie Water has good rock fishing for bream and tailor, and beach fishing for mulloway, flathead and whiting.

SHARK BAY TO BROOMS HEAD

At **Shark Bay**, you can fish from North Beach for tailor, flathead, whiting and bream. The rocks at Woody Head are a fine platform for varied fishing, with tailor and mulloway the main targets. **Frasers Rock** and **Second Bluff** are the closest rock spots to Iluka, but there is easy access to all the north shore rocks. Mulloway are again the prime target from all these rocks.

In the south, **Pippi Beach** has good fishing for flathead, bream and tailor, with mulloway around Flat Rock at the beach's southern end. The rocks around Green Point and Angourie Point attract rock blackfish, luderick and sometimes mackerel, but the main targets are mulloway, bream and tailor.

Angourie Beach is productive and runs to a rocky formation known as **One Man Rock**, a dangerous place in rough weather, but with mulloway, groper and drummer. **Shelly Beach Head** carries a similar variety of fish, but is accessible only by walking. **Brooms Head** has good fishing for luderick, bream, rock blackfish, groper, mackerel and tailor, with snapper in summer. There is reef fishing offshore, and it is possible to beach-launch from the lee of the headland.

CLARENCE RIVER

The Clarence River has tailor and mulloway around the entrance; bream and luderick around the piers and rock walls; and flathead and whiting on the sand flats along the river. The townships of Yamba and Iluka on either side of the entrance have excellent facilities for boat launching, boat hire and bait and tackle supply.

The walls at the entrance extend well out to sea, and bream, mulloway, luderick and tailor are the regular catches. **Middle Wall**, on the southern side of the river, is noted for prolific catches of bream and luderick in winter, and the same fish are targets on the northern side at **Turkeys Nest Wall** and **Collis Wall**.

Inside the river is a complex of channels, islands and sand flats. Most of the fishing is drifting for flathead and whiting, with bream and luderick around rocky banks and structures like walls and piers. The flathead and whiting are distributed up the river as far as the town of **Maclean**, but some of the best spots are downriver from **Freeburn Island**, around Sleeper Point on **Palmers Island**, where mulloway hold the deeper water, and in the oyster channel running along the eastern side of **Micalo Island** to **Wooloweyah Lagoon**. The lagoon, a popular place for mud crabbing, carries a lot of flathead and bream.

The best times to fish the Clarence are dawn and dusk. A falling tide will enhance prospects of taking the flathead and whiting in the channels.

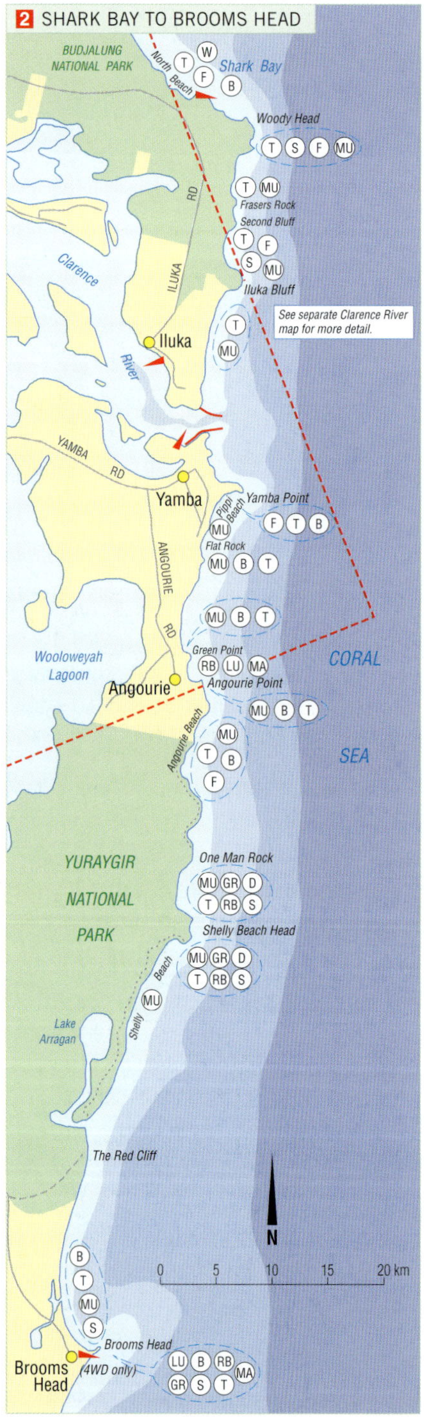

Young anglers on the lower Clarence River

GUIDE TO LOCAL FISH

	Shark Bay to Brooms Head	Clarence River	Sandon River
(B) bream	●	●	●
(D) drummer, silver	●	●	●
(F) flathead	●	●	●
(FL) flounder			●
(GR) groper	●		●
(LU) luderick	●	●	●
(MA) mackerel	●	●	
(MU) mulloway	●	●	●
(RB) rock blackfish	●		●
(S) snapper	●		●
(T) tailor	●	●	●
(TU) tuna		●	
(W) whiting	●	●	●

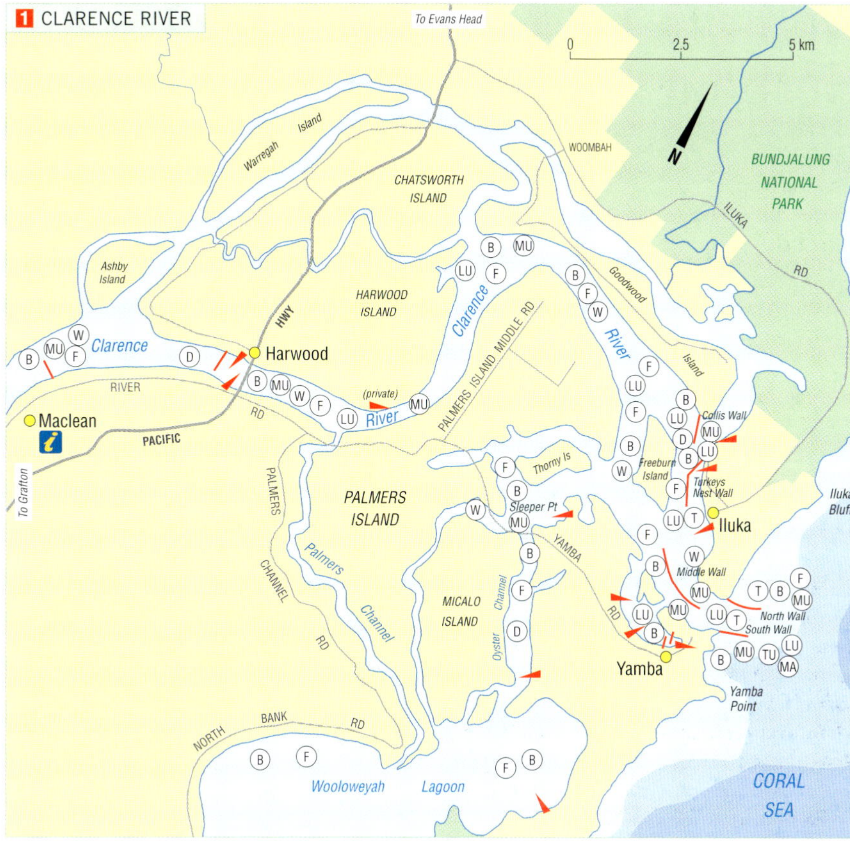

SANDON RIVER

The Sandon River region is a great fishing hideaway. The seclusion of Sandon township allows for some peaceful fishing in the river exploration of the rock and beach spots.

On the northern side of the entrance, **Plover Island**, which is connected to the mainland, can be fished from the rocks or a boat for tailor, bream and drummer, with occasional mulloway and snapper in rough weather. Boat fishing around the southern headland for the likes of rock blackfish, groper, mulloway, bream and tailor is popular. Inside the entrance, whiting and flathead are abundant around the sand flats, with the whiting best after rain. Bream and luderick are around the river mouth in winter.

Near the entrance to **Toumbaal Creek**, where the rocky bar is close to the surface, there can be good catches of school mulloway, bream and flathead on a run-out tide. The bend in the main river leads to oyster leases, and the likelihood of bream. Around the island and on to the forks in the river there are flathead, whiting in summer, and luderick and bream around rocky banks and structures. The river is shallow throughout.

The sheltered lagoon at **Minnie Water** is a fish nursery habitat and therefore a fishing drawcard, carrying bream, tarwhine, pike, sand whiting and many tropical species in the summer. Sandon and Minnie Water are part of the Solitary Islands Marine Reserve, which is subject to the control of the New South Wales Department of Fisheries and New South Wales National Parks.

Wooli to Coffs Harbour

Type of fishing
beach, creek, estuary, offshore, river, rock
Target fish
bream, mulloway, tailor, whiting

The waters between Wooli and Coffs Harbour are a delightful combination of estuaries, beaches, headlands, rock platforms and offshore islands. They include the Wooli Wooli River, which runs parallel to the coast behind Wooli, and the all-weather harbour at Coffs Harbour, one of the best established towns for fishing in Australia. A number of small rivers also run down this stretch of coast, with sand flats, channels and seagrass patches creating a varied habitat for mullet, bream, luderick, whiting and flathead. From north to south, they are **Station Creek, Saltwater Creek, Corindi River**, **Arrawarra Creek**, **Woolgoolga Creek** and **Moonee Creek**.

Fishing from the various headlands can yield snapper, tailor, groper, yellowtail kingfish, Spanish mackerel and tuna, while the main beach species are tailor, bream, whiting, flathead and mulloway. The most commonly fished headlands are at the **Station Creek** entrance, **Red Rock**, **Arrawarra**, **Woolgoolga** and **Bare Bluff**, while **Corindi**, **Woolgoolga** and **Moonee** are outstanding among the beaches along the coast.

The **Solitary Islands** are a chain of islands and other outcrops, the northernmost offshore from Wooli and the furthest south just past Moonee Beach. The warm, southward flowing current bathes the islands, creating a habitat for temperate fish and for tropical fish not found elsewhere in New South Wales. This area is a reserve, under strict controls, but line fishing is allowed in all but a few designed sanctuary zones.

North Solitary Island has snapper, yellowtail kingfish, teraglin, mulloway, pearl perch, tailor, groper, rock blackfish, silver drummer, Spanish mackerel and tuna. On the western side of the island fishing is prohibited for 200 m. **North Rock** is 3 km north of Red Rock headland, but the nearest launching places are the Wooli Wooli River and Corindi River, both with bar crossings that can only be attempted in calm water at high tide. North Rock is really twin rocks, with a sand-bottomed gutter fished for yellowtail kingfish, snapper, pearl perch, tailor, Spanish mackerel, longtail tuna and other pelagics.

North West Solitary, **South West Solitary** (known locally as Groper Islet), **South Solitary and Split Solitary islands** all have closed waters and other areas restricted to line fishing, and carry the same diversity of temperate and tropical bottom fish and pelagic species. South Solitary has the best fishing of all the islands. It is really three islands, and the northernmost, Birdie Island, often has a number of the protected grey nurse sharks in its waters.

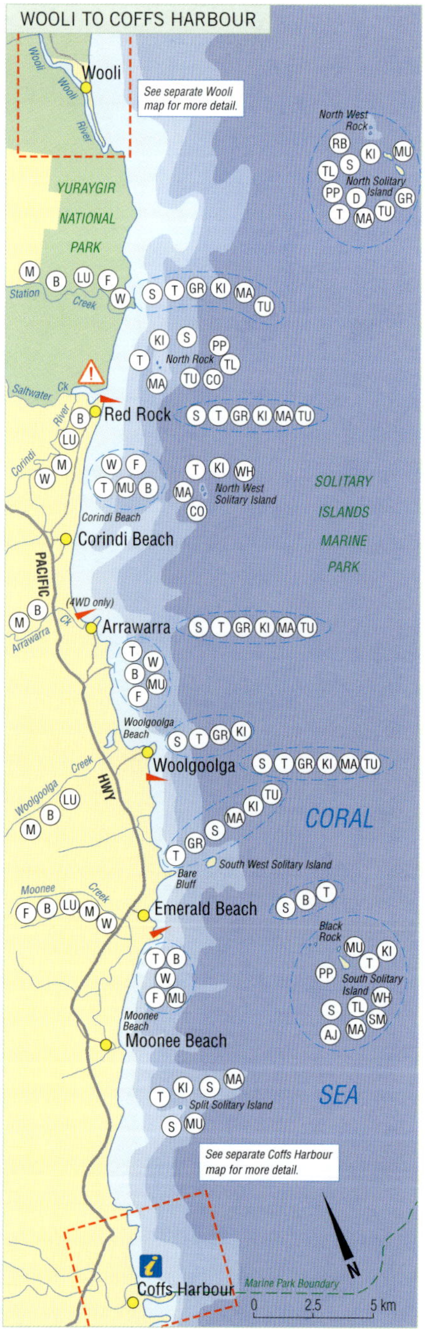

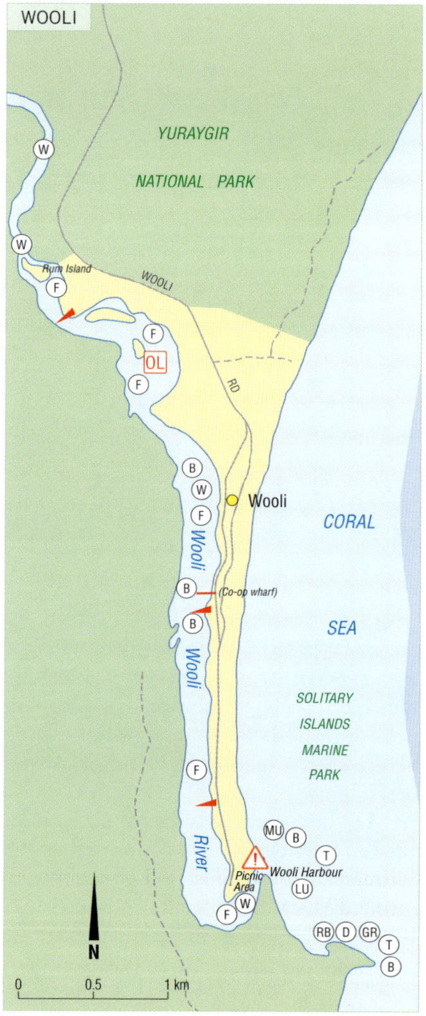

GUIDE TO LOCAL FISH

	Wooli to Coffs Harbour	Wooli	Coffs Harbour
(AJ) amberjack	•		
(B) bream	•	•	•
(CO) cobia	•		
(DA) dart			•
(D) drummer, silver	•	•	•
(F) flathead	•	•	•
(GR) groper	•	•	•
(KI) kingfish, yellowtail	•		•
(LU) luderick	•	•	•
(MA) mackerel	•		•
(M) mullet	•		•
(MU) mulloway	•	•	•
(PP) perch, pearl	•		
(RB) rock blackfish	•	•	•
(SM) samson fish	•		
(S) snapper	•		•
(T) tailor	•	•	•
(TL) teraglin	•		
(TU) tuna	•		•
(WH) wahoo	•		
(W) whiting	•	•	•

WOOLI

The **Wooli Wooli River** is shallow and the boat channel fairly winding, so care is needed. Both sides of the entrance are good for mulloway, bream, tailor and luderick. The bar is passable in southerly weather but dangerous in a north-easterly, particularly on a run-out tide. Seek local advice before attempting a crossing. A picnic area on the town side of the river has easy fishing for whiting and flathead, but there are many more spots along the river. The **Co-op Wharf** is an excellent place for bream when the fishing boats return. On the opposite side of the river, the oyster shell dumps create a habitat for large bream.

Other good spots are underneath the powerlines that cross the river near the most southerly boat ramp for flathead; around the oyster posts towards Rum Island for flathead; and in the channel on the western side of Rum Island for whiting. In its upper reaches, the river becomes a closed sanctuary zone from the point where the river branches, known as The Forks.

COFFS HARBOUR

At **Diggers Beach**, whiting, dart, bream and tailor are the main targets, with snapper around the headlands. The rock locations around **Macauleys Headland** have a variety of fish, including rock blackfish, luderick, groper, mulloway, bream and flathead.

The main surfing beach, **Park Beach**, has good gutter formations along its length for hauls of whiting, bream, school mulloway, tailor and dart. **Coffs Creek** enters the beach here, and is fished down to the Pacific Highway for flathead, and for whiting and luderick near the entrance. Offshore is **Little Muttonbird Island**, which can be reached on foot at low tide, for snapper and tailor.

Tailor abound along the state's beaches year round, with seasonal peaks in late summer and winter

Muttonbird Island was joined to the mainland in 1925 to form the northern breakwater for Coffs Harbour, and is one of the best rock fishing spots in the area, with snapper and tailor, and pelagics like Spanish mackerel, tuna and yellowtail kingfish.

The **North Wall**, which joins the island to the mainland, is fished on the ocean side for bream, tailor, snapper and drummer. The harbour is busy, but there are good hauls of yellowtail kingfish and luderick around the marina, and whiting and bream from **Jetty Beach** and the jetty itself.

The **East Wall** is fished for Spanish mackerel and mulloway on the seaward side, and bream, whiting and flathead on the harbour side. The rocks of the southern headland have many good spots to fish for mulloway, tailor, bream, luderick and snapper, including an excellent spot at the southern extremity called the Bream Hole.

Boambee Beach is another accessible and ideal fishing beach, with a plentiful supply of beach worms and pippis, and good catches of tailor, bream, whiting and school mulloway along its length.

With a good harbour and plenty of islands and reefs, Coffs Harbour offers a lot of attraction for offshore fishing. One close-in spot is the **Park Beach Bombora**, which can be located by broken water in anything from a moderate swell. Snapper, spotted and Spanish mackerel and longtail tuna are among the pelagic species here.

Offshore, the **Changte Shoal**, straight out from the harbour, is a large reef area rising to within 6 m of the surface. The reef fish include teraglin, yellowtail kingfish, cobia and snapper, and there can be good runs of school mulloway. Pelagic fish like Spanish mackerel, various tunas and even black marlin come to the shoal.

Port Macquarie Region

The combination of rock, beach, estuary and offshore fishing around Port Macquarie places this region at the forefront of Australian fishing.

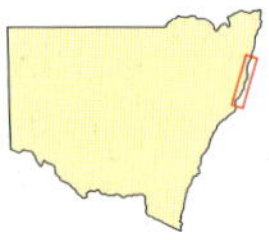

Urunga, Nambucca Heads, South West Rocks, Port Macquarie, Camden Haven and Forster–Tuncurry are just a few of the estuary spots in this region that make holiday fishing so pleasurable for the occasional angler. There are sheltered waters in which to seek flathead, whiting and bream; challenging rock areas that attract both pelagics and inshore species; and beaches with channels and gutters to try for fish such as flathead and tailor.

Boat anglers go out to the reefs, rocks, islands and bomboras for fish like snapper, pearl perch and morwong, and to the game fishing grounds for wahoo, dolphin fish, tuna and shark.

Nambucca River viewed from Nambucca Heads

WHERE TO FISH

Port Macquarie Region

SAWTELL TO NAMBUCCA HEADS ● 80

Boambee Head and Boambee Beach are a good fishing combination. Sawtell has beach, rock and river fishing, with lure fishing upriver for bream and mangrove jack. There is great land fishing around Urunga and the Kalang River. Nambucca Heads has excellent offshore and beach fishing, as well as good estuary and wall spots.

SOUTH WEST ROCKS TO HAT HEAD ● 82

The Macleay River estuary is brilliant all the way, with big mulloway at the mouth, particularly after a flood. South West Rocks is the base for some of the best light-tackle game fishing in New South Wales, with cobia caught all year round. Fish Rock, off Smoky Cape, is one of the best offshore places along this coast. The rock and beach fishing is also magical, with some superb rock spots around Hat Head.

PORT MACQUARIE ● 84

Boat anglers find wonderful sport in the Hastings River, and fine mulloway fishing around the entrance walls. There are ocean beaches on either side of Port Macquarie and reef areas close to shore, with blue water game fishing only a few kilometres out. For lovers of rock fishing, Queens Head, between Port Macquarie and Crescent Head, is the place for rock blackfish and luderick.

CAMDEN HAVEN AND MANNING RIVER ● 86

Camden Haven is a tranquil and easily fished estuary area, with big mulloway around the walls and good beach and rock areas nearby. Point Perpendicular is one of the best rock areas in the state, with high ledges and platforms over deep water. The Manning River is full of sand flats and channels for flathead and whiting.

TUNCURRY TO CHARLOTTE HEAD ● 88

The huge Wallis Lake area at Forster–Tuncurry has fine breakwall and bridge fishing. The two towns were once fishing villages, but are now boom towns. The deep-shelving rocks and cliffs around Charlotte Head allow casting with overhead and side-cast rigs for longtail tuna, yellowfin tuna, cobia and kingfish in season, while there is regular fare of tailor, bream, mulloway, whiting and salmon passing through the area during their annual migrations.

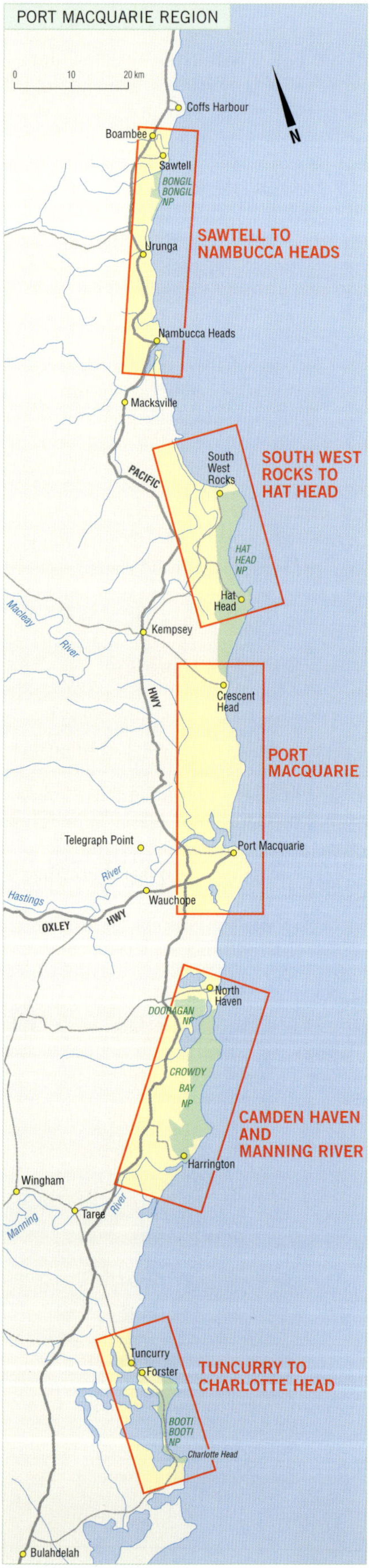

GUIDE TO LOCAL FISH

Australian salmon
bonito
bream, black
bream, yellowfin
cobia
dolphin fish
drummer, silver
flathead
flounder
garfish
groper
kingfish, yellowtail
luderick
mackerel, slimy
mackerel, Spanish
mackerel, spotted
mangrove jack
marlin, black
marlin, blue
marlin, striped
morwong
mullet
mulloway
perch, pearl
rock blackfish
shark
snapper
tailor
teraglin
trevally, giant
trevally, golden
trevally, silver
tuna, longtail
tuna, striped
tuna, yellowfin
wahoo
whiting, sand
whiting, trumpeter

Fishing boats moored at South West Rocks

FURTHER INFORMATION

Fishing and boating *NSW Fisheries has offices at 16 Jindalee Rd, Port Macquarie, tel. (02) 6581 4084; and 2/65 Muldoon St, Taree, tel. (02) 6552 6799. NSW Maritime has an office at Shop 1, cnr Uralla and Merrigal rds, Port Macquarie, tel. (02) 6583 1007. The Coastal Patrol has bases at South West Rocks, tel. (02) 6566 5240; and Forster, tel. (02) 6554 5458.*

Tourist centres *Great Lakes Tourism, Little St, Forster, tel. (02) 6554 8799; Harrington Service Station, 85 Beach St, Harrington, tel. (02) 6556 1188; Pacific Hwy, South Kempsey, tel. (02) 6563 1555; 4 Pacific Hwy, Nambucca Heads, tel. (02) 6568 6954; cnr Clarence and Hay sts, Port Macquarie, tel. 1300 303 155; Pacific Hwy, Urunga, tel. (02) 6655 5711.*

Weather

Prevailing winds in the summer months are north-north-easterlies, with westerlies dominating the winter season. The Port Macquarie region is prone to localised thunderstorms, which can bring hail, so always keep an eye out for cloud build-up to warn of impending change. The Weather Bureau can be reached on tel. (02) 9296 1555.

FISHING TIP

Over shallow tidal sand flats on a rising tide, schools of 'lano' or sand mullet can be berleyed into a reckless feeding binge with fragments of white bread. If you cast small, white, floating flies among these fish, they will readily grab them, providing fast-paced and effective fishing.

Boating

Port Macquarie has a bar, which must be carefully navigated. Local authorities always advise visitors to stay within the navigational markers. The bar is especially dangerous at ebb tides if the wind is north-easterly. The Macleay River has no navigational markers and must be negotiated with extreme caution. Laurieton, in the Camden Haven area, has a safe entrance to the sea via the Camden Haven Inlet. Further south, the two natural entrances to the Manning River are dangerous to use. For safe shelter and access to the Manning River area, use the man-made harbour and triple boat ramp at Crowdy Head, 8 km north of Harrington. This also gives the best access to Mermaid Reef. For further information, contact the local NSW Maritime office.

Sawtell to Nambucca Heads

Type of fishing
beach, offshore, river, rock, wall
Target fish
bream, flathead, luderick, Spanish mackerel

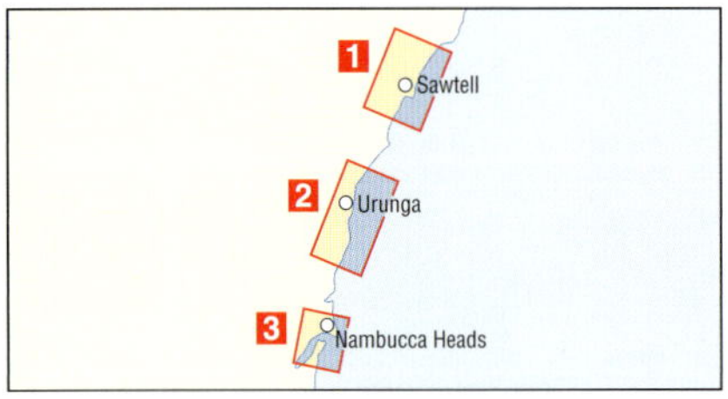

The tiny settlement of Boambee offers a smaller version of the fishing variety to the north at Coffs Harbour. Sawtell is another well-established fishing town. The Urunga area has superb river fishing just behind the coast, excellent bank and boat access, and a combination of beach, wall and rock fishing. Nambucca Heads is a major tourist town, with its river at the centre of the fishing action.

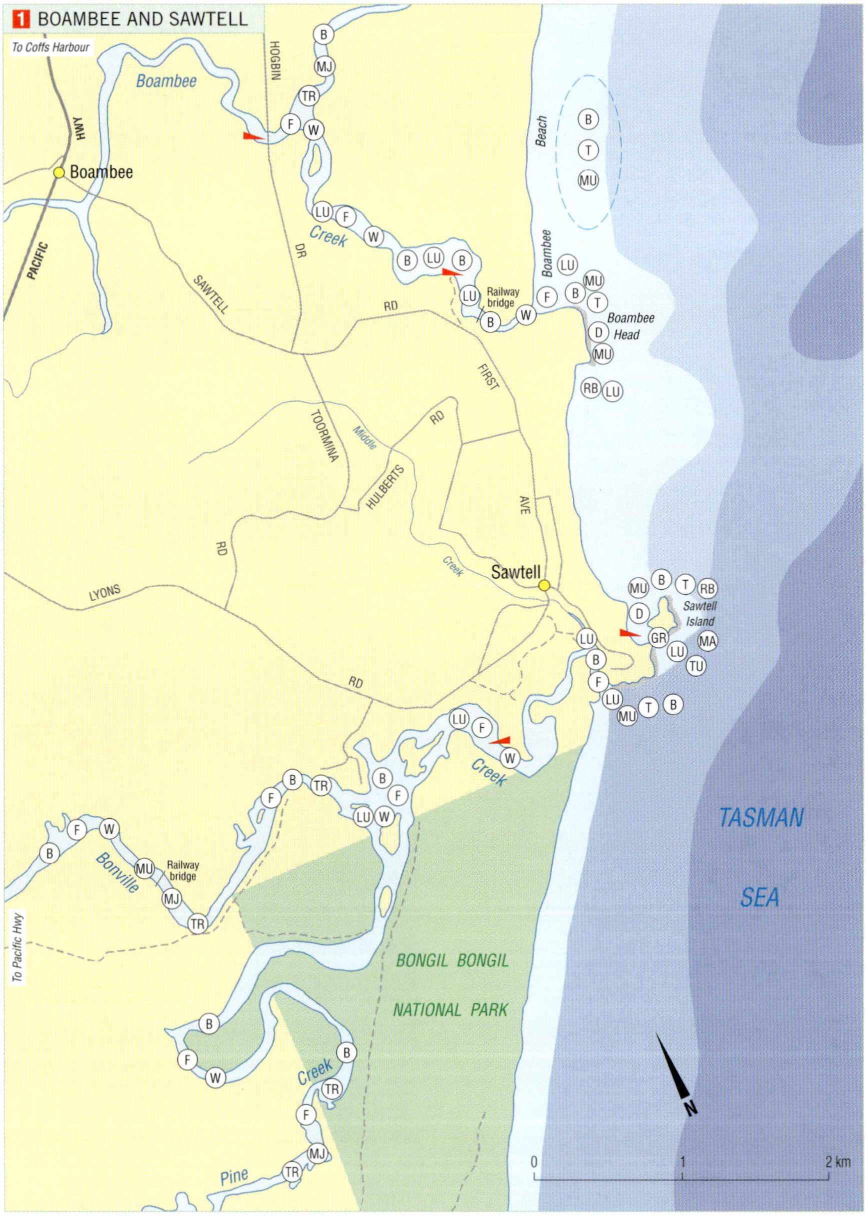

BOAMBEE AND SAWTELL

Boambee Beach has good gutters for bream, tailor and mulloway, while just inside the entrance of **Boambee Creek**, the railway bridge pylons attract bream and luderick. Past the bridge in the wider part of the creek, there are weed beds and channels where drifting can reward with flathead and whiting, and you can lure cast for bream, and flat fish for luderick.

The sand flats on the southern side of the creek, where yabbies can be pumped, have flathead and whiting. The creek narrows and forks, with mangroves along its slender northern channel providing a habitat for bream, mangrove jack and trevally in summer. There is a ramp on the southern side of the lower branch, giving access to these productive upper reaches of the creek.

Boambee Head is a combination of rock platforms and sandy gutters, with fishing for tailor, bream and mulloway. The mulloway bite best on a run-out tide, particularly after heavy rain. The southern side of the headland is rockier and provides a habitat for rock blackfish and luderick.

The headland at **Sawtell** has rock spots from which to seek tailor and mulloway, with luderick in the calmer weather. **Sawtell Island** has a good spinning platform for luderick, rock blackfish and groper, as well as tailor, silver drummer and mulloway.

Bonville Creek and its tributary **Pine Creek** get a lot of attention, as the fishing is reliable for bream, flathead, whiting in summer, and mulloway in winter.

Just inside the sheltered entrance at Sawtell, along the southern side, is an ideal luderick spot. Weed for bait can be gathered on the northern side. The creek takes a bend around a high finger of land, creating a sheltered spot, where weed and shellfish encourage the presence of bream and luderick. Opposite, there are drop-offs from the sand flats, and big flathead. A broader stretch continues this ideal situation up to the confluence of the two creeks, which is a hot spot for all these species and a great place to gather yabbies for bait. As the creeks go inland, there is lure fishing for the mangrove jack and tropical trevally that mingle with the whiting and bream.

There are school mulloway in the holes around the railway bridge over Bonville Creek, and small bass in the upper reaches, but they are too small to eat and the stock is limited so they are best released, as are the protected estuary cod, which show up occasionally further downstream.

URUNGA

The mouth of the **Bellinger River** has excellent fishing for mulloway, bream, flathead, whiting and tailor, while the southern wall is a great spot for mulloway, luderick, and large bream on a falling tide.

The footbridge is also a great fishing spot. The walls on either side of the confluence of the Bellinger and Kalang rivers are excellent for luderick, bream, flathead and whiting. **Yellow Rock Inlet** has good fishing for flathead, whiting and bream.

Further upriver near **Tuckers Island**, there are whiting and flathead, with good yabbies in the sand flats. Access is by boat from the township of Mylestom. Downstream, some 300 m from **Repton**, there is a hole for mulloway, and bream, mangrove jack and school mulloway abound in the area. Towards the road bridge, there is a sandy channel with good whiting and flathead.

The best spots on the **Kalang River** are near the bridge. You can fish from the bank or by boat for flathead and bream. A boat will take you on to the Snapper Hole, where a tributary branches off, and where mangrove jack, bream and mulloway can be in big numbers.

There is fine rock and beach fishing on either side of the estuary. The beaches produce tailor, flathead, mulloway, bream and whiting on worm and pippi baits from the sand, while snapper, rock blackfish and luderick add to the targets around Hungry Head.

NAMBUCCA HEADS

Shelly Beach has bream, flathead, tailor and mulloway among the rocks, and there is a good mulloway hole at the southern end.

2 URUNGA

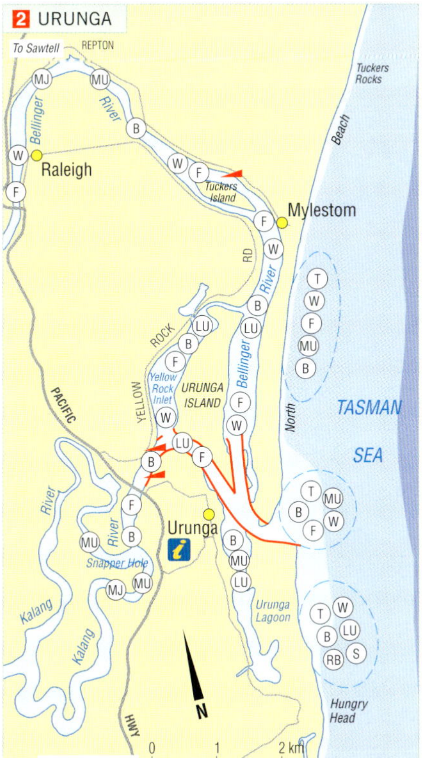

Nambucca River is silted and shallow at the river mouth, so those attracted by the prolific offshore fishing must launch from Shelly Beach. Locals can offer some good advice on the location of the reefs, which are east and north-east of the river mouth. These are worth seeking for snapper, teraglin, mulloway, pearl perch and morwong.

The headlands at the river entrance are good for spotted and Spanish mackerel in summer. The North Wall is very popular, mainly for bream, luderick and mulloway.

The wall swings south at **Vee Beach**, and creates a sheltered area where flathead and whiting come in. The action for bream, luderick and mulloway continues right along the upstream training wall. In the main channels of the river and in **Warrell Creek**, a southern tributary, the targets are flathead, whiting and bream.

South of Nambucca Heads, the beaches around **Scotts Head** and **Grassy Head** fish well, while the many offshore reefs are haunts of Spanish and spotted mackerel as well as mulloway, kingfish, cobia and teraglin. A depth sounder will help in locating these reefs and it pays to use a GPS unit to mark the reefs for future reference.

GUIDE TO LOCAL FISH

	Boambee and Sawtell	Urunga	Nambucca Heads
(B) bream	●	●	●
(D) drummer, silver	●		●
(F) flathead	●	●	●
(GR) groper	●		
(LU) luderick	●	●	●
(MA) mackerel	●		●
(MJ) mangrove jack	●	●	
(MO) morwong			●
(MU) mulloway	●	●	●
(PP) pearl perch			●
(RB) rock blackfish	●	●	
(S) snapper		●	●
(T) tailor	●	●	●
(TL) teraglin			●
(TR) trevally	●		
(TU) tuna	●		
(W) whiting	●	●	●

3 NAMBUCCA HEADS

South West Rocks to Hat Head

Type of fishing
beach, estuary, offshore, rock
Target fish
bream, luderick, whiting, yellowtail kingfish

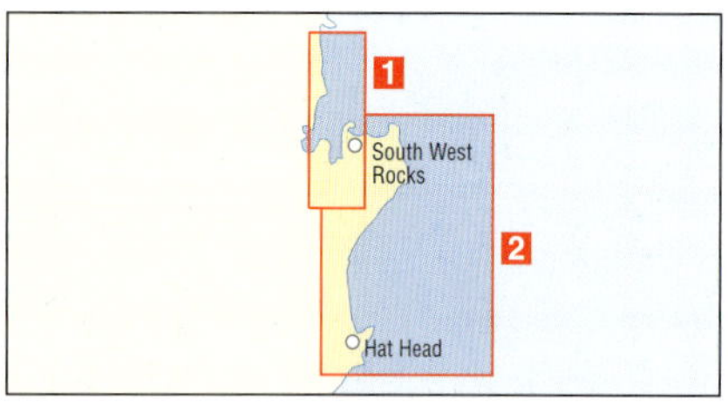

The Macleay River estuary is very productive, even into the freshwater reaches above Kempsey. South West Rocks has excellent light-tackle game fishing, with tropical and temperate fish species in the area according to the season. The coastline south of South West Rocks has some of the most magical rock and beach fishing in New South Wales.

MACLEAY RIVER ESTUARY

The action starts at the mouth of the **Macleay River**, particularly after a flood, when there can be a run of big mulloway. The mulloway anglers on the long entrance walls use up to 40-kg line with live baits or lures, and fish the area where the muddy fresh water reaches the clean ocean water. Here, the mulloway are in wait for prey washed out of the river.

The **North Wall** is best, but both this and the **South Wall** fish consistently in season for Spanish mackerel, luderick, flathead, bream and tailor. On the north side, the channels that run to the wall are fished for flathead, luderick and bream. The inner end of the wall in the north is called **Kemps Corner**, and opens into the northern stretch of the river, one of the best fishing areas. With **Shark Island** on one side and sandbanks and channels on the other, it is a great place to drift for whiting and flathead, exploring the deeper water for mulloway, and the rocks and banks for bream and luderick.

The Bay at the top of Shark Island yields bream, flathead and luderick at high tide. Further on near the oyster leases, there are channels for bream, flathead and whiting. The long run up to **Stuarts Point** may be rewarded with luderick and bream on either side of high tide. All the sandbanks in this area are great spots for collecting pink nippers.

South again, it pays to drift with pilchards in the deep channel beside **Little Shark Island**. There is an extensive weed bank at the northern end of the island, where whiting, flathead and luderick are best fished on either side of low tide. To the south, the next two sand islands have similar conditions at their northern ends. The **Clybucca Creek** entrance is excellent to drift for whiting and flathead.

Flathead Spit, on the run down to Jerseyville Bridge, is excellent drifting and spinning water, and the bridge itself attracts bream, school mulloway, flathead and tailor. It fishes well at night. The main river continues to be good for drifting for flathead, with bream and luderick around the bridges, and there are plenty of sandbanks and drop-offs yielding flathead and whiting.

Below South West Rocks, a tributary of the main river called **Spencers Creek** has flathead at the entrance, and luderick and bream along the banks, while the footbridge over **Back Creek** – known as The Spot – is reputedly the best location for luderick, and is easily accessed from South West Rocks township.

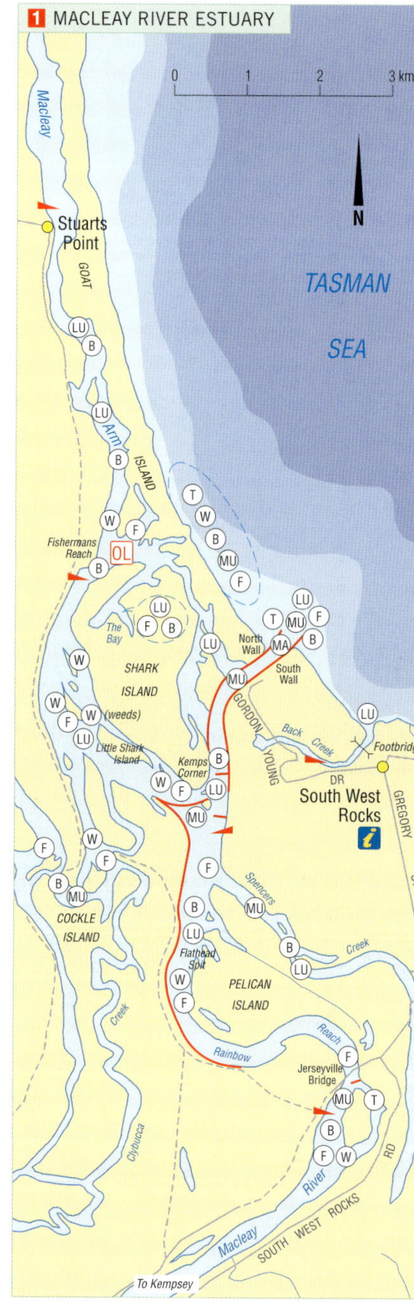

SOUTH WEST ROCKS TO HAT HEAD

Species common on the **South West Rocks** coast are Spanish and spotted mackerel from February to May, and marlin, tuna, dolphin fish, wahoo, kingfish and shark in high summer. Cobia are a lucky year-round catch.

There are also some wonderful rock spots, with the fishing peaking in autumn and winter for tailor and rock blackfish. Bream, whiting, mulloway, mackerel, drummer, luderick, snapper, kingfish and bonito are also caught from Monument Point to Smoky Cape. Some specific rock locations are the Trial Bay Gaol; Little Bay; the deep narrow bay past Green Island; the

Trial Bay Beach is a popular surf fishing venue

GUIDE TO LOCAL FISH

	Macleay River Estuary	South West Rocks to Hat Head
(BT) bonito		•
(B) bream	•	•
(CO) cobia		•
(DO) dolphin fish		•
(D) drummer, silver		•
(F) flathead	•	•
(KI) kingfish, yellowtail		•
(LU) luderick	•	•
(MA) mackerel	•	•
(ML) marlin		•
(MU) mulloway	•	•
(RB) rock blackfish		•
(SH) shark		•
(S) snapper		•
(T) tailor	•	•
(TU) tuna		•
(WH) wahoo		•
(W) whiting	•	•

2 SOUTH WEST ROCKS TO HAT HEAD

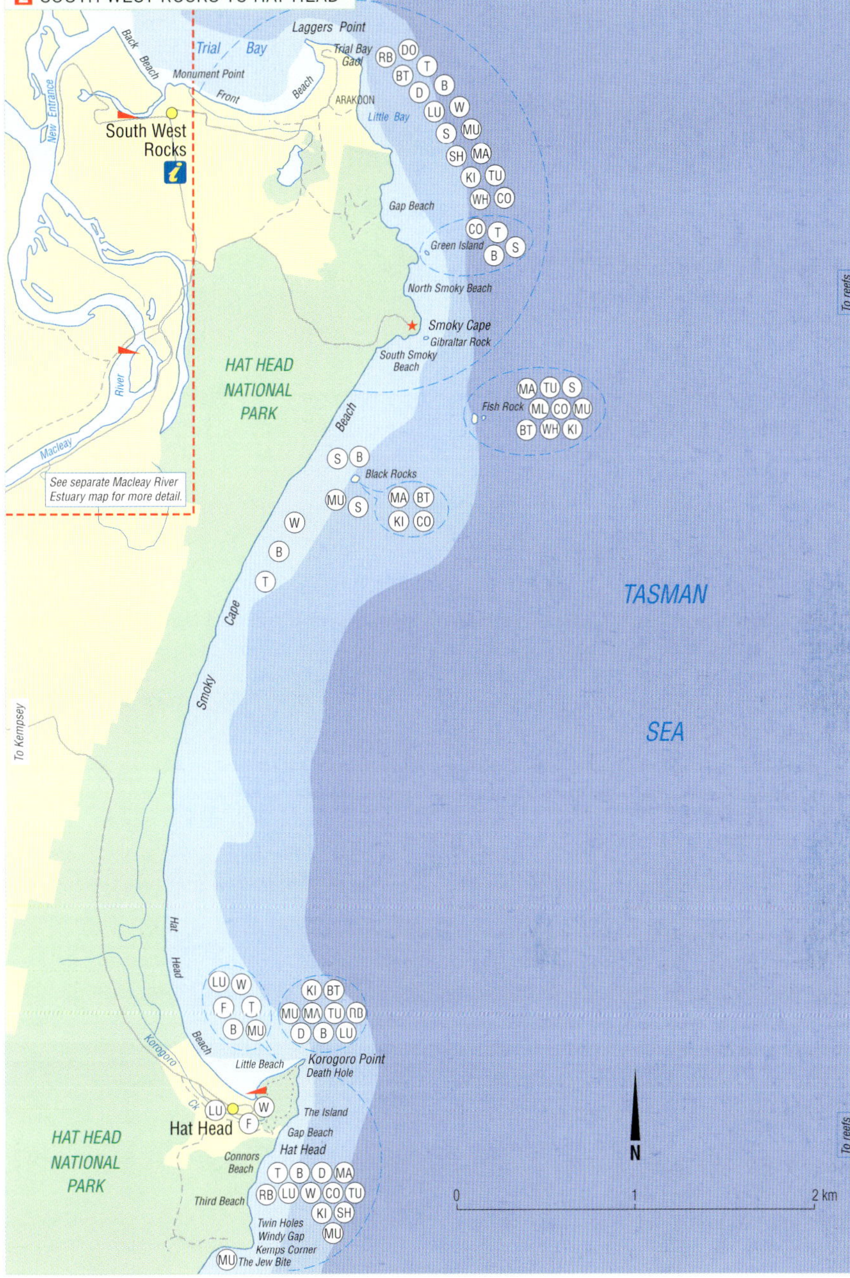

bay between Green Island and Smoky Cape; and when conditions allow safe fishing, Gibraltar Rock, just off the lighthouse point.

Fish Rock, south-east of Smoky Cape, is one of the best offshore locations along this coast, as it sits on the edge of the blue water current and has everything from game fish, such as marlin, wahoo, cobia, kingfish and tuna, to bottom fish like mulloway and snapper. Further south is **Black Rocks**. A bombora in its north-west corner is good for snapper and bream, and pinnacles just south of the rock attract mulloway and snapper. The eastern side has good trolling for Spanish mackerel, cobia, kingfish and bonito.

Smoky Cape Beach has good deep gutters, holding tailor, bream and whiting, and can be accessed with four-wheel drive. **Little Beach**, just before Hat Head, is sheltered from the southerlies, and is an excellent bream spot. Tailor, whiting, flathead, luderick and the occasional mulloway are also present.

The north side of **Korogoro Point** can only be reached by walking track, and allows casting into deep water for bonito, Spanish mackerel, kingfish and tuna, while closer in, there are rock blackfish, bream and mulloway in the rocky gutters. Around the point is the **Death Hole**, which requires ropes and care, but rewards with tailor, bream, silver drummer and mulloway. A series of bays to the south have deepwater rock fishing for the same species.

A spot called **The Island** is accessible only at low water, but is a great all-round area for rock fishing. Beyond there are some high ledges, and catches of mulloway, tailor and bream will require gaff work to bring them up. **Gap Beach** after a storm is a terrific area for luderick, rock blackfish, silver drummer, whiting, bream, tailor and mulloway. The next point south has high ledges and remains excellent for big tailor, mulloway, luderick, rock blackfish and bream.

Connors Beach has a deep gutter, protected by a sandbar, and **Third Beach** has continual wave action, so they both yield big tailor, bream and mulloway. The little finger of land between the beaches offers deepwater fishing for bream, tailor and mulloway.

The rocks around **Windy Gap** have fish, but catches can be hard to lift up onto the high ledges. The best areas are at the southern end of the point at **Twin Holes**, **Kemps Corner** and **The Jew Bite**.

Offshore from Hat Head are bomboras that provide a focus for Spanish mackerel, cobia, kingfish, tuna and shark. Out from Hat Head are **Close Reef** (4 km) and **Wide Reef** (8 km), which are good for bottom fishing for snapper, teraglin, pearl perch and dolphin fish. Off Kemps Corner, about 8 km and 9 km, are another two reef areas, which invite drifting for snapper, teraglin, morwong and pearl perch.

Port Macquarie

Type of fishing
beach, offshore, rock, wall

Target fish
bream, luderick, mulloway, rock blackfish

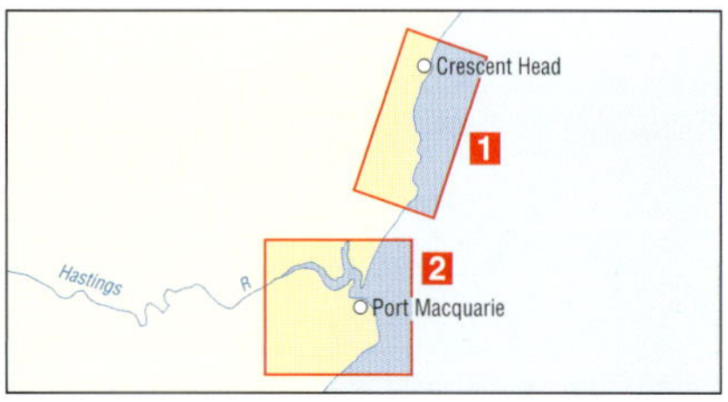

The excellent beach and rock fishing continues down this section of coast, and Port Macquarie – a historic town founded as a convict settlement – is one of New South Wales' most popular holiday resorts, offering a wonderful variety of fishing.

Fishing boats at Port Macquarie where the waters provide excellent fishing over autumn and winter

CRESCENT HEAD TO QUEENS HEAD

The area from Racecourse Head to Queens Head is dotted with many safe rock fishing spots. Tailor from 1 to 3 kg are common, and rock blackfish are a regular catch in the washes. Bream, luderick, drummer and mulloway are around in good numbers. The best fishing is in autumn and winter.

Racecourse Head allows fishing into a gutter at the end of the beach for flathead and whiting, as well as rock blackfish and luderick behind the reef in rough waters. Similar conditions exist on **Racecourse Island**, which can be waded to at low tide. **Big Hill Point** has rugged rock formations above reefs and gutters. Two favourite bream and mulloway spots are **The Arch**, accessible at low tides, and **The Stairs**, reached by following a narrow path.

The beach to the north of **Point Plomer** is sheltered in a southerly and is excellent for bream. The north side of the point is easy to fish for tailor, bream, luderick, rock blackfish, mulloway and groper. On the seaward side, fishing is for tailor off the point, and luderick and bream in the gutters. The beach on the southern side has good gutters for bream and whiting.

Barrys Bay is ideal for inshore fishing from a boat, and anglers can cast for the prime target fish caught here – Spanish mackerel, cobia and longtail tuna.

Neverfail is two rocky spurs surrounded by gutters, and is accessible in all but the biggest seas for luderick and rock blackfish close in, and bream, tailor and mulloway further out. **Queens Head** is the place for rock blackfish and luderick specialists.

PORT MACQUARIE

Of the ocean stretches near Port Macquarie, **North Beach** is just one area renowned for wonderful whiting catches on beach worm in summer, and tailor on pilchards, garfish or lures in winter.

1 CRESCENT HEAD TO QUEENS HEAD

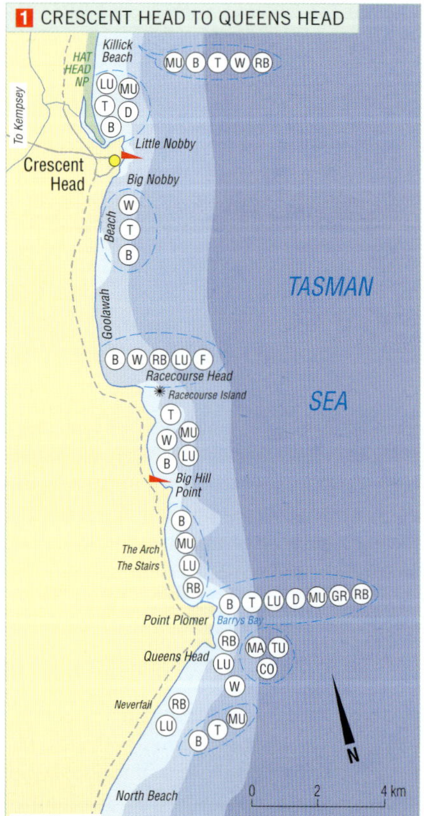

The **Hastings River** estuary provides great sport for whiting, flounder, flathead, bream and mulloway, and the weed-eating luderick, with some big tailor near the entrance in the winter.

Luderick are along the deeper banks and around the weed beds throughout the system. The best bait for them is either weed (available from local bait shops) or pink nippers, which are plentiful on the sandbanks.

The most popular fishing, however, is drifting for flathead and whiting along the

GUIDE TO LOCAL FISH

	Crescent Head to Queens Head	Port Macquarie
(B) bream	●	●
(CO) cobia	●	
(DO) dolphin fish		●
(D) drummer, silver	●	●
(F) flathead	●	●
(FL) flounder		●
(GR) groper	●	
(KI) kingfish, yellowtail		●
(LU) luderick	●	●
(MA) mackerel	●	
(ML) marlin		●
(MO) morwong		●
(M) mullet		●
(MU) mulloway	●	●
(RB) rock blackfish	●	●
(SH) shark		●
(S) snapper		●
(T) tailor	●	●
(TU) tuna	●	●
(WH) wahoo		●
(W) whiting	●	●

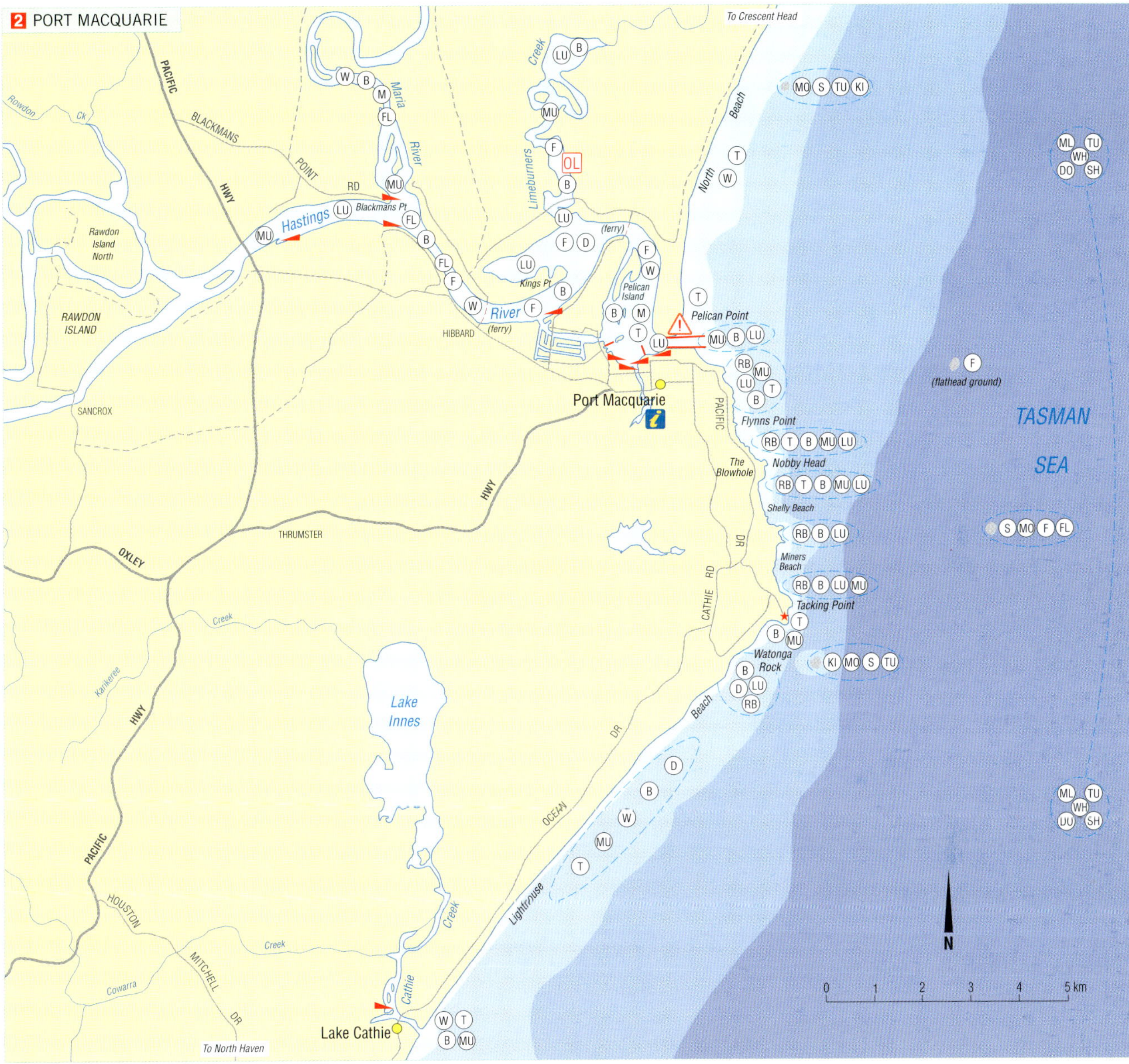

2 PORT MACQUARIE

channels and drop-offs, and over weed beds, with nippers or pilchards as bait. There are also bream, mulloway and mullet throughout the system.

Most of the mulloway are taken by fishing from the training walls at the entrance to the river with live mullet or luderick as bait, as they are the food the mulloway are naturally seeking in the area. These mulloway are big fish, requiring 20-kg line or more, with a beach rod and a big side cast or overhead reel to manage hooked fish in the tough terrain.

As the river swings north and then south inside the entrance, the water is mostly bream, flathead and whiting territory, with luderick along the banks. **Limeburners Creek** has oyster leases in the area close to its junction with the river. In the channels of the creek are big flathead, with bream in the upper reaches. In the Hastings River, the biggest mulloway are often found further upstream in deep water, past the confluence with the **Maria River**.

The rock and beach areas on the southern side of the town are convenient, offering tailor, rock blackfish, luderick, mulloway and bream. A good rock spot, though dangerous in big seas is **The Blowhole. Shelly Beach** offers excellent beach fishing.

Reefs north and south of Port Macquarie hold a good quotient of bottom and surface fish. Snapper is the prime target on the inshore reefs, taken by drifting baits down a berley stream. Straight in front of the town, from 5 to 7 km out, is a very big flathead ground. Off Shelly Beach, some 4 to 6 km, is a large area of rubble and reef attracting snapper, morwong, flathead and other reef fish.

Blue water game fishing off Port Macquarie is a growing sport, with the boats working out to areas 100 fathoms deep and more. Summer targets are marlin, wahoo, dolphin fish, yellowfin tuna and shark, and winter and early spring bring big catches of mako shark. Makos are known for their tremendous leaps from the water when hooked.

The entrance to Port Macquarie can be dangerous, particularly on a run-out tide when strong north winds are blowing. Boats can launch from Shelly Beach, or from Big Hill Point or Crescent Head for more northern offshore grounds.

Camden Haven and Manning River

Type of fishing
beach, estuary, rock, wall
Target fish
bream, flathead, luderick, mulloway

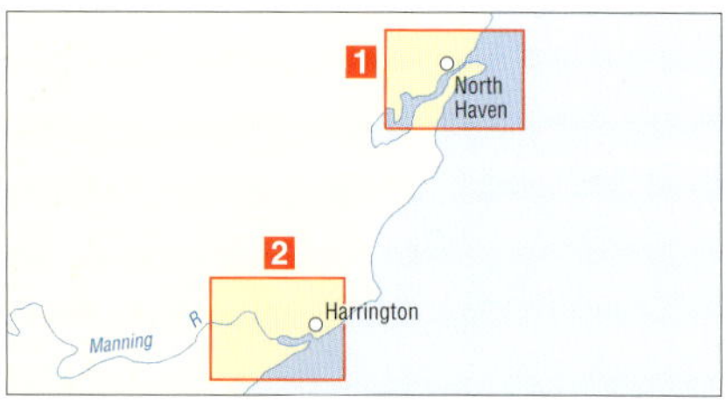

Fishing for luderick at Pilot Headland

Camden Haven is one of the most productive estuary fishing areas on the north-east coast. The Manning River estuary is not quite as good, but it is still an enjoyable place to fish, with regular and good catches of bream, flathead, whiting, school mulloway and luderick.

CAMDEN HAVEN

The fishing delights in this estuary are many. As always on the New South Wales coast, the big mulloway are around the entrance walls, particularly when rain has flushed the system and carried prey out to the estuary mouth. Bream and tailor are also common. There are ample launching ramps, and the added thoughtfulness of cleaning tables and running water to make the fishing experience at 'The Haven' as good as you can find.

The river quickly becomes shallow inside the entrance. The southern wall allows access to **Gogleys Lagoon**, also known as Lake Hope, a shallow lagoon with plenty of yabbies to gather on the sand flats. These will be taken by the flathead and whiting that congregate in the area. The main entrance to the lagoon is at **Gogleys Creek**, where big bream can be found. An Australian record bream of 4.45 kg was caught here.

Under the **North Haven Bridge**, there is a good chance for big flathead and bream. Further along this arm are channels for flathead and whiting, with bream and luderick around the rocks and banks. Because of extensive ill-marked oyster leases at the entrance to Queens Lake, the passage is difficult to negotiate, except on a high tide.

Down towards Laurieton, there are luderick around **Camden Point**, and bream on the north shore towards the Laurieton launching ramp. Weed beds, sandbars and more oyster leases all the way to **Watson Taylors Lake** ensure productive drifting for whiting and flathead.

There are some good outside areas including **Grants Beach**, an excellent spot for whiting, bream and tailor, and **Dunbogan Beach**, with its long gutters carrying whiting, flathead, bream, tailor and mulloway. **Pilot Beach**, just outside the southern wall, is a reliable whiting spot and a pleasant, sheltered place to fish.

Point Perpendicular is one of the state's best rock spots, with high ledges and platforms fronting deep water that can

GUIDE TO LOCAL FISH

	Camden Haven	Manning River
(B) bream	●	●
(CO) cobia	●	
(D) drummer, silver	●	
(F) flathead	●	●
(KI) kingfish, yellowtail	●	
(LU) luderick	●	●
(MA) mackerel	●	
(MU) mulloway	●	●
(RB) rock blackfish	●	●
(T) tailor	●	●
(TU) tuna	●	
(W) whiting	●	●

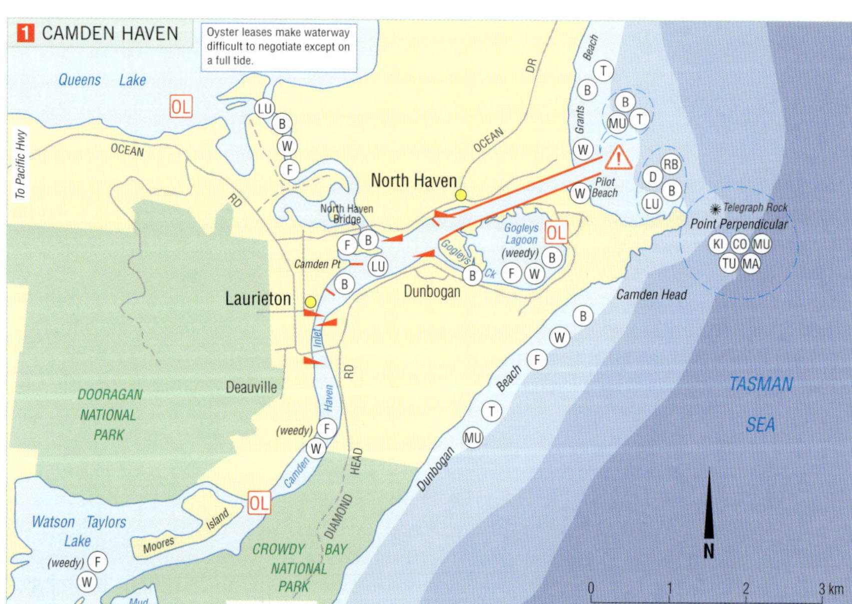

carry an abundance of yellowtail kingfish, cobia, longtail tuna, Spanish mackerel and mulloway. Bream, rock blackfish, silver drummer and luderick are among the smaller species found here. Further to the south, **Diamond Head** is another great rock fishing spot.

MANNING RIVER

The **Manning River** estuary is full of sand flats and channels, and so requires careful navigation, but these are ideal conditions to drift for flathead and whiting. School mulloway are in the deeper holes, while luderick are close to the shore, especially in weedy areas or near rocks.

At **Harrington**, the north section of the sea wall is fished for bream and tailor, with mulloway particularly active after heavy rain. Rock blackfish and luderick will bite on cunjevoi or weed at the bend, while the southern section of the wall fishes well for flathead and whiting. Mulloway, bream and luderick are the targets around **Manning Point**, a perfect jumping-off point for exploration of the river.

Cattai Bridge, on the road from Coopernook to Harrington, is an excellent land spot for bream, luderick and flathead, particularly on its eastern side. The river between **Jones and Mitchells islands** is good for boat fishing, and the best place for bream, flathead and mulloway is just out from the channel marker pole, about 500 m from Croki. **Dumaresq Island Bridge**, at Cundletown, is also productive. Beyond Dumaresq Island and just upstream from the Fishermens Co-op is a good spot for luderick.

Scotts Creek and the **Manning River South Channel** flow around Oxley Island and into **Farquhar Inlet**, a shallow sand flat and weed area, which provides great boat fishing for whiting, bream, luderick and flathead. The bridges on either creek are good land spots for bream, flathead and mulloway.

This entrance is unsafe. Small boats can launch off the beach at Old Bar, but most seagoing boats launch from Crowdy Head, 5 km north of Harrington, where there is a protected anchorage and a triple boat ramp. This also gives best access to the highly productive **Mermaid Reef**, 2 km offshore and 6 km north-east of Crowdy Head. The reef has a large number of fish, such as snapper, kingfish, mulloway, bream and bonito, and summer visits from surface pelagics like striped tuna, marlin, shark, wahoo and yellowfin tuna.

East of Crowdy Head, there are many reef formations extending some 10 km out, again with a variety of reef and game fish. Crowdy Head has great rock fishing.

The Manning River at Taree is particularly scenic although the fishing is better in the lower reaches

Tuncurry to Charlotte Head

Type of fishing
beach, estuary, offshore, rock, wall

Target fish
bream, flathead, luderick, whiting

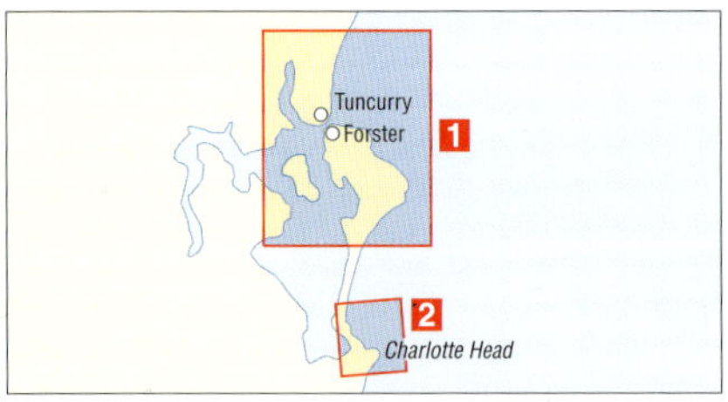

The bonanza of estuary fishing on the New South Wales coast continues at Forster–Tuncurry, once two sleepy fishing villages but now boom towns. The attractions are many, including good rock and beach areas outside the entrance to the lake, keen offshore fishing, and wonderful estuary fishing in the huge Wallis Lake area. South of Forster, Charlotte Head juts into the sea and creates an unusual combination of rock and beach fishing close to the deeper game waters.

TUNCURRY AND FORSTER

The breakwalls on both sides of the entrance fish exceptionally well for bream, tailor and flathead, while the North Wall is a mulloway hot spot. The South Wall and the southern channel attract the luderick anglers, despite the rough bottom, which can claim a lot of tackle. The **Fishermans Co-op** on the north side draws the bream when the fleet comes in.

Inside the entrance there is a bridge linking the two towns, which is usually productive for bream, tailor, flathead, whiting and garfish, but the fishing really hits the heights at night on a run-out tide. The sand spit near the bridge is a great spot to lure cast for flathead.

Straight on from the bridge is a big area of oyster leases, set in a maze of channels, which are a haven for bream and, to a lesser extent, luderick. There are many other equally productive oyster lease areas in the northern end of **Wallis Lake**.

Breckenridge Channel is one of the most consistent luderick-producing areas in the state, as it combines weed beds with the proximity of oyster leases. The **Forster Channel**, on the northern side of Godwin Island and around the south-east of Cockatoo Island, is a wonderful stretch of water for drifting for flathead, whiting and bream. The hot spot is a channel called **Hells Gate**, in the narrows between Godwin and Wallis islands.

This area, from Hells Gate to and beyond the bridge, is filled with boats at the time of the new moon on summer nights, as the channels are thick with prawns moving out to sea on a run-out tide.

South-east of **Regatta Island**, a vast area of channels and sand and weed flats is ideal for drifting for flathead, and also a great spot for whiting, bream and flounder.

The undoubted pick of the lake is on the eastern side of **Wallis Island**. One enters a rocky area called **The Stockyard**, where luderick and bream are the targets, and then continues south through barely navigable water to reach **The Step**, where the sand level at the entrance shelves into the main body of the lake. This is a magnificent location for tailor, flathead, bream and mulloway. These predatory fish wait here for small fish and crustaceans to

Boats moored at Forster harbour

Wallis Lake, a large and productive waterway, provides excellent estuary fishing, especially around the oyster leases

be swept over the edge towards them on the rising tide. Anglers should stay on the shallow side and feed their baits with the current into the drop-off area. Live poddy mullet, pilchards, whitebait or prawns, properly presented, will be snapped up. Blue swimmer crabs, common throughout the lake, are abundant in this stretch.

Offshore anglers should be wary of the Forster–Tuncurry entrance, but there are large hauls of flathead to be had outside. The reef areas are well north and south of the entrance. **Black Head**, 8 km to the north, has an extension of reefs, which carry a lot of snapper. **The Pinnacles**, east of Cape Hawke, are good for snapper, teraglin, mulloway and kingfish.

CHARLOTTE HEAD

Seven Mile Beach is renowned for tailor, which come close inshore on the steeply shelving beach as they drive the bait fish into the shallows. Bream, mulloway, whiting and salmon also come close in to this area.

The rock areas, between Booti Booti and Elizabeth Beach, are fished mainly for luderick, rock blackfish and bream among the washes, but are also good for bait casting for tailor. **Elizabeth Beach** is a good place for summer whiting, and also big mulloway, and its southern end is the place to launch boats over the sand. The headland at the southern end of the beach is easily reached from a carpark, and offers mostly bream and tailor.

The small **Shelly Beach** is protected. Big mulloway are a feature here, along with bream, tailor and whiting. Nearby **Seagull Point** is a safe place to fish in all but southerly blows and has reef fish varieties, like snapper, yellowtail kingfish, cobia and mulloway. The rocks and cliffs on the north side of **Charlotte Head** are hard to reach and exposed to the south, but can be fished in moderate weather for drummer and bream. Anglers can also target yellowfin tuna and yellowtail kingfish with lures, or by drifting out live baits.

GUIDE TO LOCAL FISH

	Tuncurry and Forster	Charlotte Head
(BT) bonito		•
(B) bream	•	•
(CO) cobia		•
(D) drummer, silver	•	•
(F) flathead	•	
(FL) flounder	•	
(G) garfish	•	
(KI) kingfish, yellowtail		•
(LU) luderick	•	•
(MU) mulloway	•	•
(RB) rock blackfish	•	•
(SA) salmon, Australian		•
(S) snapper	•	•
(T) tailor	•	•
(TU) tuna		•
(W) whiting	•	•

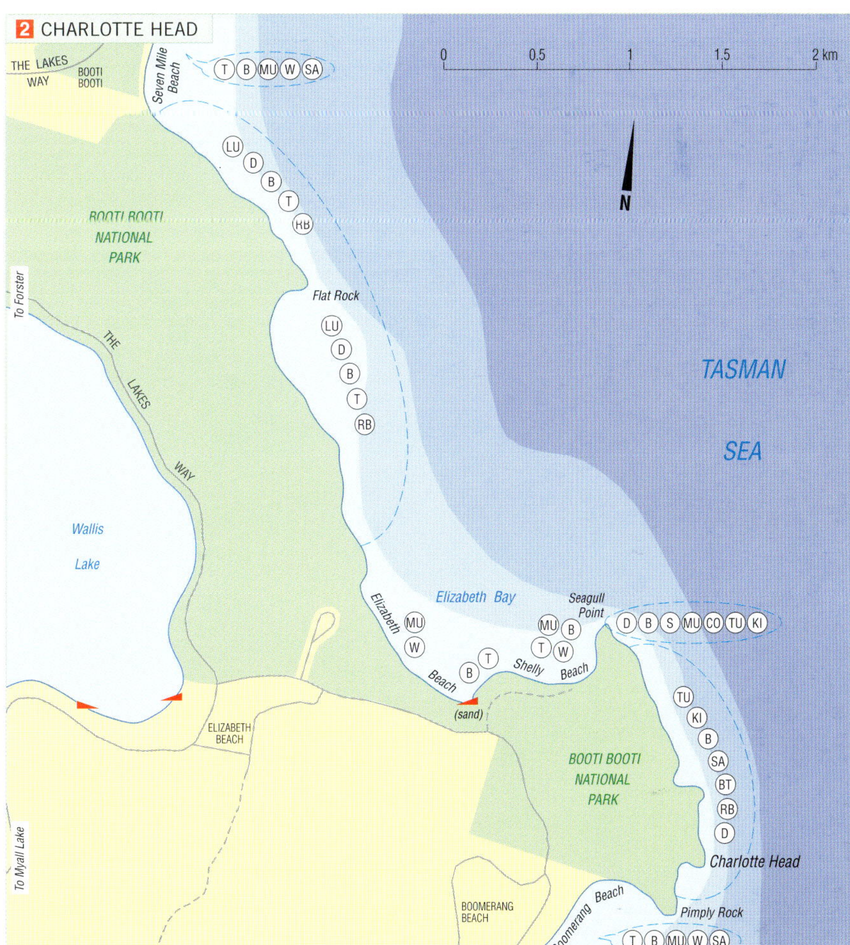

Newcastle Region

The Myall Lakes and Lake Macquarie are the main geographic and scenic features of the Newcastle region, and the fishing they offer is tranquil. Flathead, whiting, bream and luderick are usually found around the sea entrances. Outside, there is reliable beach fishing.

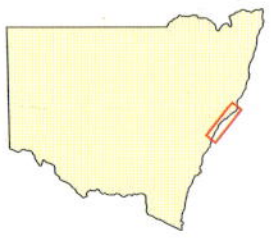

Port Stephens estuary is a busy fishing area in summer, while nearby Broughton Island is one of the best year-round snapper fisheries in New South Wales. Newcastle's industrial port does not look enticing but there is some good fishing inside and from the breakwaters. Lakes, beaches, rocks, reefs and wrecks add to the variety.

An angler fishing The Entrance for luderick, at the mouth of Tuggerah Lake

WHERE TO FISH

Newcastle Region

SEAL ROCKS AND MYALL LAKES ● 92

There is some exhilarating boat fishing near the tiny village of Seal Rocks – around the headland, offshore rocks, pinnacles and reefs. The lakes system is vast and shallow and fish can be hard to find, but there are some reliable reefs and drifts for boat anglers, and some good shore fishing places. The nearby Myall River carries flathead, whiting and luderick.

PORT STEPHENS ● 94

The Port Stephens estuary has a lot of summer fishing traffic. The Hawks Nest area is excellent for both land-based and boat fishing, and there is great rock fishing near the port entrance. Offshore islands and reefs are another attraction, with Broughton Island superb for snapper.

NEWCASTLE AND LAKE MACQUARIE ● 96

There is interesting fishing in Newcastle Harbour, from land or sea. Hairtail are caught here in winter. The entrance and Stockton Beach are well worth fishing, as are the offshore wrecks and reefs. The best fishing in Lake Macquarie is at the entrance, as the lake itself is generally featureless. However, five artificial reefs placed around the lake have attracted fish.

COASTAL LAKES ● 98

Munmorah and Budgewoi lakes have little tidal influence so the best fishing is around structures. The entrances to the power station channels are ideal spots in both lakes. Good offshore points include Birdie Beach and Wybung Head. In Tuggerah Lake, there is great fishing for the family from the park at Picnic Point, at The Entrance; and the North Channel, running between The Entrance North and Terilbah Island, is ideal for boat fishing.

TERRIGAL ● 100

Protected rocks and beaches attract big predatory fish, including tuna, bonito and yellowtail kingfish. When the lagoon is open, flathead, bream and tailor are found inside the entrance, and beaches nearby have bream, tailor and mulloway. The Terrigal coast is a good rock and beach fishery, attracting many anglers with its accessible rock platforms and varied and plentiful fish. The best rock area is The Skillion.

NEWCASTLE REGION

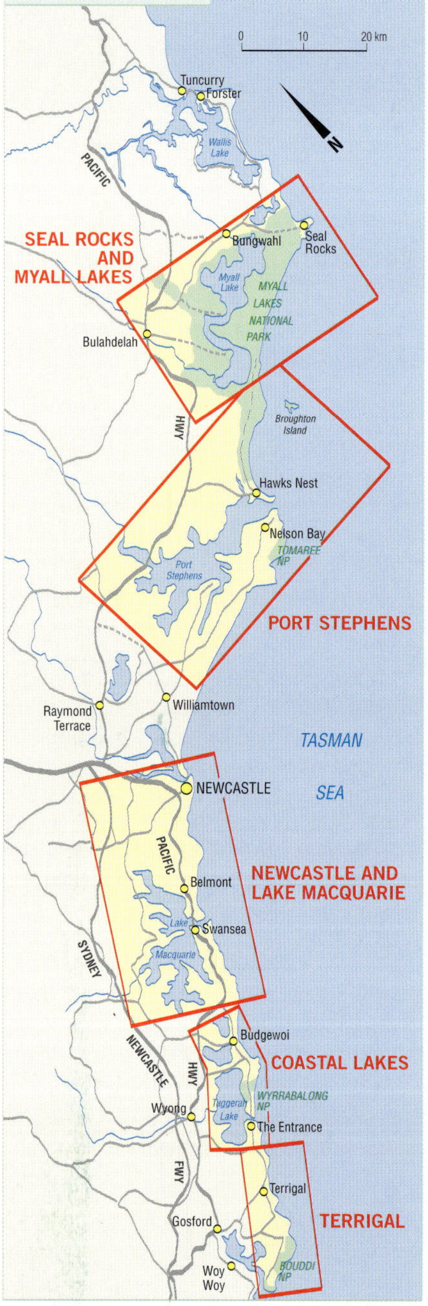

FISHING TIP

One of the best kept 'secret baits' for bream fishing is plain white bread. Some anglers prefer to use dry hard crusty bread, while others use bread as fresh as they can get it. By adding judicious amounts of water, and kneading the bread into small dollops, it is possible to return it to a dough-like texture that can be moulded onto a hook and withstand the stresses of casting. The bream often take it quite well.

GUIDE TO LOCAL FISH

bass, Australian
bonito
bream, black
bream, yellowfin
cobia
drummer, silver
flathead
flounder
garfish
groper
hairtail
john dory
kingfish, yellowtail
leatherjacket
luderick
marlin, black
marlin, blue
marlin, striped
morwong
mullet
mulloway
rock blackfish
salmon, Australian
shark
snapper
tailor
tarwhine
teraglin
trevally, silver
tuna, frigate mackerel
tuna, longtail
tuna, mackerel
tuna, striped
tuna, yellowfin
whiting, sand
whiting, trumpeter

Rods and net poised for action as the sun sets over Lake Macquarie

Weather

The prevailing winds are north-easterlies, which can reach forces up to 20 knots, creating dangerous and choppy conditions on Lake Macquarie. In summer, southerlies can come in, causing even more dangerous conditions. When boating on Lake Macquarie, always look out for these southerly changes as they can come in quickly and fiercely. For coastal forecasts, ring the Weather Bureau on tel. (02) 9296 1555 or contact local Coast Guards or the Coastal Patrol.

Boating

Boat anglers should be cautious of the bar at the entrance to the channel at Swansea Heads; it is dangerous at low tide when a north-easterly is blowing. If your vessel is too big to pass under Swansea Bridge, you will need to give the Coast Guards at least one hour's notice for the bridge to be lifted. Never anchor too close to the bridge, as tidal waters are extremely strong and could sweep your craft away. Common sense should prevail when on the water. Apart from the obvious weather check, see what the tide is doing and understand what effect the wind will have on the direction of tidal flow. Never anchor in shipping channels and always use navigation lights at night. For further information, contact the local NSW Maritime office.

Luderick

Luderick, often called blackfish, are found in estuaries, near rock walls, and in open water where there are rocky foreshores. A good specimen will weigh 1 kg.

FURTHER INFORMATION

Fishing and boating *NSW Fisheries have offices at Taylors Beach Rd, Taylors Beach, tel. (02) 4982 1311; 97 Hannell St, Wickham, tel. (02) 4927 6548; and 55 Lambton Pde, Swansea, tel. (02) 4971 1201. NSW Maritime has offices at 8 Cowper St Sth, Carrington, tel. (02) 4962 8500; and Marine Pde, Tea Gardens, tel. (02) 4997 1836. The Coast Guard has depots at Port Stephens, tel. (02) 4982 4981; and Swansea, tel. (02) 4971 3498.*

The Coastal Patrol has bases at Port Stephens, tel. (02) 4981 3585; Newcastle, tel. (02) 4927 8237; Lake Macquarie, tel. (02) 4971 3723; Gosford, tel. (02) 4325 7929; and Terrigal, tel. (02) 4384 5577.

Tourist centres *Lake Macquarie Visitors' Information Centre, 228 Pacific Hwy, Swansea, tel. (02) 4921 0740; Great Lakes Tourism, Little St, Forster, tel. (02) 6554 8799; Victoria Pde, Nelson Bay, tel. (02) 4981 1579; Wheeler Pl, 361 Hunter St, Newcastle, tel. (02) 4974 2999; Central Coast Tourism, Rotary Park, Terrigal Dr, Terrigal, tel. (02) 4385 4430; Memorial Park, Marine Pde, The Entrance, tel. (02) 4385 4430.*

Seal Rocks and Myall Lakes

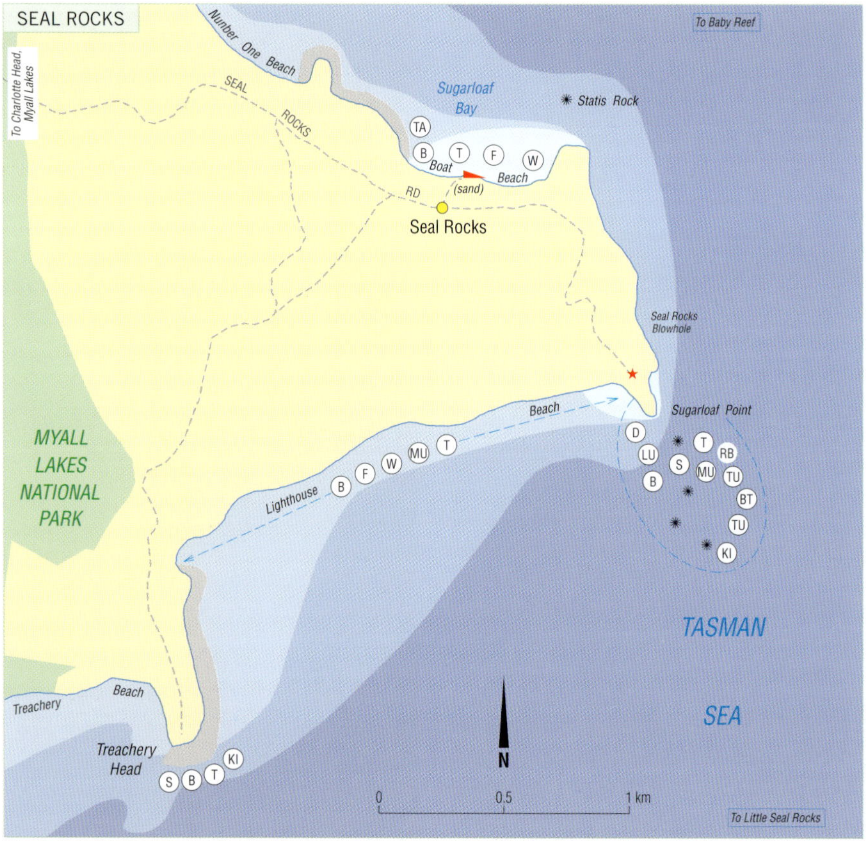

Type of fishing
beach, lake, offshore, reef, river, rock

Target fish
bream, flathead, luderick, tailor, yellowtail kingfish

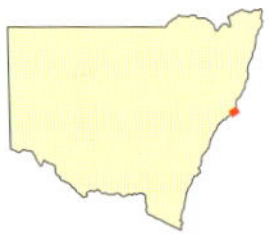

The tiny fishing village of Seal Rocks is the jumping-off point for some exhilarating boat fishing around the headlands, offshore rocks, pinnacles and reefs in the area. The Myall Lakes, surrounded by national park, have many boat ramps and camping places to allow leisurely and rewarding fishing expeditions. The long outside beach is hard to reach, but fishes very well. The Big Gibber Headland is a fine rock spot.

SEAL ROCKS

Boat launching is from the sheltered beach at Sugarloaf Bay, basic but effective for craft up to about 6 m with a suitable launching vehicle. **Baby Reef**, 5 km to the north-east of Sugarloaf Bay offers an extensive reef area. It generally rewards those drifting and bottom fishing for snapper and bream, or surface fishing for kingfish and tailor, with scope for other species.

Sugarloaf Point is an excellent rock fishing area, with good ledges that are reasonably safe and allow comfortable fishing for luderick, snapper, tailor (especially in autumn), bream, rock blackfish and mulloway. The pelagic game fish come close in past this point, and yellowtail kingfish, bonito, yellowfin tuna, longtail and mackerel tuna are just some of the species prevalent in the area. The best time to chase these pelagics is between December and April although, depending on water currents, they can be present in the winter months as well.

Boat anglers can fish the rocky islets off the point, and **Treachery Head** to the south, for snapper, bream, tailor and kingfish. Treachery Head is well named, as the waves close to shore can rise unexpectedly.

Sugarloaf Bay, looking towards Seal Rocks – a good area to fish in a southerly, with surf-dwelling species available

MYALL LAKES

The **Myall River** winds up from Port Stephens, carrying a good complement of flathead, whiting and luderick, before it runs through the vast and shallow **Myall Lakes** system, a nursery ground for many species of fish. It has good quantities of bream, mullet and luderick. Small boats and, at times, with care, even stable canoes can be used in the lakes as the waters are generally placid. There are a number of shore fishing spots, notably at Mungo Brush in the south; along the difficult road east of the Bombah Broadwater; at Nerong; the northern river mouth; Bombah Point; around the lake to Violet Hill; Neranie Head; and near Smiths Lake, in the northern-most part of the system.

The best fishing places for boat anglers are off Pigeon Point; around Sheep and Goat islands on the Boolambayte Lake; off Mayers Point; on the drift from

GUIDE TO LOCAL FISH

	Seal Rocks	Myall Lakes
(BA) bass, Australian		•
(BT) bonito	•	•
(B) bream	•	•
(D) drummer, silver	•	•
(F) flathead	•	•
(FL) flounder		•
(KI) kingfish, yellowtail	•	•
(LU) luderick	•	•
(M) mullet		•
(MU) mulloway	•	•
(RB) rock blackfish	•	•
(SA) salmon, Australian		•
(S) snapper	•	•
(T) tailor	•	•
(TA) tarwhine	•	
(TU) tuna	•	•
(W) whiting	•	•

Myall Lakes is steeped in history and this extensive estuary complex has been home to anglers and their craft for over one hundred years

Stinging Tree Point to Burrah Burrah Point; around the oyster leases in the middle of the main lake; and on the eastern side, around Shelly Point, Blossom Point and Long Point.

The coastal side of the park has long stretches of beach, which can be reached by four-wheel drive by branching off from the rather rudimentary Hawks Nest Seal Rocks Road. However, beach access for four-wheel drives is strictly limited and you should contact the Great Lakes Shire Council for information. The beach anglers' favourite fish – bream, flathead, whiting, mulloway and tailor – are in bountiful supply along these lonely shores. An accessible spot for beach anglers is the **Sand Bar Beach** near Smiths Lake, which can also fish well at times.

Offshore, some 5 km north of Seal Rocks, are the exposed **Skeleton Rocks**, a good spot for snapper, bream, mulloway and yellowtail kingfish. On calm days the best fishing is between the rocks. South-west of Seal Rocks, the **Yagon Reef** is about 1 km off the Yagon Gibber Headland and is a good place for mulloway and flathead.

Little Seal Rocks can be seen some 3 km to the south-east of Sugarloaf Point (see Seal Rocks map). Big snapper are caught here, particularly after a heavy sea, and there is also a strong possibility of mulloway. The abundant surface fish include kingfish, yellowfin tuna, and tailor and salmon (in good years) in winter.

A little to the south-west of Seal Rocks is **Edith Breaker**, which is easily found as it rises to just below the surface and creates clearly visible waves in all but the calmest seas. Fish the sides of the reef for the plentiful snapper, bonito and yellowtail kingfish.

The long beach stretching from Yagon Gibber Headland to Port Stephens offers whiting, tailor, flathead, and mulloway, while one of the best rock spots in New South Wales, the **Big Gibber Headland**, attracts bream, whiting, rock blackfish, mulloway and tailor.

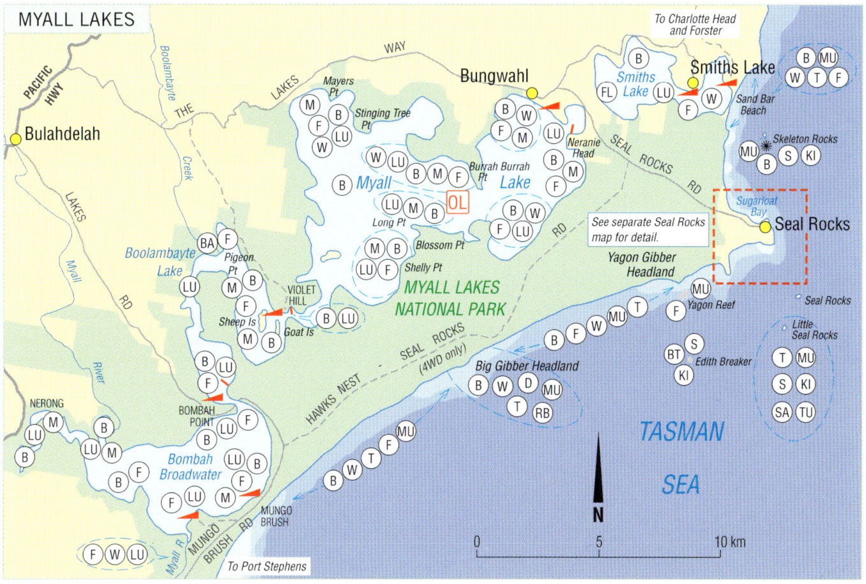

Port Stephens

Type of fishing
beach, estuary, jetty, offshore, reef, river, rock
Target fish
bream, flathead, marlin, mulloway, snapper, tuna

Port Stephens has become a major holiday destination that offers many types of fish in great abundance. A quality snapper fishery is a rarity in New South Wales waters, but the hard-bottomed reefs, washes and drop-offs at Broughton Island create ideal conditions.

PORT STEPHENS

The estuary holds up against considerable summer traffic, and at various times of the year provides good catches of mulloway, bream, flathead, whiting, flounder, tailor, crabs and other estuary species. Whiting are particularly prolific in summer, mostly around **Lemon Tree Passage**. They can be caught, along with flathead and bream on fresh baits of worms and yabbies, which can be collected at low tide on the sand and mudflats. Lure casting near oyster leases can also reward with flathead and bream.

Once a yearly event, the springtime invasion by striped and mackerel tuna is now rare. Mulloway can be caught in the deeper holes, particularly those around the Nelson Bay **Marina Breakwall**, the channel marker at Dutchmans beach, the wreck in Salamander Bay, and around **Dowardee** and **Middle islands**. Further upstream, there are good holes and channels in the mouth of the Karuah River.

One of the most accessible and exciting areas of the port is the entrance to the **Myall River**, near the twin north-shore towns of Hawks Nest and Tea Gardens. The Myall's main channel and the sand flats around it are ideal places to fish for bream, whiting, flathead and mulloway.

The jetty at **Hawks Nest** is over deep water and allows good land-based fishing for a variety of species, even for beginners. Fronting the ocean, **Bennetts Beach** provides great fishing for bream, flathead, tailor and occasional mulloway. Worms and pippis for bait are plentiful.

There are excellent rock platforms on either side of the entrance to Port Stephens. **Yacaaba Head** on the northern side is rugged and risky in rough weather, but offers bream, tailor and silver drummer. **Tomaree Head**, on the southern side, produces these same species, plus snapper and trevally, and big fish such as tuna, yellowtail kingfish, cobia, shark and even the odd marlin.

Port Stephens has outstanding attractions for offshore anglers, with reefs and islands close inshore for small boats, and excellent game fishing, from close grounds to the edge of the continental shelf, 40 km out. Close in are Cabbage Tree Island, Little Island and Boondelbah or Big Island. The eastern side of **Little Island** can produce marlin, snapper, mulloway, kingfish, bonito and various tunas, and at **Cabbage Tree Island** there are garfish, bream, snapper, rock blackfish, bonito, tuna and live bait grounds.

Port Stephens is highly regarded for its quality bream

Inshore reefs here carry teraglin, snapper, flathead, morwong and sundry other reef fish. In spring, large schools of big silver trevally visit a lot of Port Stephens' reefs. Among these is **Gunsight**

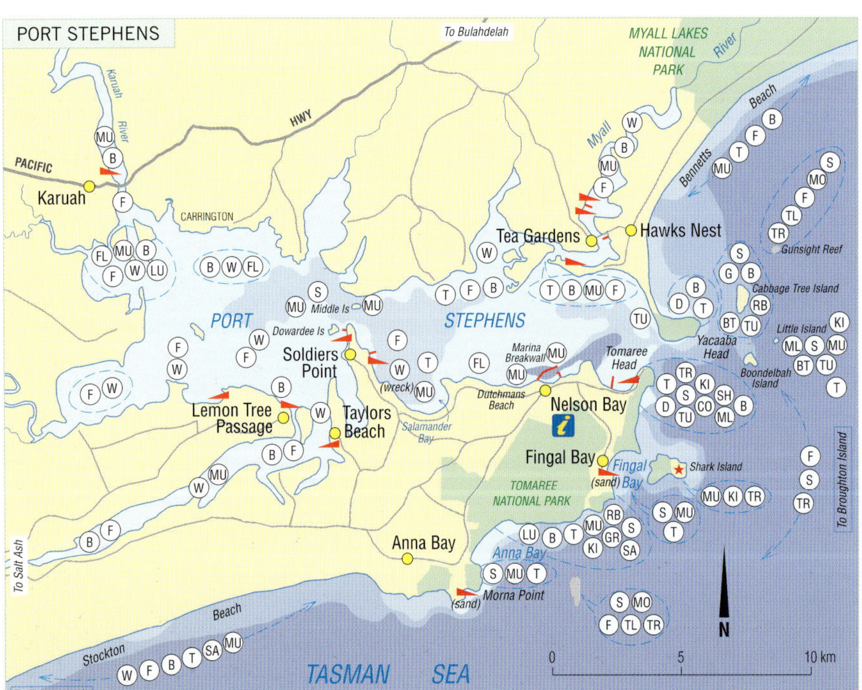

Beachworm

Beachworms are a favoured and highly prized bait. They are caught on the beach in sand on the receding wash. A berley bag is swished over the sand and as the wash carries the scent back, the beachworms poke their heads out. While experienced anglers use thumb and forefinger to extract the worms, most find it easier to use a pair of worm pliers to pull them out smoothly. They are one of the strongest and sturdiest worms available and are perfect for surf casting.

GUIDE TO LOCAL FISH

	Port Stephens	Broughton Island
(BT) bonito	●	●
(B) bream	●	
(CO) cobia	●	
(D) drummer, silver	●	
(F) flathead	●	
(FL) flounder	●	
(G) garfish	●	
(GR) groper	●	
(KI) kingfish, yellowtail	●	●
(LU) luderick	●	
(ML) marlin	●	●
(MO) morwong	●	●
(MU) mulloway	●	●
(RB) rock blackfish	●	
(SA) salmon, Australian	●	
(SH) shark	●	
(S) snapper	●	●
(T) tailor	●	
(TL) teraglin	●	
(TR) trevally	●	●
(TU) tuna	●	●
(W) whiting	●	

Reef, north of Cabbage Tree, where trevally up to 5 kg have been caught.

To the south, **Shark Island** has mulloway, kingfish and trevally around its eastern and south-eastern coast. Flathead and snapper can be found drifting between the islands, and trolling in the area will be well repaid.

A string of bays, beaches, rocky points and headlands runs from **Fingal Bay** to **Anna Bay**. The rock areas around the beaches are great casting spots for luderick, bream, salmon, tailor and mulloway. This coastline also offers superb fishing for kingfish, rock blackfish, snapper and groper. Calamari can be taken on squid jigs, and bait fish like slimy mackerel, yellowtail and garfish are seasonally abundant close in. Boats can be launched from the beaches of Fingal Bay and Anna Bay, and from Morna Point.

Stockton Beach has deep holes and gutters promising everything from whiting, flathead and bream to tailor and salmon, and big mulloway for those who put in the time.

Offshore, there are wrecks as well as reefs to hold the fish. The *Sigma* wreck has its own attractions, but serves as a mark for Carls Reef and The Gravel, which are good snapper, kingfish and mulloway areas. To the south-east of the *Sigma* is a renowned mulloway spot known as 'the mudhole'.

In recent years the offshore waters have achieved international recognition as one of the world's premier salt water fly destinations for marlin. Anglers from all over the world have come here in search of world records, and many new benchmarks have been established.

FISHING TIP

Birds can often be one of the most effective ways of finding schools of fish. A flock of birds sitting close together on the water is not often the sign of fish, but birds flying in circles, and diving into the water is a sure sign that there are fish beneath the surface. Shearwaters or muttonbirds are great hunters and a favourite for fishermen looking for schools of pelagic fish. But not all birds are as helpful. Seagulls can look like they are working when in fact all they are doing is haggling between themselves over a few scraps of orange peel.

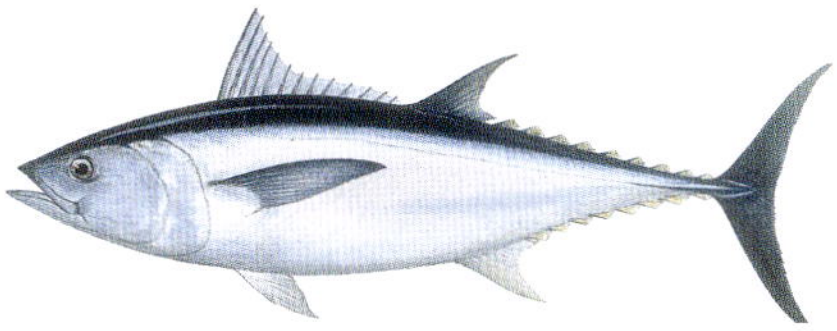

Longtail tuna

Longtail tuna is a popular inshore species keenly sought by shore-based anglers who specialise in fishing with live baits or high-speed spinning. Although this species can grow to 40 kg, it is most commonly caught from 10 to 15 kg.

BROUGHTON ISLAND

Apart from the snapper that are found around the island for most of the year, there are a lot of trevally, particularly in spring, as well as bonito and tuna over the reefs. These shallow reef areas can be drifted, or fished at anchor, and best results usually come from using light line and unweighted baits. Broughton has the advantage of some sheltered spots at Esmeralda Cove and South Cove in bad weather. The northern side has broad expanses of shallow reefs as well as deep holes and caves, which will reward with mulloway.

Fishing from the jetty at Nelson Bay

Newcastle and Lake Macquarie

Type of fishing
beach, estuary, lake, rock, wall, wharf
Target fish
bream, flathead, hairtail, luderick, mulloway

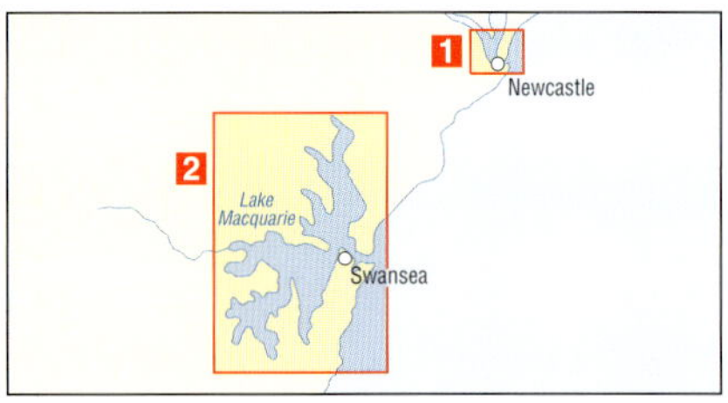

The Newcastle area boasts a good fishery that varies from rock and surf to inside fishing in the lake, estuary and harbour. The Hunter River is surprisingly resilient to the effects of heavy industry. Despite the vastness of the Lake Macquarie waterway, some of the best action is in the relatively small area around the entrance.

NEWCASTLE

Bream and school mulloway are the staple catch, but the highlight of the year is the invasion of hairtail, in winter. The harbour then becomes crowded with boats, night fishing with live and slab baits under light sticks on floats.

The two long breakwaters at the entrance to the harbour provide a good platform for fishing. The **Northern Breakwater** allows good ocean rock fishing on the outside, with a wreck as an added bonus, and estuary fishing on the inside. The best place to fish the wreck is towards the stern, and the quarry here are bream, flathead, yellowtail kingfish, tailor, morwong and john dory. Elsewhere on the wall, trevally and bream are the targets. The estuary side has bream, luderick and occasionally mulloway, with the head of the wall being the best mulloway spot in the area. There is a strong tidal flow through here, but it abates as the river bends north, allowing excellent land-based fishing from the Stockton ferry wharf for bream, flathead, mulloway and luderick.

On the southern side of the entrance, the peninsula and a constructed wall join to form a long breakwater, which offers great fishing inside and out. Snapper, tailor, mulloway, tuna and kingfish can be found at the ocean end, but the sloping rocky bottom demands that you fish beneath a float. Just inside the wall there is a deep hole, which is favoured for bream, snapper and occasionally mulloway. Luderick can be caught all the way down to the wharves.

Half-way along the breakwater, at **Stony Point**, anglers can walk out to the edge of the stones at low tide and cast a lightly weighted bait for bream and tailor. Flathead and whiting are caught from **Horse Shoe Beach**. At the end of the beach is the small harbour breakwall with bream, tailor, mulloway and flathead, and a small beach attracting tailor, flathead and whiting.

Further west, at **Queens Wharf** and other wharves nearby, there is fishing for bream, flathead and school mulloway. Further up the Hunter River, good bream, flathead, whiting and school mulloway can be taken, particularly at drop-offs and smaller creeks and channel mouths on a dropping tide.

Along the outer edge of the Southern Breakwater and stretching south-west to Nobbys Beach is a reefy area, which is ideal for snapper, particularly after a blow. Bream and luderick are also caught here. Further out is a peaked reef known as Big Ben Rock, which appears at low tide. The area should be avoided in heavy weather, but on a calm morning you can be sure of pulling snapper, mulloway and kingfish into the boat.

Inner reefs that are good for snapper, mulloway and bream are the **Middle Reef**, straight out from the port, and the **'dumping ground'**, 3 to 5 km out, where rubble from dredging the harbour has been deposited.

A popular beach fishing technique is to cast lightly weighted pilchards for tailor on sidecast tackle

There are some fine rock and beach spots to the south. **Newcastle and Merewether beaches** are good for luderick, bream, Australian salmon, tailor and mulloway.

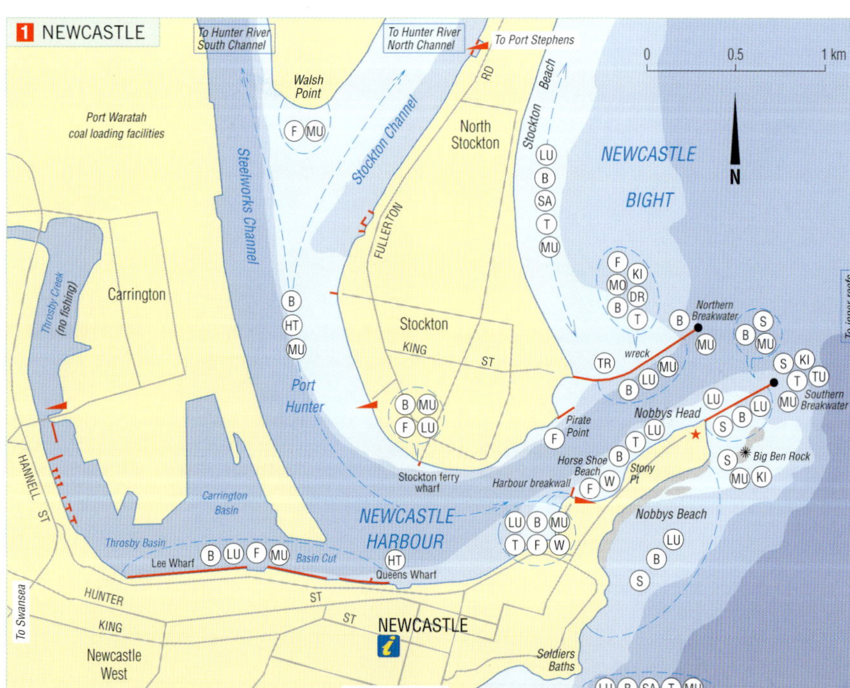

LAKE MACQUARIE AND SWANSEA

Lake Macquarie has little tidal movement, and this reduces its value as a fishery as there are few places where the fish naturally gather on the tides to feed. An attempt to enhance the fishery has been made with the placement of five artificial reefs: four just north-west of Swansea and one in Warners Bay. Bream is the main reef species.

But, generally, the target fish in the lake are bream, luderick, flathead and whiting, with the bonus of tailor and mulloway in some places. Other spots to try are around headlands or at the head of the many bays in the system. Dora Creek, entering the lake on its western side, produces bream, flathead, mulloway and luderick.

The fast flowing **Swansea Channel** carries good numbers of truly big flathead, bream, whiting, luderick, mulloway and even yellowtail kingfish. The area around the bridge is particularly good for all these species, while luderick and bream are best found around the walls at the entrance. The best spot of all is at the western end of the channel, where there is a big drop-off from the shallow channel to the floor of the lake. The biggest flathead in the state can wait here for their prey to reach them on the incoming tide, and often that prey is yellowtail or small tailor, which can be caught for live bait. The channel is also noted for its prawn runs, and prawns can be scoop netted in the two or three days either side of a new moon over summer.

GUIDE TO LOCAL FISH

	Newcastle	Lake Macquarie	Swansea
(B) bream	•	•	•
(F) flathead	•	•	•
(HT) hairtail	•		
(DR) john dory	•		
(KI) kingfish, yellowtail	•		•
(LJ) leatherjacket			•
(LU) luderick	•	•	•
(MO) morwong	•		
(M) mullet		•	
(MU) mulloway	•	•	•
(SA) salmon, Australian	•		
(S) snapper	•	•	•
(T) tailor	•	•	•
(TR) trevally	•		
(TU) tuna	•		
(W) whiting	•	•	•

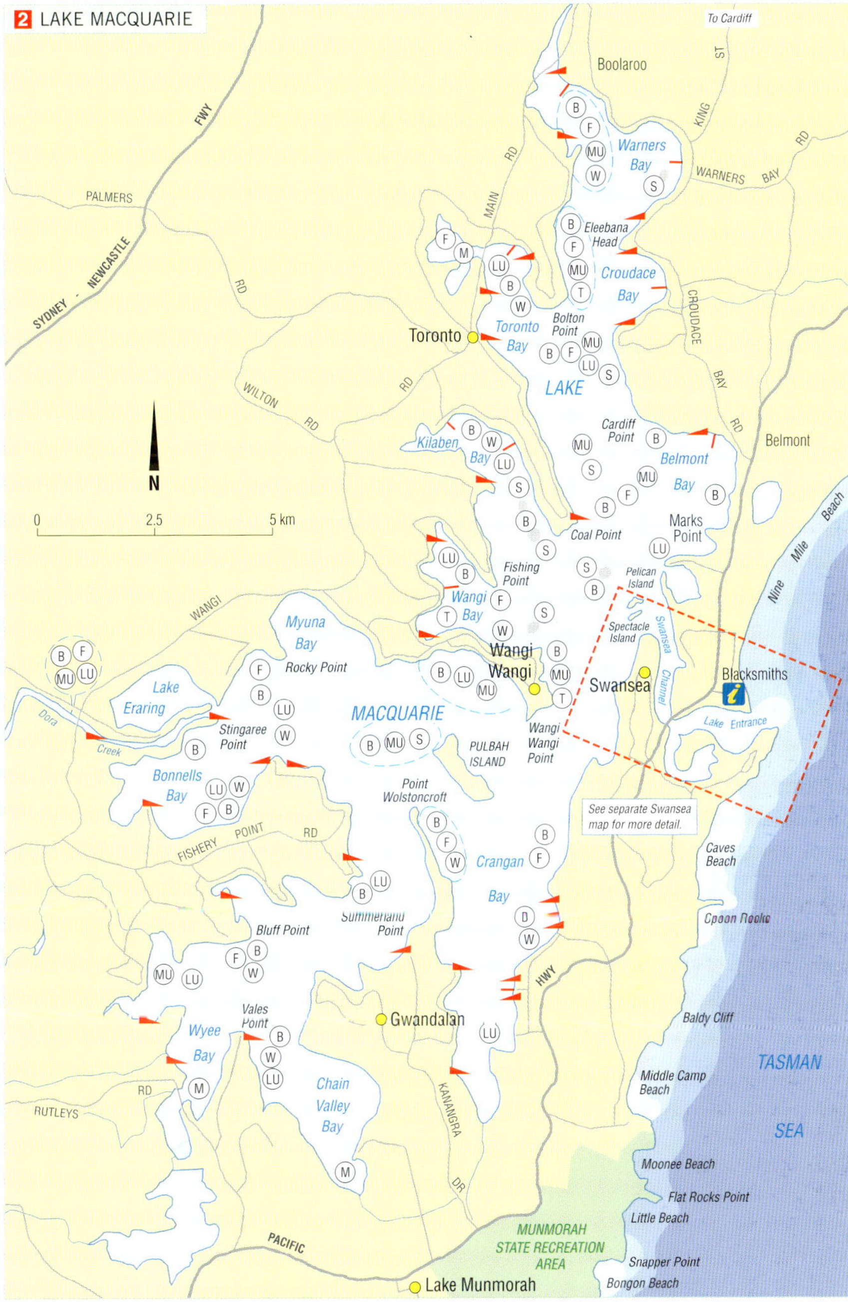

Coastal Lakes

Type of fishing
beach, lake, offshore, river, rock
Target fish
bream, flathead, luderick, tailor, whiting

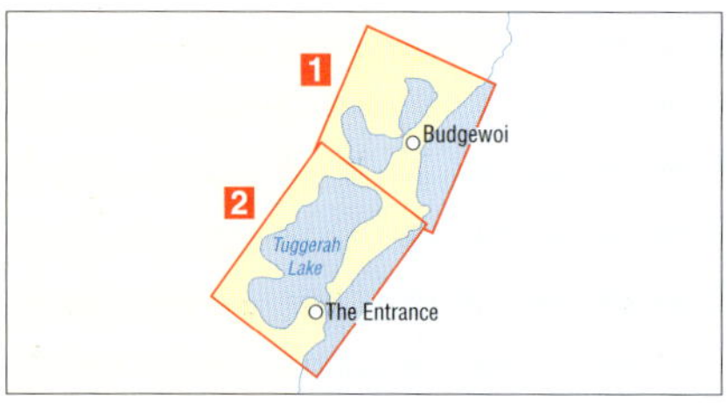

Flathead, bream, whiting and luderick are the target fish from the jetties at The Entrance

Munmorah and Budgewoi lakes, now in a built-up area within easy reach of Sydney, are fairly busy waterways. Tuggerah Lake is the most interesting fishery, with the entrance on the ocean side creating a tidal flow, as well as sand flats and channels.

MUNMORAH AND BUDGEWOI LAKES

Lake Munmorah is the northernmost and deepest of the central coast lakes and offers good fishing for flathead, bream and tailor, mostly around the banks. Because there is little tidal influence in these lakes, berley can be important, as the fish tend to gather around power station flow points and other structures around the lake rather than waiting for food washed to them by the tides.

The power station inlet, in the north-west corner, attracts luderick and bream, and the occasional tailor. Shore-based anglers can have a bonanza here at the right time. Access, however, involves a creek crossing so a four-wheel drive is needed to get to the inlet. The next best place for both boat and bank fishing in Lake Munmorah is in the south, at the entrance to Budgewoi Lake. The bridge over the entrance is a good luderick and bream spot, and the whole channel carries bream, luderick and tarwhine. It is a place for light line and minimum weights. There are some deep areas north of the entrance where it is possible to catch very big tailor.

Bream, the biggest catch in **Budgewoi Lake**, are best sought at dusk using lightly weighted baits, while drifting along the northern banks can yield good catches of whiting and flathead, and prawns. The north-west part of the lake has similar conditions to Munmorah, but here the water heated in the power station is expelled, creating a thermal attraction for a variety of species. The hot water outlet is built into a rock wall that extends into the north-west lobe of the lake and is only accessible by boat. Bream can be caught in big numbers here, but special care should be taken to release the large number of small fish that can also be taken. The immediate surrounds of the outlet are closed to fishing from May to August.

A little to the west is **Wallarah Creek**, particularly good when rough water in the lake sends fish into calmer areas. Bloodworms are easy to pump and gather in this area.

The ocean fishing is good around **Snapper Point** and **Wybung Head** to the north. This great rock location is part of the Munmorah State Recreation Area, and access is by tracks most suited to walking or four-wheel drive. Wybung is probably the best rock fishing area on the central coast, with great deepwater angling over boulders or gravel. Mulloway and snapper are the main hope, but bream, groper, luderick, rock blackfish and tailor are all in good supply around these rocks. At Birdie Beach, adjacent to Lake Munmorah, there is good

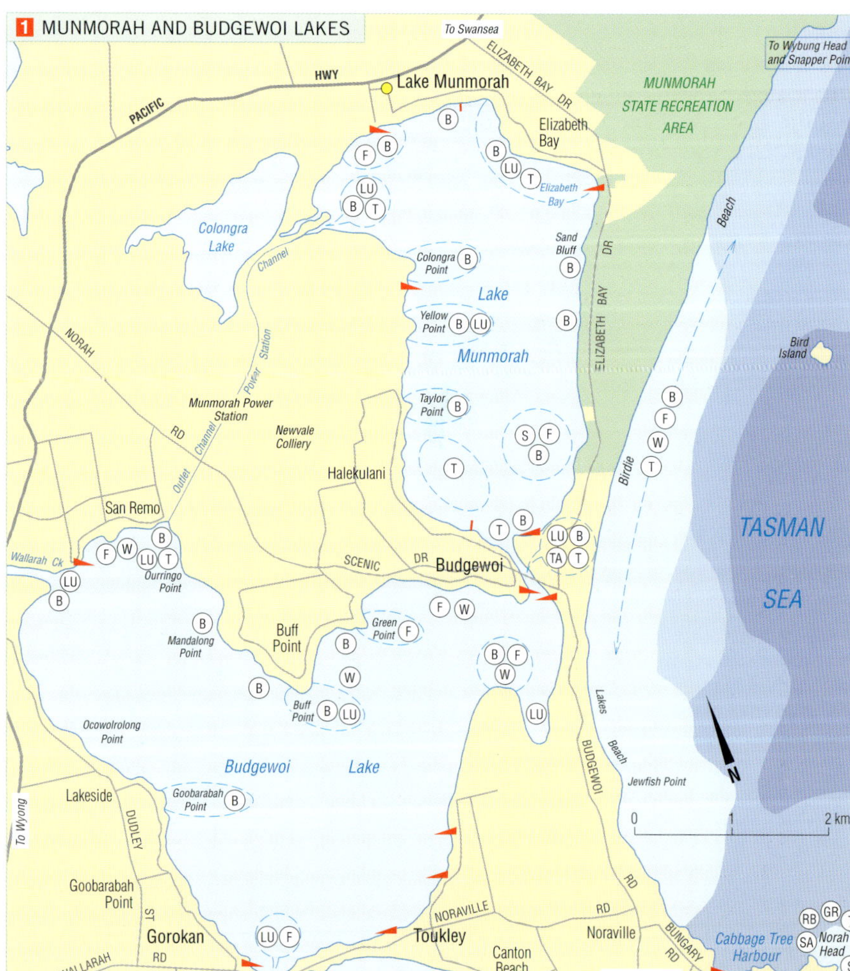

surf fishing. To the south at Norah Head, the fishing is also good for rock blackfish, snapper, groper, tailor and Australian salmon.

TUGGERAH LAKE

The mouth of **Tuggerah Lake**, known as The Entrance, is fast flowing on any tide, and should not be navigated. Fish from the land here for luderick. Prawning on a moonless night is best done when the tide is slack or turning. The sand flats just inside are good for collecting yabby and worm baits, and fishing for whiting, flathead and bream.

There is a net and trap exclusion zone in Tuggerah Lake, extending west from Picnic Point, northward past Pelican Island and eastward toward the Two-Shores Caravan Park. Bank fishing into the south channel from the park at **Picnic Point** is an ideal family pastime, as children can find other safe activities if they lose interest in the fishing. The North Channel is an ideal luderick spot on a run-out tide, with a weed bank in the shallows to provide instant bait and berley. Another channel runs past **Pelican Island** on its western side, with a drop-off ideal for boat anglers, who can anchor nearby and drift baits on light lines into the channel. Drifting past the island for flathead can be very productive.

As with the other lakes, the fishing gets harder where the tidal influence is less, and the central area of the lake does not make good fishing. The best inflow area is at **Chittaway Point**, where Ourimbah Creek runs in, and provides bream, luderick, mullet and flathead over the sand and weed flats. The fishing is excellent after heavy rain, when fish are pushed down by the fresh water. The situation is similar where the **Wyong River** enters the lake at Tacoma, and there is the extra bonus that this river can be navigated in a small boat and has surprisingly good bass fishing upstream. **Canton Beach** in the north-east is a good whiting, bream and flathead area. Bream and luderick are the main targets along the eastern side of the lake.

Outside, **Tuggerah Beach** is backed by Wyrrabalong National Park, so walking is required for those seeking the main beach fare of tailor, whiting and mulloway. Offshore, a large area of reef, known as The Shallows, runs south to Pelican Point at the northern end of Tuggerah Beach and carries snapper, mulloway and yellowtail kingfish. You can also wade to the drop-off at low tide from **Pelican Point**, provided the sea is calm, and try for tailor and mulloway. You can only fish for a short while, however, as the rising tide can cut you off from the mainland.

The best mulloway fishing is just north of The Entrance, and usually on a run-out tide, while there are snapper, drummer and mulloway on the southern side.

Further south, **Toowoon Point** creates a sheltered fishing area in Toowoon Bay, so fish back to the beach for bream and the big whiting that come into the bay. The rocky washes at the end of the point carry luderick and rock blackfish, and there are some good mulloway holes on the southern side.

GUIDE TO LOCAL FISH

	Munmorah and Budgewoi Lakes	Tuggerah Lake
(B) bream	●	●
(D) drummer, silver		●
(F) flathead	●	●
(GR) groper	●	
(KI) kingfish, yellowtail		●
(LU) luderick	●	●
(M) mullet	●	●
(MU) mulloway	●	●
(RB) rock blackfish	●	●
(SA) salmon, Australian	●	
(S) snapper	●	●
(T) tailor	●	●
(TA) tarwhine	●	
(W) whiting	●	●

2 TUGGERAH LAKE

Terrigal

Type of fishing
beach, lagoon, rock
Target fish
bream, rock blackfish, tailor, tuna

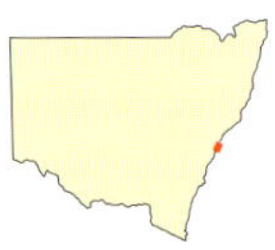

The rock and beach areas running from Bateau Bay to Box Head are heavily fished by anglers due to their proximity to Sydney and the excellent and varied fishing that they provide. More specifically, the fishing at Terrigal and Terrigal Haven features good access to the rocks and beaches and plenty of opportunities for big fish.

BATEAU BAY TO BOX HEAD

Crackneck Point and **Yumbool Point** have good rock spots, though they require some serious walking from Bateau Bay township. A few are a little low and dangerous in high seas, but in calm conditions they can offer snapper, rock blackfish, bream and groper.

Forresters Beach is very good for whiting at its southern end, particularly if the bait is beachworm taken from the beach. A high, safe rock ledge at **Wamberal Point** has good fishing for snapper, luderick, tailor, rock blackfish and bream, and the little beach beyond has bream, particularly when the swimmers are not around. When Wamberal Lagoon is open, the long stretch of **Wamberal and Terrigal beaches** fishes best near the

GUIDE TO LOCAL FISH

	Bateau Bay to Box Head	Terrigal
(BT) bonito		●
(B) bream	●	●
(D) drummer, silver	●	●
(F) flathead	●	●
(GR) groper	●	
(KI) kingfish, yellowtail	●	●
(LU) luderick	●	●
(MU) marlin	●	
(MU) mulloway	●	●
(RB) rock blackfish	●	●
(SA) salmon, Australian	●	
(S) snapper	●	
(T) tailor	●	●
(TU) tuna	●	●
(W) whiting	●	

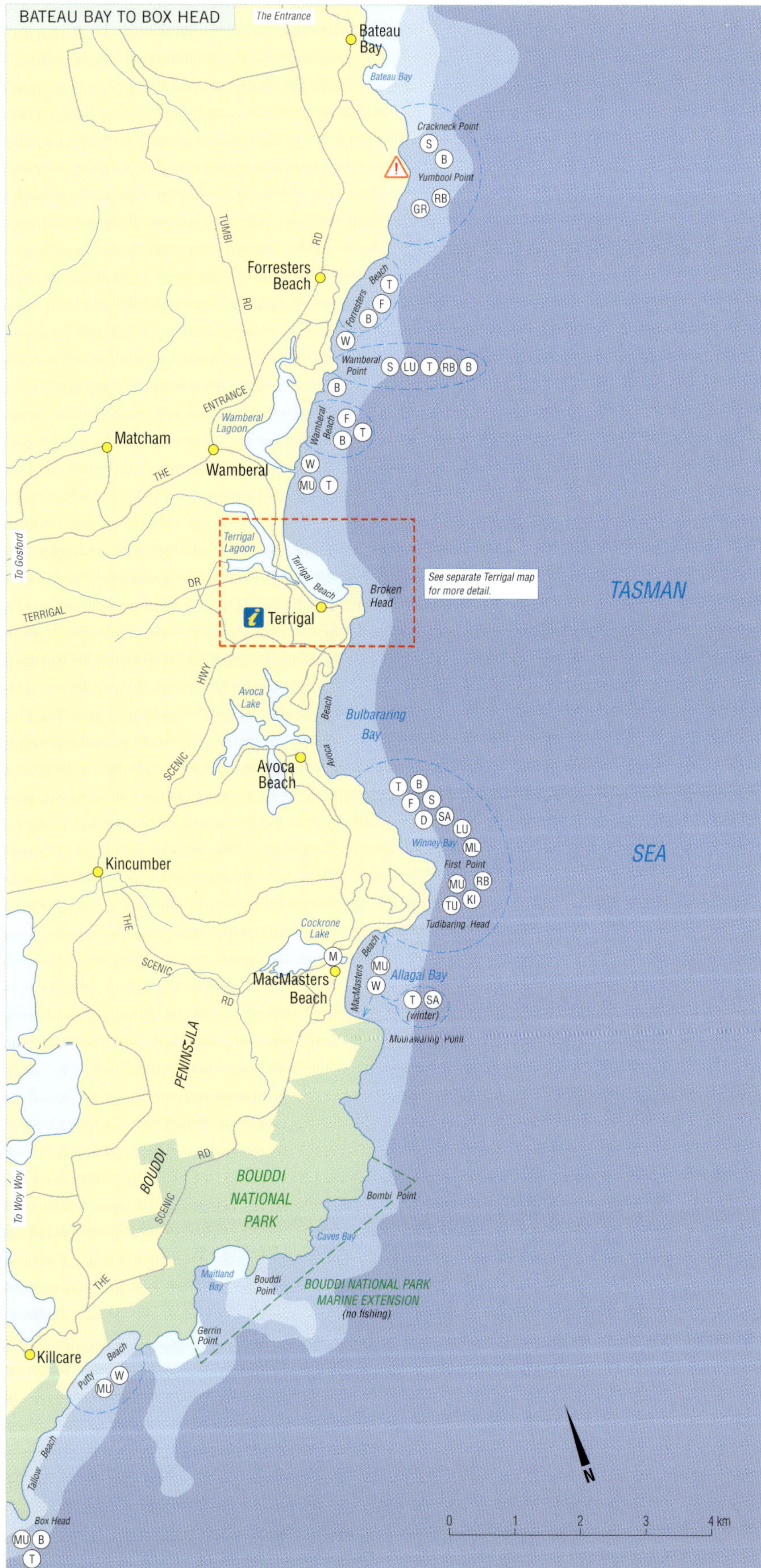

Hooked up on The Skillion

entrance. Mulloway and tailor wait here for prey to be swept from the lagoon. Otherwise, the beaches are best fished wherever the gutters are at the time, and for bream, flathead, whiting and tailor.

South of Terrigal, the large headland at **Avoca Beach** is one of the most popular rock areas in the country, as there is car parking close by. The seas have to be watched on the north side, but to the south, a long, flat ledge takes over, dropping into deep water over a sand bottom. This area is fished for flathead, bream, rock blackfish, silver drummer, snapper and mulloway. Tuna, Australian salmon, kingfish and tailor are among the surface fish that come in here, and even marlin are not out of the question. Most regulars either use lures or live bait for the bigger fish. Bream, rock blackfish and luderick are also in the washes along the rocks of this big headland area.

MacMasters Beach is backed by a large lagoon, known as **Cockrone Lake**. This is sometimes open to the sea and is a good place to get small mullet as bait. Whiting and mulloway are the main catches off the beach, with tailor and salmon in winter. Part of the Bouddi National Park – the stretch from Bombi Point to Gerrin Point – is a marine reserve, closed to fishing. To the south-west, **Putty Beach** can be easily reached for whiting and mulloway, but the big action for rock anglers requires a long walk to **Box Head**. This is at its best when the Hawkesbury River is in flood and the mulloway prowl after fish flushed from the river. At other times, Box Head generally fishes well for bream and tailor.

The rock platform at The Skillion provides a great fishing spot for anglers targeting pelagic species

TERRIGAL

The comparatively protected waters of the Haven attract some big surface fish from offshore, like frigate mackerel, bonito and yellowtail kingfish. The frigates are most prevalent around February and March. They can be fished from the shore on the inner side of the headland, if you can find standing room, and by casting small metal lures. This promontory is also good for bream and tailor, particularly in the rocky washes after a southerly blow. Luderick, rock blackfish and silver drummer are also around the rocks.

Terrigal Lagoon is often closed at the beach, but when it is open flathead, bream and tailor are caught around the entrance, and the beach fishing becomes more active for bream, tailor and mulloway. At the southern end of the beach is a high rock known as **Grannys**, which can be fished safely, with bream as the main target.

Around the headland, there are good rock spots known as the Cod Hole, Flat Rock and Splashy, and bream, luderick and rock blackfish can be caught here, particularly after a southerly swell. Flat Rock can only be fished in calmer conditions.

One of the most crowded spots in this popular rock area is **The Skillion**, which can be reached by walking through parkland. Fishing for bonito, tailor, kingfish and striped and mackerel tuna is done with lures or live baits, and the place is generally crowded at the peak fishing times of early morning and tide changes. Those with more modest ambitions can still fish close in for luderick, rock blackfish and bream. The ledges here extend around the point, creating shelter from north-east winds, and the fishing is good for bream, tailor, luderick and rock blackfish.

Wollongong Region

The beach and rock fishing in the Wollongong region starts in the unspoiled Royal National Park, within an hour's drive of Sydney, and continues in great variety all the way to Durras lake. The Shoalhaven is the only big river in the region, and the islands, sand flats, creeks and channels in its estuary are fascinating to explore by boat.

There are close-in reefs all down the coast carrying fish such as snapper, morwong, trevally, yellowtail kingfish and tuna. Minnamurra, Kiama, Gerringong and Gerroa are among a chain of fishing towns down this coast, and one of the best rock fishing spots in the region is Bass Point, which juts out into deep water. Further south a string of rock platforms, beaches, harbours, estuaries, rivers, channels and sand flats offer wonderful fishing.

Weather

As is the case along the rest of this coast, prevailing winds in the summer months are north north easterlies, with a tendency to swing sharply to the south unexpectedly. Always keep an eye on the cloud cover to ensure you are not taken by surprise. It is usually better to fish on the southern side of headlands, except during southerlies, when the northern aspect is obviously preferable. For information, ring the Weather Bureau on tel. (02) 9296 1555 or contact the local Coast Guard or Coastal Patrol. Detailed weather information can be found at: www.bom.gov.au

Boating

Tidal surges can cause problems at the Bellambi (Wollongong) and Kiama boat ramps, and the Shellharbour boat ramp is adequate, but not great. Generally anglers use Port Kembla, which has calm waters. There are bomboras off Wollongong and at the entrance to Shellharbour, so check the Admiralty Chart maps for water levels. Lake Illawarra and the Minnamurra River have bars close to their entrances, and Lake Illawarra is very shallow in parts. For local information, check with the Coast Guards, NSW Maritime and local maps.

WHERE TO FISH

Wollongong Region

ROYAL NATIONAL PARK • 104

There is camping in the national park, and walking to some spectacular deep-water rock spots and secluded beaches. One attraction is The Gulf, a deep gutter frequented by a variety of pelagics.

WOLLONGONG • 105

Port Kembla harbour has fine breakwater fishing. There are great rock and beach locations on either side of Port Kembla and Wollongong, and extensive reefs close to shore.

LAKE ILLAWARRA • 106

Lake Illawarra is very shallow and best fished near the entrance, with outstanding prawn runs in summer. Nearby Windang Island is prolific for numerous species, while Bass Point juts a long way out into the sea and attracts big surface fish as well as the close-in rock species.

MINNAMURRA TO CULBURRA • 108

This is a beautiful stretch of coast, with harbour fishing at Kiama, some great beach spots, and rock fishing at places such as Blowhole Point and Black Head at Gerroa. The Shoalhaven River is a fascinating estuary, with numerous islands, sandbars, bays and canals near the coast, creating some prime fishing locations.

JERVIS BAY TO LAKE CONJOLA • 110

There is excellent rock fishing on the Beecroft Peninsula, and good, safe land spots in Jervis Bay. Boat fishing is rewarding but unsafe in a southerly. Sir Joseph Young Banks is a large, productive reef 4 km out from the peninsula, while Sussex Inlet is good for both land and boat fishing. Lake Conjola is famous for its big flathead.

ULLADULLA TO DURRAS LAKE • 112

This area offers a combination of beach, rock, harbour and estuary fishing, while the offshore islands can teem with snapper and yellowtail kingfish.

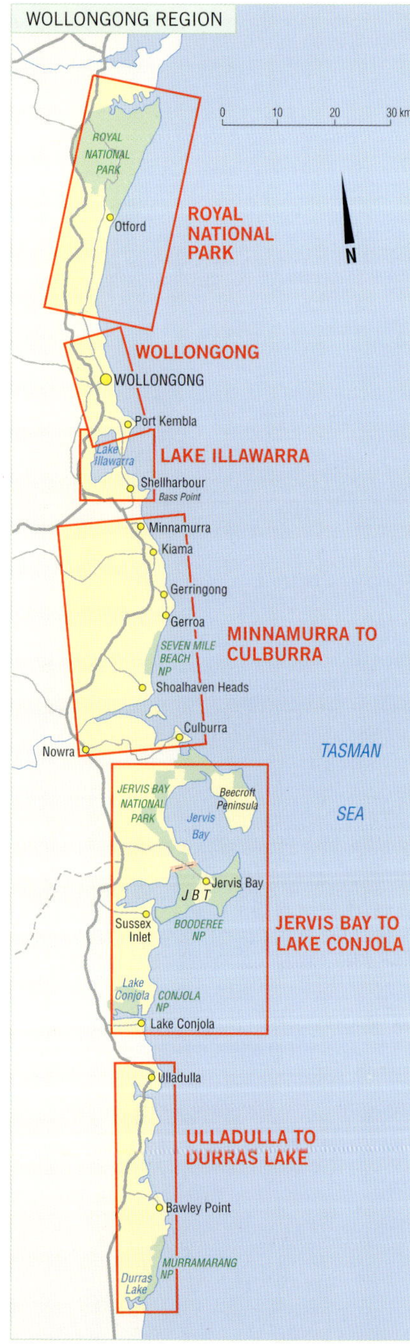

FISHING TIP

Cunjevoi is a superb bait for a number of species including snapper and bream. Also known as sea-squirts or cunje, these animals are more like plants and live in colonies along the tidal zone of rock platforms and on pier pilings. Although tough on the outside, once opened the flesh is a rich orange to purple and should be scooped out. A few cunje will generally last a reasonable period. Rather than take too many, try taking just enough because they don't breed as fast as anglers can remove them.

GUIDE TO LOCAL FISH

albacore
bonito
bream, black
bream, yellowfin
drummer, silver
flathead
flounder
garfish
groper
hairtail
john dory
kingfish, yellowtail
leatherjacket
luderick
mackerel, slimy
marlin, black
marlin, blue
marlin, striped
morwong
mullet, sand
mullet, sea
mulloway
nannygai
rock blackfish
salmon, Australian
snapper
tailor
teraglin
trevally, silver
tuna, mackerel
tuna, striped
tuna, yellowfin
whiting, King George
whiting, sand
whiting, trumpeter

Garie Beach area: the high elevation enables this angler to cast out to the back of the breakers

FURTHER INFORMATION

Fishing and boating *NSW Fisheries has offices at 43 Reddall Pde, Lake Illawarra South, tel. (02) 4295 1809; and 64 North St, Nowra, tel. (02) 4423 2200. NSW Maritime has an office at Unit 5, cnr Kembla and Beach sts, Wollongong, tel. (02) 4227 3644.*

The Coast Guard's main bases are at Bellambi (Wollongong), tel. (02) 4284 8822; Port Kembla tel. (02) 4274 4455 and Shellharbour, tel. (02) 4297 3999. The Coastal Patrol has bases at Wollongong, tel. (02) 4229 3434; Jervis Bay, tel. (02) 4441 5433; Sussex Inlet, tel. (02) 4441 1444; Kioloa, tel. (02) 4457 1109; and Ulladulla, tel. (02) 4455 3403.

Tourist centres *Blowhole Point Rd, Kiama, tel. (02) 4232 3322; Princes Hwy, Ulladulla, tel. (02) 4455 1269; 93 Crown St, Wollongong, tel. (02) 4227 5545.*

Royal National Park

Type of fishing
beach, offshore, rock

Target fish
Australian salmon, bream, snapper, tailor

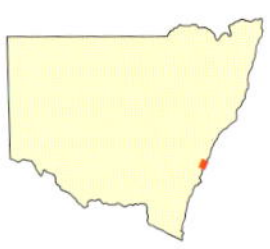

Although close to Sydney, Royal National Park is a largely unspoilt paradise for the rock and beach angler. You must be prepared to walk to your fishing spot, to carry your supplies, and to get a permit if you want to camp overnight. The good news is that the bushwalking is pleasant and the fishing wonderful.

The northernmost fishing area, known as **The Cobblers**, can be reached from the walking track that runs from Bundeena to Marley Beach. This area can be very dangerous in big seas and the high ledges make a cliff gaff essential. There is good fishing for luderick and rock blackfish in the washes and, further out, for tailor, Australian salmon and snapper.

Marley Head and the rocky ledges south of Marley Beach are good luderick, bream and rock blackfish territory. The adjoining **Marley and Little Marley beaches** are bream and whiting grounds, with tailor and salmon in winter. The ledges south of Little Marley are good casting platforms for snapper further out, and for spinning in summer for yellowtail kingfish, tuna, salmon and tailor.

The sheltered **Wattamolla Bay** can provide bream and tailor. At **Curracurrang** there is inshore fishing for luderick, rock blackfish, bream, groper and leatherjacket, with snapper, tailor, salmon and kingfish further out. A track from the Wattamolla road leads to **The Gulf**, a deep gutter running back to a large rock platform. Marlin, tuna and kingfish can be caught on live baits, while tailor, salmon, trevally, snapper and bream are targets for those spinning and baitfishing in the washes.

Further south, trevally, tailor, bream, snapper and salmon can be caught from the rocks at the north point of Garie Beach. The beaches at **South Era** are good for flathead, whiting and bream.

Offshore, there are Jibbon Bombora in the north, Marley Head, Little Marley Beach, Wattamolla and Curracurrang. There are no boat ramps in the park but boats may be launched at Cronulla. Snapper, mulloway, tailor, morwong and nannygai are likely to be caught over reefs, while there is good drifting for flathead along the entire coast. South of Royal National Park, there are extensive reefs offshore from Austinmer and Bellambi Point, with kingfish, bonito and yellowfin tuna the main catches.

GUIDE TO LOCAL FISH

	Royal National Park	Wollongong
Ⓑ bream	●	●
Ⓕ flathead	●	●
(GR) groper	●	●
(HT) hairtail		●
(DR) john dory		●
(KI) kingfish, yellowtail	●	●
(LJ) leatherjacket	●	
(LU) luderick	●	●
(ML) marlin	●	
(MO) morwong	●	●
(MU) mulloway	●	●
(NG) nannygai	●	
(RB) rock blackfish	●	●
(SA) salmon, Australian	●	●
Ⓢ snapper	●	●
Ⓣ tailor	●	●
(TL) teraglin	●	●
(TR) trevally	●	●
(TU) tuna	●	●
Ⓦ whiting	●	●

Wollongong

Type of fishing
beach, harbour, offshore, rock

Target fish
bream, luderick, mulloway, snapper, tailor

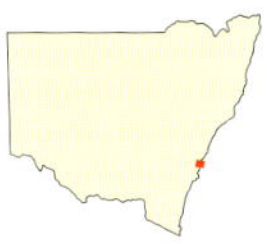

Flagstaff Point is a good spot for luderick, rock blackfish, tailor and bream, while **Wollongong Beach**, running to Port Kembla, will yield tailor, salmon and flathead. There is good fishing all around the Wollongong area, particularly in and around Port Kembla Harbour.

Like many other port locations, with piers, buoys and other structures attracting fish, **Port Kembla Harbour** has a lot to offer the land-based angler. The best spot is the Northern Breakwater, where mulloway, snapper, bream, luderick and tailor are plentiful, particularly at dawn and dusk. Hairtail are caught here at times. Those who fish outside the retaining wall, running to the breakwater, will be fishing over sand for luderick, rock blackfish, school mulloway and tailor. The Southern Breakwater is almost as good, while in the harbour the shipping wharves can be fished for school mulloway, john dory and yellowtail kingfish when ships are not tied up. The walls on both sides of the inner harbour entrance provide great locations for luderick fishing.

The rocks at **Battery Point**, near the Southern Breakwater, are great luderick and rock blackfish spots, with good weed on the rocks but a sandy bottom to protect your rig. Between Battery Point and Red Point, flathead, bream, whiting and tailor are found off the beaches.

Tailor

The tailor is one of Australia's most popular saltwater sportfish. It is found in inshore and close offshore waters from Fraser Island, in Queensland, right round the south coast to Shark Bay in Western Australia. It is a great fighting fish, requiring the use of a wire trace or ganged hooks. It will readily hit trolled or cast lures as well as static or moving baits. As a table fish, tailor is best bled immediately after capture and tastiest when freshly cooked. It does not freeze well.

Further south, the headland at the north end of **Perkins Beach** has good rock fishing for snapper, tailor and Australian salmon, but it must only be fished in calm seas, as it is not called Dead Mans Hole for nothing.

The offshore fishing in the region is consistent, without being spectacular, for those who know the right locations and tactics. There are gravel patches with good snapper possibilities about 1.5 km out from Wollongong Harbour, and a snapper reef another 1 km out. Similar gravel areas run from west of Big Island.

Off Port Kembla, The Five Islands, which include **Flinders and Bass islets** and **Big Island**, have kingfish, snapper and mulloway, with bream, tailor and salmon in the inshore washes. Boat launching can be made from Wollongong or Shellharbour, but avoid the entrance to Lake Illawarra.

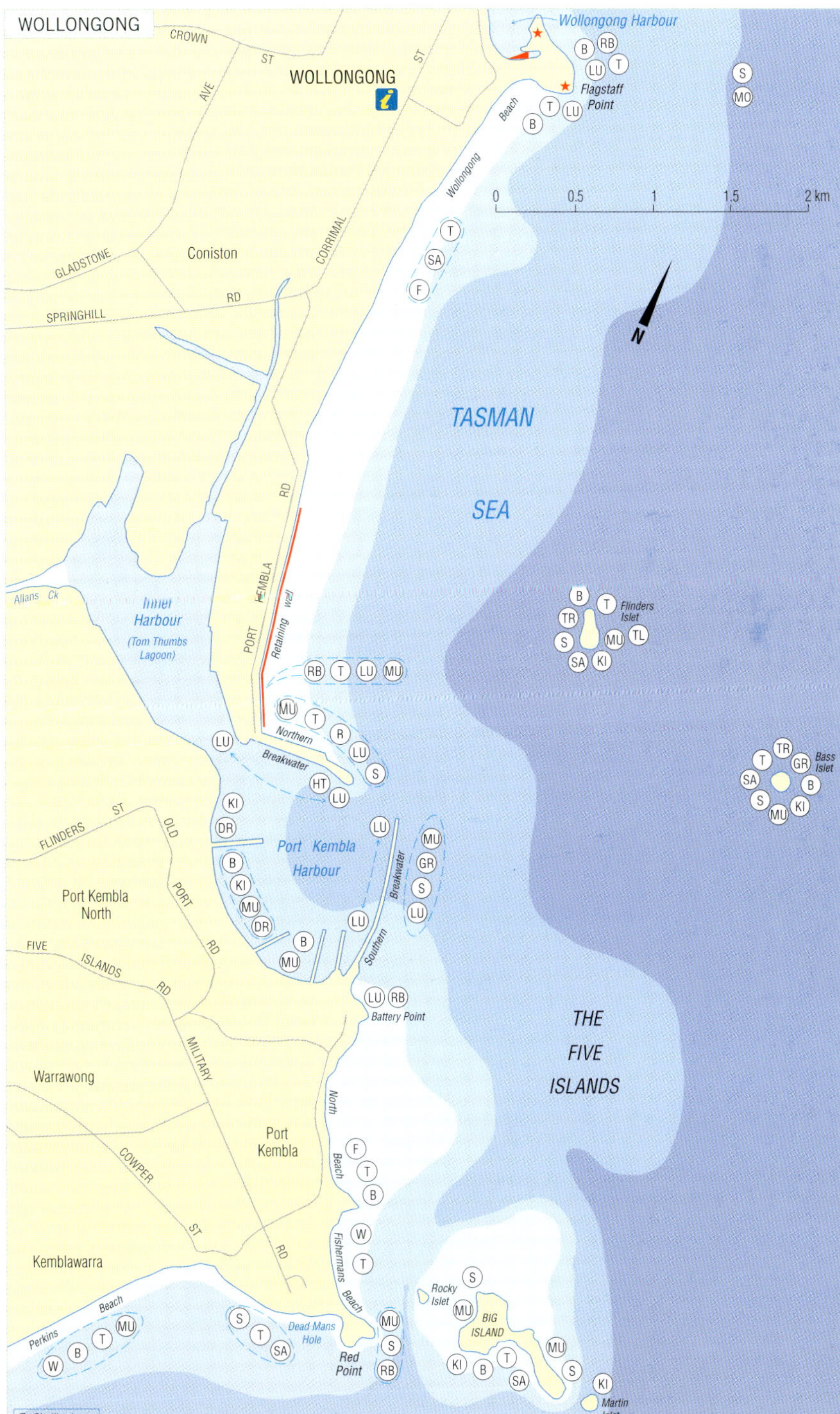

Lake Illawarra

Type of fishing
beach, lake, rock

Target fish
bream, flathead, luderick, rock blackfish, tailor, whiting

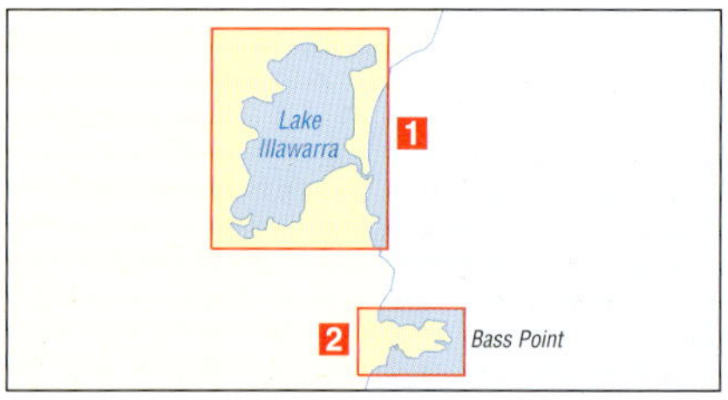

Lake Illawarra is very shallow, less than 4 m at its deepest, but it yields a lot of fish year after year, despite the pressure from both professional and recreational fishers. The best fishing along the whole Wollongong coast is at Bass Point, a wedge of land jutting into the sea just south of Shellharbour.

LAKE ILLAWARRA

Lake Illawarra's best fishing is at the entrance and around the shore, although its very shallowness makes its central waters productive also – sandbanks and gutters close in are good for whiting, using live worms or yabbies as bait. The lake can be dangerous in high winds, as the choppy conditions can easily overturn small craft. Nevertheless, the hire boats available around the lake attest to the popularity of this waterway and its general safety.

The entrance is the most prolific and crowded area of the lake, producing whiting, flathead, mullet, luderick, bream and tailor for both boat and shore anglers. The prawn runs around the entrance in summer, on the new moon, are outstanding, and hundreds of people wade the shallows with strong lights and dip nets to reap the rewards. Others operate out of boats. There are prawning areas all along the north-eastern side of the lake. On the northern shore, just inside the entrance, the flathead fishing can be good, particularly at dusk on a falling tide. Persistent holiday-makers often get their evening meal at a flathead mark just north of **Cudgeree Island**, or a bucket of prawns a little further north and near the bank. Straight in from the entrance is **Bevans Island**, which has luderick on the north side. Whiting, flathead and bream can be caught all around the island.

Several creeks run into the lake on its western side. Near their entrances, these waters provide reliable fishing for bream, and luderick, mullet and flathead are also prevalent. Fishing outside the creek entrances after heavy rain can yield big bream catches at **Mullet Creek**, **Duck Creek** and **Macquarie Rivulet**.

Outside, Windang Island is connected to the mainland by a changing tidal sandbar that sometimes blocks the southerly outflow. When this occurs, **Perkins Beach** (known locally as Windang Beach), which is one of the best south coast beaches, becomes even more prolific for mulloway, as well as bream, flathead, salmon, whiting and tailor.

Windang Island is a great place to fish, with the rocky shores attracting bream, luderick, rock blackfish, drummer and tailor to its washes, and its deep, sandy-bottomed surrounds making casting and spinning a pleasure. It is known as a bream hot spot, particularly in winter, and the best bream area is on its south-eastern shore. The north-eastern area of the island is best for snapper, while luderick can be caught from the northern shore, along with tailor and rock blackfish.

Warilla Beach fishes very well if the lake is flowing out south of Windang

Suitable tackle for the Lake Illawarra estuary

Island. The target fish are whiting, bream, tailor and mulloway. At the southern end of the beach, **Barrack Point** has rock fishing for bream and luderick, using bait under floats in the washes close-in, tailor further out, again with bait under a float, and snapper by casting well out on the bottom.

BASS POINT

The peninsula juts out into the passing currents and is a perfect venue to fish for pelagics such as tailor and tuna as well as bream, leatherjacket, luderick, rock blackfish, snapper and silver drummer attracted to the rocky washes and gutters. Baits like cunjevoi, crabs and cabbage weed are easily gathered, and there are two boat ramps in the area for those wishing to fish the currents out from the island. The ramp at Shellharbour, to the north, is the safer of the two as boat launching at Bass Point is subject to rough seas.

On the north-east shore of Bass Point, a carpark allows good access to rocky gutters that produce yellowtail kingfish, snapper and trevally. Bream, luderick and leatherjacket are also here. The eastern-most point of the peninsula, near the bombora, is the best spot to cast out for tuna, tailor, kingfish and other pelagics.

A cove, known as **Bushrangers Bay**, on the south-east corner of the point, is an aquatic reserve nursery for juvenile fish species and other marine life, and is completely protected. On the southern side there is a group of rock ledges that allows high and safe casting for the inshore rock fish, and tailor, salmon and snapper.

GUIDE TO LOCAL FISH

	Lake Illawarra	Bass Point
(BT) bonito		•
(B) bream	•	•
(D) drummer, silver	•	•
(F) flathead	•	
(G) garfish		•
(GR) groper		•
(KI) kingfish, yellowtail		•
(LJ) leatherjacket		•
(LU) luderick	•	•
(M) mullet	•	
(MU) mulloway	•	
(RB) rock blackfish	•	•
(SA) salmon, Australian	•	•
(S) snapper	•	•
(T) tailor	•	•
(TU) tuna		•
(W) whiting	•	

Lake Illawarra is a well-known estuary for land-based locations

Minnamurra to Culburra

Type of fishing
bay, beach, estuary, offshore, rock
Target fish
bream, flathead, snapper, whiting

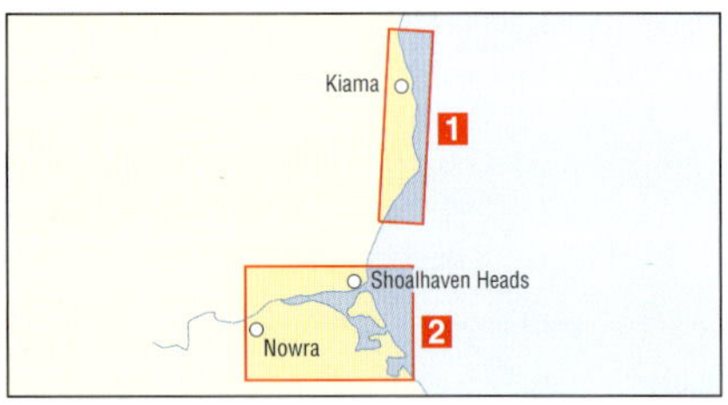

Fishing is a great part of the life of the townsfolk, retirees and vacationers on the beautiful stretch of coast from Minnamurra to Culburra. A string of rock platforms and beaches offers wonderful fishing, providing that the rock-hoppers take care as most of the locations are near sea level and very dangerous. The Shoalhaven River has many islands, sandbars, bays and canals near the coast, creating some prime fishing spots.

MINNAMURRA TO SEVEN MILE BEACH

The Minnamurra River provides relaxing fishing for luderick, bream and whiting on nippers and flathead near the mouth spinning. **Boyds Beach** is a good spot for luderick, rock blackfish and snapper, with gutters for bream and whiting from the beach. **The Boneyard** is protected, and when the huge southerlies are rolling in can still be fished for bream, luderick and snapper. **Bombo**, **Surf** and **Kendalls beaches** are all good for bream and whiting.

Land-based anglers get the best of **Kiama Harbour** after a big southerly sea, when bream, luderick and snapper come into these protected waters. For reef fishing, snapper and morwong are the main targets. Further out you can troll for striped and yellowfin tuna and marlin, with albacore out off the shelf.

Blowhole Point is one of the finest rock fishing spots on the coast, and one of the easiest to reach by road. Live baits, which can be caught in the harbour, are drifted off the point for kingfish and tuna, while snapper and salmon are also taken.

South of Kiama, **Marsden Head** is the next great spot, with big trevally in the winter, spinning for tuna and kingfish, and salmon, tailor and snapper. Further south, **Werri Beach** and **Walkers Beach** have deep gutters holding salmon and tailor, with good summer catches of bream, whiting and flathead. Big fish can be caught off the rocks all the way to Gerroa, with top places including **Big Rock**, south of

GUIDE TO LOCAL FISH

	Minnamurra to Seven Mile Beach	Shoalhaven River
(BA) bass, Australian		•
(B) bream	•	•
(D) drummer, silver	•	
(F) flathead	•	•
(FL) flounder		•
(G) garfish		•
(GR) groper	•	
(KI) kingfish, yellowtail	•	
(LU) luderick	•	•
(ML) marlin	•	
(MO) morwong	•	
(MU) mulloway	•	•
(RB) rock blackfish	•	
(SA) salmon, Australian	•	•
(S) snapper	•	
(T) tailor	•	•
(TR) trevally	•	
(TU) tuna	•	
(W) whiting	•	•

Fishing the rocks at Black Head near Gerroa

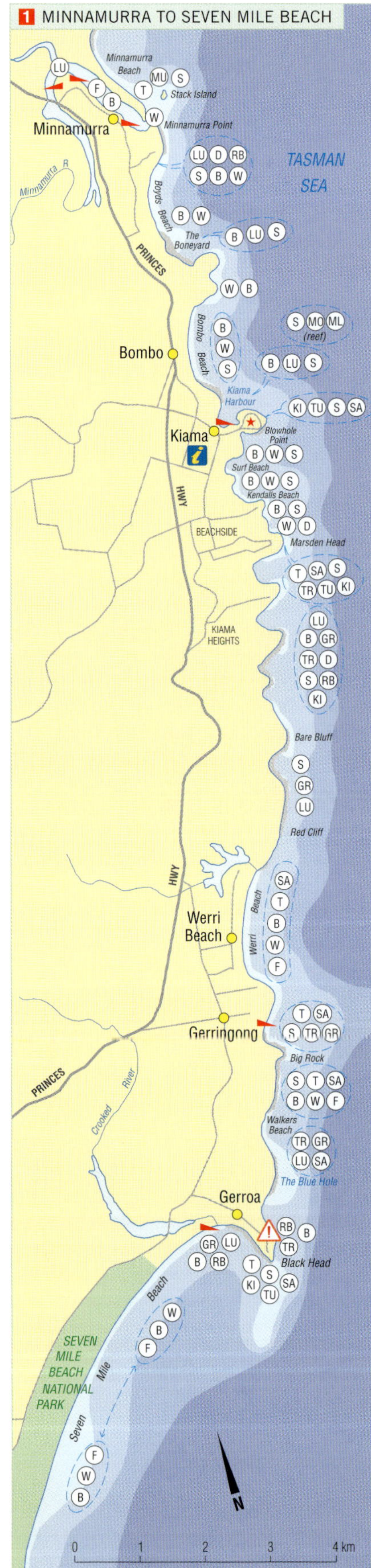

Gerringong; **The Blue Hole**, past Walkers Beach; and **Black Head**, at Gerroa. Small boats can be launched from the protected northern end of the **Seven Mile Beach** at Gerroa, and this most popular beach is wonderful for whiting and bream and the odd flathead in the summer.

SHOALHAVEN RIVER

Shoalhaven River provides a lot of interest for boat anglers who are after great estuary fare like whiting, flathead, bream, luderick, tailor and even mulloway. The best baits are right there on the sand flats – squirt worms and nippers are abundant and will catch anything you might encounter. The **Shoalhaven entrance** is often closed but sometimes opens after big floods. Fishing inside the entrance or from the beaches will yield whiting, bream and flathead, with nipper available all around the inner shore. The reef near O'Keefes Point and **Berrys Canal** are the best places for big mulloway. The canal runs down to the entrance of the Crookhaven River and its island-filled estuary, Curleys Bay, where bream, flathead and luderick are in good numbers. One hot spot for luderick is **Greenwell Point**, just south of the boat ramps, and the flathead drifting is good from Greenwell Point to the wharf just inside the entrance. Comerong Bay, behind the entrance, is very shallow, but there is drifting for flathead and good bream water near the shore. Outside, anglers will do well on the beaches in either direction, seeking whiting, bream, tailor and salmon.

Typical shoreline around the Shoalhaven district

Into the Shoalhaven proper there is an excellent flathead drifting run on the incoming tide from **O'Keefes Point** to the **Broughton Creek** entrance. The river is then split by islands and sandbars. Anchor in the sand flats east of **Numbaa Island** to catch flathead on a rising tide. Past the island, a buoy marks a sand flat that is exposed at low tide. In this area there is good drifting for flathead along the northern shore on a run-out tide. Bream, luderick, whiting and flathead are at the eastern head of **Pig Island**. On the northern bank there is a high paper mill that marks a prime spot for bream and luderick, and some really big mulloway. Beyond the island is a reef, dangerous for boating but excellent for luderick and bream at night. The Shoalhaven is well served for boat ramps.

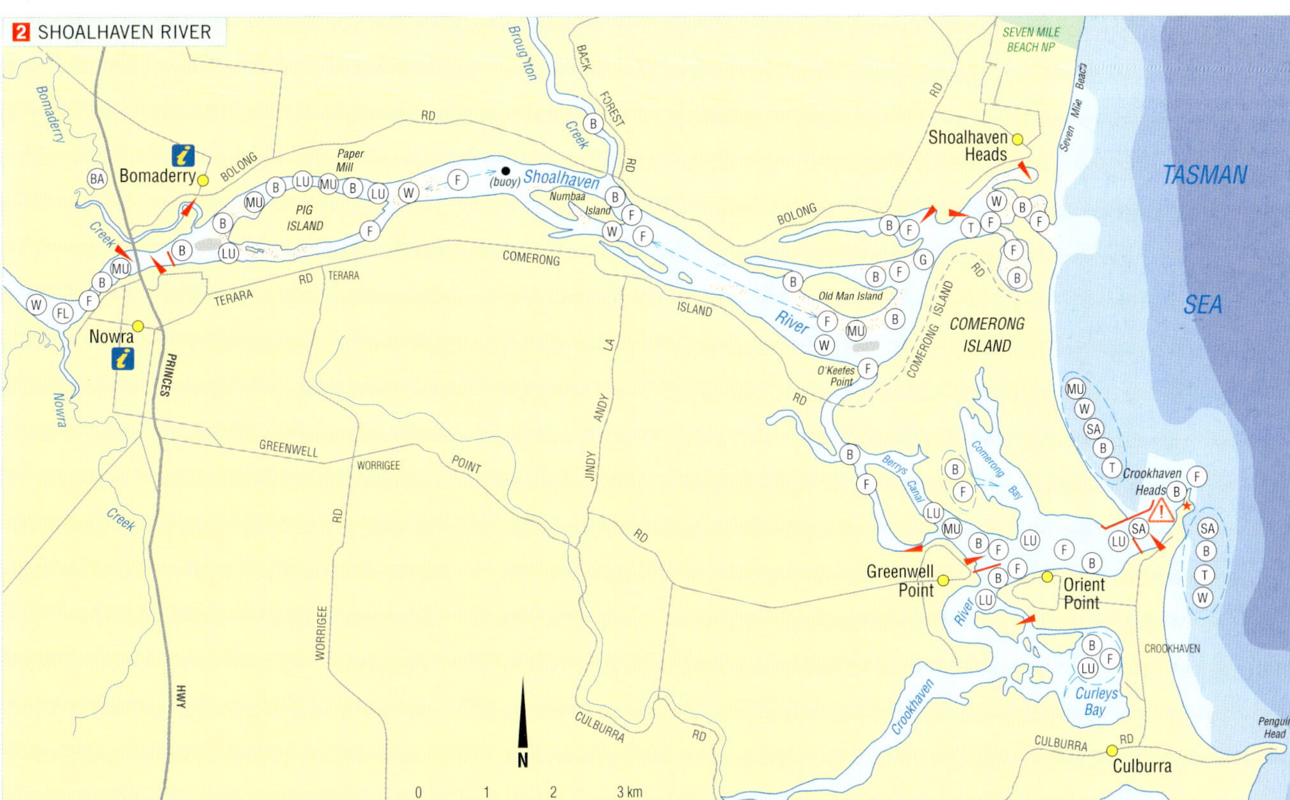

Jervis Bay to Lake Conjola

Type of fishing
bay, beach, lake, offshore, reef, rock
Target fish
bream, flathead, luderick, whiting, yellowtail kingfish

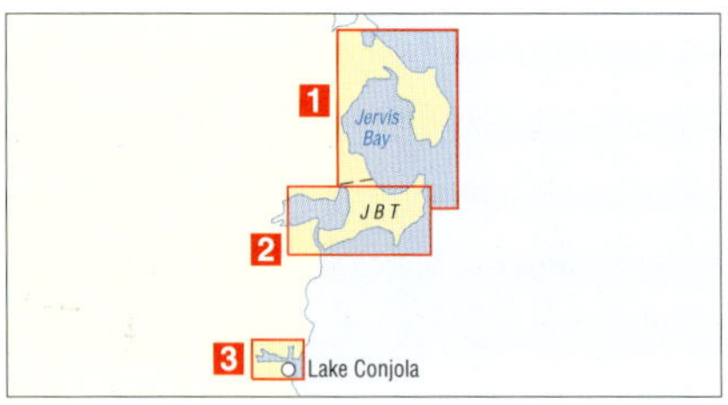

Jervis Bay offers a combination of good rock, boat and land fishing in the bay itself, and excellent offshore fishing at the Sir Joseph Young Banks. In the Sussex Inlet area, the excavation of canals has expanded the fishing water. Lake Conjola, a relatively quiet estuary, rates as one of the most pleasant places to fish in New South Wales.

JERVIS BAY

The Jervis Bay area has top rate rock fishing on the low rock ledges among the high cliffs of the **Beecroft Peninsula**. Surface fish such as kingfish, bonito and tuna are the targets, with marlin a welcome surprise, along with snapper and rock blackfish in the washes. Rock fishing at Beecroft Head, Eves Ravine, Never Fail, Devils Gorge and The Ladders is only for those with experience who can deal with the hazards of using ropes and ladders and carrying large fish.

The entrance to Jervis Bay has a reef known as the **Middle Ground**, a good drifting area for flathead and bream, but also carrying tuna, tailor, kingfish, bonito and trevally. Inside, on the south-western side of the Beecroft Peninsula, there is good land and boat fishing for snapper, rock blackfish, salmon, bream, trevally and an abundance of garfish. Further north, inshore drifting offers flathead, bream, flounder and whiting, but any southerly blow funnels through here and makes boating hazardous.

The rest of the bay is good and safe fishing, mainly from the beaches, for whiting, bream and flathead, though other species are also present.

Jervis Bay is now a marine park with the likelihood that areas within the bay will be closed to fishing. Contact Jervis Bay Marine Park on (02) 4441 7752 for details.

The greatest attraction of the Jervis Bay area is the big offshore reef known as the **Sir Joseph Young Banks**, lying about 4 km north-east of Beecroft Head and best fished from October to May. The northern end of the reef is good for snapper and big kingfish, and the outer side of the reef is frequented by marlin and tuna. Over the reef there is bottom fishing for snapper, morwong, trevally and kingfish.

Two other offshore spots are the **Nowra Hill Ground**, 4 km north-east of Penguin Head (snapper, mulloway, teraglin, kingfish) and **The Shallows** to the north of Currarong (kingfish, snapper, mulloway).

SUSSEX INLET

Access to the coast is difficult between Jervis Bay and Cape St George and the area is not heavily fished. Rock spots around **Green Rock** have luderick, rock blackfish and bream. **Cave Beach** is renowned for its salmon.

The beaches around the entrance to Sussex Inlet provide brilliant fishing for bream, salmon and tailor, while the rock platforms on the southern side of the inlet fish very well at dawn and dusk for these same fish, and also luderick.

Sussex Inlet carries bream, whiting and flathead in large numbers, with luderick in the weed beds and around rocky areas,

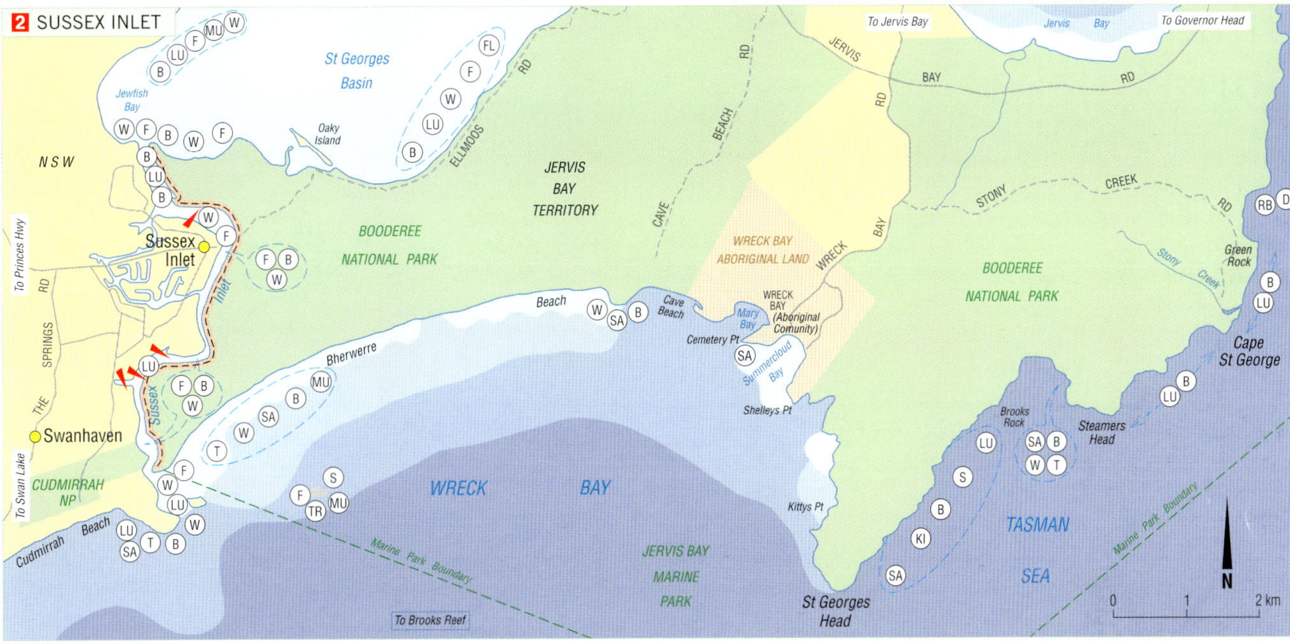

especially near the entrance. Boat fishing and shore-based angling will be rewarded here, particularly at slack water on a high tide.

St Georges Basin is best where the inlet enters the lake, either for shore angling or drifting, mainly for flathead. The shores of the lake offer good fishing, with marshes and mud banks creating natural food sources for bream, luderick, flathead and whiting. Nearby **Swan Lake** has similar fishing, with bream the target fish.

GUIDE TO LOCAL FISH

	Jervis Bay	Sussex Inlet	Lake Conjola
(BT) bonito	•		
(B) bream	•	•	•
(D) drummer	•	•	
(F) flathead	•	•	•
(FL) flounder	•	•	•
(G) garfish	•		•
(GR) groper			•
(KI) kingfish, yellowtail	•	•	
(LJ) leatherjacket	•		•
(LU) luderick	•	•	•
(ML) marlin	•		
(M) mullet	•		•
(MU) mulloway	•	•	•
(RB) rock blackfish	•	•	•
(SA) salmon, Australian	•	•	•
(S) snapper	•	•	•
(T) tailor	•	•	•
(TR) trevally	•	•	
(TU) tuna	•		
(W) whiting	•	•	•

About 1 km offshore, an extensive gravelly area is ideal for drifting for snapper, morwong, flathead and trevally, and further out Brooks Reef attracts kingfish, morwong, snapper and tuna.

LAKE CONJOLA

Lake Conjola is part of a lake system entering the sea at Cunjurong, south of Sussex Inlet. The attraction on the sand flats of the lower part of Lake Conjola is big flathead, while flounder, garfish, bream, luderick and mullet are also on the menu. The upper lake fishes well for bream, flathead, mulloway and whiting, particularly in summer. The prime position in the lake is The Steps, at the entrance to the channel between the lakes, where a drop into deep water creates an ambush point for flathead and bream.

Outside the lake is Green Island, separated from the land by a shallow sand spit. Anglers can walk across to the island on low tide or wade through chest-deep water at high tide. On the ocean side of the island groper can be caught, along with snapper, bream, luderick and rock blackfish. **Conjola Beach** is a favoured place for anglers pursuing flathead, whiting, salmon, tailor, bream and occasionally mulloway.

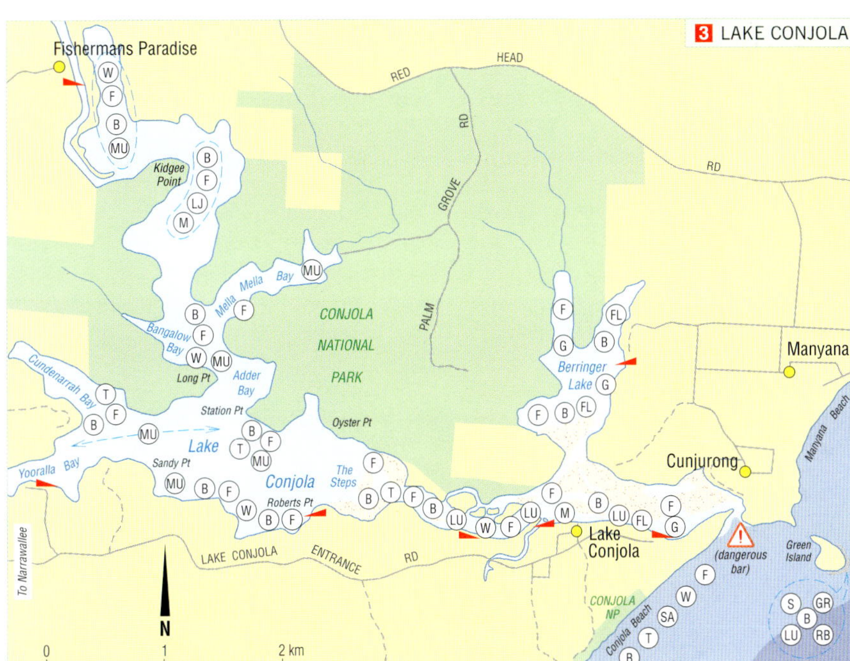

Ulladulla to Durras Lake

Type of fishing
beach, estuary, harbour, lake, rock

Target fish
Australian salmon, bream, flathead, luderick, snapper, tailor, whiting

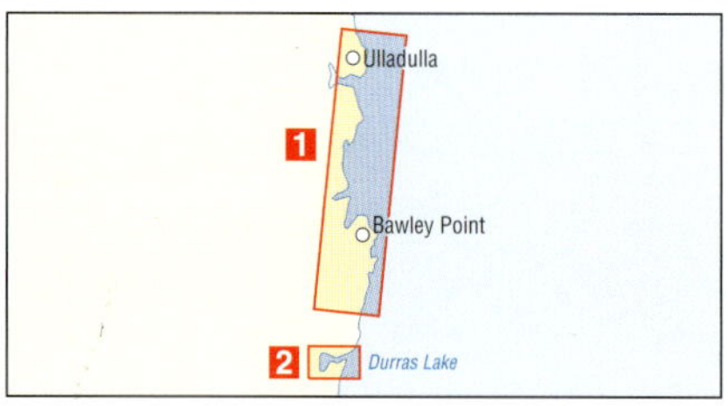

GUIDE TO LOCAL FISH

	Ulladulla to Point Upright	Tabourie Lake	Durras Lake
(B) bream	•	•	•
(F) flathead	•	•	•
(GR) groper	•		
(KI) kingfish, yellowtail	•	•	
(LU) luderick	•	•	•
(MO) morwong	•		
(M) mullet			•
(MU) mulloway	•	•	
(RB) rock blackfish	•	•	
(SA) salmon, Australian	•		
(S) snapper	•		
(T) tailor	•		
(TR) trevally	•		
(TU) tuna	•	•	
(W) whiting	•	•	•

Anglers flock to this part of the New South Wales coast for the combination of beach, rock, harbour and estuary fishing. The offshore islands between Bawley Point and Point Upright reward boat anglers with yellowtail kingfish, tuna, snapper and morwong.

ULLADULLA TO POINT UPRIGHT

North of Ulladulla, **Mollymook Beach** is a great spot for salmon, tailor, bream and flathead. **Ulladulla Harbour** should not be overlooked by anglers, as bream, tailor and salmon abound there, with luderick, rock blackfish and bream around the harbour rocks. The harbour fishes best when white water is breaking on the outer reef. Outside the reef are salmon, mulloway, snapper and trevally, but these are best sought by boat, as fishing from the exposed reef is dangerous.

There are good rock ledges around Ulladulla for tailor, bream, luderick and rock blackfish, particularly at **Warden Head**. Two of the best fishing beaches in the area are **Rennies Beach**, especially after a storm, for bream and mulloway, and **Racecourse Beach** for salmon and tailor.

Further south is the wide entrance to **Burrill Lake**, with bream and luderick the main targets from **Horseshoe Beach**, on the coast, up to the lake itself. This is a very good area for land fishing, with the **Princes Highway Bridge** excellent for bream and the odd mulloway. The sand flats and channels in the lake produce whiting and big flathead, best caught with live poddy mullet, lures or worms and yabbies taken from the sand flats. Luderick and bream are around the lake shores. Three boat ramps in the lake provide good access for boat fishing.

Lagoon Head is another of the top rock fishing spots on the coast. Fishing off the ledges here can yield tailor, bream, luderick and rock blackfish.

The very best of beach and rock fishing can be found in the beautiful stretch of

Ulladulla Harbour has resident populations of bream, luderick, rock blackfish, tailor and salmon

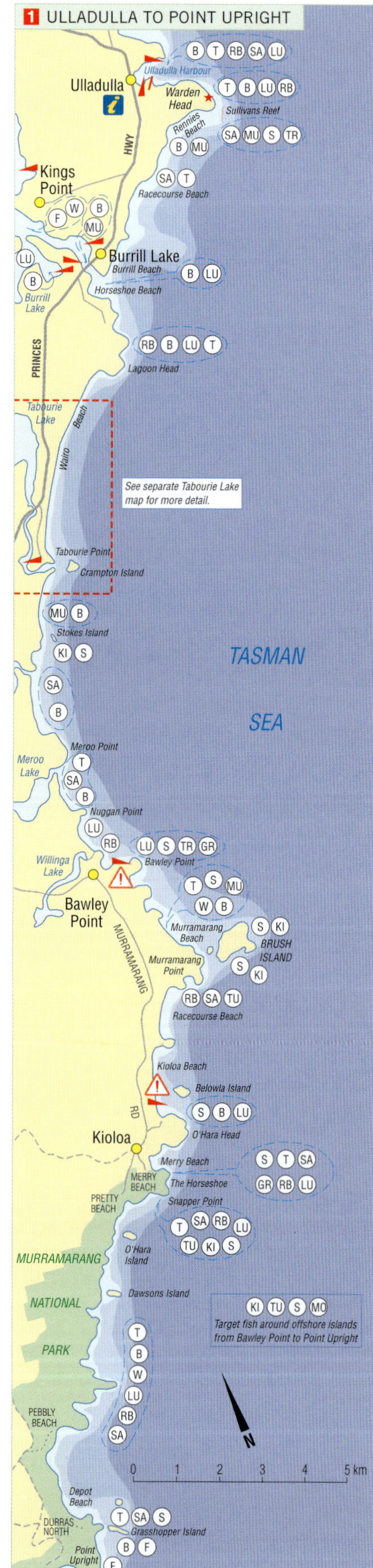

coastline from Bawley Point to south of Point Upright. The rock platforms are high and safe, and they front deep water. Offshore, many small islands attract kingfish, snapper and various tunas. Many rocks are accessible for the collection of bait like cunjevoi, crabs, shellfish and cabbage weed, while the beaches abound with pippis and worms.

Bawley Point is not typical as the rock slopes down to the sea, and it requires long casts. Luderick, snapper, trevally and groper are among the many species to be caught here. **Murramarang Beach** is best for tailor, salmon and mulloway, with some whiting and bream. Offshore, **Brush Island** often teems with snapper and yellowtail kingfish.

Merry Beach is an outstanding rock fishing area. The rocks form a crescent and the main area, known as **The Horseshoe**, is a place for experienced devotees with cliff gaffs seeking big snapper, groper, tailor, salmon, luderick and rock blackfish. **Snapper Point** is a moderately high platform with deep water close in. It attracts big fish from their offshore highway, and some notable catches of tuna and kingfish are made on live bait. There is also potential for catches of snapper, tailor, salmon, rock blackfish and luderick.

Further south, offshore from Depot Beach and around Grasshopper Island, you may be rewarded with large numbers of tailor and salmon, along with bream, flathead and snapper. Big flathead are taken on the drift outside Point Upright.

Near Lagoon Head the surf fishing from the beach is productive, especially at dawn and dusk

TABOURIE LAKE

Stretching south from Lagoon Head to Tabourie Point, **Wairo Beach** is good for whiting, bream and mulloway. **Crampton Island** can be reached across the sand at low tide, and has high cliffs on the south-eastern side, allowing spinning for kingfish and tuna. There are luderick, rock blackfish and bream close in on the south-east.

Along **Tabourie Creek** luderick, flathead and bream are the main targets. There is a safe launching ramp on the creek bank near the entrance. In the lake, drift for flathead along the channels between the sand flats, and seek whiting around weed patches.

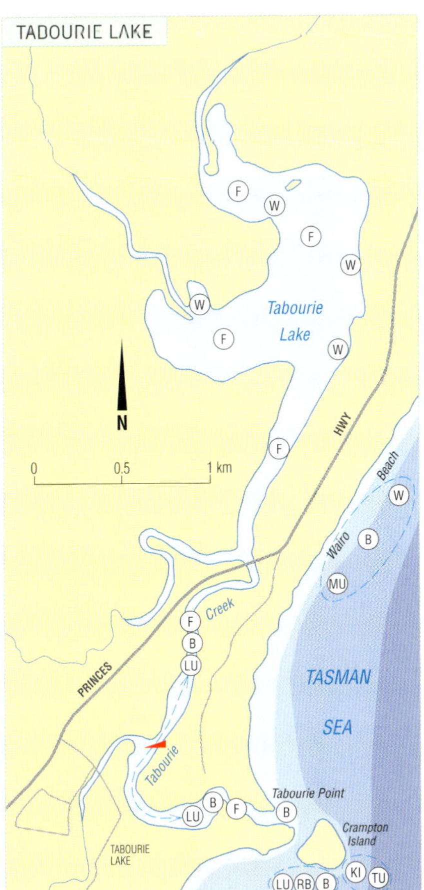

DURRAS LAKE

Throughout the year, Durras Lake is among the best bream spots along the whole New South Wales coast, although the fish have a tendency at times to retreat to the deep channels in the upper reaches. The lake is also an excellent producer of flathead, whiting and mullet. When it is open to the sea, the prawning runs on the new moon summer nights can be terrific. The lake abuts a superb surf beach, which is excellent for whiting in the summer, and is bounded by national park and bushland, which provides a tranquil fishing experience. Boats can be launched into the lake from the southern shore near the entrance.

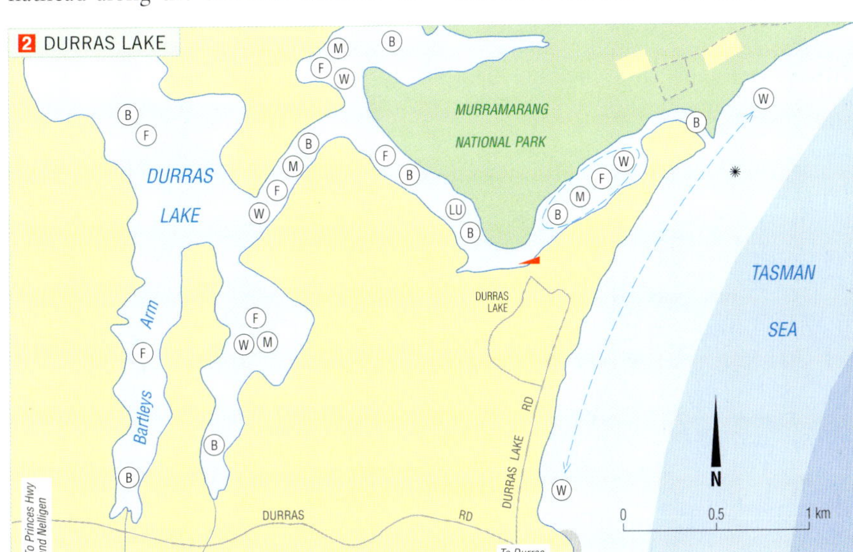

Bermagui Region

The stunningly beautiful far south coast of New South Wales is not only easy on the eye but is also almost perfect for fishing in all forms (lake, estuary, offshore and big game). Anglers can enjoy the spectacularly rugged coastline, the frequently mist-covered mountains and the unspoiled countryside.

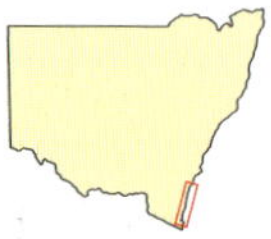

The bays and headlands provide virtually continuous rock and beach fishing, and there are many close-in gravel patches and reefs to be explored by inshore boat anglers. The beautiful estuaries are the joy of the southern scene for most anglers, with bream flathead and whiting as the main targets, and mulloway the cream on the cake. Offshore, the southern game fishing grounds are inhabited by various tunas, bonito, kingfish, blue and black marlin and sharks.

Weather

Watch out for north-easterlies, as they can be dangerous for small craft if winds are over 15 knots. Generally conditions are good, but be aware of south-west changes, which can come in very fast. The best time for fishing is early morning, from daybreak to about 10.30 a.m., before the wind comes

WHERE TO FISH

Bermagui Region

BATEMANS BAY TO BROULEE ● 116

Clyde River is an easy estuary to fish, and there is good shore fishing south of Batemans Bay. Jimmies Island provides a land and boat bonanza, and there is access to reef fishing in Broulee Bay.

MORUYA TO KIANGA LAKE ● 118

Moruya River is a perfect estuary for both land and boat fishing, with bass upstream. Tuross and Coila lakes are complex and picturesque, with plenty of fish.

NAROOMA TO WALLAGA LAKE ● 120

At Narooma, there is plenty of action in Wagonga Inlet, and good beach and rock fishing nearby. Montague Island is a mecca for boat fishers.

BERMAGUI TO WAPENGO LAKE ● 122

A succession of rocks, headlands, beaches and inlets makes this one of the most interesting stretches of fishing coastline in New South Wales.

TATHRA TO PAMBULA ● 124

Tathra has good beach, estuary and bay fishing, but the high Tathra Wharf is the supreme fishing spot in the area. Good bay, river, lake, rock and beach angling prevail along the coast, with reef fishing offshore.

EDEN TO GREEN CAPE ● 126

The wharves at Eden are very popular with holiday anglers, Twofold Bay has a huge and sheltered inshore area with deepwater fishing, and there is great and rugged rock fishing at Green Cape.

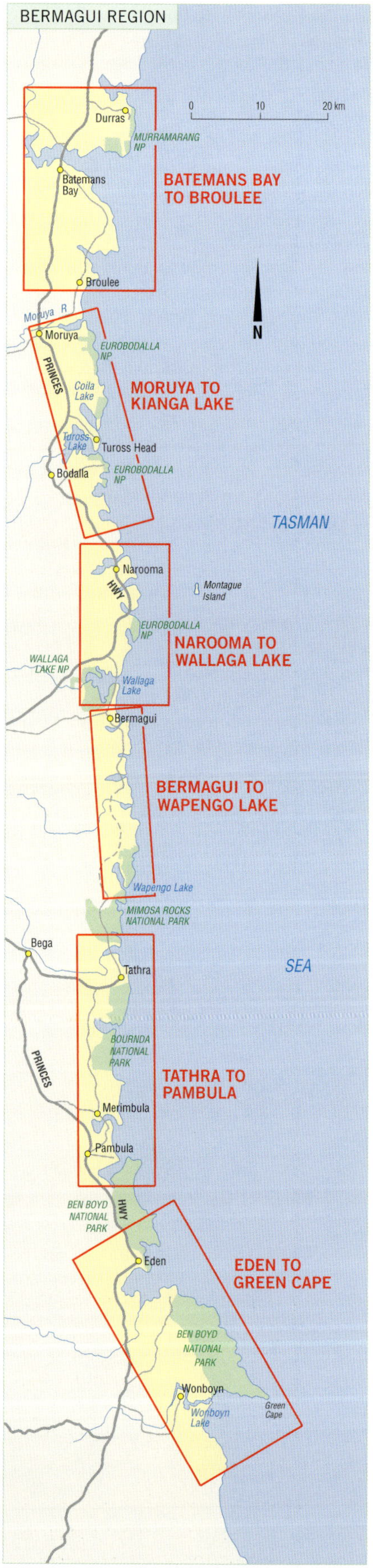

Boat fishing on the Clyde River at Nelligen near Batemans Bay

GUIDE TO LOCAL FISH

barracouta
bass, Australian
bonito
bream, black
bream, yellowfin
drummer, silver
flathead
flathead, dusky
flounder
garfish
groper
gurnard
john dory
kingfish, yellowtail
leatherjacket
luderick
mackerel, slimy
marlin, black
marlin, blue
marlin, striped
morwong
mullet
mulloway
nannygai
pike, striped sea
rock blackfish
salmon, Australian
shark
snapper
sweep
tailor
tarwhine
teraglin
trevally, silver
trumpeter
tuna, bigeye
tuna, mackerel
tuna, longtail
tuna, southern bluefin
tuna, striped
tuna, yellowfin
wahoo
whiting, King George
whiting, sand
whiting, trumpeter

Many large sharks have been caught from the Tathra Wharf as well as smaller resident fish such as trevally, yellowtail, salmon and tailor

up. At Eden, the north-easterly blows in mid-morning, but the area generally has calm water inshore and rough water out wide. Contact the Coast Guard, Coastal Patrol, or Weather Bureau on tel. (02) 9296 1555 or visit the website: www.bom.gov.au

Boating

It is worth investing in Admiralty charts if you are navigating this coast, as there are dozens of bomboras and hazardous rocky headlands and features such as Black Rock, near Batemans Bay. There are a considerable number of dangerous bar crossings: the bar at Tuross Lake should never be attempted by boat; the Narooma bar at the entrance to Wagonga Inlet can be fearsome and should only be attempted by experienced boaters; the bars at Merimbula and Pambula require careful navigation; and the bar at Wonboyn Lake is shallow and hazardous.

Safety comes first when you have to negotiate a bar crossing. Some bars, such as the one at Merimbula, can appear relatively calm but you should never go out to sea with the idea that crossing any bar will be easy. It pays to observe the bar before attempting passage. If you haven't crossed the bar before then seek local advice and check with a local NSW Maritime officer.

FURTHER INFORMATION

Fishing and boating *NSW Fisheries has offices at Suite 8, Braysyth Bldg, Cnr Beach Rd and Orien St, Batemans Bay, tel. (02) 4472 4032; 13 Cocora St, Eden, tel. (02) 6496 1377; and Riverside Drive, Narooma, tel. (02) 4476 2072. NSW Maritime has an office at 95 Campbell St, Narooma, tel. (02) 4476 2006. The Coast Guard has a base at Bermagui, tel. (02) 6493 4506. The Coastal Patrol has bases at Batemans Bay, tel. (02) 4472 3060; Moruya Heads, tel. (02) 4474 2770; Narooma, tel. (02) 4476 1443; Merimbula, tel. (02) 6495 3331; and Eden, tel. (02) 6496 2167.*

Tourist centres *Cnr Princes Hwy and Beach Rd, Batemans Bay, tel. (02) 4472 6900; 91 Gipps St, Bega, tel. (02) 6492 2045; Lamont St, Bermagui, tel. (02) 6493 3054; Princes Hwy, Eden, tel. (02) 6496 1953; Beach St, Merimbula, tel. (02) 6497 4900; Princes Hwy, Narooma, tel. (02) 4476 2881.*

Batemans Bay to Broulee

Type of fishing
bay, beach, estuary, offshore, reef, river, rock

Target fish
Australian salmon, bream, flathead, luderick, snapper

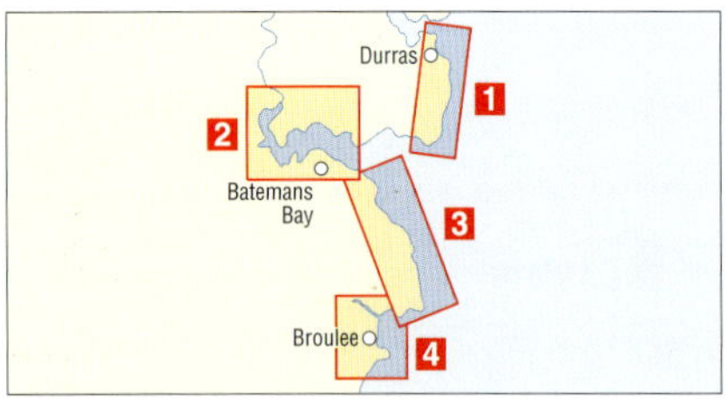

The remote coastal country between Durras and Batemans Bay allows solitary and rewarding fishing for adventurous anglers, while Batemans Bay itself, with its wide but sheltered bay, its navigable river entrance and a vast and sheltered estuary region, is one of the most popular fishing areas of the south coast. Batehaven to Burrewarra Point is great flathead drifting territory.

DURRAS TO NORTH HEAD

Four-wheel drive and walking tracks provide the only access to the rugged rock locations and small beaches in this area, where snapper, Australian salmon, bream, tailor, luderick and rock blackfish can be sought.

Wasp Island lies off the southern end of Beagle Bay. Boat anglers can catch snapper close to the island, while morwong, teraglin and kingfish can be taken on the drift on the eastern side. Further out is good live bait or trolling water for yellowfin tuna and marlin. The shoal area to the south of Wasp Head should only be fished in calm conditions, but it does carry a lot of snapper.

Along this stretch of coast, the most accessible places are **Flat Rock Island** for big luderick, rock blackfish, snapper and bream; **Myrtle Beach** for snapper, salmon and tailor; **Green Point** for snapper, bream, luderick and rock blackfish; **Richmond Beach** for salmon and tailor, with snapper and groper off the rocks; **Oaky Beach** for salmon, tailor and snapper, and the rocks at its southern end for luderick, drummer, snapper and groper; **North Head** for snapper, groper, luderick, bream and tailor; and **Acheron Ledge**, where snapper and kingfish are the main targets.

BATEMANS BAY AND CLYDE RIVER

Batemans Bay is a big camping and accommodation centre, and the supply of bait, tackle, boat hire and ramps leaves little for the angler to desire. Boating provides enormous variety, but there are plenty of productive places for land anglers.

Square Head, at the northern entrance to the bay, is a good land spot for yellowtail kingfish, tailor, bream and whiting. On the opposite shore, in the township of **Batemans Bay**, fishing from the rock will yield flathead, mulloway and luderick.

The river and estuary area is exciting. The caravan park beach is a good spot for bream and whiting, and ideal for children on their first forays into fishing. The jetties on the southern bank are also good, particularly for bream.

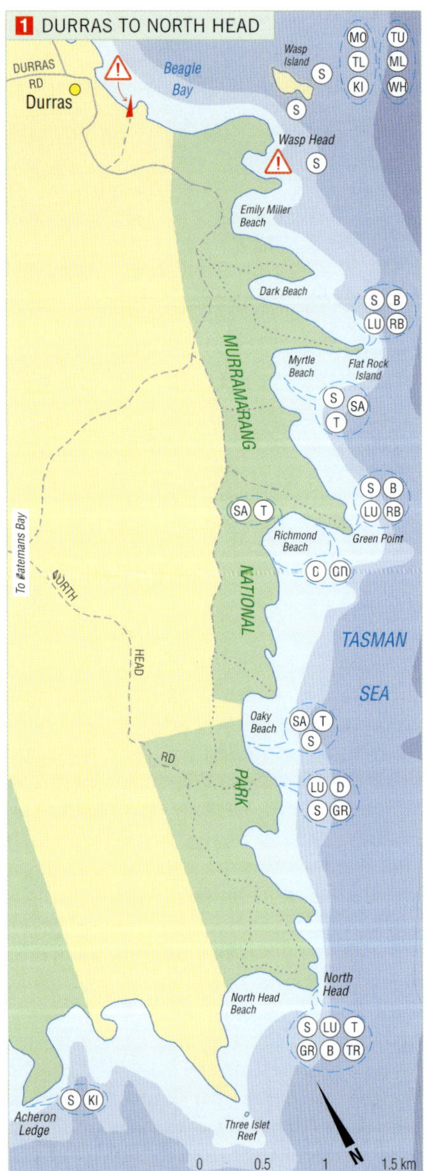

Most of the estuary is best tackled by boat anglers, and can be fished as far up as Nelligen and beyond. The Clyde River Bridge, fished by boat on a falling tide, can produce some large mulloway. Between the bridge and the powerlines is best for bream, with good possibilities for flathead, mulloway and whiting. Beyond the powerlines are the oyster leases, always a haunt for bream, especially at high tide.

The estuary narrows to **Chinamans Point**, where shallow reefs are frequented by mulloway, and in the bay on the opposite shore there is a deep hole carrying very big flathead and mulloway.

Drifting for flathead will take you up the estuary, past the navigable eastern side of **Big Island**, where it may pay to anchor on the falling tide and baitfish for flathead. Further along the Clyde to Nelligen, anglers can try for bream, flathead, flounder and mulloway. Beyond Nelligen there is some of the best water for bass.

BATEHAVEN TO BURREWARRA POINT

The south-west side of **Snapper Island** is excellent for bream and the eastern side produces flathead and whiting. When boating in this area beware of breaking waves. There is land-based angling at Observation Head.

The run down from the southern end of Batemans Bay to Burrewarra Point has some good shore fishing spots. **Corrigans Beach**, on the west side of Observation Head, is particularly good for tailor, and trolling close to the shore between Point Pleasure and Denhams Beach can yield yellowtail kingfish.

Offshore, about 4 km east of Denhams Beach, are the **Tollgate Islands**, where good numbers of flathead are taken on the shallow sands to the south and east of the islands. Snapper and morwong may be caught closer in, while there are often large numbers of bait fish sheltering between the islands. Trolling out to the east can yield good catches of yellowfin and mackerel tuna, wahoo and marlin.

The headland at **Lilli Pilli** has a rough bottom and a float will be required, although a cast of 70 m on the southern side will drop a bait into a deep snapper hole. Tailor, salmon, bream and rock blackfish are the close-in fish. About 1 km offshore, **Black Rock** has a reef extending out to the east, again good for snapper and morwong.

Mosquito Bay, which has a launching ramp, and **Garden Bay** are great spots for garfish and bream. **South Head** has a rough area close inshore, but this attracts snapper,

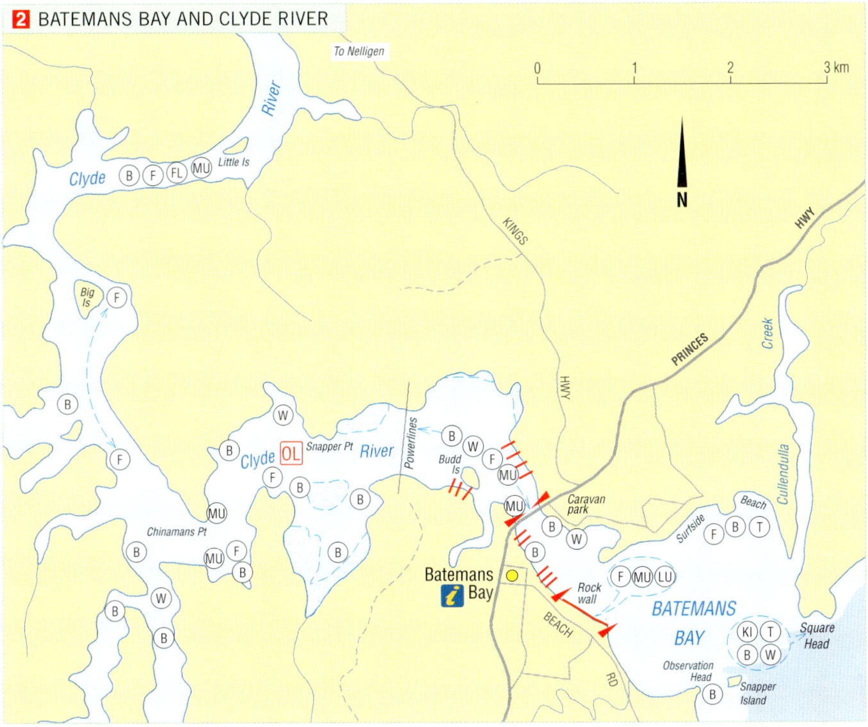

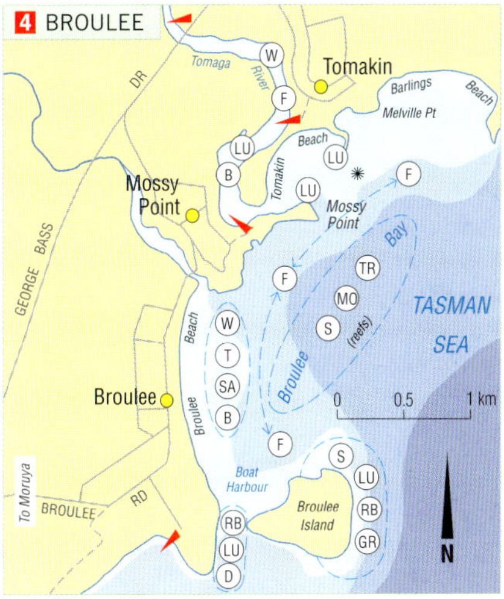

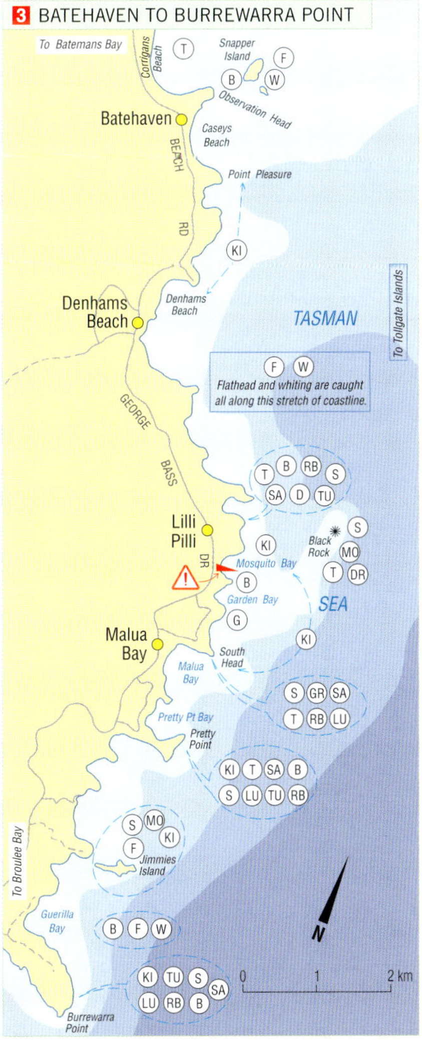

groper, salmon and tailor, along with weed-eating rock blackfish and luderick.

South Head attracts the inshore rock fish, but boat anglers can take big hauls of kingfish just offshore. **Pretty Point** is a rope and ladder location for the hardy, but they can lure cast or baitfish for kingfish and tuna, as well as going after the good numbers of salmon, tailor, bream, luderick, snapper and rock blackfish.

Jimmies Island, connected to the mainland, is surrounded by mixed reef and sand bottom, making it a great spot for land and boat anglers alike. Snapper, morwong, flathead and kingfish are the main targets in an area that can provide a bonanza at times. At **Guerilla Bay** you can launch your boat from the beach to head north to Jimmies Island, or fish within this delightful bay for bream and flathead, with whiting a possibility in autumn and winter.

Burrewarra Point projects well to the east and attracts ocean fish. Kingfish and tuna are the targets for spinning, and it can produce snapper, bream, Australian salmon, luderick and rock blackfish close inshore. It is a long walk to the point but the effort can be well worthwhile.

BROULEE

The main catch in the **Tomaga River** is bream, but there are luderick around weed beds and on the rocky parts of the shore, and flathead and whiting around the sand flats. The river provides safe access to the sea for boats and a relatively sheltered bay outside (except in a southerly), where there is good reef fishing for snapper, morwong and trevally, and drifting for flathead. Boat anglers can fish for the snapper, luderick, rock blackfish and groper close in to **Broulee Island**.

Broulee Beach is ideal for whiting, using the worms that are plentiful on the beach. There are also tailor, Australian salmon and bream off the beach, and luderick, rock blackfish and some silver drummer around the headland, which also creates a sheltered place for beach launching.

GUIDE TO LOCAL FISH

	Durras to North Head	Batemans Bay and Clyde River	Batehaven to Burrewarra Point	Broulee
(B) bream	•	•	•	•
(D) drummer, silver	•		•	•
(F) flathead		•	•	•
(FL) flounder		•		
(G) garfish			•	
(GR) groper	•		•	•
(DR) john dory			•	
(KI) kingfish, yellowtail	•	•	•	
(LU) luderick	•	•	•	•
(ML) marlin	•			
(MO) morwong	•		•	•
(MU) mulloway		•		
(RB) rock blackfish	•		•	•
(SA) salmon, Australian	•		•	•
(S) snapper	•		•	•
(T) tailor	•	•	•	•
(TL) teraglin	•			
(TR) trevally	•			•
(TU) tuna	•		•	
(WH) wahoo	•			
(W) whiting		•	•	•

Moruya to Kianga Lake

Type of fishing
beach, estuary, lake, reef, river, rock
Target fish
Australian salmon, bream, flathead, tailor, yellowtail kingfish

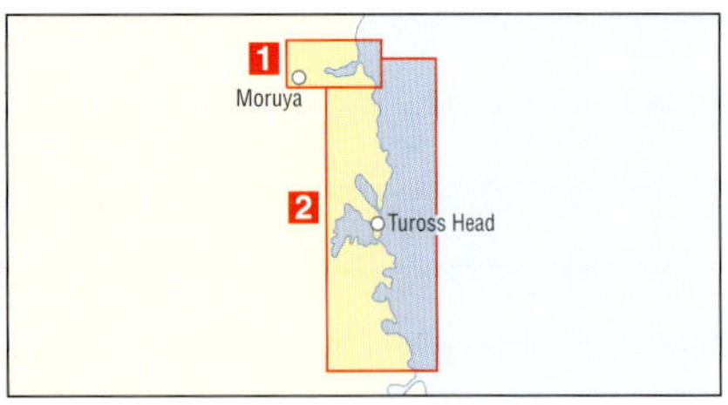

A feature of **Congo Point** is a long low rock shelf, and anglers must be aware of the tide and any build-up of waves. The shelf takes the angler to the trevally, bream and drummer, with snapper prevalent in winter.

Mullimburra Point attracts bream, rock blackfish, luderick, snapper and mulloway, with Australian salmon and tailor in summer. But the most popular rock location is **Bingie Bingie Point**, a low headland of rock, which is protected from north and south winds and has reliable fishing for salmon and tailor.

Past the Tuross Lake complex is **Potato Point**, where there are good rock platforms. Yellowtail kingfish come in over the summer period and can be caught on live baits, fish strips or lures. There are rock blackfish, sweep, salmon and tailor close in, and salmon and tailor are the targets from the beach north of Potato Point. There are reefs all around, creating good snapper and morwong grounds. Pinnacles due east of the point provide a focus for the best fishing.

Tarourga, Brou and Mummuga lakes are seldom open to the sea, but still carry flathead, whiting and bream. When the lakes are first open each year, the bream gather around the lake entrances to spawn, and the hauls are large. East of the lakes is **Brou Beach**, where there are plenty of worms for bait, and tailor and salmon are again the target fish. A reef about 1 km out from the beach attracts schools of bait fish and, in turn, kingfish, yellowfin tuna, marlin and shark.

Off Yellow Head, at **Dalmeny**, a reef extends 2 km or so out to sea, again providing good snapper and morwong fishing. The Dalmeny boat ramp is exposed to the ocean swell and is unsuitable in north-easterlies.

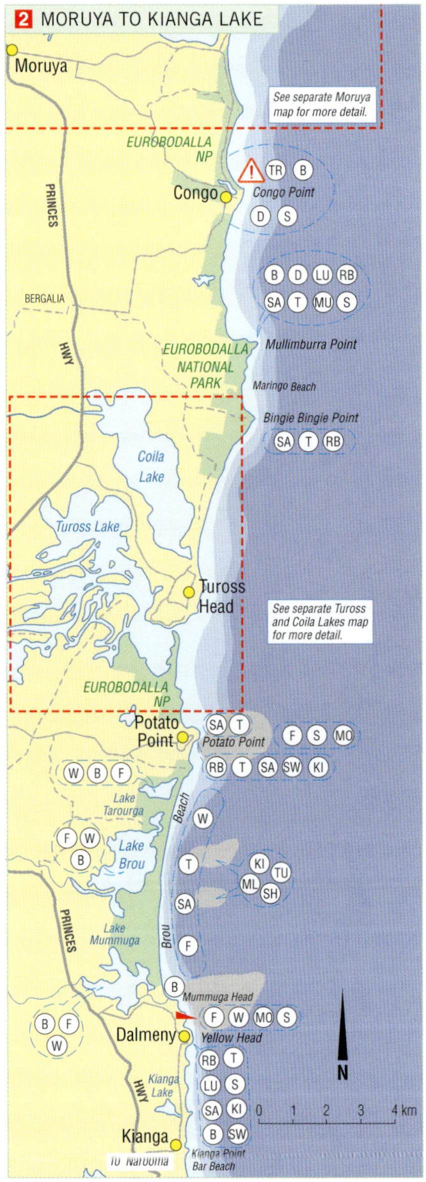

Outside the reef areas, drifting about 500 m offshore will produce big flathead and whiting over the sand and weed areas. The rock ledges at Dalmeny are dangerous in high seas, but the fish variety is great, including rock blackfish, luderick, sweep, salmon, bream, tailor, snapper and small kingfish.

The beaches between Dalmeny and Narooma are very popular as they are easy to reach. One of the best spots is a rock ledge near **Kianga Lake**, which allows casting behind the breakers.

MORUYA

The **Moruya River** winds down from deep in the hinterland and has bass fishing in the upper reaches. Its estuary fans out near the coast through oyster leases, channels and patches of sand, mud and mangrove, providing perfect conditions for flathead, whiting, bream, luderick and mulloway. The rock walls on both sides of the entrance are great platforms for seeking bream and flathead, while the channels and sandbanks running down to the river mouth are best in summer, when flathead and whiting are particularly prolific. Boating newcomers must take care because some sandbanks are just covered by water at high tide. The entrance to **Malabar Creek** on the northern side is the only exit for prawns when they are running with the new moon. The Princes Highway Bridge is also a fish attractor, with flathead, mulloway and schools of mullet.

Outside Moruya Heads, the **Bengello Beach** stretches some 5 km to the north, and it is known as a good spot for Australian salmon and tailor on pilchard bait, with flathead and john dory also present. Two parallel reefs, out from the airport and some 2 km offshore, create a wonderful kingfish ground. There is trolling for yellowfin tuna, and snapper and morwong between the reefs. On the south side of the heads, **Toragy Point** can be a good place for rock blackfish, salmon and snapper, with yellowtail kingfish a possibility. A long reef runs from Toragy Point to Pedro Point, and kingfish and snapper abound in this area, from about 500 m to 1.5 km out. Beyond that is fairly shallow sand, ideal for flathead, with some deeper holes for morwong.

GUIDE TO LOCAL FISH

	Moruya to Kianga Lake	Moruya	Tuross and Coila Lakes
(B) bream	●	●	●
(D) drummer, silver	●		
(F) flathead	●	●	●
(FL) flounder			●
(G) garfish			●
(DR) john dory		●	
(KI) kingfish, yellowtail	●	●	
(LU) luderick	●	●	●
(ML) marlin	●		
(MO) morwong	●	●	
(M) mullet		●	
(MU) mulloway	●	●	●
(RB) rock blackfish	●	●	
(SA) salmon, Australian	●	●	●
(SH) shark	●		
(S) snapper	●	●	
(SW) sweep	●		
(T) tailor	●	●	
(TR) trevally	●		
(TU) tuna	●	●	
(W) whiting	●	●	●

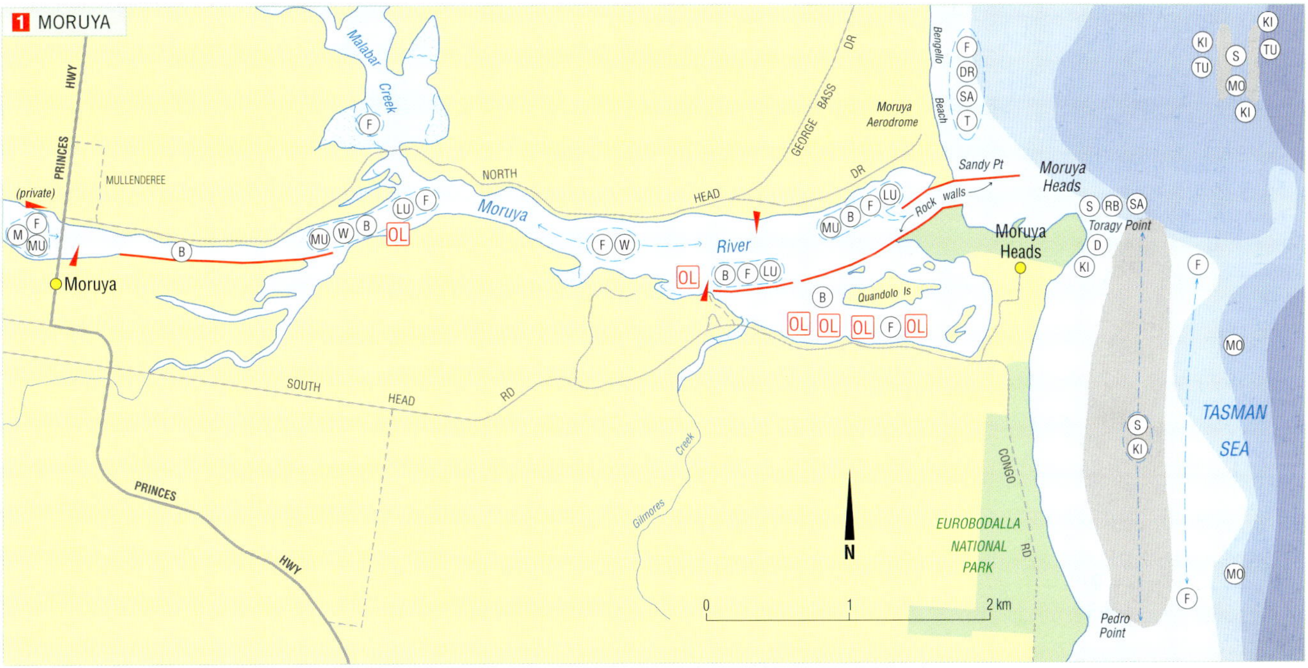

TUROSS AND COILA LAKES

The Tuross area, a complex and picturesque waterway, has everything for the estuary angler – hire boats, tackle and bait supplies, bait gathering spots and a variety of holiday accommodation. Coila Lake is often closed to the sea, but when it is open, particularly after heavy rain, the bream move down from Coila Creek. The target fish in the lake are bream, flathead, whiting and flounder. **Coila Creek**, running into the north-west of the lake, is great for bream, particularly if you fish from the southern bank in the Princes Highway Bridge area. Prawn or mullet gut baits, and berleying, will yield the best results.

Tuross Lake is sometimes closed, but even when it is open the bar should never be attempted by boat. **Sandy Point** is hailed as the best luderick spot in the state, while the channel past **Horse Island** carries big mulloway. The oyster leases north of Reedy Island are thick with bream on a high tide, while **Four Ways**, between Reedy and Cooper islands, attracts flathead, bream, luderick, whiting, flounder and mulloway. The **Tuross River** is good drifting for garfish and flathead before it branches into **Borang Lake**. This lake is very shallow and requires some careful navigation, but fishing the channels of the southern bank for enormous flathead is an exhilarating experience. The Tuross River becomes a bass haunt beyond the Princes Highway Bridge (not shown on the map).

Near the entrances to the lakes, anglers can fish for flathead, whiting, mulloway, bream and Australian salmon.

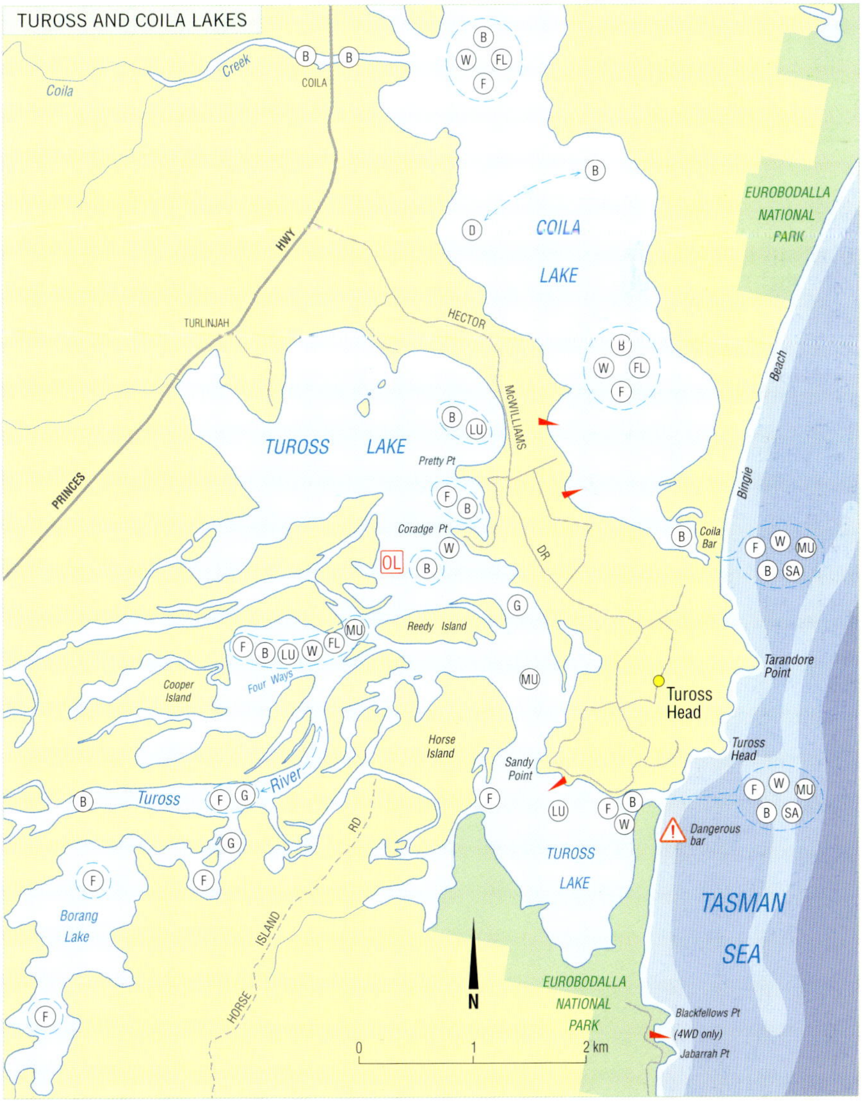

Naroomma to Wallaga Lake

Montague Island is one of the most famous game fishing spots on the south coast

Type of fishing
bay, beach, estuary, lake, offshore, rock, wharf
Target fish
bream, flathead, whiting

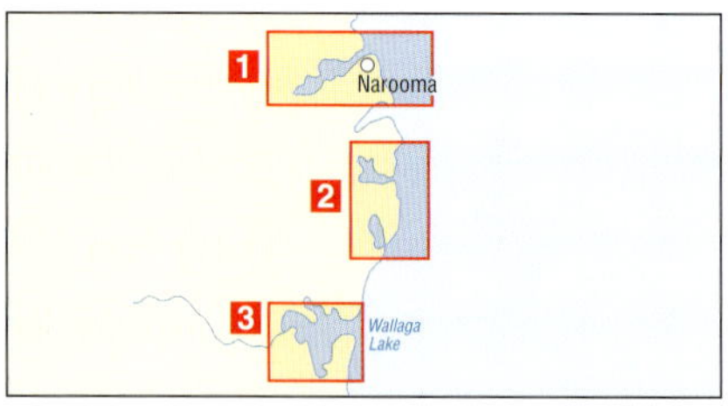

Wagonga Inlet, and further south, Corunna Lake, have large and varied fish populations, with plenty of bait. But the real action is at Montague Island or out past the reefs and onto the 100-fathom line, about 20 km out, which is legendary kingfish, tuna, marlin and general game fish territory. The shallow but extensive waters of Wallaga Lake, north of Bermagui, are popular for estuary fishing.

NAROOMA

Wagonga Inlet provides plenty of action for shore anglers and those people in boats who prefer estuary fishing to braving the Narooma bar. The sand flats, running from the entrance to the Princes Highway Bridge, are mainly flathead and whiting grounds, while the trawler wharf is a good luderick spot, and the trainer walls at the entrance are platforms for bream and tailor fishing.

West of the bridge, there are abundant flathead in the channels and some big mulloway in the holes, bream around the oyster leases, and some whiting and garfish. The inlet is well sheltered and the whole area has fine boat launching, boat hire and fishing facilities.

Outside, there is easy rock fishing from **Wagonga Head**, with tailor, bream, luderick and rock blackfish the main targets, while **Bar Beach** and **Narooma Beach** have Australian salmon, tailor and flathead, with bream and whiting in the gutters. Offshore, Narooma Beach also has fine flathead drifting over the sand for around 3 km. Similar conditions occur offshore from Little Dromedary Mountain down to Wallaga Lake.

The jewel of the coast between Narooma and Bermagui is **Montague Island**, 6 km east of Narooma and 22 km north of Bermagui. Narooma is the closest access, but its bar is dangerous and only those with experience or those prepared to listen to local advice should attempt the crossing.

Once at the island you will find an abundance of fish, particularly large yellowtail kingfish around the north-west side. The north shore generally produces yellowfin tuna, marlin, wahoo, dolphin fish and kingfish, with snapper plentiful for the bottom anglers. Schools of kingfish congregate in the south-east, and yellowfin tuna and marlin can be trolled on the eastern side. The **Aughinish Rocks**, south of the island and 3 m under water, can reward close-in anglers with snapper. Care should be taken in heavier weather, as waves can break over the reef.

CORUNNA LAKE AREA

This stretch of coast is secluded and difficult to access. The best of the coastal features are **Bogola Head** for tailor, salmon and bream; **Mystery Bay** for these same fish and also

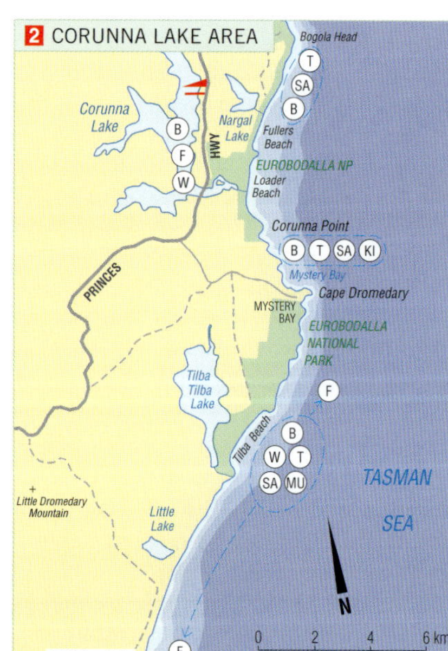

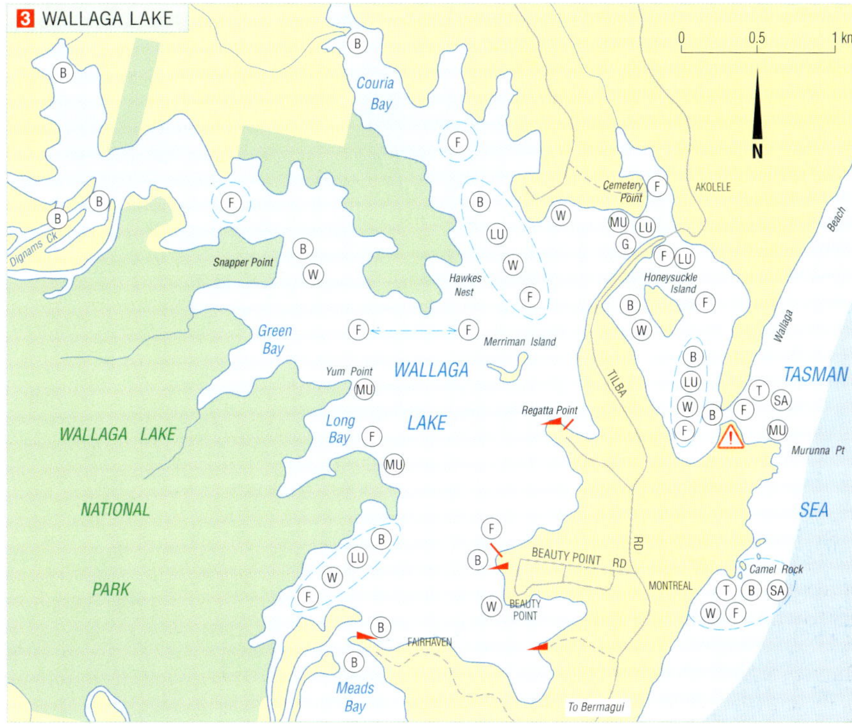

yellowtail kingfish; and **Tilba Beach** for bream, whiting, salmon, flathead, tailor and mulloway. There is a boat ramp at Mystery Bay suitable for small craft up to 4.5 m. Access to offshore grounds is possible from here. **Corunna Lake** is a poor fishery, but an excellent place to find weed bait for luderick. The lake itself can offer bream, flathead and whiting.

WALLAGA LAKE

Wallaga Lake is not always open to the sea, and the entrance is impassable at any time. When it is newly opened the fishing can be excellent. It is known for its flathead, which can reach 2 to 3 kg. The lake is wide and exposed, presenting a problem for small boat anglers in the wind, as it becomes very choppy.

GUIDE TO LOCAL FISH

	Narooma	Corunna Lake Area	Wallaga Lake
Ⓑ bream	●	●	●
Ⓕ flathead	●	●	●
Ⓖ garfish	●		●
(KI) kingfish, yellowtail		●	
(LU) luderick	●		●
(MU) mulloway	●	●	●
(RB) rock blackfish	●		
(SA) salmon, Australian	●	●	●
Ⓣ tailor	●	●	●
Ⓦ whiting	●	●	●

There are some good spots for shore-based anglers all around the estuary, but the best areas are in the entrance to the lake, between Honeysuckle Island and the bridge, and along the channel, which skirts along the northern shores of the lake and is deepest off Cemetery Point. Bream and sand whiting are taken on the incoming tide, while flathead are best caught on the outgoing tide. Sand flats at low tide are revealed around the entrance area, where nippers can be pumped.

Mulloway are not prolific in the lake, but they can be fished at low tide in the deeper areas off **Cemetery Point** and around **Yum Point**, on the southern side.

Luderick and garfish are sought near the **Tilba Road Bridge**. Use a float rig and bread or weed for bait. Bream tend to retreat into the remote and shallow arms of the lake – **Dignams Creek** contains bream, but the mouth is difficult to navigate. The easiest spot for land-based anglers is the **Beauty Point Road Jetty**, where flathead may also be taken.

Outside the lake, to the south, **Camel Rock** is a good location for tailor, bream, Australian salmon, whiting and flathead.

Camel Rock, to the south of Wallaga Lake entrance, is a popular beach fishing area

Bermagui to Wapengo Lake

Type of fishing
estuary, lake, offshore, reef, rock

Target fish
bream, flathead, whiting, yellowfin tuna

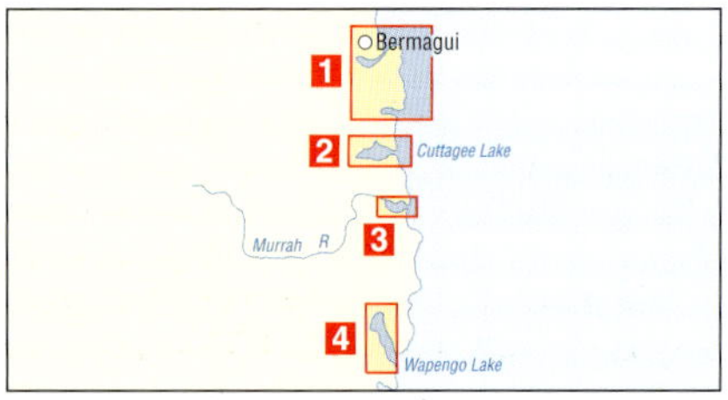

Bermagui is legendary for its fishing. It is the home of the first game fishing club in Australia and to a big trawler fleet, which can take advantage of the proximity of the deep waters beyond the continental shelf. The Bermagui River has something to offer both the land and boat angler.

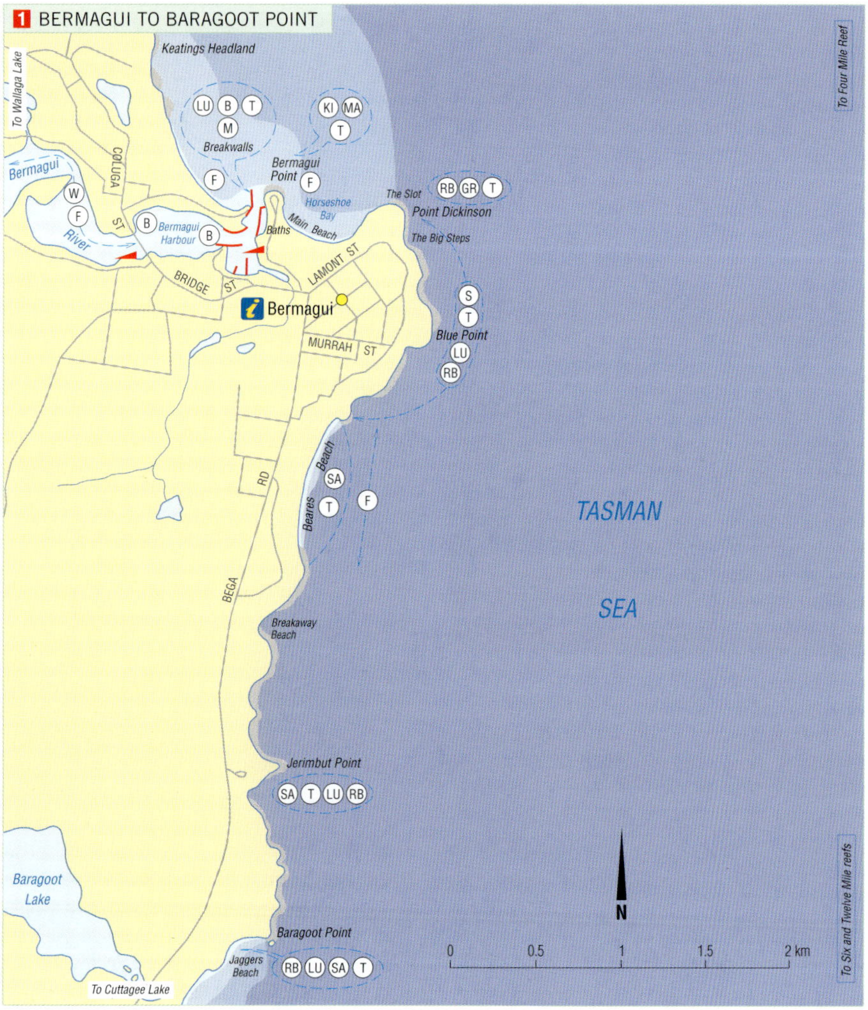

BERMAGUI TO BARAGOOT POINT

Bermagui is the best place for those wishing to take yellowfin tuna, as the offshore waters contain the hottest areas for these majestic and hard-fighting fish. Many anglers prefer the longer run to Montague Island from Bermagui to avoid the Narooma bar, as the Bermagui bar is more predictable. There is plenty of boat action over the three reefs situated out from Bermagui. **Four Mile Reef** is straight out from Keatings Headland, and can be fished for snapper, morwong, tuna and marlin. **Six Mile Reef** attracts these same fish, while the long **Twelve Mile Reef** abounds in snapper, morwong, marlin, shark and yellowfin tuna.

On either side of the entrance of the **Bermagui Harbour**, some 500 m out there is fine flathead drifting. Close in to **Bermagui Point** there is good bait fishing in the kelp beds. The entrance has various rock breakwalls, and tailor, bream and luderick can be taken there at most times of the year. Mullet are also plentiful.

Upriver is pleasant drifting in the channels for flathead and whiting, but the water becomes too shallow for boating about 2 km from the entrance. Bream concentrate around the trawling fleet when it returns to harbour.

From Bermagui south to Baragoot Point there are a number of rock and beach spots worth trying. Outside Bermagui Harbour, Bermagui Point is good for yellowtail kingfish, slimy mackerel and tailor caught on bait, while **The Slot** has rock blackfish, groper and tailor. Around the headland, the rocks from Point Dickinson to Beares Beach are good for rock blackfish, luderick, tailor and snapper.

Beares Beach has Australian salmon and tailor, while **Jerimbut Point** has the same species, and luderick and rock blackfish in the washes. The next safe area is **Jaggers Beach**, which attracts snapper, luderick, rock blackfish, salmon and tailor.

Game fishing craft crowd each other to catch live bait in Horseshoe Bay prior to motoring offshore

CUTTAGEE, MURRAH AND WAPENGO LAKES

Cuttagee, Murrah and Wapengo lakes all have whiting, flathead and bream present.

GUIDE TO LOCAL FISH

	Bermagui to Baragoot Point	Cuttagee Lake	Murrah Lagoon	Wapengo Lake
(B) bream	•	•	•	•
(D) drummer, silver			•	
(F) flathead	•	•	•	•
(FL) flounder			•	•
(GR) groper	•			
(KI) kingfish, yellowtail	•			
(LU) luderick	•	•	•	•
(MA) mackerel, slimy	•			
(M) mullet	•			•
(MU) mulloway			•	
(RB) rock blackfish	•			
(SA) salmon, Australian	•	•	•	•
(S) snapper	•		•	•
(T) tailor	•	•	•	•
(TA) tarwhine				•
(TR) trevally		•		•
(W) whiting	•	•	•	•

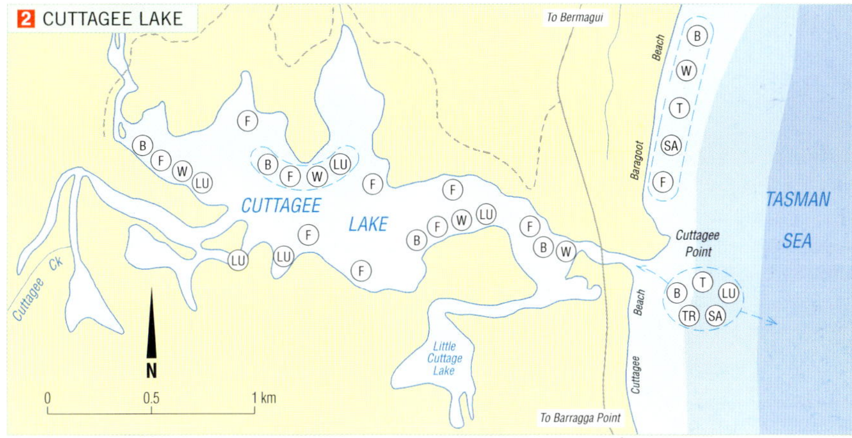

These waters are best for shore-based fishing as they are reached from the coastal road, which branches off the Princes Highway. Worm and nipper baits can be found on the sand flats, and bait fish like poddy mullet can be trapped. Wading the sand flats with fresh bait, or spinning with a lure, can be very worthwhile.

Although usually open to the sea, a break-through of a temporary closure of **Cuttagee Lake** gets fish moving and improves fishing near the mouth. An outgoing tide can see a gathering of predators on the ocean side of the entrance and an incoming tide will bring bream, tailor, luderick, trevally and Australian salmon inside the entrance. The staple fish for anglers, however, are bream, flathead, whiting and luderick. The weedy areas around the edges of the lake are fine for luderick fishing, while the channels and sand flats close to the shores are a haven for flathead. Outside the lake's entrance, the long **Baragoot Beach** is good for collecting worms and catching flathead, salmon, tailor, whiting and bream. South of Cuttagee Beach, **Barragga Point** has rock fishing for salmon, tailor, bream, rock blackfish and luderick.

Murrah Lagoon is bounded by private properties and can only be reached by a rough road to the southern shore, near the mouth, where small boats can be launched. Flathead congregate near the entrance on the end of a rising tide, and retreat to the sand flats and channels at the head of the lake as the tide recedes. Fishing in this area with nippers, worms or prawns can bring catches of flathead, bream, flounder, luderick and salmon. Fishing the deeper holes with small live mullet can yield some very big flathead. Outside at **Murrah Head**, and south of the inlet at **Goalen Head**, there is good rock fishing for a variety of species, including snapper and mulloway.

Wapengo is the biggest of the lakes, and a small boat is almost mandatory. Launching is over the sand near the oyster farmers' sheds, half-way down the eastern shore of the estuary. The variety of fish is overwhelming, as anything from big flathead, bream, snapper, flounder, luderick, trevally, tailor, salmon or tarwhine may be caught and, very rarely, gurnard. There are oyster leases all around the lake, many close to shore, so that shore anglers may cast near them on a high tide, with an unweighted prawn bait used with berley to get quick bream action. Boat anglers can use the same technique. The sandbanks in the lower half of the lake require some negotiation, but the flathead are in the channels on an ebb tide. For boat anglers, drifting the upper lake from north to south will produce flathead. Outside the entrance and to the north, **Bunga Head** has good rock fishing.

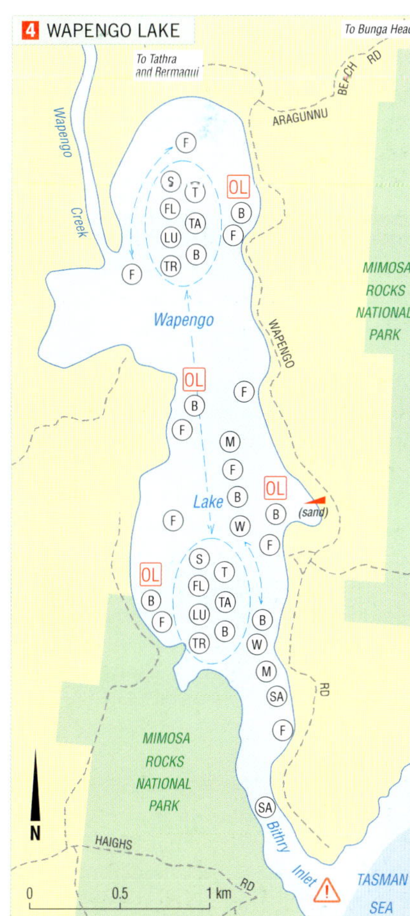

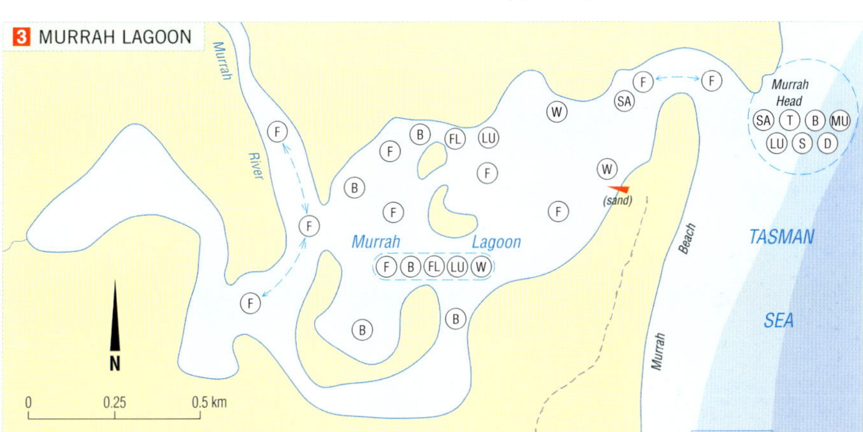

Tathra to Pambula

Type of fishing
beach, estuary, offshore, reef, rock, wharf
Target fish
Australian salmon, bream, flathead, tailor, tuna, yellowtail kingfish

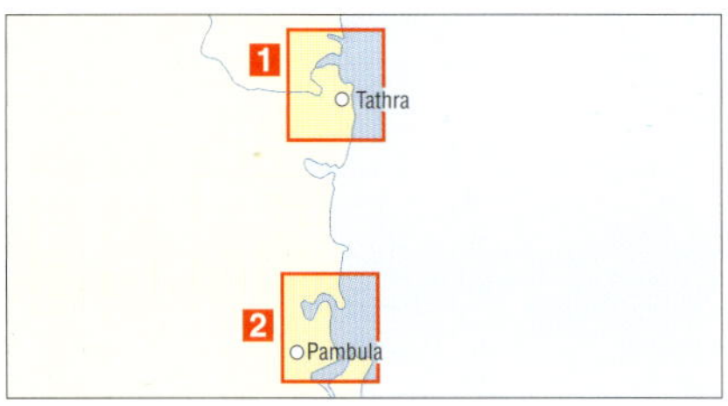

There is little to surpass the beauty and fishing variety of the short strip of coastline north of Tathra. Rocky headlands plunging into deep, clean-bottomed water, long ocean beaches, the peaceful and productive Bega River and many lakes and lagoons create an angling paradise. Tathra Wharf is the best fishing spot, closely followed by the wharf at Merimbula.

Tathra to Merimbula is forest country, for the most part, and the tracks to the coast can be a bit rough. One of the best rock places south of Tathra is **Kangarutha Point**, which has a reef, and is good for Australian salmon, tailor, snapper, bream, rock blackfish and leatherjacket. **Turingal Head** can also be reached by a track. The rocks require an awkward climb down, but it is worth fishing for the salmon and tailor around the entrance of Wallagoot Lake, when it is open.

There is a close-in area from Kianinny Bay, near Tathra, down to Turingal Head, for leatherjacket, snapper and morwong. Turingal Head marks a good spot, about 2 km out, for yellowfin tuna and marlin.

Wallagoot is usually open to the sea and is ideal for flathead, bream and prawns. The beach outside carries whiting, bream, salmon and tailor. **Bournda Island** is attached to the beach at low tide, and has prolific tailor fishing on the north side, but the south should be avoided in big seas. Rock blackfish and bream are close to the rocks.

Tura Head works so well for rock anglers that, despite the rough drive in, overcrowding can be a problem in summer. There are bream, rock blackfish, tailor, salmon and luderick, and deep water is close in, with kingfish, bonito and yellowfin tuna.

Flathead grounds are found about 1 km out from Tura Head. **Short Point Beach** is best at its northern corner, near Tura Head, and near the rock outcrop halfway down the beach. The target fish are whiting, bream, salmon and tailor.

TATHRA

To the north of Tathra, **Middle Beach** has good beach fishing for bream, flathead and salmon, and when **Middle Lagoon** is open this is enhanced after heavy rain with bream, mulloway, tailor and flathead around the lagoon entrance. **Gillards Beach** and **Cowdroys Beach** are split by a rock formation, particularly good for snapper and silver drummer after heavy weather. The best fishing at **Baronda Head** is on its north side, for luderick, rock blackfish and snapper.

Nelson Lagoon is small and remote but it has plenty of flathead, luderick and bream, with whiting near the mouth in summer. Overall the fishing is good, but a small boat or canoe is required as there is no launching ramp. Anglers must drive in and carry their craft across the sand.

Wajurda Point has snapper, leatherjacket and rock blackfish in close, and attracts tuna and kingfish and other pelagics. The rocks running down to **Mogareka Inlet** are excellent for spinning for salmon and tailor, but are dangerous in a southerly.

The **Bega River**, running from Mogareka Inlet, feeds two lagoons, which abound in bream and flathead. There are a number of holes for night fishing for mulloway, bream and flathead. The river can be drifted for flathead. A particularly good spot for big flathead is the mouth of **Chinnock Lagoon**. There is good bass fishing upstream, but silting has affected the quality.

Tathra Beach has salmon, tailor, bream, flathead and mulloway, and whiting at its northern end.

Tathra Wharf has been described as being like a land-based boat, but it is better than that as fish congregate around it in big numbers. Yellowtail, trevally, pike and slimy mackerel swarm under the pier at dawn and dusk but devotees are more interested in the sharks, very big tuna, snapper, salmon, mulloway and yellowtail kingfish.

GUIDE TO LOCAL FISH

	Tathra	Merimbula to Pambula
(BT) bonito	●	●
(B) bream	●	●
(D) drummer, silver	●	●
(F) flathead	●	●
(G) garfish	●	
(GR) groper	●	
(DR) john dory		●
(KI) kingfish, yellowtail	●	●
(LJ) leatherjacket	●	●
(LU) luderick	●	●
(MA) mackerel, slimy	●	
(ML) marlin		●
(MO) morwong	●	●
(M) mullet	●	
(MU) mulloway	●	●
(NG) nannygai		●
(PI) pike	●	●
(RB) rock blackfish	●	●
(SA) salmon, Australian	●	●
(SH) shark	●	
(S) snapper	●	●
(SW) sweep		●
(T) tailor	●	●
(TR) trevally	●	●
(TU) tuna	●	●
(W) whiting	●	●

The most unusual anglers on the wharf are the shark hunters, who use the biggest of tackle and make a practice of paddling their bait out into the bay by canoe or surf ski. The wharf can get very crowded in peak summer months, so patience waiting for fishing spots and dealing with tangled lines is important. It is essential to have a long-handled net or cliff gaff, as the platform is around 6 m above the water, depending on the tide.

Tathra Head is a good deepwater spot, with tailor, salmon, big bream, groper, bonito and snapper the targets, and rock blackfish and luderick close in. It is dangerous in a heavy swell. In the small bay to the south anglers can spin or fish with live bait as the water is very deep and carries morwong and groper, along with salmon, tailor, tuna, rock blackfish and luderick.

Kianinny Bay is protected from the weather and is a good shore fishing location when there is not too much boat traffic from the angling club ramp. Fish and berley in the channel on the southern side for bream, luderick and rock blackfish. Schools of garfish and mullet may be berleyed at the head of the inlet.

Offshore fishing in this area originates mostly from the Kianniny Bay ramp, as the Merimbula entrance is for experts only.

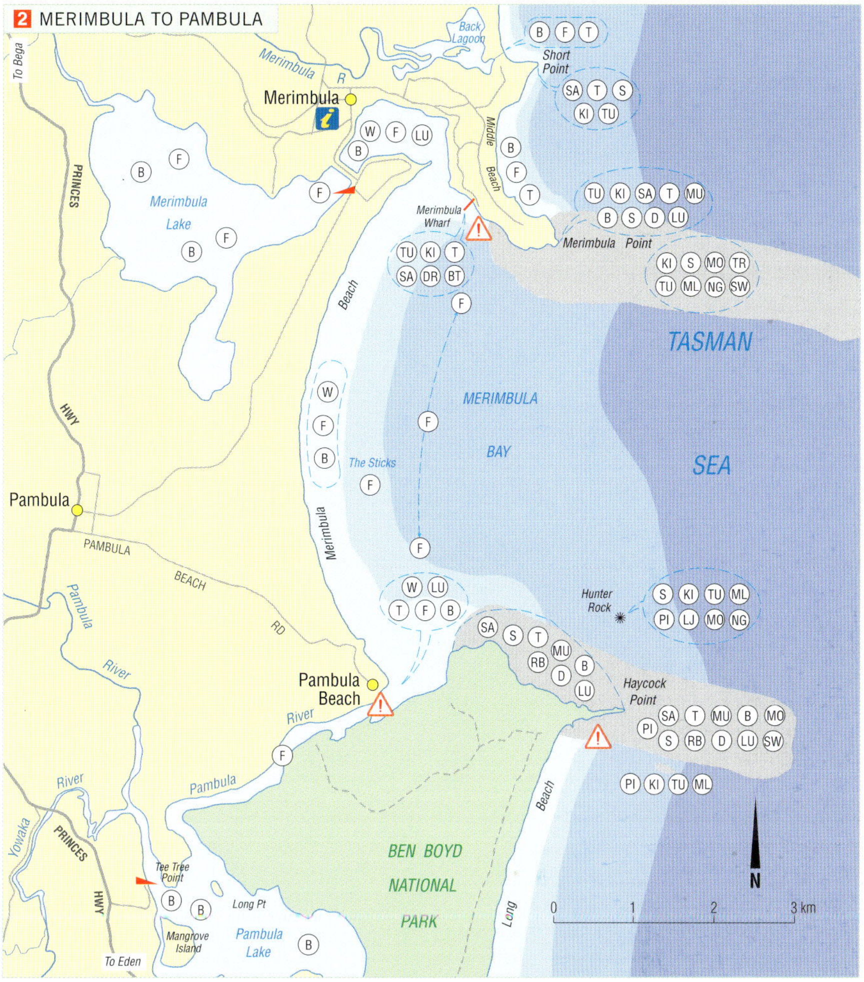

MERIMBULA TO PAMBULA

Merimbula has excellent and varied fishing even during crowded summer periods. Just north of the town is **Black Lagoon**, a hot spot for bream, flathead and tailor when the lagoon occasionally breaks out onto the beach. **Middle Beach** has the same fish, plus snapper, and is bounded by two rocky points, **Short Point** and **Merimbula Point**. These should be fished in calm seas, for salmon, tailor, snapper, kingfish and tuna. There are reefs off Merimbula Point running east with pinnacles and drop-offs, which attract yellowtail kingfish, sweep, snapper, morwong, trevally, tuna, marlin and nannygai.

The channel into **Merimbula Lake** is terrific for whiting, flathead and luderick, with the causeway concentrating the prawns into a narrow run-out area on nights of the new moon. Past the causeway, flathead are almost certain, and Merimbula Lake abounds in bream and flathead.

Merimbula Wharf is just outside the entrance and is almost as famous as Tathra Wharf. Targets are mainly tuna and kingfish, but there is also a wide range of smaller fish, including tailor, salmon, john dory and bonito. **Merimbula Beach** is relatively sheltered, good for collecting worms and pippis for bait, and producing whiting, flathead and bream. Offshore, **Merimbula Bay** is fished for flathead, and the best area is **The Sticks**, 800 m out from a prominent patch of dead trees half-way along the beach.

Tailor, flathead, bream, whiting and luderick are concentrated at the entrance to the **Pambula River**, while **Pambula Lake** has many good areas for bream, with the best place being around **Tee Tree Point**. The lake has launching facilities for offshore fishing, but the bar needs caution.

Rock anglers can fish from **Haycock Point**, near Pambula, which is safe on its north side and provides a wide range of fish – salmon, tailor, mulloway, bream, snapper, rock blackfish, silver drummer and luderick. The point is also surrounded by extensive reefs. A bombora 150 m south-east of the point, dangerous in any sea, is a good fishing area, as well as **Hunter Rock**, 1 km north of the point, which breaks in heavy seas. Snapper, kingfish, tuna, marlin, pike, leatherjacket and morwong can all be caught here.

Eden to Green Cape

Type of fishing
bay, beach, jetty, offshore, reef, rock
Target fish
Australian salmon, bream, flathead, tuna, yellowtail kingfish

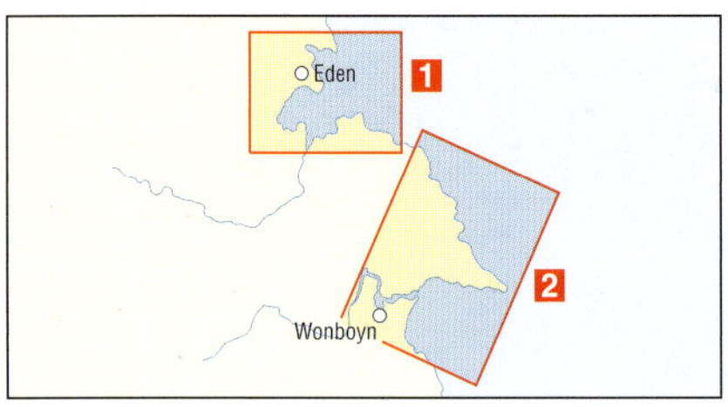

Eden provides anglers with rock, beach, jetty and boat fishing in and around the large expanse of Twofold Bay. The coastline from Twofold Bay to Green Cape and Disaster Bay is rugged national park bushland, with a few vehicle and walking tracks. It is a place for people who love fishing and the bush and don't mind a bit of hardship and exercise.

EDEN AND TWOFOLD BAY

There are some top rock fishing places north of the town of Eden, although they should only be considered in calm seas. Bream, snapper, sweep, trevally, rock blackfish, pike, luderick, Australian salmon and tailor abound, while floating live baits may take tuna, kingfish or shark.

Worang Point, at the southern end of the Ben Boyd National Park, fishes well for all rock species. This whole area is dangerous in easterly or southerly weather. **Aslings Beach** is a fine fishing spot for salmon, tailor, bream and whiting. Boat fishing behind the breaks yields flathead. The small **Curalo Lagoon**, west of the beach, offers bank fishing for bream and flathead and is ideal for youngsters and beginners. It is also an excellent prawning area in summer.

The fishing wharves at **Eden** are popular with holiday anglers, and are very productive. With the aid of berley, some mullet gut or prawn bait, there is a good chance of bream, flathead, leatherjacket and trevally. Shore anglers can also fish from the headlands and beaches in sheltered **Quarantine Bay**, where flathead and bream are the main catches, and snapper and yellowtail kingfish are a chance. At the south of Twofold Bay is Kiah Inlet, fed by the Towamba River. Access is by boat across the bay as there is extensive private land around the estuary. It holds flathead, bream, garfish and mullet. Outside Kiah Inlet there is excellent boat fishing from **Whale Beach** for whiting, flathead, bream and snapper, with occasional schools of tailor and salmon. Trolling for salmon and tailor in the bay can be very productive. Flathead and whiting can be taken from **Fisheries Beach**.

On the south-east side of the bay there is some rock fishing for bream, snapper,

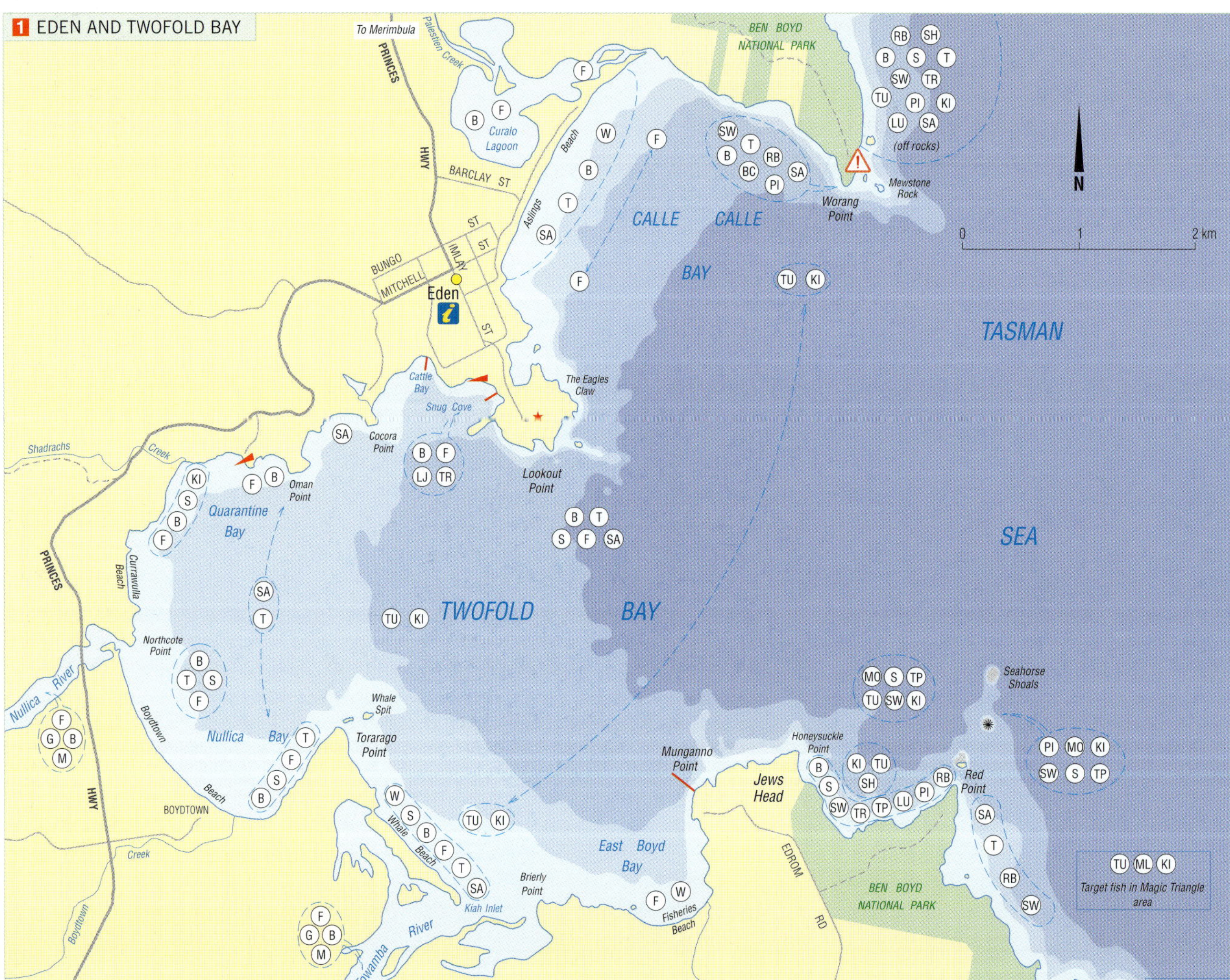

sweep, trevally, rock blackfish, luderick and pike close in, and kingfish, tuna and shark for heavy tackle anglers. **Jews Head** and **Red Point** are the main fishing places, but conditions must be calm. Red Point has a rough bottom, so float rigs with bait and lure casting are the best ways to fish.

Twofold Bay is very deep, so boat anglers seeking the deepwater species do not have to stray outside the line from Worang Point to Red Point, and those operating in the south will be in the most protected water. A depth sounder will help locate the reefs where morwong, kingfish, trumpeter and snapper are the main catches. Trolling in the bay will yield catches of tuna and kingfish.

For those boat anglers who venture outside the bay, the action starts at the **Magic Triangle**, which is an area between Red Point and Morwarry Point. Game fish abound here, and the main catches are bonito, yellowfin tuna, kingfish and marlin.

GREEN CAPE AND WONBOYN LAKE

This is one of the most exciting areas in Australia for land-based game fishing, with some brilliant offshore action for prudent boat people. However, it is also a place where the weather has to be watched, from land or sea.

GUIDE TO LOCAL FISH

	Eden and Twofold Bay	Green Cape and Wonboyn Lake
(BC) barracouta	●	
(BT) bonito		●
(B) bream	●	●
(D) drummer, silver		●
(F) flathead	●	●
(G) garfish	●	
(KI) kingfish, yellowtail	●	●
(LJ) leatherjacket	●	●
(LU) luderick	●	●
(ML) marlin	●	●
(MO) morwong	●	●
(M) mullet	●	●
(MU) mulloway		●
(PI) pike	●	●
(RB) rock blackfish	●	●
(SA) salmon, Australian	●	●
(SH) shark	●	●
(S) snapper	●	●
(SW) sweep	●	●
(T) tailor	●	●
(TR) trevally	●	
(TP) trumpeter	●	
(TU) tuna	●	●
(W) whiting	●	●

Pulpit Rock on Green Cape: hundreds of large tuna and kingfish have been hooked, lost or landed here

Morwarry Point has tailor, Australian salmon, snapper in the washes, and tuna and yellowtail kingfish for boat anglers. A reef 1 km from Mowarry Point holds a lot of snapper and morwong on the bottom, and kingfish and tuna near the surface. **Saltwater Creek** is reached from Green Cape Road. The beach there carries salmon, tailor and bream. The rocks to the north of the beach have bream, silver drummer, and sweep close in, and are good platforms for spinning for tailor, salmon, pike and bonito. Offshore, there is trolling near the southern headland for bonito and salmon.

Bittangabee Bay also has road access, a camping area and a place to launch small boats straight off the beach in good weather. The inlet carries mainly bream and flathead, and there is bait on the mud and sand flats. The rocks on the north side can produce snapper and rock blackfish or try spinning for tailor, salmon, bonito and other pelagics. Similar fishing can be had along rocks to the south of the bay, reached by a walking track. For boat anglers, Bittangabee Bay is a welcome place to run to if weather conditions change, and a reef about 300 m offshore carries snapper, morwong and leatherjacket.

Pulpit Rock is reached by track from the Green Cape Road. It is renowned as one of Australia's best rock fishing platforms for game fish. Lure casting and live baiting are the practice here, for tuna, kingfish, shark, and occasionally marlin.

Green Cape is easily reached from the picnic spot near the lighthouse. Fishing at the tip of Green Cape is not recommended. On the south side is City Rocks, another famous platform for pelagic species, and offshore there is good game fishing. **Disaster Bay** holds pelagics as well as being an excellent drift for flathead.

Wonbyn Lake is in a remote area and runs out at Disaster Bay. It is favoured by the small band of devotees who go there every year. They camp or stay at the resort, and boat hire is available. Mulloway can be caught off the northern shores of the lake. The lower lake, with its dangerous bar, is very shallow and requires careful negotiation, but there are big flathead on the banks and luderick among the weed. Oyster leases yield bream particularly at dawn and dusk on a rising tide. Yabbies and sandworms are readily available on the banks. A prominent red rock on the edge of the channel is a good spot for all the fish inhabiting the lake – flathead, mulloway, luderick, whiting, tailor, mullet and bream. At the end of the channel, a sand spit is a hot spot for whiting. Fishing the spit is also good, as is the drop-off for flathead, whiting and bream. The upper lake is well stocked with tailor, and bream is the main catch in the **Wonboyn River**.

On the coast, **Wonboyn Beach** is good for flathead, tailor and salmon on the north side, and mostly salmon in the south. The beach is best reached by boat, tying up inside the entrance.

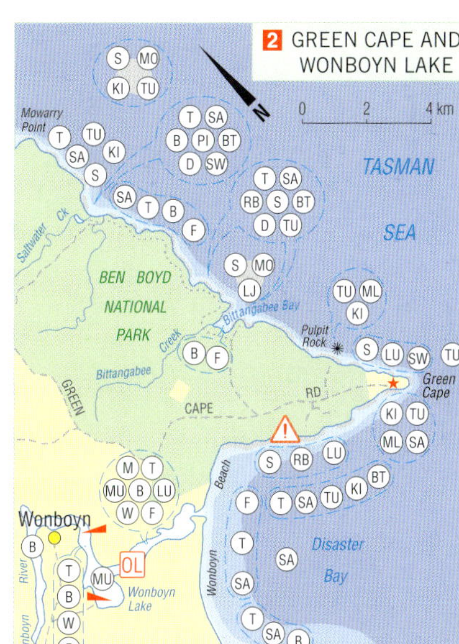

Inland Fishing

Golden perch to 10 kg, Murray cod up to 50 kg, excellent trout fishing and the best bass fishing in Australia – New South Wales has it all. You can fish quietly on a mighty western river or fly cast in the Snowy Mountains – New South Wales provides variety as well as quality in freshwater fishing.

Land shape and climatic peculiarities within New South Wales mean that the bulk of freshwater fishing is concentrated within quite a small proportion of the state. Some 60 per cent, or nearly 500 000 sq km, is open, generally flat country, only sparsely laced with rivers, and lacking the steeply folded landforms needed to trigger rainfall, or accumulate and conserve water.

The Great Dividing Range is the geographic feature that determines the freshwater fishing in New South Wales. The coastal strip to the east of the Divide has a regular rainfall and the easterly flowing rivers are significant waterways despite their relatively short length.

The mountain range is the home base of the great New South Wales trout fisheries. In the north and centre of the Divide, the New England, Upper Hunter and Central Highlands regions have trout lakes and rivers, and in the south the Snowy Mountains and Monaro boast numerous trout lakes and streams. The impoundments on the western slopes provide some of the best native species fishing for golden perch, Murray cod, silver perch and redfin, and trout in higher dams.

To the west of the Divide, the rainfall is erratic and the major rivers are wider, with slower flows and long, deep pools. Trout and bass are replaced here by Murray cod, golden perch, silver perch, redfin, carp and catfish.

The state also encircles the Australian Capital Territory, with some significant fisheries in substantial dams near Canberra, stocked with trout and native fish species.

Anglers are required to have a licence to fish all waters in New South Wales. Check with your local fisheries office for up-to-date information on recreational fishing regulations.

Protected species

In New South Wales, four species of fish are totally protected. They are trout cod, eastern freshwater cod, Macquarie perch and Australian grayling. These fish must be released unharmed.

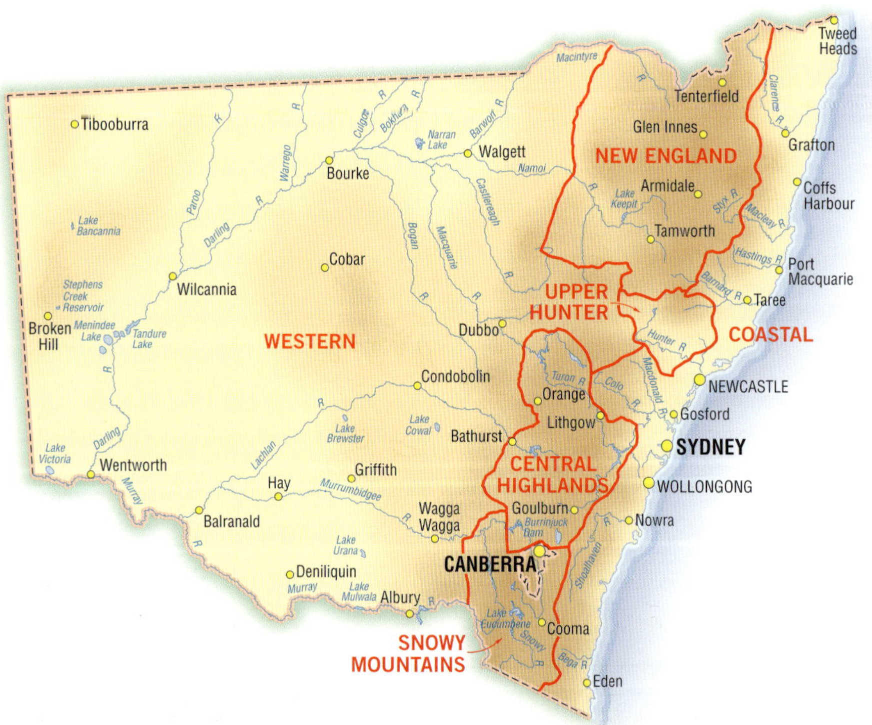

WHERE TO FISH

Inland

COASTAL REGION ● 130

Along more than 1000 km of coast, the main freshwater species is Australian bass. There are catfish, mullet and the endangered eastern freshwater cod in the north, mullet and catfish along the central coast, and mullet and the now rare Australian grayling on the south coast.

NEW ENGLAND REGION ● 134

The New England Region blends history, great fishing and a variety of spectacular scenery among rich grazing lands, plateau forests and fertile lowland farms. The region is dominated by trout in the rivers. There is some good fishing in reservoirs and several of the rivers for native fish.

UPPER HUNTER REGION ● 138

This freshwater fishery comprises about eight major rivers and four dams. Numerous small trout inhabit the cool streams of the Barrington Tops, while bass, herring, mullet, catfish and carp thrive in the eastern and southern waters. The region's dams hold trout, bass, silver and golden perch, catfish and eels.

CENTRAL HIGHLANDS REGION ● 142

This region embraces pine-clad snowline peaks, rugged sandstone escarpments, eucalypt forests and rolling grasslands. Most rivers are small, but hold either brown or rainbow trout. In warmer reaches, there are native species such as catfish, Murray cod, golden and silver perch. There is some fantastic stillwater fishing in the region.

SNOWY MOUNTAINS REGION ● 148

Here is some of the best trout fishing in mainland Australia. The slow, weedy Monaro streams provide blue-ribbon fly fishing that attracts visitors from all over the world. The huge Snowy Mountains' impoundments offer a totally different experience. In addition to fly fishing, they are especially suited to bait fishing, trolling and spinning.

WESTERN REGION ● 154

This large region includes a few incredibly productive dams and rivers. It is the home of Murray cod and golden and silver perch, although the introduced European carp can be a nuisance in some areas.

Trolling on Lake Jindabyne

Fishing regulations

There are some 15 common freshwater angling species of finfish available within New South Wales. Four of these are totally protected: trout cod, eastern freshwater cod, Australian grayling and Macquarie perch. If caught, none of these protected fish may be kept, but must immediately and carefully be returned to the water unharmed. Other threatened species, such as the purple-spotted gudgeon, may have little direct angling significance, but are nonetheless important, as they provide part of the forage base for fish that anglers do catch. All recreational anglers within New South Wales are required to hold a current 'all-waters' fishing licence. Some exemptions do apply to certain age groups and various holders of Government exemption cards. Details are available from New South Wales Fisheries. New South Wales recreational fishing licences are available from several outlets, including Fisheries offices and authorised fishing tackle shops, or by phoning 1300 550 474. All enquiries regarding current fishing regulations can be made by phoning this number or by visiting the Fisheries website at www.fisheries.nsw.gov.au

GUIDE TO LOCAL FISH

- bass, Australian
- blackfish, river
- carp, European
- catfish, eel-tailed
- cod, Murray
- crayfish, Murray
- eel, long-finned
- herring, freshwater
- mullet, bully
- mullet, pinkeye
- perch, estuary
- perch, golden
- perch, redfin
- perch, silver
- perch, spangled
- salmon, Atlantic
- trout, brook
- trout, brown
- trout, rainbow

Boating regulations

All powered craft capable of speeds greater than 10 knots must be registered with NSW Maritime and to drive such vessels, you must be licensed. All craft registered within New South Wales must also carry a hull identification number, known as a 'Boatcode'. Enquiries regarding Boatcode, licensing procedures, registration of power craft, required safety gear and 'rules of the road' can be made by contacting NSW Maritime on 131 256 or by visiting the website at www.maritime.nsw.gov.au

FURTHER INFORMATION

Fishing *For full details of fishing regulations, contact NSW Fisheries at 202 Nicholson Pde, Cronulla, tel. (02) 9527 8411, its regional offices or its website, www.fisheries.nsw.gov.au. There is a general Fisheries information line on 1300 369 365. Obtain Fisheries publications from its offices, bait and tackle shops or its website.*

Boating *NSW Maritime is at James Craig Rd, Rozelle, tel. (02) 9563 8511, and has many regional offices. It produces a variety of boating maps, guides and videos on waterways regulations and boat safety that are available from Maritime offices. Also see its website, www.maritime.nsw.gov.au. Weather forecasts and information are available from the Bureau of Meteorology, tel. 1900 955 361.*

An excellent catch of Murray cod

Coastal Region

Along more than 1000 km of coastline, the principal freshwater species on offer is Australian bass – a pugnacious, cover-loving species with the endearing tendency to strike at anything that comes within range.

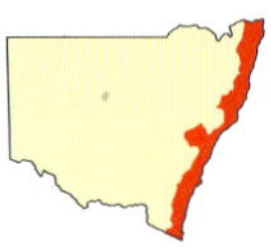

Bass move around during the year, migrating downstream to the brackish water in late autumn and winter to spawn. In spring, they work their way upstream again, to feed during summer in the best stretches they can find. Their upstream progress is generally halted when they encounter a major obstruction, such as a weir or a waterfall, as nearly all major New South Wales streams and rivers, except the Clyde River, have been dammed or altered in some way. Bass are frequently caught on lures, either by trolling or casting. In recent years bass numbers have increased as a result of intensive stocking programmes in suitable impoundments. This in turn has led to a growth in bass fishing tournaments.

Sometimes a canoe and four-wheel drive are needed to get to the best water

WHERE TO FISH

Coastal Region

NORTH COAST ● 131

The pristine Timbarra and Nymboida rivers, below the falls, are home for bass and the protected eastern cod.

CENTRAL COAST ● 132

This area fishes well for bass, freshwater herring, pinkeye and bully mullet, and catfish. Bass and eel are found in many impoundments, while mullet and some bass can be caught within the Sydney area.

SOUTH COAST ● 133

The Shoalhaven River offers limited bass fishing from about Burrier to as far up as the Tallowa Dam wall. Further south is the Clyde River, and there are a host of dams, such as the Brogo Reservoir near Bega.

GUIDE TO LOCAL FISH

bass, Australian
catfish, eel-tailed
eel, long-finned
eel, short-finned
herring, freshwater
mullet, bully
mullet, pinkeye
perch, estuary
perch, golden
perch, silver
redfin
trout, rainbow

FURTHER INFORMATION

Fishing and boating *For details of coastal offices of NSW Fisheries and NSW Maritime, see Coastal Fishing Further Information listings: Sydney Region, page 46; Grafton Region, page 66; Port Macquarie Region, page 78; Newcastle Region, page 90; Wollongong Region, page 102; and Bermagui Region, page 114.*

Tourist centres *Cnr Princes Hwy and Beach Rd, Batemans Bay, tel. (02) 4472 6900; Pacific Hwy, Coffs Harbour, tel. (02) 6652 1522; Princes Hwy, Eden, tel. (02) 6496 1953; Great Lakes Tourism, Little St, Forster, tel. (02) 6554 8799; Central Coast Tourism, Rotary Park, Terrigal Dr, Terrigal, tel. (02) 4385 4430; cnr Ballina St and Molesworth St, Lismore, tel. 1300 369 795; Wheeler Pl, 363 Hunter St, Newcastle, tel. (02) 4974 2999; cnr Spring St and Pacific Hwy, South Grafton, tel. (02) 6642 4677.*

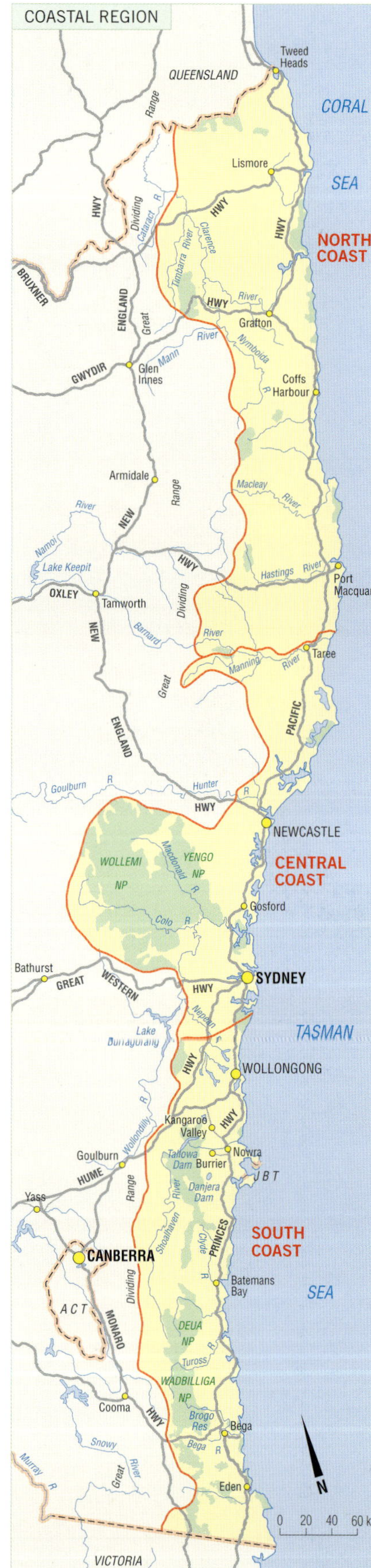

North Coast

Type of fishing
dam, lake, river
Target fish
bass

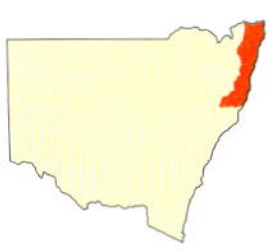

The remote north-western pristine rivers such as the **Timbarra** and **Nymboida** are wilderness fisheries, mainly accessible by raft or canoe. Catch and release, self-restraint, and the use of barbless hooks all go a long way towards experiencing this wilderness fishery without damaging it. Responsible professional guiding outfits also operate in the area.

Bass inhabit much of the freshwater reaches of the **Brunswick, Richmond, Orara, Bellinger, Nambucca, Macleay, Wilson, Hastings, Camden Haven, Stewarts** and **Lansdowne rivers**. The eastern cod is still found in the upper Clarence and Nymboida and has been stocked back into the Richmond system. It is, however, a protected species. It is superficially similar in appearance but more aggressive than the Murray cod, which is a native of the western plains and slopes. The eastern cod is slow growing and, with its aggression, is very vulnerable. This species, which nearly became extinct before a breeding program stocked important waters, was once so common it was used as pig food.

More accessible bass rivers include the Bellinger, Nambucca, Wilson, Brunswick and lower Clarence. In fishing these waters a small craft is very handy, and lures – either trolled past rock walls or deep snags or cast close to cover – produce very good results. The very best way to catch the large hard fighting bass is to drift a live shrimp about 2 m deep under a light float, along rock edges or snags. Hang on because these bruisers will try to bury you very quickly. Most of these rivers have a measure of accessible bank angling.

Freshwater herring occur as far north as the **upper Richmond**, but these fish are more often found in the central and southern sectors. *Tandanus tandanus*, a species of eel-tailed catfish, is native to the freshwater sections of most coastal rivers and found wherever de-snagging, pollution, or fishing pressure has not wiped them out. Mullet are widespread along the coast, both the true freshwater pinkeye and also juveniles of the marine bully species.

Freshwater dams in this area include **Clarrie Hall Dam**, south of Murwillumbah (bass and golden perch), and **Toonumbar Dam**, west of Kyogle (silver perch, bass and catfish). All these dams rely on stocking.

Bass country on the upper Clarence River

GUIDE TO LOCAL FISH

bass, Australian
catfish
eel, long-finned
herring, freshwater
mullet, bully
mullet, pinkeye
perch, golden
perch, silver

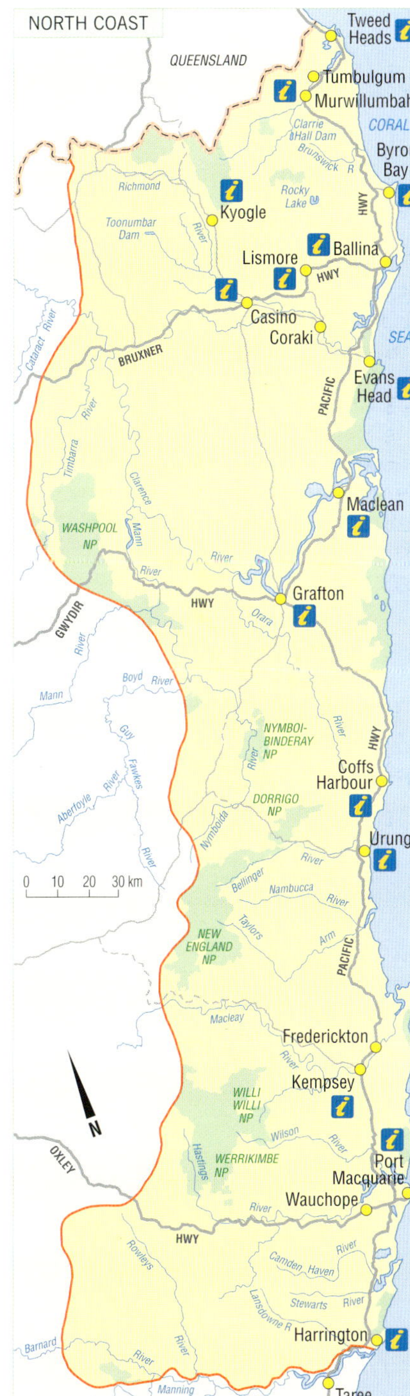

Central Coast

Type of fishing
dam, lake, river
Target fish
bass, catfish, mullet

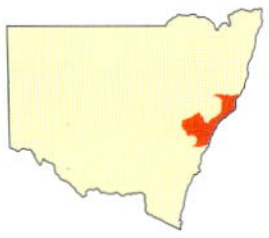

The riverine fresh water of the Central Coast, from the Manning River to the Sydney area, offers bass, freshwater herring, pinkeye and bully mullet, and catfish. It is noticeable, however, that the closer you get to heavily populated areas, the more anglers there are and the harder it is to catch fish.

Despite this, the fishing is worthwhile in streams such as the **Wallamba**, near Nabiac, the upper **Karuah**, and the **Williams River**, on which **Seaham Weir** is located. The weir has bass, mullet, catfish and eels. There is very good bass fishing downstream of Seaham Weir during late winter and early spring. The fishing is also worthwhile in **Dora and Wyong creeks**, which run into the central coast lakes, in the **Colo River**, and in the **Nepean and upper Hawkesbury system**. The upper Hawkesbury above Wisemans Ferry is a major freshwater fishery for Australian bass, with some surprisingly large fish still taken. Various tributaries, such as **Mangrove, Cattai** and **Webbs creeks**, are all classic bass and mullet habitats. Both **Nortons** and **Bents basins**, on the Nepean River at Wallacia, carry bass, mullet, catfish and herring.

A boat is a useful asset when fishing the central coast rivers, and lure fishing an excellent technique to bag a bass. These areas are heavily fished and suffer decreasing water quality due to urban sprawl and pollution. There is still good bass fishing available and those who experiment with deep diving, surface and soft plastic lures as well as flies and bait will most often take these educated fish. Dawn and dusk and into the night during warmer months are the best times. Surface lures on a warm summer night can provide some of the most exciting fishing imaginable as bass crash into lures, shattering the silence. In cooler weather, fish closer to brackish water, using small diving lures or bait.

The bass is a territorial fish. One method of encouraging a strike on surface lures is to cast the lure and allow it to sit for 10 or 15 seconds before starting the retrieve.

Central coast impoundments, such as **Grahamstown Dam, Brooklyn Dam** and **Lake Parramatta** have bass and eels in them. **Manly Dam** also has redfin and silver perch. Check boating regulations as outboard motors are generally disallowed.

Within the Sydney metropolitan area, the **upper Georges River** near Liverpool, and the **Hacking River**, above Audley Weir, have mullet – and some very educated bass.

Some coastal freshwater pondages, like this one south of Taree, have been stocked with bass and golden perch

GUIDE TO LOCAL FISH

	Central Coast	South Coast
bass, Australian	•	•
catfish	•	
eel	•	
herring, freshwater	•	
mullet	•	•
redfin	•	
perch, estuary		•
perch, silver	•	
trout, rainbow		•

Eel-tailed catfish

The Tandanus tandanus *species of catfish is found throughout the island and coastal fresh water of much of south and eastern Australia. The dorsal and pectoral spines can inflict nasty wounds.*

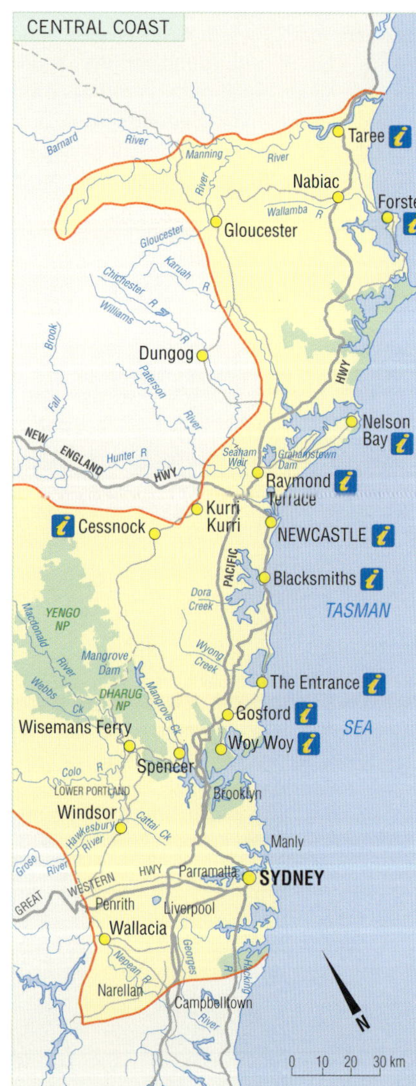

South Coast

Type of fishing
dam, river

Target fish
bass, estuary perch, mullet

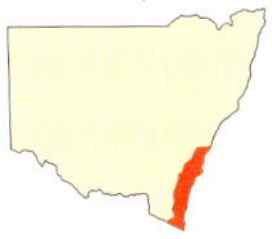

Some of the best water here cannot be fished. Sydney water supply dams are closed to fishing, which means that the productive Cataract Dam is not accessible. Near Nowra, the **Shoalhaven River** offers quality bass fishing from about Burrier, as far up as the Tallowa Dam wall. **Broughton Creek** can yield bass up towards Berry.

Stocking **Tallowa Dam** with bass in recent years has seen the emergence of a 'put and take' fishery to offset the loss of the Shoalhaven's capacity to self-regenerate its bass following construction of the dam, which stopped bass migrating. It is early days, but indications of the new fishery are promising.

Further south, there are short fresh-water stretches in **Wandandian** and **Conjola creeks**, but the next major freshwater stream southwards is the **Clyde**, where bass are present. The best section begins around Shallow Crossing and extends to the Budawang Range. The Clyde produces large numbers of small bass, but big fish, though present, are difficult to catch.

The **Deua River**, upstream of Moruya, and the **Tuross** above Bodalla, are also good streams to try. The **Murrah** and **Brogo rivers** have mullet, and sketchy populations of bass, while there are both these fish and estuary perch in the **Bega** and **Towamba rivers**, and estuary perch in the **Wallagaraugh**.

South coast dams include **Fitzroy Falls Reservoir**, above Kangaroo Valley, **Tallowa** and **Danjera dams** near Nowra, and **Brogo Reservoir**, near Bega. There are bass in Tallowa, Danjera and Brog and rainbow trout in Fitzroy Falls Reservoir, where canoe access (no motors) is available exclusively to members of the Campbelltown Sportfishing Club and then only from September through October. There is however about a kilometre of bank access on Fitzroy's eastern shore for public angling.

Fitzroy Falls, Morton National Park

New England Region

There are two separate and recognisable sectors within this region, divided by a central spine of granite-studded highlands running generally north and south with cool streams, which drain east and west.

Copeton Dam is well known for its large golden perch, which are caught near rocky points

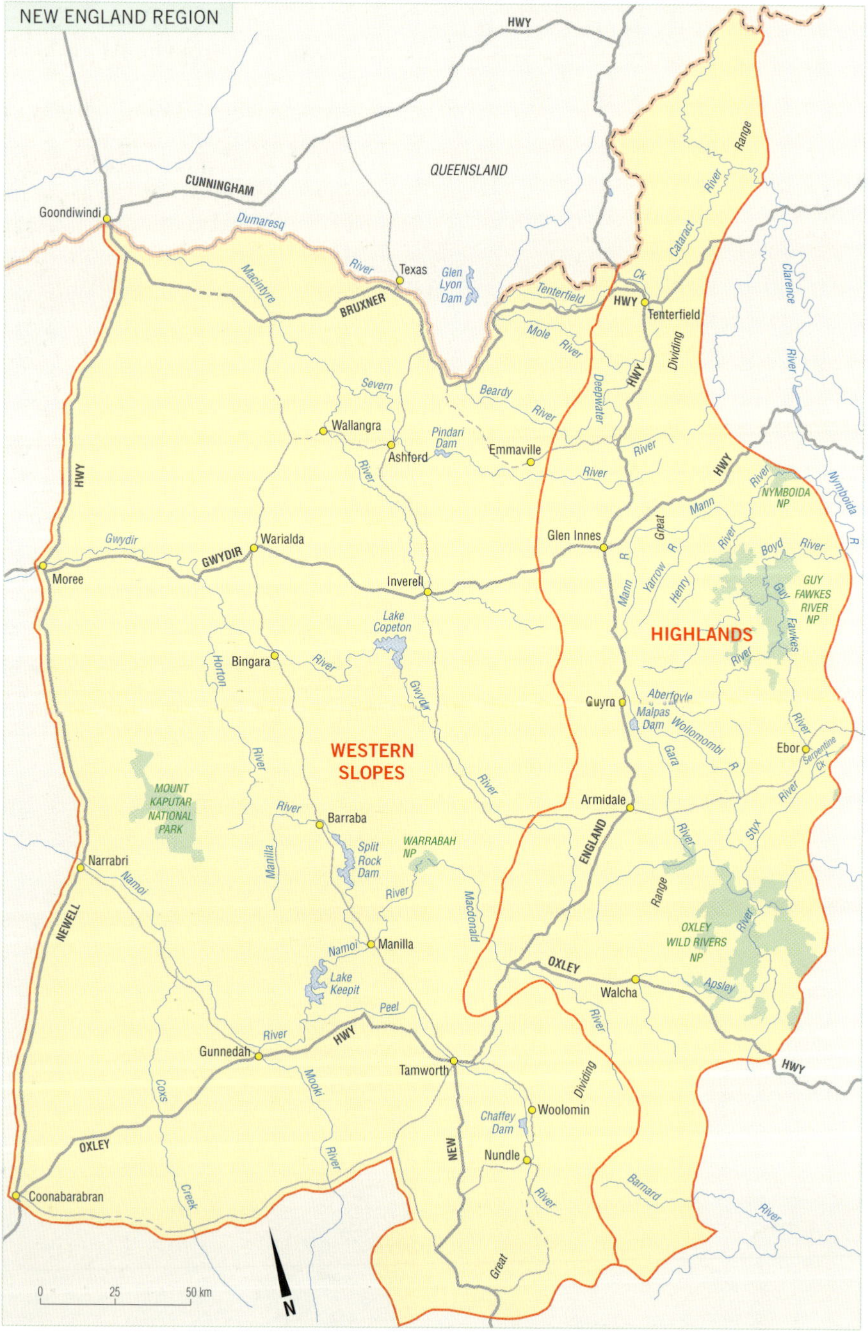

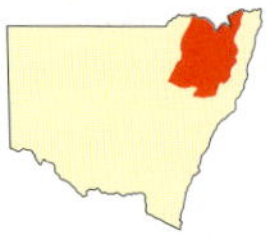

These cool rivers are the adopted homes of brown and rainbow trout. To the west and south, among the slopes and foothills, a scattering of key dams are fed by warmer rivers that carry Murray cod, catfish, golden and silver perch, and redfin.

However, many of the dams were built for irrigation and are subject to fluctuations in water levels that can be dramatic in drought years. Some of the best fishing is along the original river beds, and where the feeder streams flow into these dams. The tourist value of many of these dams is highlighted by the accommodation available, much of it aimed at the families who fish.

Many of the west-flowing rivers enter and continue beyond impoundments, some of them having good populations of native fish both above and below the dam walls, as a result of either natural breeding or restocking. These north-western river systems eventually feed into the mighty Murray–Darling river complex, the breeding heartland of our Murray cod and golden perch fisheries.

Rainbow trout have been acclimatised to the high plateau streams of the New England Region, and are also stocked in numerous private farm dams

WHERE TO FISH

New England Region

HIGHLANDS ● 136

Good trout waters in this area include the Deepwater in the north, the Gara and Wollomombi rivers near Guyra, and the Apsley, Styx, Serpentine and Guy Fawkes rivers. Bass have been stocked into Malpas Dam, near Guyra, where there are also redfin.

WESTERN SLOPES ● 137

Water temperatures are often too warm here for trout. Most likely fish are native species such as Murray cod, golden and silver perch and catfish. Redfin and carp are also found. Productive native fish streams include Tenterfield Creek, and the Mole, Severn, Dumaresq, Macintyre and Gwydir rivers. There is also excellent fishing in major dams and lakes such as Chaffey, Keepit, Copeton, Split Rock and Pindari.

GUIDE TO LOCAL FISH

- bass, Australian
- carp, European
- catfish
- cod, Murray
- eel
- herring, freshwater
- redfin
- perch, golden
- perch, silver
- trout, brown
- trout, rainbow

FURTHER INFORMATION

Fishing and boating *NSW Fisheries offices at 24 Andrews St, Inverell, tel. (02) 6722 1129 and at 72 Gunnedah Rd, Tamworth, tel. (02) 6765 4591. NSW Maritime office at Shop 16, Tamworth Arcade, Peel St, Tamworth, tel. (02) 6766 9839.*

Tourist centres *82 Marsh St, Armidale, tel. 1800 627 736; 116 Queen St, Barraba, tel. 1800 242 881; Newell Hwy, Coonabarabran, tel. (02) 6842 1441; Church St, Glen Innes, tel. (02) 6730 2400; Water Towers Complex, Campbell St, Inverell, tel. (02) 6728 8161; Lyle Houlihan Park, Cnr Newell and Gwydir hwys, Moree, tel. (02) 6757 3350; cnr Peel St and Murray St, Tamworth, tel. (02) 6755 5300; 157 Rouse St, Tenterfield, tel. (02) 6736 1082.*

Mann River landscape

Highlands

Type of fishing
dam, river
Target fish
trout

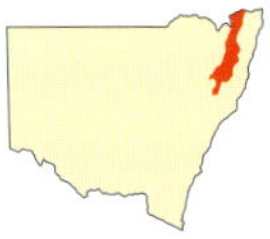

The trout angler has a good chance of catching trout in the many highland rivers that have been stocked with fish produced at the Dutton Trout Hatchery at Ebor. Between one and two million trout fingerlings and fry per year are stocked into the New England and Barrington Tops area. However, remember that these waters are subject to low flows in drought years and the quality of the trout angling will deteriorate in these conditions.

Trout rivers of the area include the **Deepwater**, which runs through the town of Deepwater, south of Tenterfield. Downstream from the New England Highway, golden perch and cod can be caught along with trout. Other trout streams are the **Wollomombi and Gara rivers**, east of the New England Highway, the **Styx**, which begins in the Oxley Wild Rivers National Park and the **Apsley**, which rises near Walcha. The **Guy Fawkes River**, a major trout stream of the area, draws water from the Aberfoyle and Sara rivers and runs northward through rugged forest country in the eastern section of the New England plateau. There is good fishing near the Chandler River, Oaky River and Serpentine Falls. Further south, the **Macdonald River** rises to the east of Niangala and runs westward, to eventually flow into the Namoi River. All these rivers can be accessed by road.

The rivers mentioned above, and some other smaller streams, have cool temperatures for trout, especially in their upper reaches, enabling them to contribute something to the overall trout fishery of New England.

Beardy Waters, just east of Glen Innes, contains large numbers of redfin, which are also found in a number of other waters. Malpas Dam, south of Guyra, has been largely unsuccessful for trout and contains redfin. In an attempt to establish this fishery it has now been stocked with bass.

GUIDE TO LOCAL FISH

	Highlands	Western Slopes
bass, Australian		
carp, European		•
catfish		•
cod, Murray	•	•
eel		
redfin	•	•
perch, golden	•	•
perch, silver		•
trout	•	•

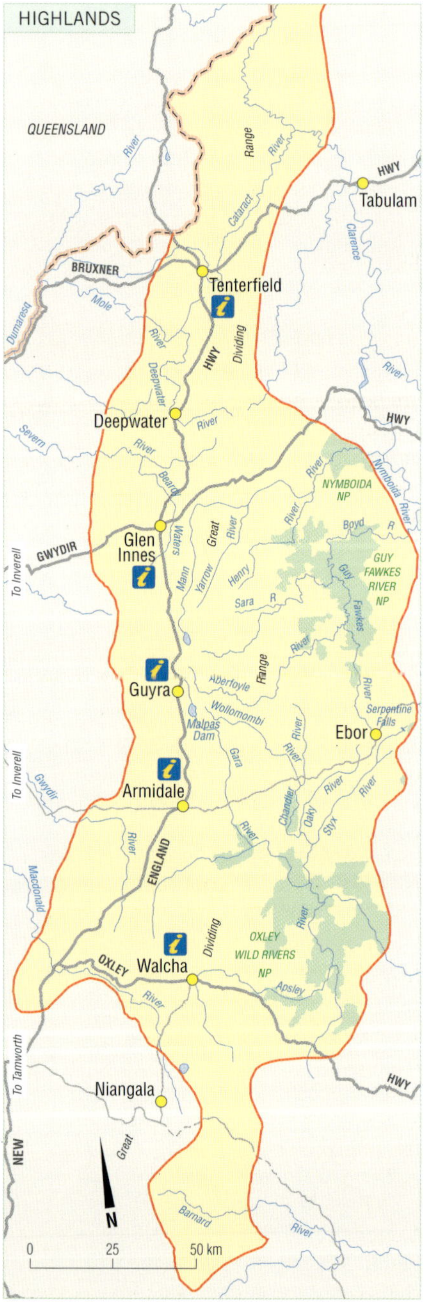

Lower Allans Water near Ebor

Western Slopes

Type of fishing
dam, lake, river

Target fish
catfish, golden perch, Murray cod, silver perch

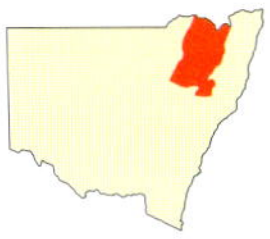

The **Dumaresq River** has many productive rocky stretches where Murray cod or golden perch can be trolled or spun from snags and corners. Good streams for native fish include **Tenterfield Creek**, which holds some excellent Murray cod.

The **Mole River**, rising south of Tenterfield, can hold trout in its upper waters, but for much of its length is best fished for natives. The **Severn**, rising in the ranges north of Glen Innes, feeds Pindari Dam, before joining the **Macintyre River** just north of Wallangra. All these waters hold native species like Murray cod and golden perch, which can be readily taken on lures when the rivers run clear, but when the water is coloured by heavy rain, species such as silver perch and catfish may be better sought with baits. Few of these rivers are boating propositions. There is fantastic fishing in rock granite gorges, although access is difficult. Keen anglers should refer to topographical maps and seek local advice. There is also great fishing in the Severn near Emmaville and in the Gwydir near Bingara because of the tremendous efforts of locals.

Pindari Dam, near Ashford, has been enlarged by five times, and has native species like golden and silver perch, Murray cod and catfish, as well as redfin. **Lake Inverell**, near the town of Inverell, has catfish, as well as golden and silver perch, while nearby **Lake Copeton** has a full complement of native species – Murray cod, catfish, golden and silver perch and large numbers of redfin. The fishing for giant golden perch is excellent in Copeton, but overcommitment to irrigators sees its level drop alarmingly over summer, which can turn the fish off. Boating is allowed on Pindari and Copeton – casting lures, trolling lures or bait fishing are all successful. In spring, land-based anglers should fish the rocky shores of these impoundments, near the dam walls, for golden perch.

The **Gwydir River** supplies Lake Copeton, and has Murray cod and golden perch. There is reasonable trout fishing in the Macintyre River above Lake Inverell where, around Elsmore, cod and trout can be taken together.

Split Rock Dam, which is fed by the Manilla River, and **Lake Keepit**, which is most easily approached from the Oxley Highway, are strongholds for golden perch. Bait fishers in Keepit generally 'bob' yabbies over submerged treetops along the old riverbed of the Namoi. Lure fishers work those same areas or troll or cast around points and ledges, and jig bladed spinners or rattling plugs over any horizontal sunken timber they can find to take goldens and cod. Keepit is now stocked with cod, golden and silver perch.

South-east of Tamworth is **Chaffey Dam**. Chaffey has Murray cod, golden and some quality silver perch and catfish. Its numerous large European carp will take wet flies and nymphs.

All these dams fish best in spring and early summer, before irrigation drawdown is greatest. They fish well again in autumn until about Easter. The state's stocking program for natives in impoundments is terrific and will ensure continued quality fishing.

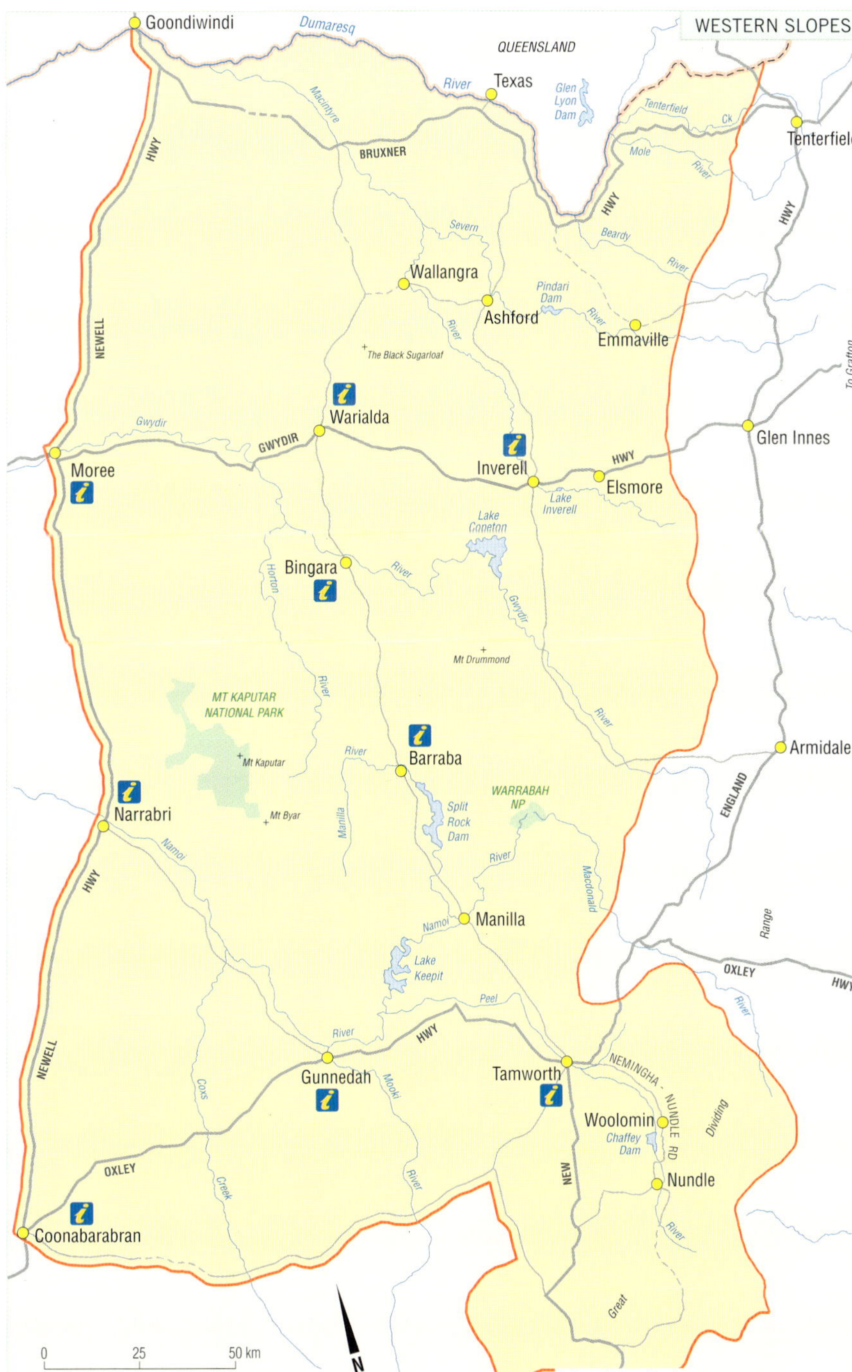

Upper Hunter Region

The countryside of this region changes in character as you descend – from semi-alpine summits, belts of wet sclerophyll and temperate rainforest where trout can be caught, down through rolling grasslands to the coastal flood plain, a section that yields native fish in abundance.

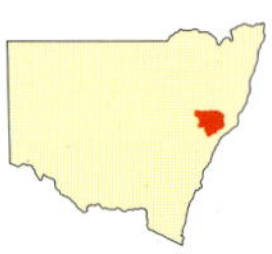

The Upper Hunter's rivers, streams and dams contain both trout and native species. Freshwater impoundments, such as Lake St Clair, Glenbawn and Lostock dams, can provide fishing for golden perch and Australian bass.

Most of the region's freshwater starts in the complex of peaks and ridges known as the Tops. The Barrington and Gloucester Tops extend, like a spread hand, roughly south, west and east from the junction of the Liverpool and Hastings ranges.

Trout have been long-time imports to the highland streams of the Top district, but it is rare for them to achieve any great size. Carp, on the other hand, present in various warm lowland streams, often reach 3 kg or more. Bass have been stocked in dams and streams, as well as catfish. While the introduced bass seem to grow rapidly in these impoundments, they cannot breed. Catfish, on the other hand, do breed and have done so very well.

In common with many other parts of New South Wales, much of the land adjacent to streams in the upper Hunter region is privately owned. While inhospitality is rare, landowners can by law deny access across their property to fish a river. Aside from public right of way, the title of rural land in New South Wales most often only extends to the high water mark, but in a handful of cases, can also include the river bed beneath the water as well, to the middle of the stream. In theory this can preclude even wading the river. However, if the stream is large enough to support a canoe or small boat, you can avoid such problems and fish the river quite legally, never needing to touch the bank or the bottom.

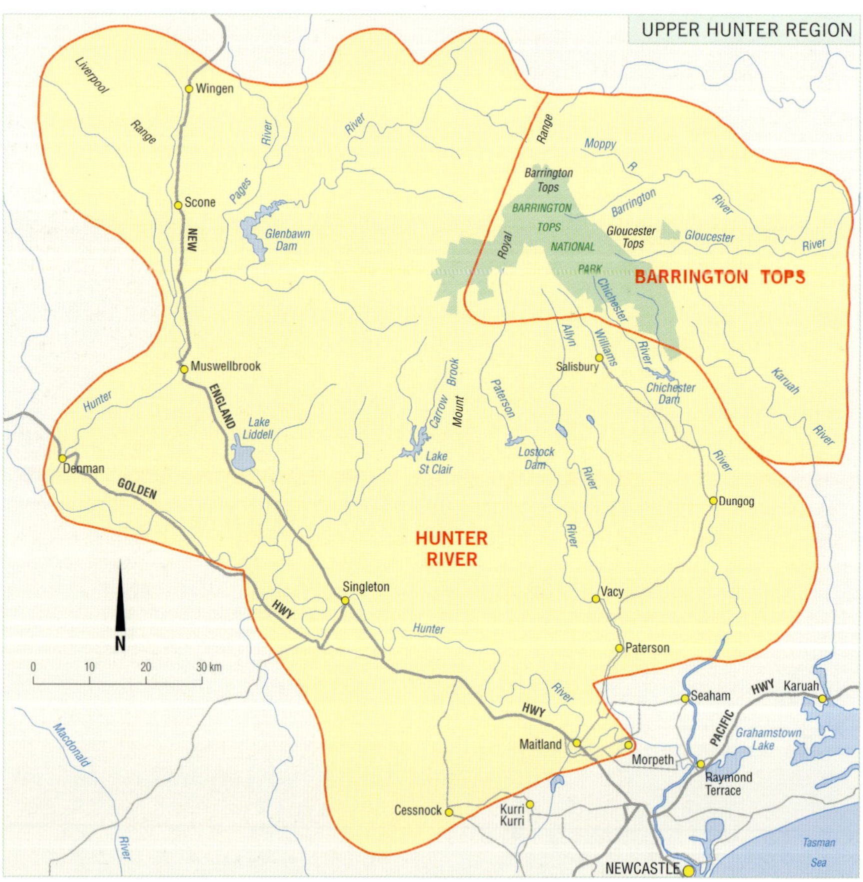

WHERE TO FISH

Upper Hunter Region

BARRINGTON TOPS • 139

The eastern slopes of the Tops can be fished for trout, and the lowland reaches of the Barrington, Moppy and Gloucester rivers provide anglers with bass, catfish and mullet. The Chichester, Allyn, Williams and Paterson rivers rise on the southern slopes and hold trout in their upper reaches.

HUNTER RIVER • 140

In the east, the southern side of the Tops (encompassing the Chichester, Williams, Allyn and Paterson rivers) has trout up high and natives down low. Dams and lakes have bass, catfish, mullet, golden perch and eels. The rest of this area essentially follows the floor of the Hunter, where bass and mullet are predominant. Glenbawn Dam has mullet, bass, golden and silver perch, Murray cod and catfish; the Hunter down to Maitland has the odd bass.

GUIDE TO LOCAL FISH

bass, Australian
carp, European
catfish
cod, Murray
eel
herring, freshwater
mullet, pinkeye
perch, golden
perch, silver
trout, brown
trout, rainbow

FURTHER INFORMATION

Fishing and boating *NSW Fisheries has an office at the Newcastle Fishermen's Co-op Building, 97 Hannell St, Wickham, tel. (02) 4927 6548 and at 55 Lambton Pde, Swansea, tel. (02) 4971 1201; NSW Maritime has an office at 8 Cowper St Sth, Carrington, tel. (02) 4962 8500.*

Tourist centres *198 Dowling St, Dungog, tel. (02) 4992 2212; 27 Denison St, Gloucester, tel. (02) 6558 1408; cnr New England Hwy and High St, Maitland, tel. (02) 4931 2800; 87 Hill St, Muswellbrook, tel. (02) 6541 4050; cnr Susan and Kelly sts, Scone, tel. (02) 6545 1526; 39 George St, Singleton, tel. (02) 6571 5888.*

Barrington Tops

Type of fishing
river
Target fish
bass, catfish, mullet, trout

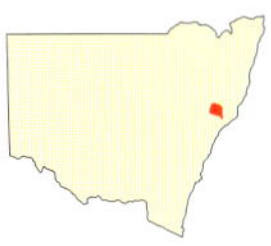

The rivers and streams of the Tops can be a challenge to fish. Access is limited by the rugged topography of the Barrington Tops National Park. The best tactic is to walk a kilometre or so from an access point before starting to fish. These streams warm up in summer so fish in the aerated water of riffles and at the heads of pools as the season progresses. Flies, jigs and spinners work well in the tight waters.

East-flowing streams such as the **Moppy, Barrington** and **Gloucester rivers** and their tributaries rise in the Tops district, and hold brown and rainbow trout in their upper reaches, but rainbows are the most commonly caught. The water temperature in these streams rises as they reach lower country and, providing no obstructions exist to prevent free movement from downstream, bass, mullet and catfish can start to put in an appearance. Even though, in strict drainage terms, the rivers mentioned do not fall within the Upper Hunter system (they feed the Karuah's system, not the Hunter's), they are commonly regarded as being within the Hunter's angling scope and promoted as such in tourist and angling literature.

Some streams are overstocked and have large numbers of small fish. Anything over the old pound mark can be considered a good catch, but this is challenging fishing and very enjoyable and rewarding.

Elk Hair Caddis

The Elk Hair is a good imitation of one of our most important trout stream insects.

GUIDE TO LOCAL FISH

bass, Australian
catfish
mullet
trout, brown
trout, rainbow

One of several small streams carrying trout in the Barrington Tops area. The fish are rarely large, but thrive on a diet of terrestrial and aquatic insects in this picturesque country

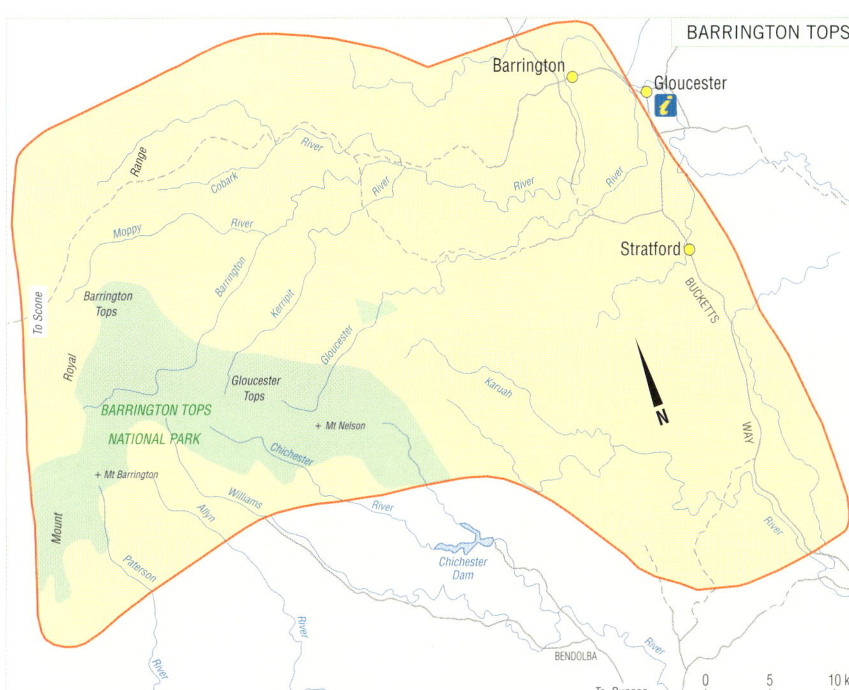

Hunter River

Type of fishing
dam, lake, river
Target fish
bass, catfish, golden perch, mullet, trout

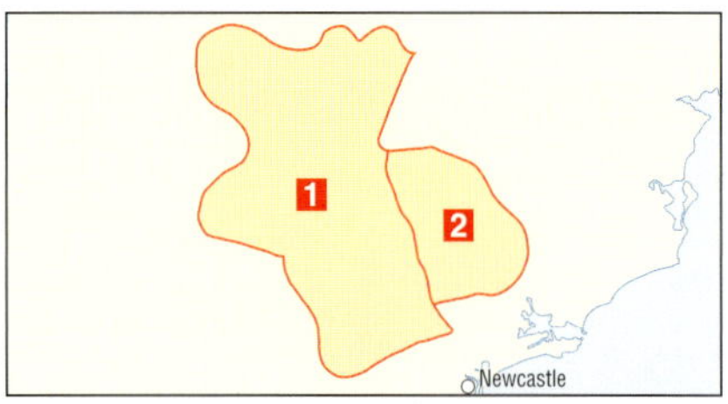

The Hunter River rises above Glenbawn Dam, picks up the Paterson River at Morpeth and receives tribute from other rivers rising in the Barringtons, such as the Chichester and Williams, where the Williams River joins the Hunter at Raymond Terrace before flowing to the coast. Other south-flowing streams from the Barrington Tops, such as the Paterson and its tributaries, feed the Hunter at Morpeth.

WILLIAMS–PATERSON RIVERS

This sector contains an interesting collection of rivers and dams. The **Chichester, Williams, Allyn** and **Paterson rivers** hold trout in their upper reaches, and have quality bass, mullet and catfish further down.

Angling is prohibited in Chichester Dam, and the Hunter Water Corporation,

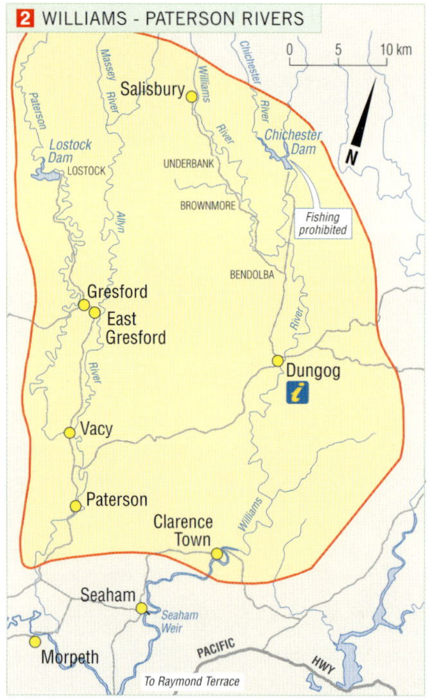

which controls the Chichester Catchment Area, actively discourages entry.

The **Williams River** runs alongside small farming communities between Salisbury and Bendolba, but fishes best from Dungog down, continuing through Clarence Town and on to Raymond Terrace.

The **lower Allyn River** can produce some good mullet fishing as far down as its junction with the Paterson River near Vacy, on the road between Paterson and East Gresford. The Paterson feeds **Lostock Dam**, a small irrigation impoundment that

GUIDE TO LOCAL FISH

	Williams–Paterson Rivers	Hunter River
bass, Australian	•	•
carp, European		•
catfish	•	•
cod, Murray		•
eel	•	
herring, freshwater		•
mullet	•	•
perch, golden		•
perch, silver		•
trout	•	•

has been stocked with bass, and also has catfish. Although Lostock is improving, fish don't come easily.

Below Lostock, the **Paterson River** continues roughly south-east to Morpeth, and in this stretch it has good numbers of freshwater mullet, with some good bass water downstream towards its junction with the Hunter.

HUNTER RIVER

From the west-facing peaks of the Barrington Tops, **Polblue Creek** and **Moonan** and **Omadale brooks** run towards the headwaters of the Hunter River, carrying trout as far down as about 800 m elevation. The fishing is often patchy though, because the western streams warm more quickly than their eastern counterparts, and for much of the year they have temperatures unsuitable

Lake St Clair, near Singleton, suits small boat fishing and supports an excellent fishery of bass and golden perch, with some catfish, mullet and eel as well

for trout. The **Hunter River**, with its source in the Liverpool–Hastings range, picks up these tributaries and irrigates the fertile valley that bears its name. Flowing south, and to the east of Scone, the Hunter supplies Glenbawn Dam, above which it carries little except mullet.

Glenbawn Dam itself holds Australian bass, golden and silver perch, Murray cod (which have been stocked illegally), mullet and catfish. It is by far the biggest and most heavily fished impoundment in the area. Catfish, in particular, have found Glenbawn to their liking. The bass are mostly chunky middleweights, but some are large and powerful fish. While the silver perch fishery is not remarkable, the goldens make up for it, with 2-kg fish being common. A huge 16-kg golden perch was caught from this dam and fish over 8 kg are taken by those who put in the time. Glenbawn's obvious potential as a bass and golden perch fishery is fast becoming legend. Land-based angling is limited to the lower section of the dam, but boating is allowed and is usually rewarding. Glenbawn is one of the state's few impoundments where access is permitted along the dam wall. Trolling or casting the wall is most productive, although rocky points are also good.

Below **Glenbawn Dam**, the Hunter sweeps through stock and crop country past Muswellbrook, then, through Denman, eastward to Singleton and Maitland, before picking up the Williams River at Raymond Terrace – the freshwater extent of the system. The freshwater species on offer are principally mullet, bass, herring, catfish and European carp.

Freshwater fishing in the Hunter is no longer as good as its size might suggest. This once-great river is only a shadow of its former self. Massive demands on its water frequently reduce its volume and water quality markedly, and that it survives to be worth fishing in its lower freshwater reaches is due largely to the inflow of the comparatively unscathed Paterson and Williams rivers.

Lake St Clair, fed by Carrow Brook and the now-drowned Glennies Creek, has catfish, eels, bass and golden perch. It is the best of the still waters in the area and boats are permitted. Glennies Creek below the dam can be very sandy and shallow, but reasonably good fishing can be found by casting to small, deep pockets of cover. Try the crossing a few kilometres downstream of the dam wall and around Aberdeen for better results, although bass can be caught around Muswellbrook, Denman and Jerrys Plains for those who make the effort.

Glenbawn Dam offers good fishing for Australian bass, golden perch and some Murray cod

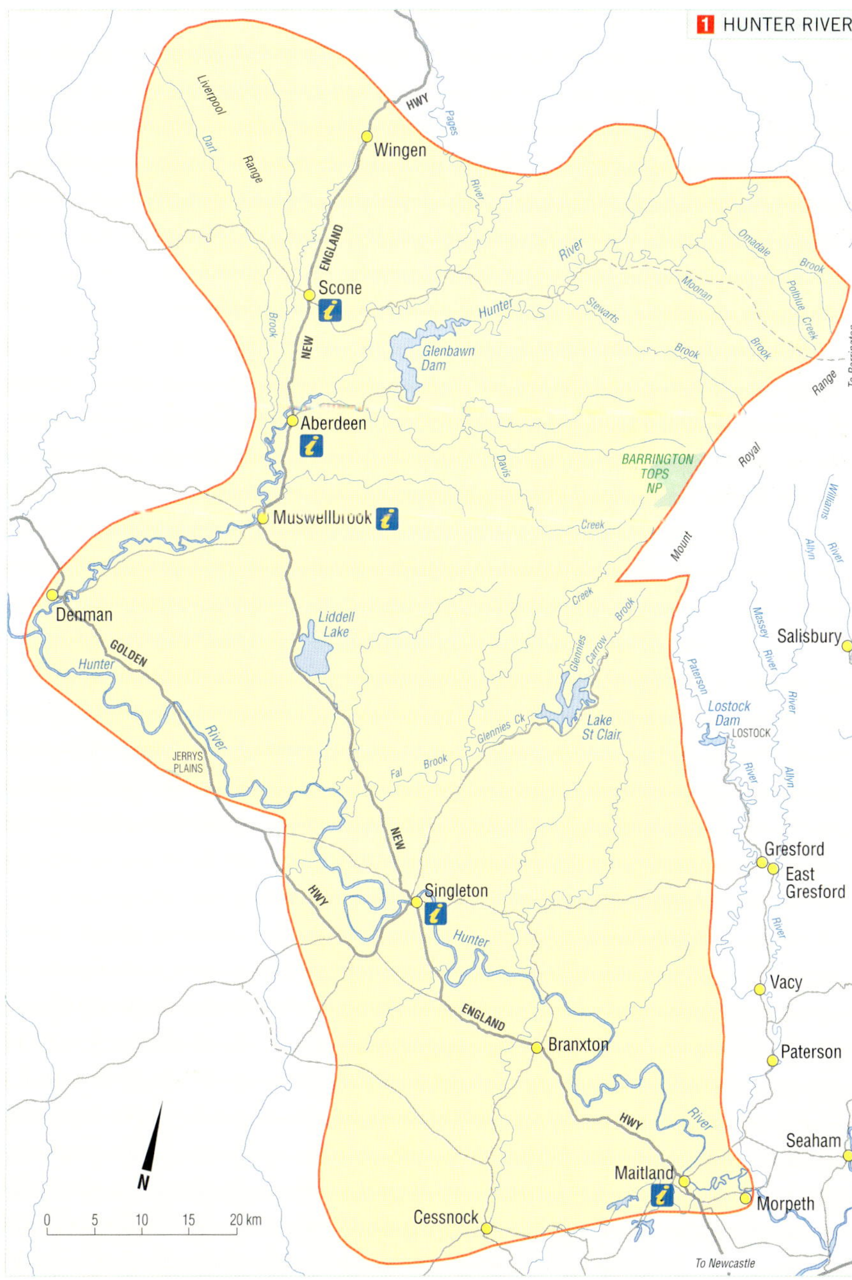

Central Highlands Region

This region offers tremendous variety, with small fly fishing waters for educated trout, larger rivers and tailraces where trophy trout can be found and some fantastic impoundment fishing for trout and native species.

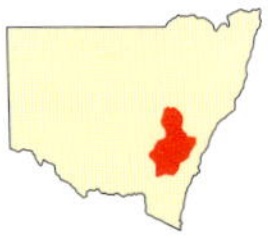

When heavy rain falls, some waters become turbid because of run-off, but this usually clears quickly. In dry spells, the same rivers can nearly stop flowing, and suffer from algal blooms. Given regular rain, however, most streams in the area provide good fishing for much of the season.

Access to the streams in the region can be difficult. The bulk of the best water runs through private property, so reaching it often means getting through gates, and good fishing relies heavily on grace and favour arrangements with local landowners. Many farmers, however, have had bad experiences with anglers in the past and are cautious about allowing them on their properties. While riparian rights legislation in New South Wales provides theoretical access to all rivers, real life access depends on finding out who owns or controls the land, making the necessary overtures to gain permission, and getting your public relations skills up to speed.

The difficulty of accessing these rivers encourages many people to fish the many large dams in the region. Wyangala and Burrinjuck lakes have trout and native fish species.

There are three superb trout fishing lakes in the Lithgow district. Lake Lyell on the Cox's River near Bowenfels is the largest, Lake Wallerawang (Lake Wallis) at Wallerawang is next in size and Thompson's Creek Dam, also near Wallerawang, is both the newest and the smallest. Powerboats are allowed on Lake Lyell but not on Lake Wallerawang and no boats of any description are allowed on Thompson Creek Dam.

GUIDE TO LOCAL FISH

- Atlantic salmon
- blackfish, river
- carp, European
- catfish
- cod, Murray
- crayfish, Murray
- redfin
- perch, golden
- perch, silver
- trout, brown
- trout, rainbow

Brown trout

This fish, considered a great sporting challenge, was introduced to Australia from Europe in the 1880s. Those caught by most anglers average around 1 kg, although large specimens can reach 10 kg. They are brown to blackish brown in colour, with red and black spots covering their sides.

WHERE TO FISH

Central Highlands Region

MUDGEE ● **144**

Lake Windamere, Rylstone Weir and Lake Burrendong are great native fisheries, as are the Cudgegong and Macquarie rivers, which feed these impoundments. Lake Wallerawang near Lithgow, and its tributary streams, hold brown and rainbow trout, as does the Macquarie below Burrendong.

BATHURST ● **145**

This area forms the nucleus of the Central Highland's freshwater fishery, with the complex of rivers that feed Lake Burragorang providing some of the best trout waters in the state. There are natives and redfin in some rivers and dams.

GOULBURN ● **146**

Streams such as the Wollondilly, Crookwell and Abercrombie have trout, as do some of their tributaries. Lake George has native fish, and there are trout in both the Pejar and Redground dams.

YASS ● **147**

Lake Wyangala and Burrinjuck Dam hold native fish and trout. Both have excellent tailrace fisheries for larger trout. There are redfin and golden perch in Carcoar Lake to the north.

FURTHER INFORMATION

Fishing and boating *NSW Fisheries has offices at Research Station Dr, Bathurst, tel. (02) 6331 1428; 30 Warne St, Wellington, tel. 1300 550 474; and at 25 Warroo Rd, Yass, tel. (02) 6226 3867. The nearest NSW Maritime office is at 2/43 Macquarie St, Dubbo, tel. (02) 6884 5355.*

Tourist centres *28 William St, Bathurst, tel. (02) 6332 1444 or 1800 681 000; Shire Council, 91 Adelaide St, Blayney, tel. (02) 6368 2104; 44 Goulburn St, Crookwell, tel. (02) 4832 1988; Great Western Hwy, Glenbrook, tel. 1300 653 408; 201 Sloane St, Goulburn, tel. (02) 4823 4492; Echo Point Rd, Katoomba, tel. (02) 4780 5729; 1 Cooerwull Rd, Lithgow, tel. (02) 6353 1859; 84 Market St, Mudgee, tel. (02) 6372 5875; Civic Gardens, Byng St, Orange, tel. (02) 6393 8226; Bridge View Inn, Louee St, Rylstone, tel. (02) 6379 1807; Cameron Park, Nanima Crs, Wellington, tel. (02) 6845 1733; Coronation Park, Comur St, Yass, tel. (02) 6226 2557; 2 Short St, Young, tel. (02) 6382 3394.*

Casting from shore at Lake Windamere is an excellent fishing method for golden perch, the resident sportfish

Mudgee

Type of fishing
dam, lake, river
Target fish
golden perch, silver perch, trout

The **Cudgegong River** rises above **Lake Windamere**. Below Windamere, it runs through Mudgee and into **Lake Burrendong**, which has Murray cod, golden and silver perch, catfish and countless redfin. **Rylstone Weir** will take small boats, and has golden perch, catfish and river blackfish. It is ostensibly a picnic spot, with angling as an added attraction.

Lake Windamere, near Mudgee, by contrast is a spectacular and versatile fishery. Access is good and you can fish from a boat, from the shores – reached by road – or from the road rock walls. The dominant species are golden and silver perch, with an improving Murray cod fishery and no carp or redfin. Goldens and silvers can be caught here in reasonable numbers and are of good size. Baits, lures or flies work, and while trolling is popular, one of the best ways to fish – for goldens in particular – is to walk the banks while wearing polarised sunglasses to spot fish before casting to them. Murray cod introduced into the lake are starting to do well, with catch rates climbing all the time.

This area also takes in the headwaters of the south-flowing **Coxs River**, the source for Lake Wallerawang, and further to the north, the west flowing **Turon River**, which joins the Macquarie north of Bathurst. Both these rivers are excellent trout fisheries. **Lake Wallerawang** holds brown and rainbow trout, most of which are less than 1 kg, although there are occasional trophy-sized specimens. The banks fish particularly well for big rainbows in the evening with fly.

There is also good fishing around Orange and Molong in the small creeks. Lake Canobolas was once a small but premier trout fishery before redfin were introduced. It is now stocked with golden perch to supplement the trout and redfin. The protected trout cod has been stocked into the upper reaches of the Turon River and should be returned to the water if caught.

The Macquarie River, in the waters below Burrendong, holds both brown and rainbow trout. Good cod are also caught in the river, especially around Long Point.

Lake Windamere, where the angler can fish from a boat, from shore or from the road rock walls

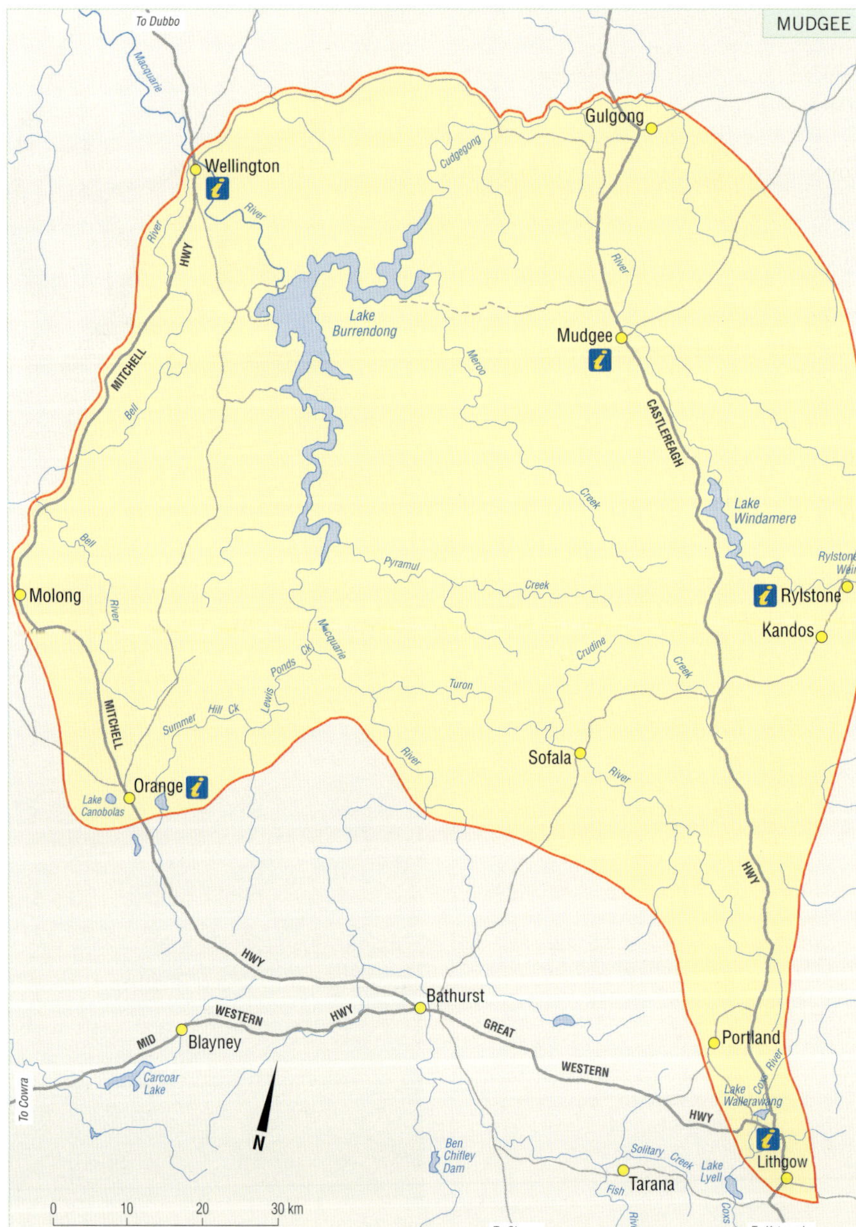

Bathurst

Type of fishing
dam, lake, river
Target fish
trout

In this area, the major towns of Bathurst, Lithgow and Oberon are centres for trout fishing, and most of the trout streams are within a day-trip of these towns. The upland streams forming the nucleus of the Central Highlands' freshwater fishery rise in high forests to the south of Oberon. The **Fish, Duckmaloi** and **Campbells rivers** all drain roughly northward and are all trout waters.

At **Lake Oberon** (near the town), fishing from boats is not allowed, but the lake can be fished from the banks right through the year. It yields good-sized browns and rainbows on lures, baits or fly.

Ben Chifley Dam, south of Bathurst, can be fished from bank or boat, and has some brown but mostly rainbow trout, a few Murray cod and golden perch, and heaps of tiny redfin.

In the south-west, the Isabella and Retreat (also known as Little) rivers flow southwards, their waters eventually running into Lake Wyangala. These south-flowing streams also carry trout. In the north-west the lower reaches of the Macquarie River is a trout water, but carries native species, too.

In the east, the other major drainage system in the area comprises the Kedumba, Coxs, Jenolan, Tuglow, Kowmung, Tonalli, Wollondilly and Nattai rivers and the Blackheath and Butchers creeks, which all wind up in Lake Burragorang, Sydney's main water supply dam. The lake itself is prohibited to public access but the vast bulk of the huge canyons and extensive rivers above it are not. The principal stream in this complex is the **Coxs River** which, with the **Jenolan, Tuglow** and **Kowmung rivers**, forms Burragorang's northern catchment. Access to these upper reaches is limited to dirt tracks, suitable only for four-wheel-drive vehicles. Some more remote sections can only be reached by hiking. On the Coxs River, near Lithgow, **Lake Lyell** holds brown and rainbow trout, as does Lake Wallerawang and the Thompson Creek Dam.

In the northern reaches of the Kedumba River, the **lake at Wentworth Falls**, near Katoomba, has both brown and rainbow trout.

An idyllic Central Highlands trout stream: Solitary Creek near Tarana

GUIDE TO LOCAL FISH

	Mudgee	Bathurst
blackfish, river	•	
catfish	•	
cod, Murray	•	•
redfin	•	•
perch, golden	•	•
perch, silver	•	
trout, brown	•	•
trout, rainbow	•	•

Goulburn

Type of fishing
dam, lake, river
Target fish
golden perch, silver perch, trout

The rivers in this area hold good numbers of both brown and rainbow trout, with fishing best in cooler months although good results can be had during the summer hopper season, especially by walking some distance from major roads before starting to fish.

Two major trout rivers have their headwaters in the southern highlands around Goulburn and Crookwell: the **Wollondilly**, which runs north into Lake Burragorang; and the **Crookwell**, which runs north-west into the Lachlan River.

To the north, the **Abercrombie River** also has trout, and natives such as silver, golden and Macquarie perch. The Macquaries and recently stocked trout cod are protected, however, and must be released alive if caught.

Redground Dam, or Crookwell Reservoir, near Crookwell, has trout, Murray cod, golden and silver perch and catfish. **Pejar Dam**, north-west of Goulburn, offers excellent fly fishing for large trout in the cooler months. While power boats are not permitted on the dam, some anglers use float-tubes to reach otherwise inaccessible banks and are rewarded with large fish. Lake Sooley is the water supply dam for the town of Goulburn, and no fishing is allowed. To the south of Goulburn, **Lake Bathurst** holds few fish.

Lake George, which periodically dries up, has been stocked with golden perch, silver perch and Murray cod. Fishing can be very good for those who find deeper water with cover that holds fish.

GUIDE TO LOCAL FISH

	Goulburn	Yass
Atlantic salmon		•
carp, European		•
catfish	•	•
cod, Murray	•	•
redfin		•
perch, golden	•	•
perch, silver	•	•
trout, brown	•	•
trout, rainbow	•	•

There are plenty of back country streams in this area holding some beautiful trout

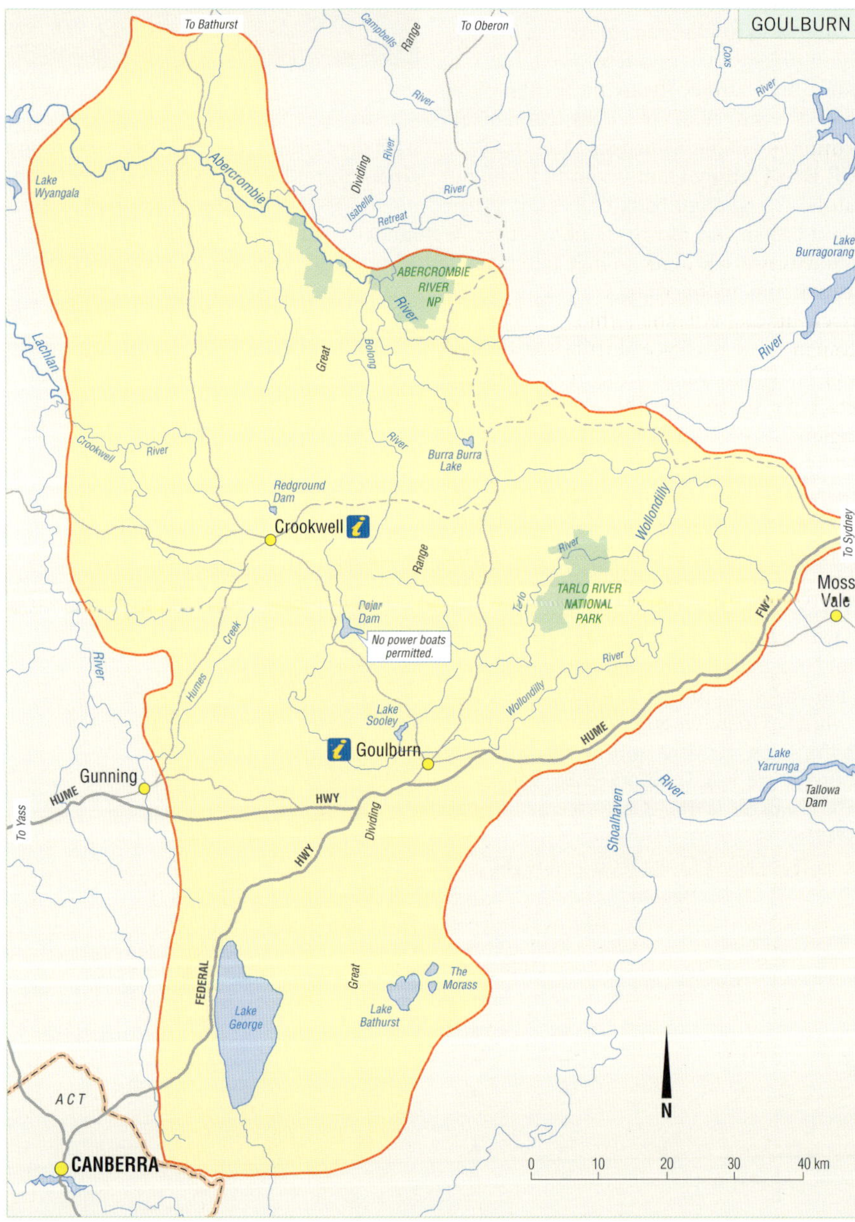

Yass

Type of fishing
dam, lake, river
Target fish
Atlantic salmon, golden perch, Murray cod, silver perch, trout

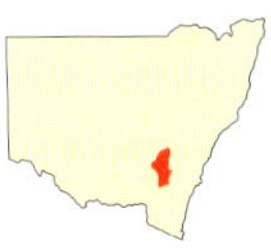

Lake Wyangala and Burrinjuck Dam are fed by extensive catchments, while Carcoar Lake is more modest. **Carcoar Lake** accepts boats and bank anglers, but is relatively featureless and sometimes malodorous. Its major attraction is tonnes of redfin, some of which can be sizeable. It carries some golden perch and recent stockings of Murray cod. While the goldens are known to eat redfin, the survival of the cod fingerlings is as yet unproven. If they do become established, they too will feed well on the abundant redfin. If the cod fingerlings survive, they will have plenty of redfin to eat, so growth rates may prove to be excellent.

Lake Wyangala, near Cowra, has both golden and silver perch, and Murray cod. It also has a rainbow trout fishery that is at times excellent, and Atlantic salmon and brown trout in the cool tailrace water below the dam wall. This dam is one of the most popular west of Sydney, with good facilities for boat anglers and plenty of access to the shores for land-based enthusiasts. Bush camping is allowed all around the lake and there are a number of excellent caravan parks.

The **Lachlan River**, which flows through Lake Wyangala, and the Abercrombie River, hold trout in the reaches above the lake. Sizeable fish can be found at Reids Flat early and late in the season, but they are either there in numbers or not at all. Below the lake the Lachlan tailrace contains some trophy brown trout, as well as large, hard-fighting rainbow trout. Atlantic salmon have also been stocked here.

Burrinjuck Dam, is a huge reservoir that offers golden and silver perch, Murray cod, carp, redfin, catfish, trout and Atlantic salmon. Macquarie perch are also here, but this protected species must be released alive if taken. Land-based angling is popular but the best results are from a boat. The Murrumbidgee offers good fishing above and below the lake, while the Yass is a mediocre stream.

Further south, the Goodradigbee River at Wee Jasper is a well-known trout area and contains monster cod in lower reaches during the closed season.

Wyangala Dam contains both native fish and trout

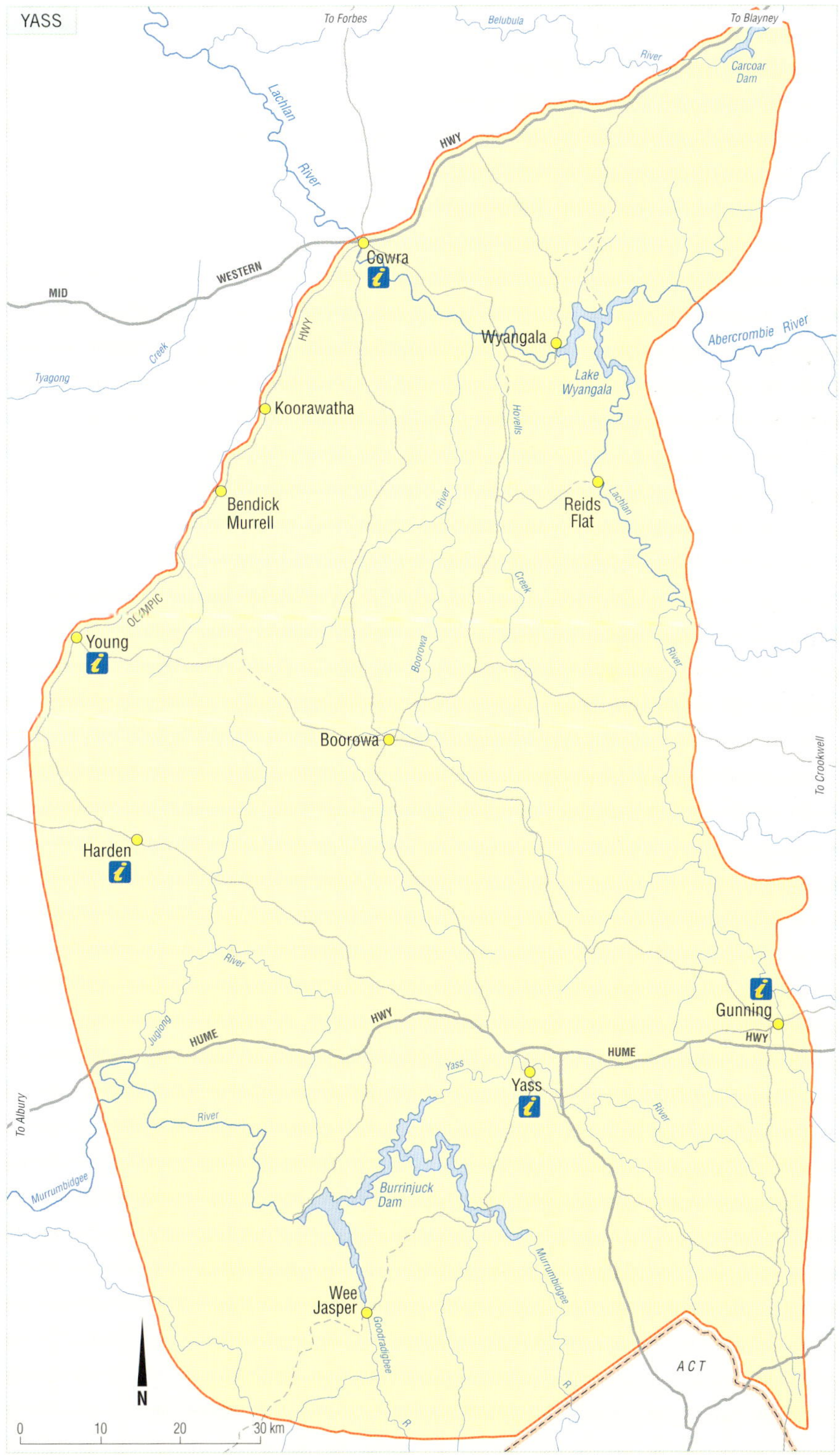

Snowy Mountains Region

This area is the premier trout fishery in New South Wales. Views of the snow-covered peaks of the main range are commonplace and the scenery is spectacular. The large impoundments provide fishing fun for thousands of anglers every year, and attract large numbers of boat anglers. The big waters are well suited to the practice of trolling artificial lures behind boats, a method of fishing that is easy and relaxing for the whole family.

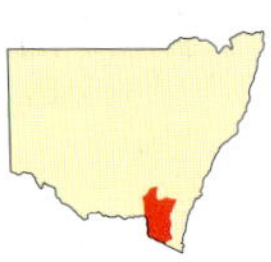

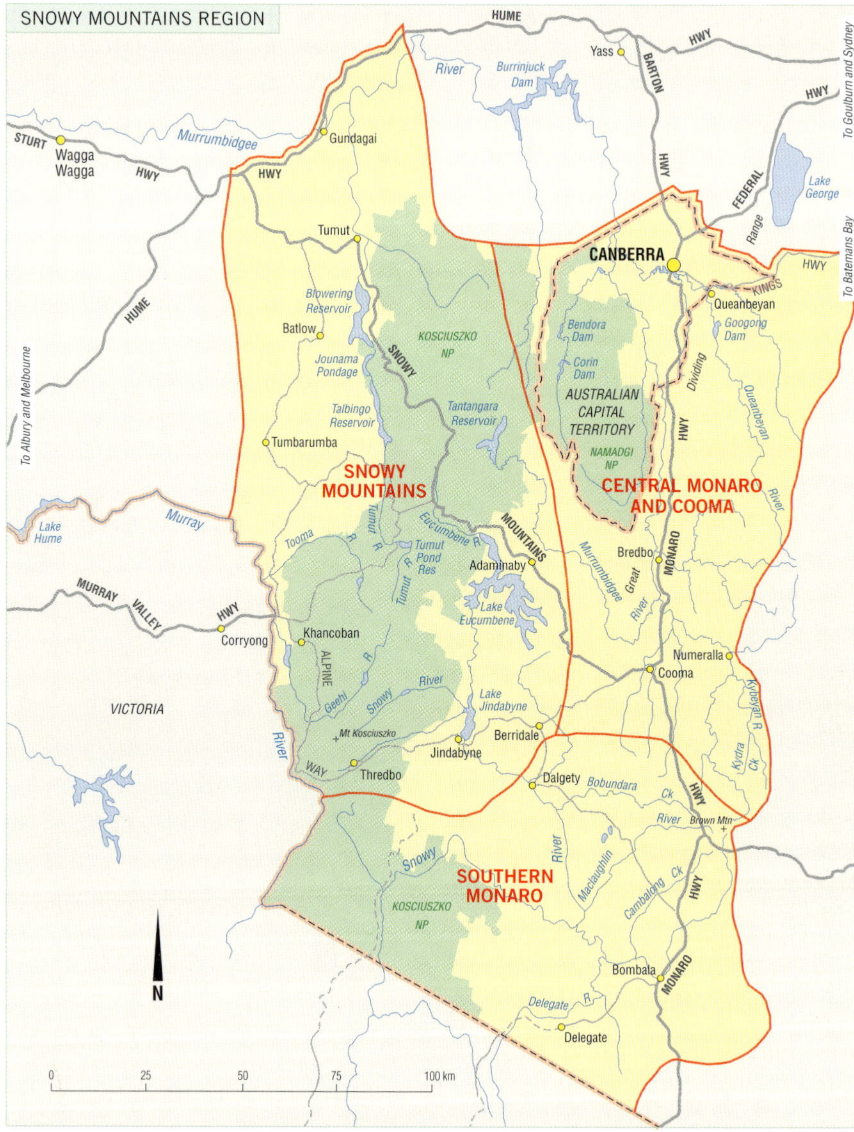

The highest mountains in Australia provide the run-off for the streams and rivers of this region. Rivers such as the Thredbo and the Eucumbene are swift and cold and they feed the huge, cool Jindabyne and Eucumbene lakes. There are other smaller dams, built as part of the Snowy Mountains Hydro Scheme, such as Tantangara, Island Bend and Talbingo, and these waters, too, often produce exciting trout fishing. On the Monaro plateau the rivers and creeks are more sedate, and the Murrumbidgee, Maclaughlin, Kybeyan and Numeralla rivers, and the Rock Flat, Bobundara, Kydra and Cambalong creeks, meander along in a series of weedy pools.

Trout are the main quarry for anglers in the region and the two main species present are browns and rainbows. The rainbow trout is an important contributor to the impoundment fisheries and the brown is the blue-ribbon target of the fly fisher in the streams. The flowing waters offer a wide range of fishing options, with the large gravel-bottomed rivers favouring spin and fly fishing amidst rugged mountain scenery, the high plains streams catering for the true fly enthusiast, and the headwaters of the eastern-flowing creeks offering a pleasant diversion for the casual spin fisher. Atlantic salmon are also found in Lake Jindabyne and brook trout are a rare catch in Lake Jindabyne and other waters.

The western slopes hold good native populations and the Murray crayfish is a tasty catch from the Murrumbidgee River.

The lakes and ponds of the Snowy Mountains offer great fly fishing in summer

WHERE TO FISH

Snowy Mountains Region

CENTRAL MONARO AND COOMA ● 150

This area lies between the mountains and the coastal escarpment, with the Australian Capital Territory within its western boundary. This is one of Australia's most challenging trout fisheries and the Monaro rivers offer some of the best fly fishing in the world. Many of the streams here can be affected by low summer flows.

SOUTHERN MONARO ● 151

The Southern Monaro straddles a steep escarpment: to the east, the lower streams flow to the Tasman Sea and they can be marginal for trout because of high temperatures. West of Brown Mountain there are high growth-rate basalt streams that fly fishers rate highly. The fishing can be technical and difficult but to a keen devotee of the sport this only makes it more desirable. There is a small hydro lake known as Cochrane Dam at the top of Brown Mountain, however, that is well stocked with small rainbows, and this venue is suitable for beginners.

SNOWY MOUNTAINS ● 152

Many of the region's rivers have been dammed to form the famous Snowy scheme, and the resultant impoundments have achieved high status as trout waters. The streams in this area are cool and fast-flowing, with gravelly bottoms and rapids. Trout are smaller than in the Monaro streams, but generally more abundant. This area is magnificent and encompasses one of the finest all-round fisheries in the country. Native fish can be caught in Blowering Reservoir and the lower Murrumbidgee River.

GUIDE TO LOCAL FISH

- Atlantic salmon
- carp, European
- cod, Murray
- crayfish, Murray
- redfin
- perch, golden
- perch, silver
- trout, brook
- trout, brown
- trout, rainbow

Fly fishing the Thredbo River

Special status streams

Several streams in the Snowy Mountains have been classified as 'catch and release only' or have reduced bag limits. For details contact NSW Fisheries.

Rainbow trout

The rainbow trout, native to America, can reach 10 kg, but 2-kg specimens are more likely. It is greenish in colour on its back, with red markings along its sides, which brighten in the breeding season. The underbelly is silver.

FURTHER INFORMATION

Fishing and boating *NSW Fisheries has offices at 39 Bombala St, Cooma, tel. (02) 6452 3411; Kosciuszko Rd, Jindabyne, tel. (02) 6451 3400; and 64 Fitzroy St, Tumut, tel. (02) 6947 4188. NSW Maritime has an office at 1/1 Buttle St, Queanbeyan, tel. (02) 6297 4985, open Thursday and Fridays.*

Tourist centres *119 Sharp St, Cooma, tel. (02) 6450 1742; Canberra Visitors Centre, Northbourne Ave, Dickson (Canberra), tel. 1800 100 660; Snowy Region Visitor Centre, Kosciuszko Rd, Jindabyne, tel. (02) 6450 5600; National Parks and Wildlife Service, Scott St, Khancoban, tel. (02) 6076 9373; cnr Farrer Pl and Lowe St, Queanbeyan, tel. (02) 6298 0241; 31 The Parade, Tumbarumba, tel. (02) 6948 3444; 7 Adelong Rd (Snowy Mountains Hwy), Tumut, tel. (02) 6947 7025.*

Central Monaro and Cooma

Type of fishing
dam, river
Target fish
brown trout, rainbow trout

Googong Dam catchment, south-east of Queanbeyan, is a fine fishery, with brown trout, rainbow trout, golden perch, Murray cod and the protected Macquarie perch. Redfin now make up the bulk of the catch. Trolling is the preferred method here as the banks are steep and difficult to access. Boats may be powered with electric motors or oars – petrol motors are banned.

The **Murrumbidgee River** is an excellent stream that has a good head of rainbow and brown trout, as well as small pockets of the protected trout cod. Murray cod and silver perch are also present. Popular spots include Pine Island and Casuarina Sands. In the main, the section of river that flows through this area is fished for trout. Bait drifting with natural grasshoppers is popular and there are regular evening hatches of aquatic insects to keep the fly fisher happy. Spinning for the rainbows with Celta-style lures or jigs also works well in the faster water. The majority of the fish are small, with the average being well under 1 kg, but there have been some large brown trout over 3 kg taken from this water. European carp are now seen in the lower reaches.

Small brown and rainbow trout are taken from the **Bredbo River**, but the lower reaches tend to overheat and it doesn't have a high reputation. The **Numerella River** is formed when the Kydra and the Kybeyan join and it then flows into the Murrumbidgee. Both rainbow and brown trout can be taken and small lures and flies are the best producers. The river forms long shallow pools with gravel runs between them.

Kydra Creek winds its way through thick tussock country and wooded hills, and carries brightly coloured small brown trout. The occasional fish does reach 1 kg but the stream is fished fairly hard and big ones are rare. There are good rises to mayflies and grasshoppers, and the Kydra is a delightful dry fly stream if rainfall has been reasonable.

Running through extremely fertile country, the **Kybeyan River** is sometimes almost choked up with weed. The dense weed, however, provides great cover for brown trout and plenty of food in the form of mayfly nymphs, damsel flies and caddis. The fish run up to 1.5 kg, with the odd bigger one showing up at times. Warm spring days often herald frantic action as fish jump for mayfly 'spinners'.

Another of the slow weedy creeks that often produce outsized brown trout, **Big Badja River** is predominantly a fly fishing water featuring rich weed beds crawling with insect life. Good fishing depends to a large degree on the rainfall – if the seasons have been good for a few years the Badja can fish brilliantly, but significant fish-kills during droughts often reduce the fish population.

Rock Flat Creek is a fertile stream plagued by a low water flow. In good seasons both brown and rainbow trout rise freely to mayflies and beetles. Fish can attain a good size here and some approaching 4.5 kg have been taken. The area is most suited to fly fishing. While not being a recognised water, **Cooma Creek** does have a trout population.

Near the western border of the Australian Capital Territory and within easy reach of Canberra, the **Goodradigbee River** is heavily fished, but it is possible to take brown trout and rainbows in picturesque settings. Summer fishing with grasshoppers and their imitations can be very successful.

The Molonga River can be patchy, but produces reasonable trout as well as Macquarie perch.

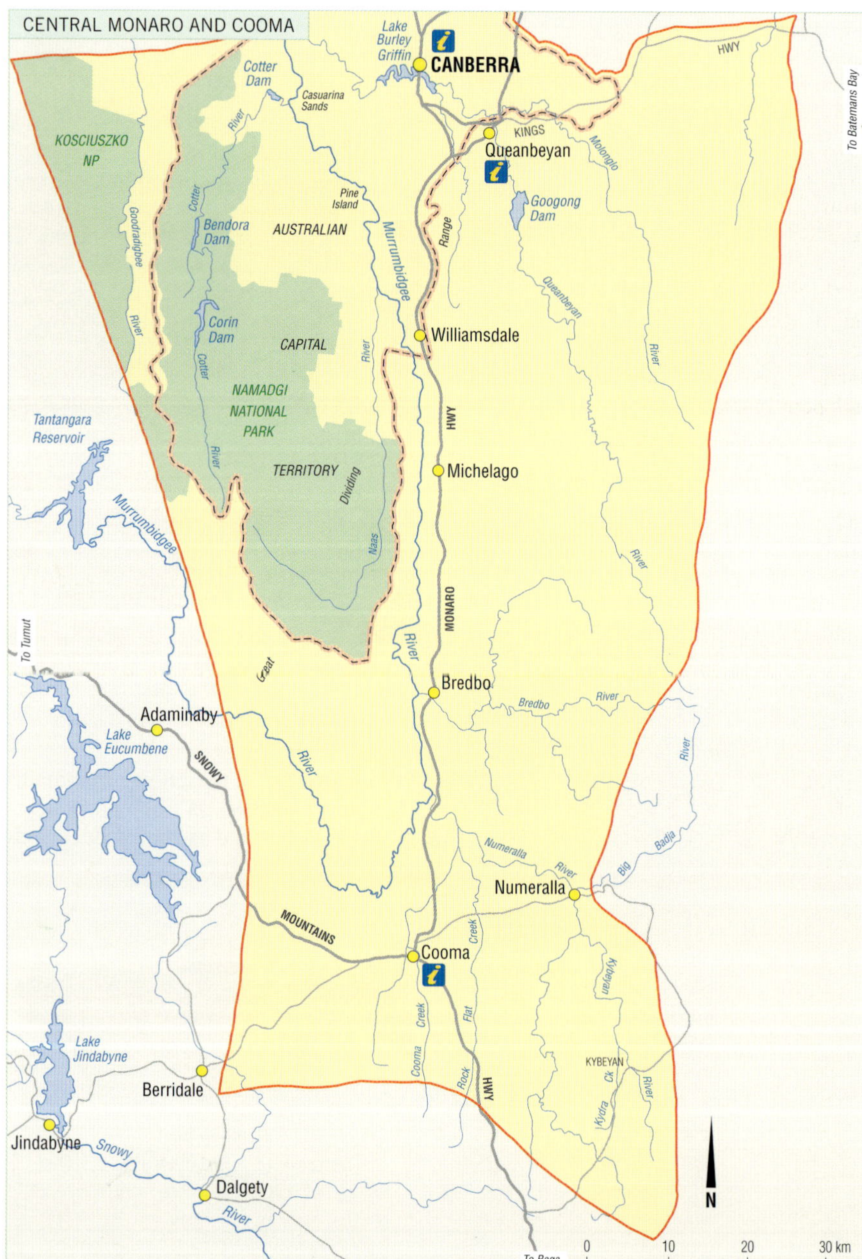

Southern Monaro

Type of fishing
river
Target fish
brown trout, rainbow trout

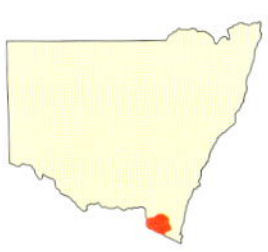

This whole area is lightly populated but there is increasing fishing pressure because trout fishing is undergoing something of a boom and the Southern Monaro is recognised as a prime location. Scenically, the area is very attractive and it has enormous potential for eco-tourism activities.

The **Maclaughlin River** is affectionately known as the 'Mac' and is a prominent attraction. It is a stream made up of shallow stony runs and long still pools. It produces brown trout with an average weight of around 1 kg and occasional specimens over 3 kg. Fly fishing is the most successful method. Small nymphs and dry flies are recommended here. Public access points are few but landowners will generally allow entry to responsible anglers prepared to seek permission.

Cambalong Creek has a mixed population of brown and rainbow trout in its deep still pools – best fished with nymphs and small dries as well as small bladed lures. Some of the rainbows can reach significant size. Often affected by dry conditions, the **Bombala River** is slow and weedy and has a reasonable population of brown trout. Fly fishers often do well on ant patterns as much of the river has timbered banks.

The **Coolumbooka River** suffers from a small catchment area and is in an unreliable rainfall pocket. Shallow areas allow the river to heat up quickly and it only holds quantities of reasonable-sized fish in wet seasons. A marginal brown trout water with fish up to 1 kg in high rainfall years, **Saucy Creek** can have a heavy weed growth problem.

Only a short section of the **Little Plains River** flows through New South Wales before it runs into the Delegate, but it maintains a good head of smaller brown trout that rise freely to grasshopper-pattern flies and take small lures.

The **Delegate River** rises in Victoria, in high rainfall country, so it fishes well when other rivers in the southern Monaro are drought-affected. Early morning and especially evening hatches of mayflies can be spectacular. Tiger snakes abound in the marshy areas above Delegate township.

Fishing in the **Snowy River** has suffered from a restricted flow since the Jindabyne dam was completed, but in wet seasons there are brown trout in the section from the junction with Bobundara Creek to the base of the dam wall. Extensive erosion has also shallowed the river and decreased its potential as a good fishery.

In good seasons, **Bobundara Creek** produces large brown trout from its slow weedy pools. It has acquired a reputation as a tough but rewarding water for the dedicated fly fisher. Large hatches of turkey brown mayflies offer exceptional fishing in the spring if water levels have been high. Unfortunately this productive stream suffers badly in times of drought.

An angler at Bobundara Creek plays a strong Monaro brown

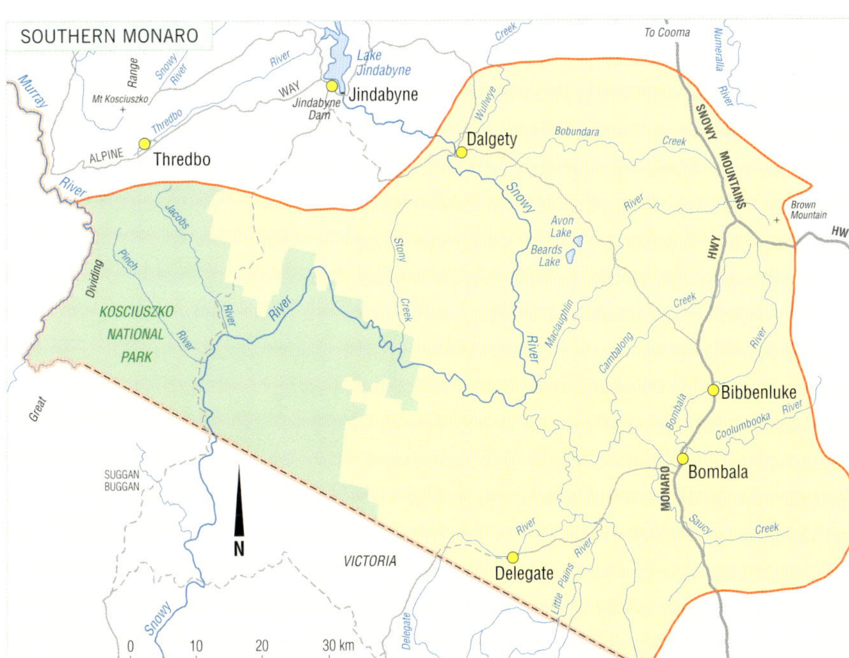

GUIDE TO LOCAL FISH

	Central Monaro and Cooma	Southern Monaro
carp, European	•	
cod, Murray	•	
redfin	•	
perch, golden	•	
perch, silver	•	
trout, brown	•	•
trout, rainbow	•	•

Snowy Mountains

Type of fishing
dam, lake, river
Target fish
trout

The rivers draining the western side of the Snowy Mountains are snow plain waters in their upper reaches, steep and rocky in their middle reaches, grading to medium-paced with gravel beds further down. The Indi (upper Murray), Geehi, Swampy Plains and Tumut are all very good trout streams, with the last two benefiting from tailrace influence in their lower sections. The Tooma is also a reasonable river, as are the Goobarragandra, Yarrangobilly and Paddys rivers.

Blowering Reservoir has rainbow trout, brown trout and redfin, and native fish such as golden perch and Murray cod. Fishing from the bank in spring is the best way to find trout, while the natives, particularly golden perch and Murray cod, respond well to trolled lures when the water heats up in the summer. The tailrace below Blowering can produce huge trout but flows vary due to irrigation demand, while further down native fish and Murray crayfish are found.

Talbingo Reservoir is a steep-sided, crystal clear body of water, mainly suited to boat trolling for trout. Access is limited to the dam wall and at the top end known as Sue City. Redfin and the protected trout cod (must be released alive) can also be caught.

The eastern slopes are generally less precipitous than those further west. Gravel and rock bottomed streams of moderate gradient dominate. The upper Murrumbidgee and its major tributaries like Tantangara Creek are good trout

GUIDE TO LOCAL FISH

cod, Murray
crayfish, Murray
perch, golden
redfin
salmon, Atlantic
trout, brook
trout, brown
trout, rainbow

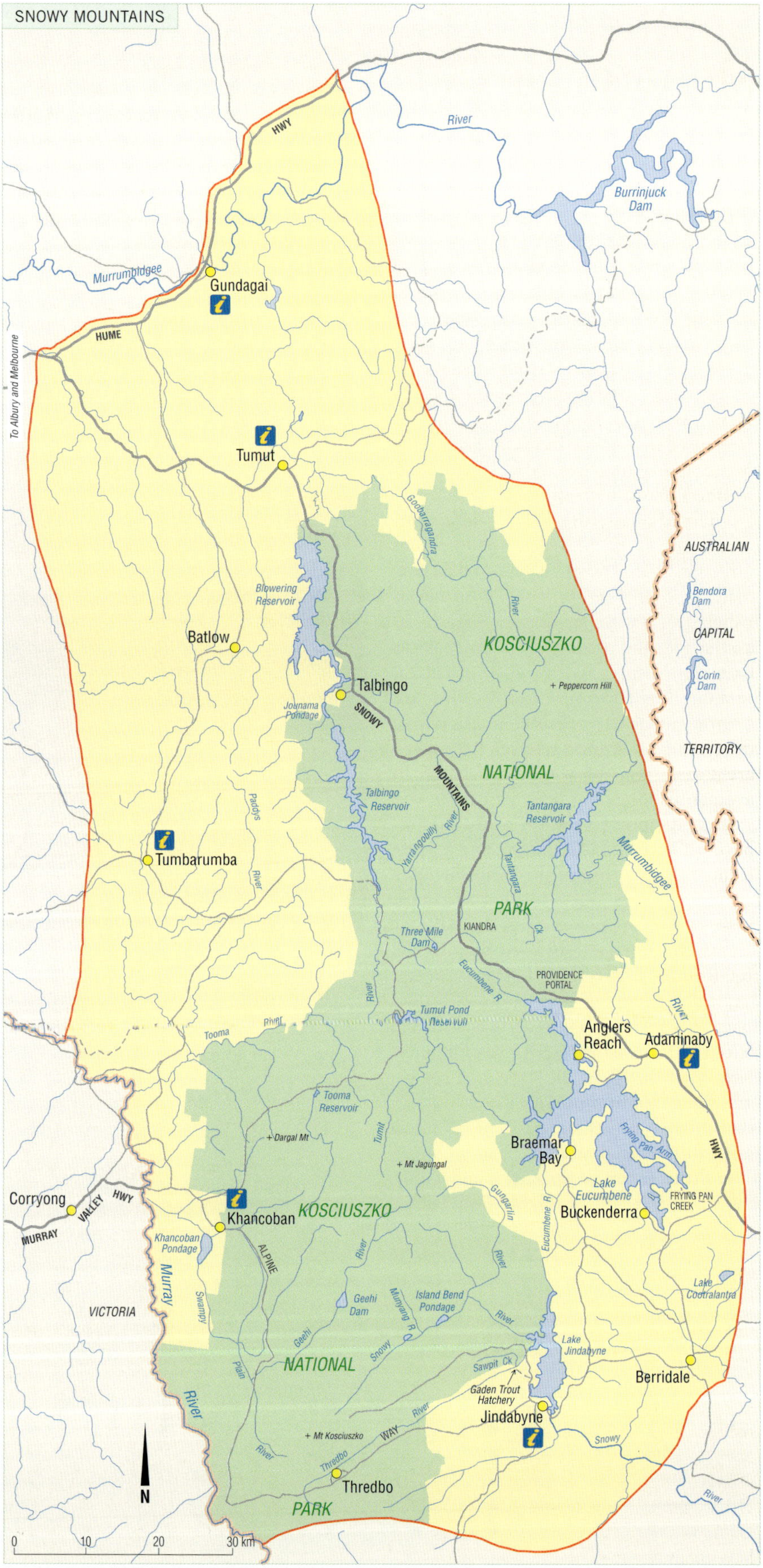

streams, while the upper Snowy and tributaries like the Munyang and Gungarlin contain plenty of smallish trout. The Eucumbene River and Thredbo River are major spawning streams, and contain large lake fish for a period in autumn and early winter prior to their seasonal closure. The Eucumbene, in particular, continues to offer good fishing during the warmer months.

Tantangara Reservoir is one of the most exposed lakes in the area. Although subject to sudden rises and falls, this water has fair populations of both brown and rainbow trout. In spring, when the tunnel through to Lake Eucumbene is closed, the lake tends to fill fast and good fishing can be had from the bank. At other times, trolling from boats is the favoured option.

Lake Eucumbene is a huge lake where brown trout and rainbow trout are both prolific, but the rainbows are the main targets for the trollers and bait fishers that flock to its shores. Mudeyes and scrubworms are the most common baits employed here, but wood grubs and small yabbies also work well. The stealthy brown trout are a prized catch for the fly fishers who stalk the shores, and large fish are taken on a fairly regular basis. The average fish is likely to be around 500 g Fish caught from Lake Eucumbene often have bright red flesh and make delicious eating.

The barren shores of **Lake Jindabyne** belie the lake's productivity. Brown trout are prolific and each year fish in the old-fashioned double-figure (pounds) are landed. There are also plenty of rainbows in the lake, and they grow fat on a diet of midges, caddis, snails and yabbies. Small but significant populations of Atlantic salmon and brook trout are also present. Bait fishing, fly fishing and trolling are all successful techniques here.

The trout in **Geehi Dam**, one of New South Wales' most remote impoundments, are generally small rainbows and browns, and they take surface food readily. The best methods are mudeyes under a bubble float, trolling, or lure casting near the river entrances. A small craft is necessary.

Rainbows and browns inhabit the scenic **Khancoban Pondage**, but the fishing does not seem to be as good as it once was. Trolling from boats is the favoured method of fishing this water. Other quality waters such as Three Mile Dam, Tooma and Happy Jacks Pondage all have their devotees.

You can rely on the Pan

Hearing the mighty wallops and seeing the heavy boils of feeding fish is reason enough for many anglers to return to the Frying Pan year after year.

Frying Pan Arm on Lake Eucumbene is about the most reliable place I know to catch trout – its sheltered bays suit just about any fishing technique – and it offers easy access. An affordable lakeside caravan park offers anglers basic accommodation and boats can be launched from the park or from an old gravel road that runs straight into the lake opposite.

You can fish the 'Pan' with artificial flies or natural bait or lures cast from the shore or your boat. If you decide to try some lure trolling from a boat, the best tactics involve trolling slow Flatfish-style lures up the main arm of Frying Pan Creek in front of the park, and as far up the creek as you can comfortably run your boat. Under high water conditions the arm extends a long way up the creek, but when the lake is low your options are more limited.

If there is a wind blowing down the lake, this area is difficult to fish, so it pays to head for sheltered Muzzelwood Inlet, less than 10 minutes from the caravan park by boat. The best lures for trolling in this area include small Flatfish in Frog and Perch Scale colours, Tassie Devils in hot pink, and green and gold, Old Cobbers in No. 26 and a black and white spotted colour scheme known as Corroboree. The best trolling speed for the Flatfish is dead slow, but you can increase your speed for the Devil-style lures until your rod tip is performing a distinct nod. This indicates that the lure has achieved optimum speed and is darting around enticingly. If you go too fast the lure will spin and your rod will buckle over in a steady curve. Make sure that you set a light drag on your reel because the fish often hit hard.

The 'Pan' is a great place to fish with bait off the bank. Even the kids can get into the act here as it isn't hard to rig up a small hook and a running sinker and heave the whole thing out into the lake. The best baits to use on the bottom are scrubworms and wood grubs. If the lake is rising in the spring, plenty of scrubworms can be found around the edges of the water right in front of the park. Another successful tactic is to rig a mudeye 50 cm or so under a partly-filled clear plastic bubble float. This works particularly well early in the morning or late in the evening during the warmer months. If the action is slow you can continually cast this rig out and carefully wind it in to attract extra strikes. Substituting a wet fly for a natural mudeye can also give outstanding results. You don't need deep water to catch trout on bait, and the shallow flats directly opposite the caravan park often produce good fishing.

During the summer and autumn months the Frying Pan draws fly anglers like a magnet. When conditions are right there are spectacular hatches of caddis moths and midges, while sporadic falls of beetles and ants occur on hot thundery days. In a good year the mudeye migration is an exciting event that brings some of the big brown trout that Eucumbene is famous for into the shallows. Hearing the mighty wallops and seeing the heavy boils of feeding fish is reason enough for many anglers to return year after year.

Time seems to stand still at the park as you are lulled to sleep by the not-so-distant barking of dogs and the weird cries of peacocks. The rest of the world flies past but nothing ever changes here! Long may it be so. I guess the whole charm of one of my favourite spots is that it is just a good honest fishing spot where everyone gets to have some fun.

– Kaj Busch

Western Region

The western rivers invite a more relaxed style of fishing that often attracts repeat visits year after year. Holiday makers camping on the banks of these slow but beautiful waters will find fishing is just one of the attractions.

Type of fishing
dam, river
Target fish
catfish, golden perch, Murray cod, redfin, silver perch

The western rivers, in particularly the **Barwon, Bokhara** and **Colgoa** in the north, as well as the **Warrego** and **Paroo**, all hold Murray cod, golden perch, silver perch, European carp and catfish, as do the northward flowing **Bogan, Macquarie** and **Castlereagh**. All these rivers eventually flow into the Darling, which joins the Murray River at Wentworth, before continuing on to South Australia. In the Riverina belt, the Murray is also joined by the **Murrumbidgee**, and around Wagga Wagga, Narrandera and Hay you know you are in serious fishing country. Those with local knowledge do particularly well for goldens, cod and redfin. **Lake Albert** in Wagga provides quality angling as can **Lake Talbot** at Narrandera and **Lake Centenary** at Temora.

The **Lachlan** is the other major tributary of the Murray–Darling system. It provides the worst fishing generally and cod numbers have been seriously depleted. Carp is the main species caught and Lake Cargelligo, Lake Brewster and Lake Caval average 10 to 20 huge carp for every golden perch. **Lake Forbes** provides good native fishing.

The **Murray** itself still provides some quality fishing in spite of intensive river management. The best area is above Hume to around Tocumwal, with the area downstream of Lake Hume producing some of the largest brown trout in the state as well as good golden perch fishing.

Lake Mulwala is one of the best Murray cod fisheries in the country, and the river downstream of the Yarrawonga Weir offers some of the best river fishing for native species in the region and is one of the last strongholds of the protected trout cod.

The fishing downstream of Tocumwal is less predictable, but there is still good fishing in the **Edward** (upper reaches are good for crayfishing), **Wakool** and **Niemur rivers**. From Echuca, the fishing is fairly poor.

Up north, where the **Darling** and its tributaries flow through seemingly interminable dry plains, the drainage is typified by sluggish flows for much of the year. But when heavy rains come down from Queensland and fill them, these rivers can unleash awesome power. Fishing these rising rivers can be very productive. One of the best spots in the whole Western Region is the regulator at **Menindee Lakes**, where golden perch can congregate in large numbers. The much degraded Darling River still produces some quantities of native fish (as well as blue-green algae) and a week-long trip beyond 'the back of Bourke' is a must-do for serious freshwater fishers.

In the northern reaches of the Darling River and in other northern streams, small spangled perch can be taken. Although not a popular sportfish they play an important role as food for larger species.

When the western rivers of the vast open plains swell in flood, they spread over a huge area, filling creeks, depressions and dried billabongs, providing native fish, such as Murray cod and perch, with a brief opportunity to spawn in the warm shallows and swollen feeder creeks before the waters subside again.

These rivers can be turbid for much of the year, so local practice is usually to baitfish them, but they can be successfully lure fished too. The most effective lures are usually those that send out strong sonic pulses. In slightly less dirty water, lures with fluorescent or metallic hues can work, as can those with inbuilt rattles, or the sonic beat and visual attraction of revolving blades. Baits in the region include live yabbies, worms, bardi grubs, and big insects, like crickets and grasshoppers.

In long slow reaches of inland rivers, the only visible sign of fish-holding territory might be the top of a fallen tree sticking out of the water. Or it could be a stand of river gums, which offer tangled roots and fallen limbs underwater, and shade above it.

Bends in the stream create deeper holes on their outside curves, and creek mouths, rock bars, or any narrowing of the river bed can provide fish with convenient places to feed or rest. Actively fishing such features will prove far more productive than merely soaking a setline along just any old stretch of river.

FISHING TIP

Murray cod are not reckless fish but they are fearless. Many experienced anglers contend you need to 'wake up' these essentially lazy fish by bumping the boat or lures into the snags where they lie. Another part of that same approach is to present large, noisy lures, repeatedly, in areas of likely looking water. If you see fish on an echo sounder, or deduce from the terrain that cod are likely to be present in an area, it can pay to persevere, making repeated casts or trolling passes to goad the fish into striking.

GUIDE TO LOCAL FISH

carp, European
catfish
cod, Murray
redfin
perch, golden
perch, silver
perch, spangled
trout, brown

FURTHER INFORMATION

Fishing and boating *NSW Fisheries has offices at 3/556 Macauley St, Albury, tel. (02) 6042 4200; 27 Mitchell St, Bourke, tel. (02) 6872 2077; and 449 Charlotte St, Deniliquin, tel. (03) 5881 9999. NSW Maritime has offices at 440 Swift St, Albury, tel. (02) 6021 7188; 159A Eighth St, Mildura, tel. (03) 5023 4610; and 104/110 Banna Ave, Griffith, tel. (02) 6964 0147.*

Tourist centres *cnr Blende and Bromide sts, Broken Hill, tel. (08) 8087 6077; Railway Station, Hovell St, Cootamundra, tel. (02) 6942 4212; 88 Sanger St, Corowa, tel. 1800 814 054; Peppin Heritage Centre, George St, Deniliquin, tel. 1800 650 712; cnr Newell Hwy and Macquarie St, Dubbo, tel. (02) 6801 4450; cnr Banna and Jondaryan aves, Griffith, tel. (02) 6962 4145; 407 Moppett St, Hay, tel. (02) 6993 4045; 10 Yanco Ave, Leeton, tel. (02) 6953 6481; cnr Thomas St and Newell Hwy, Parkes, tel. (02) 6862 4365; Tarcutta St, Wagga Wagga, tel. (02) 6926 9621; McCann Park, Newell Hwy, West Wyalong, tel. (02) 6972 3645; Shire Offices, Reid St, Wilcannia, tel. (02) 8091 5927; Gateway Visitor Information Centre, Lincoln Causeway, Wodonga, tel. 1300 796 222.*

The Darling River at Wentworth. This much degraded river still produces good quantities of native fish

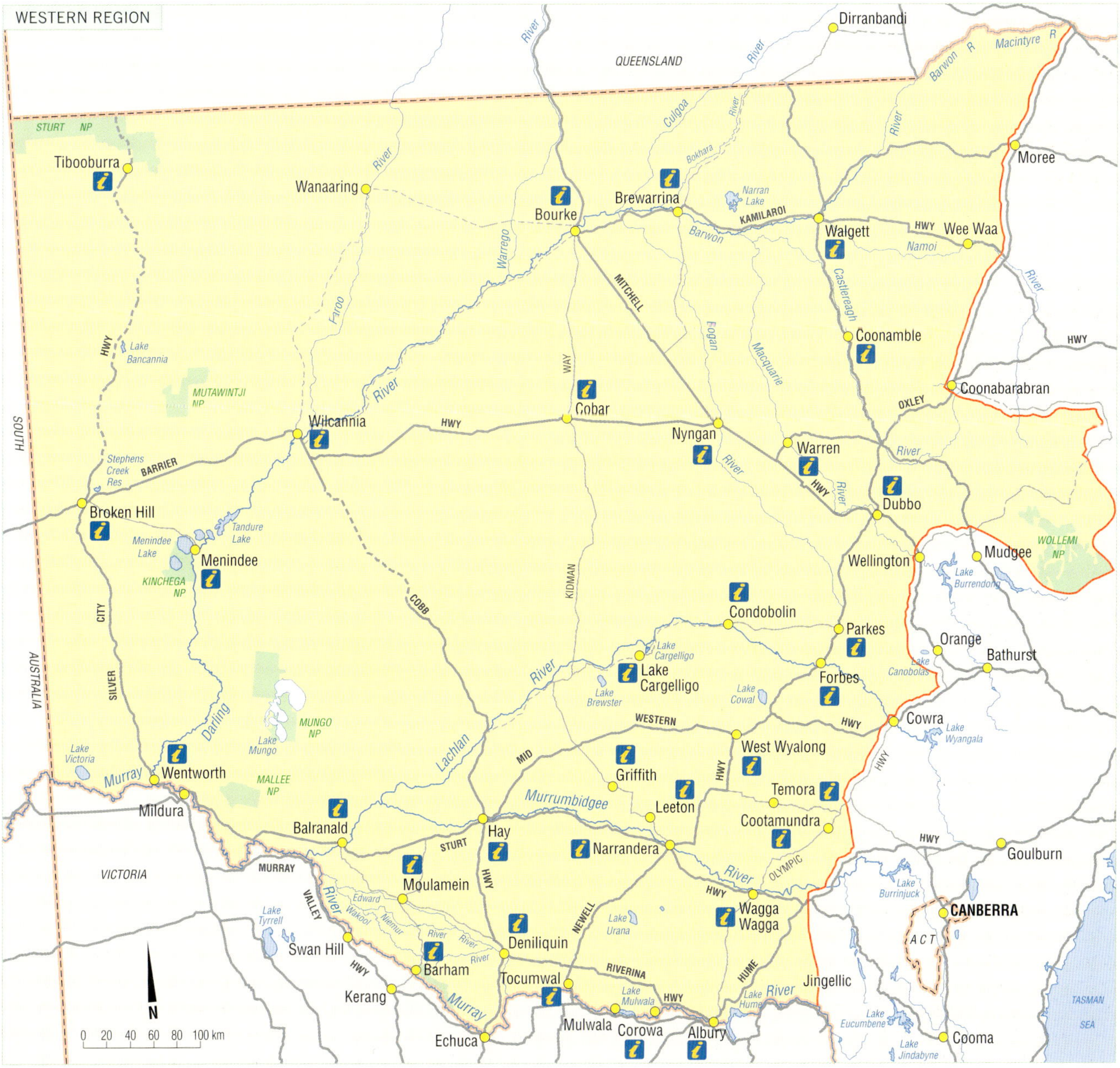

IDENTIFYING YOUR CATCH

FISH	LOCATION/DESCRIPTION	FISHING METHOD

ALBACORE
Thunnus alalunga

Also known as longfin tuna.

Found in offshore waters and usually in schools, the albacore is recognised by its exceptionally long pectoral fins, which extend well beyond the second dorsal. Although it can grow to 40 kg, it is commonly captured at 2 to 5 kg. The fish is irridescent blue along the top with a silvery belly. It is prized for its fight, particularly when encountered in a large school. Its table quality is also excellent, the meat being almost white when cooked, whereas the meat of other tunas is mostly red and oily.

This fish is mostly caught by trolling or jigging with lures, live baiting with yellowtail or slimy mackerel, or drift fishing with berley and bait of cubed fish flesh. It inhabits the warm ocean currents in waters well offshore.

BARRACOUTA
Thyrsites atun

Also known as axehandle, couta, pickhandle.

The barracouta is a pelagic, schooling, cold-water fish. When caught in warmer waters it is rarely good eating because of parasitic worms and 'milky' flesh, but it is a regularly sold commercial species in Australia's south. This long, slender fish is fast and voracious but even a 1.5 m specimen will not weigh much more than 5 or 6 kg. It is blue-black on top, fading down the sides to a silvery belly. The black dorsal fin is long and low, and the protruding jaws are lined with large, needle-sharp teeth.

Barracouta will bite anything (a piece of red or white rag, even a bare shiny hook), but is usually fished by trolling or casting with whitebait, bacon rind, fish strips, or a variety of lures. A trace is necessary because of its teeth.

BASS, AUSTRALIAN
Macquaria novemaculata

Also known as bass, perch.

This native freshwater fish hits lures and baits with an aggression out of proportion to its size, and it fights hard when hooked. It naturally inhabits southern and eastern coastal freshwater and estuarine river systems, but has recently also been established in freshwater dams and impoundments through artificial stocking. Bass prey on insects, shrimp, small fish, frogs and earthworms, and favour snaggy corners and bank sides strewn with logs, reeds and boulders. They require brackish water to spawn in late winter.

Anglers now fish for bass with lures instead of baits. Lures work just as well, are more fun to fish with, and suit catch and release fishing. Trolling and lure casting work well in both rivers and impoundments. As a sportfish, bass is usually released on capture.

BLACKFISH, ROCK
Girella elevata

Also known as black drummer, blackfish, pig.

The rock blackfish grows to around 8 kg, but the most common catch ranges from 1 to 2 kg. It is a dark, rotund, small-mouthed herbivorous species with the occasional urge to eat meat, and with the ability to romp happily in rocky water rough enough to smash lesser fish to a pulp. It is found all along the east coast of Australia from Noosa Heads in Queensland to Victoria, but not in western Victoria or South Australia. Its western relative, *G. tephraeops*, is found on coastal reefs of south-western Western Australia.

Serious rock blackfish anglers use stout rods, sidecast reels and line from 10 to 20 kg. Bobby corks help to minimise tackle losses, and hooks should be double or triple X strong in sizes from #1 to 2/0.

BONITO
Sarda australis

Also known as bonnie, horse mackerel, horsie.

Found in coastal waters of New South Wales, southern Queensland and southern Western Australia, this member of the tuna family has horizontal dark stripes on its back and sides, differing from the similar oriental bonito *(S. orientalis)*, a west coast species, striped only on its upper half. Another species, Watson's leaping bonito *(Cybiosarda elegans)*, is found in east coast waters and is characterised by a high dorsal fin, belly stripes and broken wavy markings from shoulder to tail on its back.

Strip baits or small live fish can be used, but bonito is best caught by trolling or casting with lures: usually small chromed metal slices, swimming minnows or saltwater flies. Top time is dawn. Bonito frequent wash areas of headlands and inshore islands.

FISH | LOCATION/DESCRIPTION | FISHING METHOD

BREAM, BLACK
Acanthropagrus butcheri

Also known as southern black bream, southern bream.

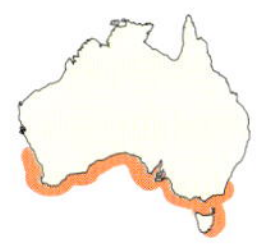

Black bream is the most commonly found member of this family in southern waters. It favours estuaries and inshore waters where it feeds on various marine worms, crustacea, shellfish, juvenile molluscs and finfish. Anglers can expect to catch a few good-sized examples of this fine table fish in any southern estuary. Its body colour varies between dull gold and silvery olive-brown. Similar in colouration but of different body shape, the pikey bream *(A. berda)*, is found only in the tropics.

Light lines from 2 to 6 kg, depending on terrain, and baits of worms, nippers or even tuna strips are best. Black bream (and pikey bream) will also attack small lures if they are accurately cast and worked close to structures where these fish lie in wait.

BREAM, YELLOWFIN
Acanthropagrus australis

Also known as eastern black bream, sea bream, silver bream, surf bream.

Yellowfin bream has a much narrower geographical range than black bream. This handsome silver fish has bright to dull yellow pelvic and anal fins. The head is more sharply pointed than the black bream and the clear to yellowish tail has a distinct black trailing edge. It inhabits surf beaches as well as estuaries in northern and central New South Wales, and in Queensland. In common with other members of the bream family, it becomes extremely cunning as it matures. It is a popular table fish.

Popular baits include live nippers, live or dead crabs, prawns, shrimp, live marine worms, strip baits of fish flesh, squid or octopus, or whole pippis or other shellfish. Yellowfin bream will also take small lures.

CARP, EUROPEAN
Cyprinus carpio

Also known as common carp.

This fish is extremely widespread, from the sub-tropics to the alpine regions of Victoria, New South Wales and, recently, Tasmania. Of the various imported species of fish introduced into Australian waters, carp is considered the greatest pest. It is neither a good table fish nor a good sportfish, and it threatens the habitat of many native species. Its feeding techniques stir up silt, which reduces the oxygen output of native aquatic plants and smothers the eggs of trout and native fish. Popular with some anglers but certainly not all.

Carp respond to berleying and fishing with baits of maggots, sweet corn, dough, bardi grubs or scrubworms. Fisheries regulations in enlightened states require that once caught, carp should never be put back.

CATFISH, EEL-TAILED
Tandanus tandanus

Also known as dewfish, freshwater catfish, kenaru, freshwater jewfish.

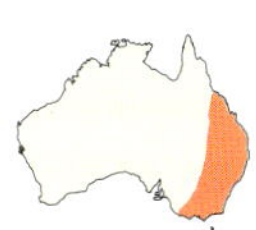

Eel-tailed catfish occur in various forms; the *Tandanus* species is found throughout the inland and coastal freshwater of much of south and eastern Australia. It has thrived in many water supply impoundments. This species is usually mottled grey to russet brown and averages 1 to 2 kg. Like many catfish, the dorsal and pectoral spines can inflict nasty wounds. It needs careful handling when brought in. Despite its appearance, the catfish is considered by some to be a prize table fish, once the skin has been peeled away.

Catfish is not generally caught on lure or fly. It is more usually targeted with baits of peeled crayfish tail, a bunch of worms or bardi grub. Fish these baits on light line with a running sinker rig over a shelving soft bottom, especially at night.

COBIA
Rachycentron canadus

Also known as black king, black kingfish, cobe, crab-eater, ling, sergeant fish.

The cobia is a handsome game fish, found in oceanic waters from temperate to sub-tropical climes. It frequents areas around navigation beacons, deepwater wharves, headlands, offshore islands and over reefs. It is blackish-brown with a creamy stripe along its sides, and its streamlined shape can lead anglers to mistakenly identify it as a shark. Growing to over 50 kg and being common between 10 and 20 kg, cobia is recognised as one of the toughest fighting fish in Australian waters.

Cobia is taken by trolling, jigging or casting lures toward washes and island corners, drifting live baits over reefs or from ocean rock locations. Lines should be around 10 to 15, or even up to 24 kg. Traces of 40 to 60-kg nylon will suffice.

FISH | LOCATION/DESCRIPTION | FISHING METHOD

COD, ESTUARY
Epinephelus coioides

Also known as brown-spotted rock cod, greasy cod, north-west groper.

In Australia the name 'cod' has been given indiscriminately to a large number of fish including members of the Serranidae family. This family has a number of species, including estuary cod *(E. coioides)*, the most common at around 2 to 4 kg, but growing in excess of 50 kg. Others include the black cod *(E. damelli)*, the Queensland groper *(E. lanceolatus)* and the potato cod *(E. tukula)*. In New South Wales, estuary cod, black cod and Queensland groper are all totally protected.

Cod are common captures in tidal creeks, large inshore bays, and around some headlands and island groups. A short trace of heavy nylon or wire is advisable.

COD, MURRAY
Maccullochella peeli peeli

Also known as goodoo, Murray, codfish.

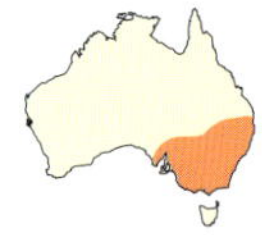

Considered to be the largest and most famous native freshwater table fish (although those caught by anglers usually average from 6 to 8 kg), the Murray cod is actually found well beyond the confines of the Murray River, being distributed throughout the Murray–Darling Basin. It has also been stocked in many popular impoundments and now has a wide distribution through Queensland, New South Wales and Victoria. Related species include the protected trout cod, the Clarence River cod, the Mary River cod and the protected eastern cod.

Cod will take lures, flies and baits. Tackle should be 4 to 10 kg depending on the terrain; in the Murray River, where the fish are big, 15 kg is not too heavy. They can be taken by trolling or casting lures, bottom fishing or 'bobbing' baits of bardi grub, worms or crayfish.

DART, SWALLOWTAIL
Trachinotus coppingeri

Also known as billy lids, dart, surf trevally.

A thin, deep-bodied and agile fish, the swallowtail dart is commonly found along surf beaches swimming among the waves with great speed and dexterity. It will snatch at baits, but when hooked, will hang out there with tenacity beyond its size. A relative, the common dart *(T. botla)*, is found in Western Australia and a smaller, spotted east coast cousin, the black-spotted dart *(T. bailloni)*, has a distribution that overlaps that of the swallowtail.

Dart will take beachworm and pippi baits, or thin strips of fish flesh, and even small lures on occasion. Light beach rods with 3 to 7-kg line are suitable. Cast towards any deep holes adjacent to broken water and move the bait or lure steadily.

DOLPHIN FISH
Coryphaena hippurus

Also known as dollies, dorado, Mahi Mahi.

The dolphin fish, not related to the mammalian dolphin, is one of the most beautiful species of fish; its colours vary from blue to green, and silver to gold. Its dorsal fin stretches from the top of the head to the tail butt, and it has tremendous speed and agility. Preferring warmer waters, it is found northward from New South Wales in the east and from Bunbury in the west. The average size of this species is 2 to 5 kg, but may exceed 25 kg.

Dolphin fish tend to school near reefs, or fish aggregating devices such as fish trap buoys, floating objects like rafts, weed, logs or even a length of rope. Troll or cast lures or whole fish baits so they travel past such 'habitats'.

DORY, JOHN
Zeus faber

Also known as St. Peter's fish, dories, johnnies.

The john dory visits central New South Wales estuaries each winter and becomes an inshore angling target. The related mirror dory *(Zenopsis nebulosus)* and silver dory *(Cyttus australis)* are only obtained by commercial deep trawling. Aside from its habit of taking inshore winter holidays, the john dory can be distinguished from its relatives by a dark 'thumbprint' either side of its body and by the long spines on its dorsal fin. It is one of Australia's best table fish.

Squid strips, fish flesh or live prawns are good, but the best bait is a small live yellowtail with its tail fin clipped, and suspended under a float on a sharp 3/0 or 4/0 suicide hook. A take is indicated by the float moving out and down steadily.

FISH	LOCATION/DESCRIPTION	FISHING METHOD

DRUMMER, SILVER
Kyphosus sydneyanus

Also known as buffalo bream.

The silver drummer *(K. sydneyanus)* is a streamlined fish with a dull metallic hue. Often caught from ocean rocks in rough seas, it is quite a brawler when hooked. The popularity of this tough tenacious fighter relates to its fighting qualities rather than its table quality. It has relatives such as the western buffalo bream *(K. cornelii)* and low-finned drummer *(K. vaigiensis)*. The silver drummer is very popular in South Australia.

The silver drummer is found around reefs and rocky shores, and hence the need to avoid snags and to prevent the fish reaching rocky hideaways when making its run. It is best fished for with a paternoster rig using baits of bread, cunjevoi and abalone gut.

EEL, SHORT-FINNED
Anguilla australis

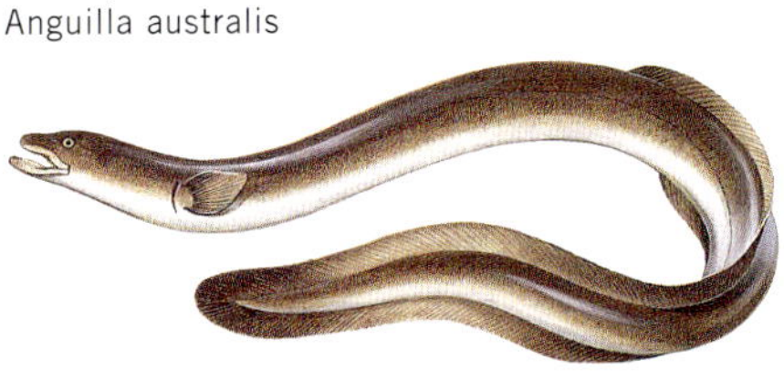

Also known as freshwater eel, silver eel.

A freshwater species that migrates to salt water to spawn, the short-finned eel is common in dams, swamps, rivers and estuaries throughout much of eastern Australia, including Tasmania, and extending offshore to Lord Howe and Norfolk islands, and New Zealand. Olive-green to brown in colour, it grows in excess of 6 kg and over 1 m in length. This eel will eat almost anything that presents itself, whether alive or dead, but is essentially carnivorous.

Baitfishing with fish strips, worms or bardi grubs is best. Hooks can be 1/0 to 2/0, rigged with a small running sinker. Use 4 to 6-kg line or risk having the line broken by the eel's vigorous struggles, particularly when it is about to be landed.

EMPEROR, SPANGLED
Lethrinus nebulosus

Also known as iodine bream, yellow sweetlip, north-west snapper.

A handsome fish with a yellow-golden body with blue spots, the spangled emperor is renowned for its excellent table quality. Average size is from 2 to 3 kg with good specimens reaching 6 kg. Other common emperors are the long-nosed emperor *(L. olivaceous)* and the yellow-tailed emperor *(L. atkinsoni)*. The spangled emperor is found in northern waters from northern New South Wales in the east around to southern Western Australia. It prefers a loose rocky bottom of gravel or broken coral and inhabits shallow reefs.

Bottom fishing on anchor with a paternoster rig and cut baits is best. The fish will occasionally strike at jigs worked near the bottom. Best baits include fish, crab, prawn and squid.

FLATHEAD, DUSKY
Platycephalus fuscus

Also known as black flathead, flatty, lizard.

Of the fourteen common species of flathead in Australian waters, the largest by far is the dusky flathead. This elongated fish takes its name from the colour of its head. It is common in estuaries along the east coast from around the Whitsundays in Queensland to as far south as Victoria. Growing to 15 kg, it is more commonly encountered from 1 to 3 kg. Dusky flathead is a bottom dweller, usually found in shallow water (1 to 6 m) in estuaries, bays and surf beaches.

From a boat, drift baits of fish strip or whole prawns, rigged to bounce along the bottom behind a sinker heavy enough to stir up sediment. From shore, flick out into deep channels and allow the tide to sweep the bait around. It responds well to lures or saltwater flies.

FLATHEAD, SOUTHERN BLUE-SPOT
Platycephalus speculator

Also known as yank flathead, long nose, sandies (incorrect), shovel nose.

This fish inhabits the Victorian coastline from New South Wales to South Australia, and also the waters of northern Tasmania and southern Western Australia. The southern blue-spot species resembles the dusky in appearance and occupies a similar range of habitats. It is commonly caught by drift fishing over sand and it is distinguished by the dark bars across its back. In Port Phillip Bay, Victoria, it is the predominant 'larger' specimen caught. It is an excellent table fish.

Strip baits of fish, or prawns, whole small fish, etc. are best, but lures will also work. Mostly caught by boat anglers, but land-based anglers can cast baits into bankside channels and across weed beds in southern estuaries.

FISH	LOCATION/DESCRIPTION	FISHING METHOD
FLOUNDER, SMALL-TOOTHED Pseudorhombus jenysii 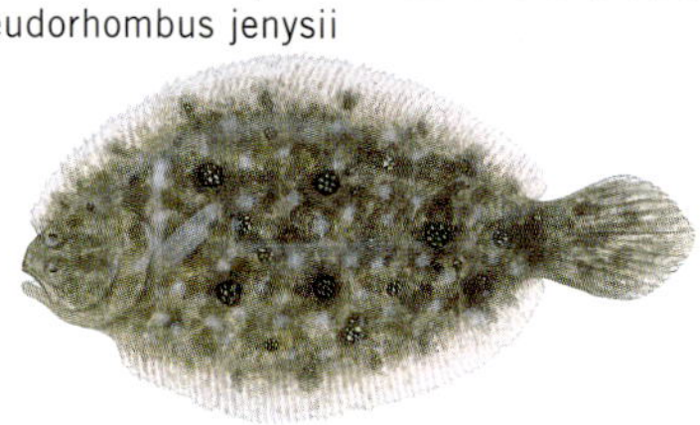	 The flounder begins life with an eye on each side of its head, but metamorphoses into adulthood with both eyes on the same side. The small-toothed flounder is found in both eastern and Western Australia, is dark coloured and carries five to six eye-like blotches spread around the body. Other species include the large-toothed, elongated, long-snouted and green-back flounders. They are common in southern esturaries, and are considered to be fine table fish.	Flounder may be speared in some states, but are usually caught with lines from 2 to 4 kg, small long shanked hooks and small pieces of bait, fished on the bottom from a drifting boat. Popular baits include fish strips, peeled prawn, marine worms or whitebait.
GARFISH, EASTERN SEA Hyporhamphus australis  *Also known as garie, beakie, red beak.*	 The slender, bony sea garfish is a common species on the east coast, targeted both for bait and food. The flesh, despite its small size and large number of bones, is keenly sought for its outstanding flavour. A southern form, *H. melanochir*, is similar in all respects to *H. australis* but grows larger, to the delight of South Australian and Victorian anglers. The garfish is found around jetties and other estuary and bay structures, and is most active in the summer and autumn months.	Sea garfish can be readily line-caught, and are also netted professionally. To catch garfish, berley with bran or bread, and use small baits of fish or prawn flesh (or dough), on tiny long shanked hooks on a float rig.
GROPER, BLUE Achoerodus viridis  *Also known as bluey.*	 The eastern blue groper inhabits the waters of mid-Queensland and New South Wales and commonly grows to around 15 kg. A western species, *A. gouldii*, also exists, distributed from South Australia around into Western Australia, and can grow in excess of 30 kg. The western female is greenish, the eastern is reddish brown (called red groper), and the juveniles of both are a grey-brown in colour.	To withstand the tug of war involved in landing a groper, use heavy line, extra strong hooks from 1/0 to 6/0 to carry the large favoured baits of cunjevoi, red crab or abalone gut, and a powerful rod. The fish is usually caught by land-based fishing from rocks.
HAIRTAIL Trichiurus lepturus 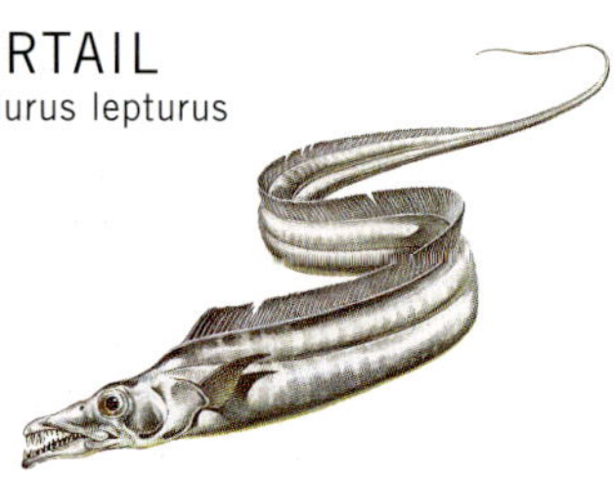 *Also known as Australian hairtail, Cox's hairtail, largerhead hairtail.*	 The hairtail is a long fish with a fearsomely toothed head, a scaleless body and a tail tapering to a thin, thread-like end. The body colour is a brilliant silver, like polished chrome. This fish is found in coastal bays and estuaries of Australia's east and west coasts. Growing in excess of 2 m and weighing over 4 kg as an adult, the hairtail is most active at night. Usually found in deep holes in estuaries, but unpredictable as to when it will bite, it provides exciting sport for anglers.	Most regular hairtail anglers use from 4 to 10-kg line, a 1/0 to 4/0 hook, and always with a short (15-cm) wire trace as insurance against those teeth. Favoured baits include fillet of yellowtail or slimy mackerel and whole or half pilchards.
HERRING, OXEYE Megalops cyprinoides 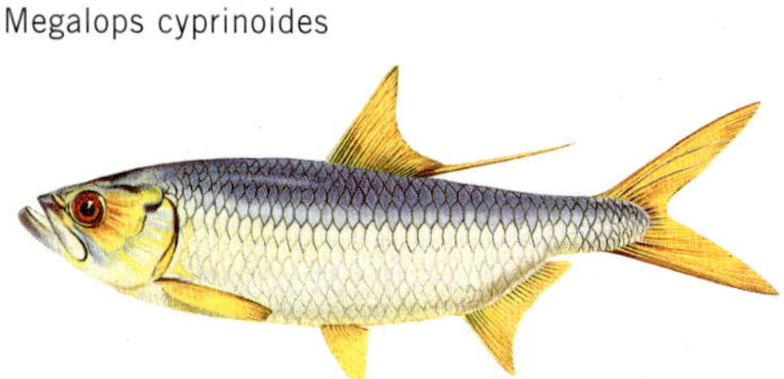 *Also known as tarpon.*	 Found in tropical water, from far northern New South Wales, throughout Queensland and across the Gulf of Carpentaria to the Northern Territory, this species is an active, shiny, large-scaled fish, mostly silver in colour, and a great lure and fly taker. It provides a light-tackle diversion for anglers taking a break from barramundi and saratoga. Oxeye are commonly fished for sport as they are very fast and resist until exhausted. It is not highly regarded for its table quality and is usually released unharmed.	Best caught using casting lures, especially small lead-headed jigs with either feather, fibre or soft plastic tails. Larger specimens will take small swimming plugs, and small surface poppers are also particularly useful, whether cast with fly tackle or spinning gear.

FISH	LOCATION/DESCRIPTION	FISHING METHOD

JACK, MANGROVE
Lutjanus argentimaculatus

Also known as creek red bream, dog bream, red bream, jack, mangrove snapper, rock barramundi.

Mangrove jack is common throughout the tropical north, as far south as Coffs Harbour in the east and Exmouth in the west. A dark red, powerfully built fish, mangrove jack up to 3 kg are prevalent in tidal creeks and estuaries. Larger fish tend to move out into bays and on to onshore reefs. Some monster specimens of 11 kg or more have been taken from offshore reefs in New South Wales. A good table fish, it should not be confused with red bass (which has a distinctive 'pit' in front of each eye), which is often toxic.

Mangrove jack has canine teeth, sharp spines and gill blades. It lives around oyster-encrusted rocks, mangrove roots and various other line-cutting structures. Line classes upwards of 6 kg are adequate. The fish will hit lures, baits or flies, then dash for cover.

JAVELIN FISH
Pomadasys kaakan

Also known as barred grunter, trumpeter, spotted grunter, spotted javelin fish.

This fish's other common name, grunter, evolved because of its habit of emitting loud grunting sounds on capture. The name 'javelin' fish comes from the heavy spear-like anal fin that is capable of inflicting severe wounds on anglers who handle this fish carelessly. Commonly found in estuarine rivers, especially close to the sea, javelin fish live in far northern New South Wales, Queensland and the Northern Territory and parts of Western Australia. This fish is great table fare and good sport on reasonable tackle.

Fish strips or prawn baits are best. Most anglers fish with 6 to10-kg tackle and just enough sinker weight to get the bait down in a tidal run. Because the javelin often lives near line-cutting structures, a heavier trace of 25 kg is sometimes used.

JOB-FISH, ROSY
Pristipomoides filamentosus

Also known as king snapper, rosy snapper.

Plentiful within the warmer waters of Queensland and far northern New South Wales, the rosy Job-fish is also caught around Lord Howe Island, and off Australia's north-western continental shelf. Growing in excess of 7 kg, it is a handsome, top-grade table species, with the same colouration as adult snapper, but much more streamlined. Related to the small toothed Job fish *(Aphareus furca)* and green Job-fish *(Aprion viriscens)*, it is known for its sad look and hence the biblical reference in its common name.

Fished for over reefs in 50 m or more of depth, the rosy Job-fish bites best on cut fish baits at night, and is an excellent table fish as are all Job-fish. Solid tackle with 10-kg line or even higher is useful due to the depth of water it inhabits.

KINGFISH, YELLOWTAIL
Seriola lalandi

Also known as bandit, hoodlum, king.

A fish of exciting power and glamorous appearance, it has the nasty habit of taking lures and bait rigs and refusing to give them back. This very popular sportfish can be caught off the rocks or from a boat. It is usually associated with reef areas and often schools. It is found in waters from southern Queensland, to New South Wales, Victoria, South Australia and as far west as Shark Bay in Western Australia. Growing to 50 kg or better, this species averages from 4 to 10 kg.

Use lures, strip baits, cube baits or live baits, fished over reef, around deepwater wharf pylons and channel markers, from boats or the ocean rocks. Berley works well. The selection of a breaking strain in line should reflect the size and strength of the fish.

LEATHERJACKET, TOOTHBRUSH
Acanthaluteres vittiger

Also known as jackets, pale brown leatherjacket.

Leatherjacket is easily recognised by the prominent dorsal spine above the eyes, which in some species, including *A. vittiger*, folds completely into a groove when not in use. Its other distinguishing feature is the leathery skin rather than scales. It is a peaceful breed of fish that mooches around reef and weed beds grazing daintily with its small but chisel-toothed mouth. The toothbrush leatherjacket is commonly found around southern Australia, from Coffs Harbour, New South Wales, to Western Australia's Jurien.

The shearing teeth make long shank hooks necessary. Baits should be small and soft, such as peeled prawn, fish flesh, skinned octopus or squid meat. An unweighted or lightly weighted bait allowed to sink slowly is the best method.

FISH | LOCATION/DESCRIPTION | FISHING METHOD

LONG TOM, SLENDER
Strongylura leiura

Also known as hornpike long tom, needlefish.

The long tom has jaws of equal length, studded with rows of tiny, needle-sharp teeth. The slender long tom is distinguished by the black bar on the side of the head. It is found in Australia's northern and temperate waters, and is related to the barred long tom *(Ablennes hians)*, which is purely tropical, the stout long tom *(Tylosurus gavialoides)* and the crocodilian long tom *(Tylosurus crocodilus)*, the last two being much larger fish and found in both tropical and temperate waters.

Long tom are surface cruisers, preying on small fish, which they herd and slash at in spectacular fashion. They are easy to draw strikes from with small lures, but not so simple to hook, there being little soft tissue among all those teeth.

LUDERICK
Girella tricuspidata

Also known as blackfish, darkie, nigger.

A fish of the estuaries and inshore rocks mainly along the eastern seaboard, luderick is most commonly found in New South Wales. This chunky little fish is usually encountered around a half to 1.5 kg. Essentially vegetarian, the luderick will take baits of marine worms, prawns and nippers on occasion. A good table fish if prepared correctly, it is often kept alive in net bags, then bled, cleaned and skinned immediately before the angler leaves for home.

Float fishing is best with green weed or sea lettuce baits from the ocean rocks, river breakwalls or within estuaries from bank or boat. The float is weighted with either running barrels, beans or crimped split shot, and hooks should be small.

MACKEREL, SLIMY
Scomber australasicus

Also known as blue mackerel, common mackerel, slimies.

This speedy little baitfish is excellent live or cut bait for larger quarry such as snapper, mulloway, yellowtail kingfish and tuna. Usually caught from 15 to 25 cm in length, this species prefers cooler areas and often forming extensive surface shoals. It is most common inshore in the southern half of Australia, where it schools over reefs, around islands and headlands, and occasionally enters bays. Its skin is soft and slippery to touch – hence its common name.

Light handlines or flick rods are used to cast tiny metal lures or flies, small pieces of cut bait or multi-hook live bait jigs. These fish respond to berley and can be kept alive in a large container of sea water, provided the water is constantly exchanged.

MACKEREL, SPANISH
Scomberomorus commerson

Also known as narrow-barred mackerel, narrow-barred Spanish mackerel, Spaniards, Spanish.

The largest member of the mackerel family and a fast swimming oceanic species, the Spanish mackerel can grow to 30 kg or more, but is commonly encountered around 5 to 10 kg. It ranges throughout the tropics and as far south as Montague Island on the east coast and Rottnest Island in the west. A streamlined fish, it is all about speed and slicing power. Its serrated rows of dagger-like teeth interlock like shears. It is an extremely popular game fish and fair table food.

Mackerel teeth mean wire traces are a must, or at least ganged hooks. Mackerel can be trolled, or spun to with lures, especially surface poppers. They love live baits as well, and dead baits are useful. Mackerel usually hit first to maim the bait then come back to inhale it.

MACKEREL, SPOTTED
Scomberomorus munroi

Also known as Japanese mackerel, snook, spottie, Australian spotted mackerel.

As its common name indicates, numerous small spots on its body distinguish this species. The spotted mackerel frequents a similar area to Spanish mackerel *(S. commerson)*, although it rarely moves further south than Forster, on the New South Wales coast. Slightly smaller than the Spaniard, it averages around 3 to 5 kg, with a really big fish being around 8 or 9 kg and probably coming from a north Queensland offshore reef. Found offshore in schools, its presence is usually signalled by wheeling and diving birds.

Trolling lures or live baits, or drifting with live or cut baits over inshore plateaus of reefs is best. Mackerel teeth mean wire trace is essential or at least ganged hooks. This fish will often move up a berley trail behind an anchored boat.

FISH | **LOCATION/DESCRIPTION** | **FISHING METHOD**

MARLIN, BLACK
Makaira indica

Also known as black, silver marlin, silver.

Black marlin is a fast swimming, highly prized big game fish. Available offshore right down the east and west coasts of Australia, the black marlin becomes less common the further south you go. In Queensland and throughout much of New South Wales, marlin of various sizes are regular summer visitors to waters as shallow as 40 m or less. Many game fishers suspect big fish inhabit deeper offshore trenches year round. The largest known aggregation of giant black marlin is around the Great Barrier Reef north of Cairns.

Giant black marlin of 500 kg are taken trolling large baits well offshore. Smaller blacks, around 100 kg, are regularly taken closer inshore. Boat anglers troll large skirted lures, bibless minnows or whole fish baits – either dead or alive.

MARLIN, BLUE
Makaira nigricans

Also known as blues, Indo-Pacific blue marlin.

The blue marlin inhabits much the same waters as the black marlin *(M. indica)*, but is less common and appears to prefer the deep, oceanic currents and to be more tolerant of cooler water temperatures. It has been caught as far south as Storm Bay in Tasmania. It is a prized game fish, and some anglers consider it a tougher opponent than equivalent sized black marlin. Large blue marlin have been captured offshore of Bermagui, south of Sydney. Once hooked, a marlin of any size will put up a tremendous fight.

Lure fishing works best, especially over deep offshore canyons where the bigger fish prowl. Lures need to be large, as do the rods, reels and line classes, as when hooked, big blue marlin are capable of stripping over 1000 m of line from a reel.

MARLIN, STRIPED
Tetrapturus audax

Also known as stripey.

Far more prevalent along the eastern seaboard than in the west, the striped marlin is generally a lighter built fish than either the black or blue of the same length. It makes up for this lack of bulk by being the most spectacular of all the billfish when hooked, often racing across the sea making immense leaps. It is not unknown for a prime adult striped marlin to jump more than thirty times during a fight, and twenty consecutive jumps are common. It takes its name from the bluish stripes that extend across its body.

Small trolled live baits, such as slimy mackerel and yellowtail, are favoured. Trolling an array of skirted lures intended for blue marlin will often land this fish. It will respond to live baits cast across its path when cruising the surface.

MORWONG, BLUE
Nemadactylus douglasii

Also known as grey morwong, mowie.

Commonly found throughout the inshore coastal reef waters of southern Queensland, all of New South Wales and the eastern part of Victoria, the blue morwong is also an occasional catch in Tasmania's warmer northern waters. A fish that favours moderately deep reef areas and rubble bottom, morwong is a popular charter-boat fish for handline anglers bouncing baits off the bottom. While not highly rated as a sporting fish, despite its size and fight, it is a fair table fish.

It is best caught with baits of fish strip and peeled prawn, fished as close to the vertical edges of reefs as is practicable. As charter boats drift fish, such precision is not always achieved, but anglers in charge of their own craft should do a better job.

MULLET, SAND
Myxus elongatus

Also known as lano, sandie, tallegalane.

The sand mullet is widespread throughout New South Wales and South Australia, and occasionally in southern Western Australia. A solid-bodied streamlined fish, with a straight back, large eye and small, pointed snout, it also has a large black spot at the base of the pectoral fin. Its rows of well-developed teeth distinguish it from other members of the mullet family. Caught mostly from sand flat areas in estuaries or from beaches, sand mullet is excellent bait for larger fish, but also a good table fish in its own right.

Small baits of fish flesh, peeled prawn, marine worms or dough are best. These can be fished on the bottom, or unweighted, but more success will be enjoyed if you berley heavily with bread and fish these baits under a slim quill float. Hooks should be small.

FISH | LOCATION/DESCRIPTION | FISHING METHOD

MULLET, SEA
Mugil cephalus

Also known as bully mullet, hardgut mullet, poddy mullet, grey mullet.

The sea mullet is a much larger mullet than most, growing to an astonishing 8 kg or more, but is rarely seen above 2 kg. It is a temperate species of fish that spends part of its life in freshwater reaches of coastal rivers and lakes. It travels to sea as an adult and runs up the east coast in huge schools for annual spawning migrations. The eggs are carried southwards until the young have developed enough to enter bays and harbours. These bully mullet are a common catch in coastal rivers of New South Wales.

Float fishing in estuaries is best, or fishing baits on the bottom in either estuaries or surf. It forages in freshwater reaches of rivers over weed beds, but can be caught on small trout flies. It is not easy to tempt and is rarely taken by line in Western Australia.

MULLET, YELLOWEYE
Aldrichetta forsteri

Also known as pilch.

A similar fish to sand mullet, this species is distinguished by a rounder back, absence of the black spot near the pectoral fins and having a large, prominent yellow eye. It shares similar distribution to the sand mullet, but is found much further west. In Western Australia it is known as 'pilch', and is taken from both estuary and surf. The yelloweye mullet is predominant in Victoria where it is a major part of the surf angling catch. It is a good table fish, with firm white fillets ideal for cooking.

In the surf the paternoster rig is best using small pieces of fresh tuna, or better still, pippis, mussel or other shell baits. The yelloweye mullet responds well to berley and is found in gutters close to shore and in estuaries.

MULLOWAY
Argyrosomus hololepidotus

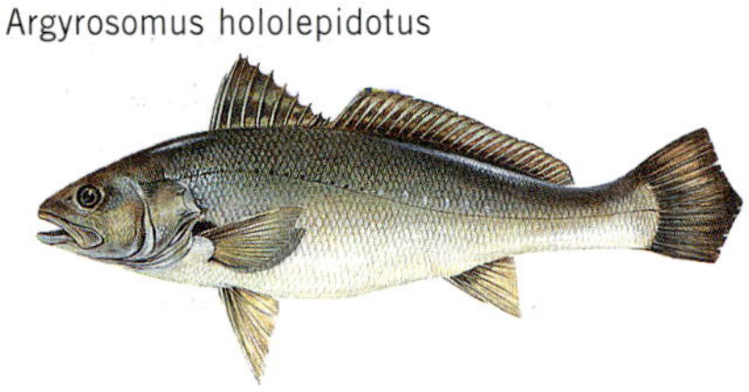

Also known as butterfish, jew, jewie, jewfish, river kingfish, soapie (juvenile).

Known by a host of confusing names, this large species is a predator of major southern estuarine river and lake systems, surf beaches and offshore reefs. Growing in excess of 50 kg, most adult mulloway are caught between 10 and 15 kg. The smaller juveniles, up to 4 kg, are known as 'soapies' because of their soft flesh. They will often follow squid and sometimes develop a fixation for these cephalopods. The mulloway is considered an important sportfish and respected for its table quality, particularly in South Australia.

Use strip baits in the surf; live baits of pike, yellowtail scad, slimy mackerel, or mullet, in estuaries or over reefs. Hooks should be 5/0 to 8/0, lines from 6 to 10 kg, but over reefs or from the rocks, 15 to 20-kg line may be more sensible. Mulloway will also take lures.

NANNYGAI
Centroberyx affinis

Also known as 'gai, goat (nanny-goat), nanny, redfish.

A deepwater species found in New South Wales, Victoria and Tasmania, the nannygai is a prime commercial fish occasionally caught by anglers fishing deep reefs for snapper or morwong. The nannygai is conspicuous by its colouring, which is deep pink to red with metallic-silvery tints. An acceptable to good table fish, growing over 2 kg but being common at about half that size, nannygai is also a prized live bait for yellowfin tuna. A similar species, the red snapper (*C. gerrardi*), is found in southern waters.

Strip baits of fish flesh, mounted on hooks from 1/0 to 4/0 are best, as this small fish has a large mouth. Rigs commonly are of the paternoster type, with a large sinker hung below several short dropper lines, each carrying its own hook and bait.

PERCH, ESTUARY
Macquaria colonorum

Also known as Australian perch, freshwater perch, perch.

Estuary perch is found in the brackish reaches of coastal fresh water from around Lismore in New South Wales, down the southern New South Wales and Victorian coast and around to the Murray mouth in South Australia. Some isolated populations also exist in northern Tasmania. Similar to bass (*M. novemaculata*) in appearance and habit, this fish will be found relating strongly to snags, creek mouths, reefs and rock-wall structures in mid to upper estuarine sections of coastal rivers.

The perch loves baits of live prawns, crickets, worms, tiny poddy mullet and crabs, but will occasionally take trolled, or cast, lures and flies. Its activity is quite tide-related, and tide changes and either dawn or dusk are prime fishing times.

FISH | LOCATION/DESCRIPTION | FISHING METHOD

PERCH, GOLDEN
Macquaria ambigua

Also known as callop, yellowbelly.

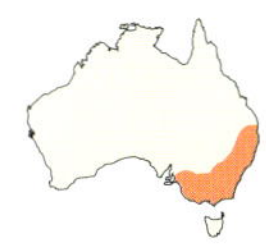

Naturally occurring throughout the Murray–Darling system in New South Wales, and southern Queensland, into Victoria and South Australia, the golden perch has also been artificially stocked in a number of alpine and coastal drainage impoundments. Stocky, deep-bodied fish, goldens commonly range from 1 kg to 3 kg in rivers and farm dams, and can reach 5 or 10 kg in major impoundments. It is a popular fish with anglers for its table quality.

Baits of crayfish, bardi grub and shrimp are effective, as are diving lures with the capability of diving to 3 to 5 m. Casting or trolling lures around suitable stands of drowned timber is effective in impoundments. Bait fishing is more effective in turbid (muddy) rivers.

PERCH, MACQUARIE
Macquaria australasica

Also known as mackas, Macquarie, mountain perch, silvereye, black bream.

The Macquarie perch is a shy, cryptic fish of freshwater streams. Competition from introduced species and the erection of weirs and dams restricting its spawning grounds have caused the reduction in numbers. The best places to catch a Macquarie perch are in Lake Dartmouth and the upper Mitta Mitta River in Victoria. While it does exist in some New South Wales rivers such as the Lachlan, Nepean and Shoalhaven, its threatened status means it is totally protected in that state.

A light paternoster rig with worm or mudeyes as bait is best. Also good is jigging small spoons around sunken timber, using tiny minnow lures or trout flies. The fish is usually found in between 5 to 10 m of water around trees in Lake Dartmouth.

PERCH, MOSES
Lutjanus russelli

Also known as Moses sea perch, Moses snapper, black-spot sea perch.

The Moses perch is a similar fish to fingermark and is often confused with that fish. It is probably the dominant species of the two in Western Australia. Found around inshore reefs and mangroves in tropical estuaries, it is more prevalent across the top of Australia. It is usually found in pairs or small groups, sometimes hiding under ledges or gutters. The Moses perch is reasonably small, averaging between 400 g and 1.5 kg, and is frequently considered a nuisance fish by amateur anglers hoping to catch larger fish.

Moses perch can be caught on lures and with both dead and live bait. Lures cast close to mangroves and meant for barramundi or mangrove jack can induce strikes from Moses perch.

PERCH, PEARL
Glaucosoma scapulare

Also known as eastern pearl perch, pearlie, nannygai.

This species frequents offshore deep water over rubble beds and low reef areas. It is found from central Queensland through northern New South Wales, to as far south as Newcastle. Those caught usually average around 1 to 2 kg. It has a deep, laterally compressed body, large eye and a black-skinned bony extension to the top of the gill cover. Beneath the thin black membrane, this bony plate is pearly – hence its common name. It is widely regarded as one of Australia's best table fish.

Only fresh fish strip baits are likely to be taken, or small squid. Hooks of 3/0 to 6/0 are suitable, with lines usually being 4 to 8 kg on rods and 15 to 20 kg for handlines.

PERCH, SILVER
Bidyanus bidyanus

Also known as bidyan, black bream, silvers.

The natural distribution of this fish is throughout the Murray–Darling Basin, but it has been translocated to impoundments throughout southern Queensland, much of New South Wales and into Victoria, with minor stockings in parts of South Australia. Once considered the carp of the inland, silver perch are now rare in rivers. Silver perch prefer timbered and weedy water with moderate depth and good clarity. The silver perch is an acceptable table fish, having firm, dry, white flesh.

Best baits are worms, grubs, crickets, grasshoppers, mudeyes and yabbies. Riverine dwellers seem to prefer small wobbling or spinning lures, but larger impoundment fish can fall for lures aimed at golden perch or Murray cod.

FISH | LOCATION/DESCRIPTION | FISHING METHOD

PIKE, LONG-FINNED
Dinolestes lewini

The long-finned pike grows in excess of 2 kg but is common at less than 1 kg. Often confused with the smaller seapike *(Sphyraena obtusata)*, it is best distinguished by the longer length of its anal fins and is a more stoutly bodied fish. Distributed throughout the mid to southern coastlines of Australia, it is variously described as a poor food fish, a bait-stealing pest, an entertaining light-tackle lure chaser, but most importantly, as a prime live bait for large yellowtail kingfish, mulloway and snapper.

Small whole fish such as whitebait, fish strips or lures, moved erratically in the manner of wounded bait fish is best. Its dagger-like teeth mean a short trace of heavier nylon is useful. Trolling from boats and also lure casting from rocks is common.

REDFIN
Perca fluviatilis

Also known as English perch, reddies, redfin perch.

The redfin, an introduced species, has a propensity to overbreed and produce what is called a 'stunt' fishery of voracious tiddlers. If kept in check by predators, the redfin can grow to a respectable size and is quite good food and fair sport too. Its track record of taking over to the detriment of native species means it should never be stocked or returned to the water once caught. This fish has now infiltrated most of the eastern states' fresh water, petering out in the warmer waters of Queensland.

Any freshwater bait, such as worms, crickets, mudeyes, yabbies or bardi grubs, is best. They will take almost any small lure or fly, particularly small metal fish-shaped lures, jigged in deep water over schools located by echo sounder.

SAILFISH
Istiophorus platypterus

Also known as sails.

Found throughout Queensland and the Top End, and south as far as Exmouth in Western Australia, the sailfish is most plentiful off the Pilbara coast in the west and in the east in Moreton Bay and throughout the island complexes of the Great Barrier Reef. This most elegant of the billfish family is a prized game fish, which has in recent years become a regular target for anglers in small boats. Fish in the 20 to 40-kg bracket will gather in schools around reefs or sandy tidal bays where currents aggregate bait fish.

A Queensland technique is to locate a pod of midwater bait on the sounder, jig up a supply on multihook baitjigs and either rig these for trolling, or present them as live baits on casting tackle to surface swimming sailfish.

SALMON, AUSTRALIAN
Arripis trutta

Also known as bay trout, blackback, cockie salmon, colonial salmon, kahawai, salmon trout, sambo.

Prized more as a fighting fish than table fare, the Australian salmon is no relation to the European salmon. It moves in schools, leaving sheltered estuary and inlet waters in its second or third year for beach, reef and ocean rock environments. The two species are the eastern salmon *(A. trutta)*, which is commonly 2 to 4 kg, and a western salmon *(A. truttaceus)*, which can easily top 8 kg. Adult salmon are silvery with an olive-grey back, while juvenile salmon have brown markings on their backs and sides.

Favourite baits are beach and bloodworms, pilchards, garfish, pippis and a variety of lures and saltwater flies. The bite of a salmon can be indecisive and its mouth is soft, so sharp hooks and a careful hand are needed to avoid it tearing free.

SAMSON FISH
Seriola hippos

Also known as sambos, samsons, sea kingfish.

The samson fish can vary considerably in shape and colour, causing much confusion. Often mistaken for a differently coloured yellowtail kingfish, the samson fish is generally stouter in build and uniformly bronze to grey-green across the back. Common in Western Australia it inhabits the coastal waters of Australia's east and west coasts. It is found over reefs and in water to 50 m in depth, and can top 40 kg. This large powerful game fish fights savagely when hooked; it is an excellent table fish, particularly when juvenile.

Bottom fish with large, live or strip baits of squid or fish, or cast, jig or troll lures. Lines can be from 6 to 8 kg but should more probably be 10 to 15, with 24-kg line. Samson fish respond to berley.

FISH	LOCATION/DESCRIPTION	FISHING METHOD

SERGEANT BAKER
Aulopus purpurissatus

Also known as sarge.

Plentiful on both deep and inshore coastal reefs throughout much of the lower two-thirds of the continent, the sergeant baker commonly sits perched tripod-like on its fins, on boulders, reef bottoms or in crevices. It can be caught from boats or ocean rocks, and in some exceptionally deep and clean harbours, such as Jervis Bay in New South Wales. This fish apparently takes its common name from a sergeant with the First Fleet, who reportedly first spotted it. They are a reasonable table fish.

Use fish baits, and allow the bait to settle where rock bottom turns to sand. Also put lures close to the bottom where this fish spends most of its time.

SHARK, BRONZE WHALER
Carcharinus brachyurus

Also known as cocktail shark, copper shark, whaler.

One of many 'whaler' sharks, the bronze whaler is perhaps the best known, by reputation if not personal encounter. A potentially dangerous shark to swimmers, it is inquisitive, aggressive and when excited, quite fearless. Found with related species almost all around Australia, it roams between offshore reefs, surf beaches, estuaries and bays, and along the ocean rocks. It can be targeted by land-based gamefishers from piers and rocks. It is happy to switch from being a hunter to a scavenger as the need arises.

Use large, live or dead, whole fish baits, or large slabs of cut bait, squid, fish heads, or whatever, suspended under a balloon for a float. Large forged game hooks and traces of 7 to 49-strand cable wire are usually employed.

SHARK, SCHOOL
Galeorhinus galeus

Also known as greyboy, grey shark, snapper shark, tope.

Together with the gummy shark *(Mustelus antarcticus)*, pencil shark *(Hypogaleus hyugaensis)* and whiskery shark *(Furgaleus macki)*, the school shark does not attack swimmers. Unlike the gummy shark, however, it has small sharp teeth that can inflict a painful bite to a careless angler's hands. It is found offshore and within enclosed waters from Brisbane, throughout New South Wales, Victoria and Tasmania, to South Australia and just north of Perth in Western Australia. It is a small species of around 1 m in length.

Most often trawled or long-lined by professionals, this shark will take fish-flesh baits in estuaries or over shallow reefs. It is a common catch along north-eastern Victorian beaches and estuaries.

SNAPPER
Pagrus auratus

Also known as cockney bream, red bream, reddies, schnapper, squire (juvenile).

The snapper is widely distributed from central Queensland, throughout New South Wales, Victoria and the two gulf regions of South Australia, into Western Australia as far north as Shark Bay. Inhabiting inshore to moderate-depth reefs, snapper is also found in major estuaries and bays. The juveniles inhabit bays and estuaries as nurseries, but the adult fish will enter large bays such as Port Phillip in Victoria. The biggest snapper are found in the gulf waters of South Australia and Shark Bay, Western Australia.

Fresh baits of whole or cut fish or squid, or live baits, such as yellowtail scad, slimy mackerel and garfish are best. Use needle sharp hooks from 2/0 to 6/0, line of 4 to 8 kg and a running sinker rig with a minimum of sinker weight. Berley helps.

SNOOK
Sphyraena novaehollandiae

Also known as pike, short-finned seapike.

This member of the pike family inhabits cool southern waters from around Port Stephens, New South Wales, southward around the coast to Island Point in Western Australia. Favouring shallow waters to 20 m with sand to weed bottoms, the snook preys upon small bait fish, juvenile squid and various crustaceans. It is often found in the same places over periods of weeks or even years, in season. Fish average under 1 kg, but can reach over 2 kg. It is a very popular angling species in South Australia.

Small fish strip baits or even lures are taken, it being best to 'jig' the offering. A trace of heavier monofilament can help. Use bluebait or whitebait presented on linked #1 to 2/0 hooks.

FISH	LOCATION/DESCRIPTION	FISHING METHOD

SWEEP
Scorpis aequipinnis

Also known as sea sweep.

Juvenile sweep inhabit the New South Wales coastal estuaries and close inshore on the rocks where it is regarded as a nuisance. Larger specimens are found over reefs. In Victoria and South Australia sweep can grow in excess of 2 kg. These fish are good table fare and on some parts of the coast highly sought after by anglers. Sweep seem to favour the tip of breaking water near the edge of bomboras and the like. Drifting in a boat close to the white water of breaking reefs can make serious sweep fishing a dangerous proposition.

Regular sweep anglers berley over shallow reefs. Small hooks, baited with peeled prawn, squid or fish flesh are drifted down on lightly weighted rigs.

SWEETLIP, GRASS
Lethrinus laticaudis

Also known as brown sweetlip, snapper bream, grass emperor.

The grass sweetlip is an attractive, powerful fish of exceptional table value. Its distribution ranges from temperate to tropical waters, favouring rocky or coral reefs according to latitudes, and the species is apt to follow warm coastal currents in summer from its usual tropical haunts as far south as central New South Wales. Common in sizes from 2 to 3 kg, sweetlip may surpass 6 kg, but such fish are rare these days as fishing pressure mounts on tropical coral reefs.

Present fresh bait close to, but just off, the bottom. Use leadhead jigs, tipped with baits of squid or fish strip, to get the bait down past the swarming lesser fry. This rig, however, must be 'worked' or jigged up and down.

SWEETLIP, RED-THROATED
Lethrinus miniatus

Also known as red-throated emperor, sweetlip, sweetlips emperor, tricky snapper.

The attractive, powerful, red-throated sweetlip is one of the most common of the Lethrinidae family of emperors and sweetlips. It ranges from temperate to tropical waters, favouring rocky or coral reefs according to latitudes and is apt to follow warm coastal currents south from its usual tropical haunts to central New South Wales. Common in sizes from 1 to 2 kg, sweetlip rarely surpass 4 kg. It provides excellent eating but it has been associated with ciguatera – in north-eastern regions only.

Fresh bait presented just off the bottom is best. Leadhead jigs tipped with squid or fish strip baits can be used to ensure the bait is not taken by other fish on the way down. If using this rig, it must be jigged up and down.

TAILOR
Pomatomus saltatrix

Also known as chopper (juvenile), pomba, skipjack.

A saltwater favourite found throughout New South Wales, southern Queensland and the Western Australian coast south of Shark Bay, the tailor seldom attains more than 4 kg. Fish of 9 or 10 kg create a sensation when caught. Tailor frequent surf beaches, rocky headlands, offshore islands and wash areas, and can often be seen tearing up the surface under a canopy of screeching sea birds. The Fraser Island tailor run is the best known in Australia.

Troll tidelines and the edges of ocean rock washes, and also cast with lures, or whole fish baits on ganged hook rigs, usually comprised of three, four or even five hooks from 2/0 to 5/0 in size.

TARWHINE
Rhabdosargus sarba

Also known as silver bream.

This member of the same family as bream and snapper has a smaller, slightly undershot mouth and a pattern of golden, wavy, horizontal lines on a silver background, which distinguish it from the similar looking yellowfin bream. Tarwhine is distributed throughout shallow reef, surfline and estuary environments, from southern Queensland, throughout New South Wales, Victoria, part of South Australia and southern Western Australia. Fish over 2 kg are occasionally caught, but half to 1 kg is the average size.

Baits of marine worms or prawns, nippers or shrimp are effective, particularly at coastal lake entrances during a prawn run. Tarwhine also inhabit the surf and will take baits of pippi. Hooks need to be slightly smaller than for an equivalent-sized bream.

FISH	LOCATION/DESCRIPTION	FISHING METHOD

TERAGLIN
Atractoscion aequidens

Also known as trag, teraglin-jew.

The southern teraglin is similar in appearance to the juvenile mulloway, but where the mulloway's tail is convex, that of the teraglin is concave, almost crescent shaped. It is commonly found from just south of Fraser Island in Queensland to Bermagui in New South Wales, and over reefy bottom in depths of something around 60 m. This species is related to the silver teraglin *(Otolithes ruber)* found in more tropical waters and sometimes called 'wiretooth' or 'yankee whiting'. Both species are top-rate table fish.

Use baits of fish strip mounted on two linked 5/0 hooks on a short trace below a running sinker. This rig is night-fished over suitable reef area – full moon is best. Handlines around 15 to 20 kg are necessary as a lost fish can put the school off the bite.

TREVALLY, GIANT
Caranx ignobilis

Also known as lowly trevally, turrum.

This fish is a strong opponent on any line class and is a slab of raw swimming power weighing in excess of 30 kg. A surface hit from one of these fish is awesome and the run is often unstoppable. The giant trevally is distributed throughout the tropics and is occasionally found in more southern waters on the east and west coasts during summer, a result of following the warm currents. It prefers rocky corners of reefs, partially submerged bomboras or the narrow tide-race passages between tropical islands and coral formations.

Baits of dead or live fish, or whole squid, or a variety of lures, especially surface poppers, are best. Troll or cast these and retrieve them quickly over or past preferred habitat. Giant trevally sometimes band up in packs and savage schools of smaller fish.

TREVALLY, SILVER
Pseudocaranx dentex

Also known as blurter, croaker, silver, skipjack trevally, skippy, white trevally.

By far the most common trevally in cooler southern waters, this fish is normally caught in sizes ranging from juveniles weighing half a kilogram in estuaries, to adults from 3 to 5 kg around reefs and open headlands. The silver trevally is distributed from southern Queensland through New South Wales and into Victoria, extending southward to Tasmania and westward through South Australia into Western Australia and as far north as North West Cape. It is renowned as an excellent table fish.

Use strip baits of fish or squid, whole peeled prawns or small chrome lures. The fish often school offshore over reefs in 5 to 40 m of water. Depending on local conditions, you can anchor or drift over them, drop baits or lures, and expect to capture fish up to 5 kg.

TROUT, BROOK
Salvelinus fontinalis

Also known as brookies, brook char.

Brook trout, actually a form of North American char, were first introduced in the 1870s, but have not acclimatised with the same success as browns and rainbows. Their distribution is patchy in most alpine regions of Australia, notably within Lake Jindabyne, and some streams within the New England area of New South Wales. One of the most important populations is present in Tasmania's Clarence Lagoon. Common sizes are between half a kilo and 2 kg.

Flies, bait or lures can be used. In lakes, they respond to fly fishing from the bank perhaps more readily than to other methods, and opinion is divided whether bait fishing or fly fishing is better in streams.

TROUT, BROWN
Salmo trutta

Also known as brownie, brown, German trout, Englishman.

The brown trout originated in Europe and has been successfully introduced into New South Wales and Victoria, with Tasmania having perhaps some of the best wild, brown trout fishing in the world. Nearly all alpine regions capable of sustaining trout have been stocked with browns, most notably Lake Eucumbene in New South Wales, which has a successful spawning run most winters into the Eucumbene River. Browns are commonly caught from half a kilo up to 2 kg, but can exceed 5 kg in some waters.

The best methods are wet or dry fly fishing, spinning with small-bladed lures, or using Glo-bugs and trailing nymph rigs on fish that gather in pre-spawning aggregations. Browns also readily take baits of worms, yabbies, mudeyes, live crickets and grasshoppers.

FISH	LOCATION/DESCRIPTION	FISHING METHOD

TROUT, RAINBOW
Oncorhynchus mykiss

Also known as bows, rainbows, sea-run trout, steelhead.

This flashy, attractively coloured fish needs artificial stocking to maintain numbers. This is due to the fact that it spawns after the brown trout and the results are less productive. Distributed widely throughout Tasmania, Victoria and alpine regions of New South Wales, the rainbow seems to prefer faster, rocky streams, and deeper, colder lakes. It is also found in certain areas of South Australia and Western Australia. This fish commonly attains 1 to 2 kg, but is capable of growing to 6 kg or more.

Best methods are bait fishing, trolling and spinning for most small to average fish, and fly fishing for the large specimens. Trolling very early in the morning is preferred once the warmer weather arrives.

TRUMPETER, BASTARD
Latridopsis forsteri

Also known as silver trumpeter.

This species is said to have earned its common name because it is difficult to catch. It is found in the cool marine environments of the southern states, inhabiting areas from deep offshore reefs to shallow rocky inshore waters. Its distribution is similar to the Tasmanian trumpeter *(Latris lineata)*, but it is often found in shallow waters while the Tasmanian is not. The bastard trumpeter is not a large fish, averaging 1 to 2 kg, whereas the Tasmanian can grow to well over 10 kg. Both are good table fish.

Not a common catch on hook and line, but best baits include crab, prawn and squid fished on or near the bottom. The Tasmanian trumpeter is often taken on bait or jigs fished on the bottom in deep water from 20 to 160 m.

TUNA, LONGTAIL
Thunnus tonggol

Also known as northern bluefin tuna, northern blue.

This species is common at 10 to 15 kg and is known to exceed 40 kg. It has a similar distribution to mackerel tuna. It is regularly taken each summer and autumn by rock anglers in New South Wales who use live bait with slimy mackerel, garfish or yellowtail scad. In Moreton Bay and various other more northerly Queensland locations, it may be spun for from boats by approaching surface feeding schools. Of only passable food value, northern blues are essentially a sportfish or a source of bait.

Best methods include lure casting or live baiting from either ocean rocks, large river breakwalls, or boats. Some anglers berleying and cubing for yellowfin tuna around Bermagui have taken exceptional specimens of this fish, to 35 kg or better, on live baits.

TUNA, MACKEREL
Euthynnus affinis

Also known as kawakawa, mack tuna, mack, oriental bonito.

The mackerel tuna is a robust, tapering fish found in northern New South Wales, Queensland, Northern Territory and the west coast of Western Australia. A fish of both open ocean and inshore waters, it often schools with Spanish and spotted mackerel. In spring, schools of this fish gather inshore to harass glass bait fish and may enter large bays. However, these incursions are not as common as they once were, due perhaps to natural cycles of abundance and scarcity, or overfishing.

Lure casting metal lures such as those that imitate small bait fish is successful from boats or ocean rocks. Also fishing small live fish under a bobby cork is useful when they are not evident. Trolling is not a preferred option.

TUNA, SOUTHERN BLUEFIN
Thunnus maccoyii

Also known as southern blue.

A more rotund and stocky tuna, the southern bluefin is one of the largest marine game fish in southern Australia. It was once a profitable and rich fishing resource of Australia's southern oceans. Overfishing and poor resource management led to the collapse of southern bluefin stocks. It is found in coastal offshore waters throughout southern Australia, from southern New South Wales to the coast of Western Australia. An acceptable barbecue fish, the main use of southern bluefin is for canned tuna.

Lures, live baits and strip baits are best. It is normally taken by trolling small feather jigs at a fairly fast troll speed. At times it is best to lure cast from a boat. Taking from shore is rare.

FISH | LOCATION/DESCRIPTION | FISHING METHOD

TUNA, STRIPED
Katsuwonis pelamis

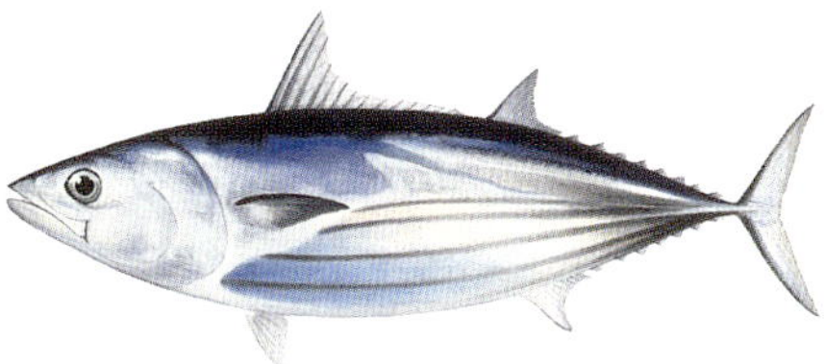

Also known as skipjack tuna, stripey.

Striped tuna are found usually in large schools all around Australia, particularly in coastal waters of southern Australia. Commonly trolled from the 100-m line off coastlines from Queensland through New South Wales to Tasmania, this species is a vital intermediate forage link in the food chain between small ocean species and the larger game fish. Although well regarded as a sportfish, it is of poor food value unless steamed commercially, and is most often killed for bait or berley.

Spinning or trolling with lures from a boat is best, but it can be taken from the shore with long casts by rock anglers. Lines can be down to 3 or 4 kg, but reels must have good drags and carry enough line to exhaust this determined and powerful little battler.

TUNA, YELLOWFIN
Thunnus albacares

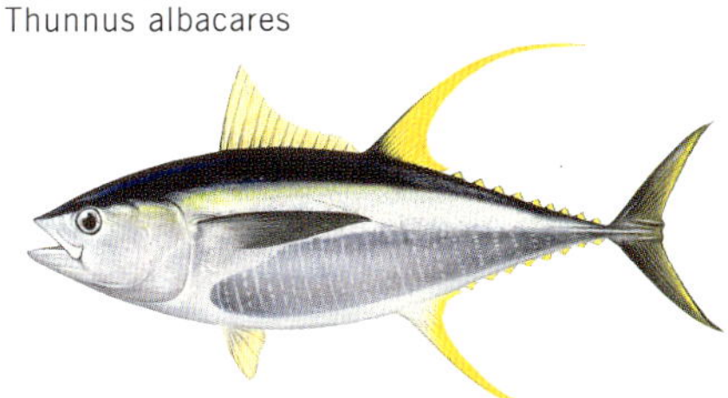

Also known as 'fin, Allison tuna.

An important commercial species, which in angling terms has come to mean 'a threatened resource', yellowfin tuna has been targeted more in the last twenty years than in the previous hundred, probably because of the aggravated decline of southern bluefin. Found all around Australia, yellowfin comes within reach of coastal anglers most often in late summer and early autumn, when fish can vary between 15 to 50 kg. Known to grow in excess of 100 kg, this is a magnificent food and sportfish.

Best methods include trolling lures or live fish, such as striped tuna and frigate mackerel, or skipping dead rigged garfish. Cubing – a technique of feeding baits and berley out into a current – practised from an anchored boat is very successful.

TUSKFISH, VENUS
Choerodon venustus

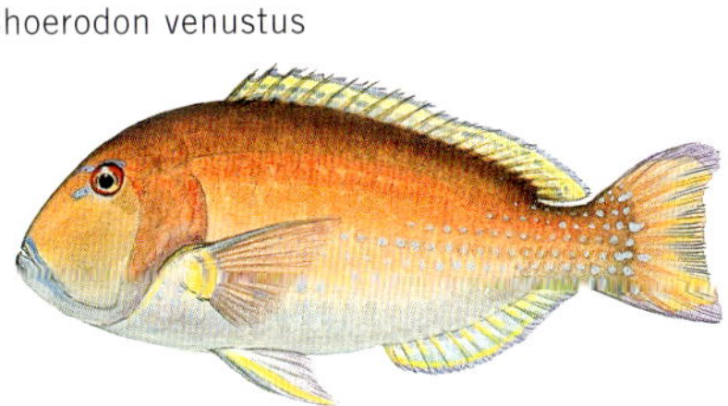

Also known as bluebone tuskfish, venus parrotfish.

The Venus tuskfish is a member of the wrasse family and not hard to recognise due to its bright colouring of purples, silver and pink. This fish is found along the east coast, north of Sydney, and across the top half of Australia. Its size varies from 2 to 5 kg, with larger specimens reaching 7 to 8 kg. Another species (*C. rubescens*), found in Western Australia between Coral Bay and Geographe Bay, grows to over 10 kg. Both species are superb fish to eat.

Baits of crab and cut fish are best, with double extra strong hooks and lines. Rod and reel anglers might get by with 15 to 25-kg line on the smaller fish, which average around 5 to 6 kg, but the big adults can require heavy handlines.

WAHOO
Acanthocybium solandri

Also known as Doctor Hoo, 'hoo.

A tropical species of fish, loosely related to the mackerels, wahoo is found around coral reef areas of northern New South Wales, Queensland and Exmouth in Western Australia. It strays as far south as Sydney and the Sir Joseph Young Banks off Nowra, when warm northerly currents create the sparkling clean, deep blue ocean water in which you would expect to see this fish. The wahoo's speed and willingness to put up a fight make it a game fish of international note. The average size is about 15 kg.

Rarely caught from shore, it is usually encountered when trolling lures from a boat. Lures must be rigged on wire. Be prepared in the event of an accidental strike. Wahoo earn the ire of many marlin anglers, being capable of severing a carefully rigged marlin bait.

WHITING, KING GEORGE
Sillaginodes punctata

Also known as black whiting, South Australian writing, spotted whiting.

The King George whiting, the largest and tastiest of the whiting family, is plentiful in Victoria, South Australia and southern Western Australia. It is only an occasional capture in New South Wales and Tasmania. It is native to the shallow grassy flats with sand and mud bottom, although some larger fish prefer scattered offshore reefs. It grows to an impressive 60 cm or more, which translates into weights in excess of 2 kg. An important commercial catch, it is an excellent table fish.

Baits of mussel, pippi, skinned squid and octopus tentacle, live marine worms and pink nippers are all used. Hooks need to be small, but this can mean up to #1 or 1/0 for the larger fish, and #6 to #4 for the average size. Line need only be 3 to 4 kg.

FISH	LOCATION/DESCRIPTION	FISHING METHOD
WHITING, SAND Sillago ciliata  *Also known as bluenose whiting, sandie, silver whiting, summer whiting.*	 Abundant on the east coast, the sand whiting is commonly caught by anglers. It is found along the east coast from Cape York, south along the New South Wales coast and into the East Gippsland–Lakes Entrance region of Victoria. Tasmania has a few on the eastern seaboard. Common from half to three quarters of a kilo, the sand whiting can grow in excess of 1 kg and has sweet tasting, firm flesh. It is a willing, straightforward biter on most marine worm and shellfish baits, and is fun to catch.	Small-gape long shanked hooks from #6 to #2 are usual in estuaries; bigger beach fish will take baits on a size #1 if hungry enough. Good baits are bloodworms, squirt worms, beachworms, garden worms, pippis, cockles, mussels and small soldier crabs.
WRASSE, CRIMSON-BANDED Pseudolabrus gymnogenis  *Also known as white spotted parrotfish.*	 This commonly encountered fish is one of several species known as parrotfish, so-called because of the formation of the front teeth, which form parrot-like shears. A related species, the rosy wrasse *(P. psittaculus)* is fairly common in reef areas of coastal Victoria and Tasmania. The white-spotted parrotfish commonly attains weights of 1 kg, but may be caught at several times that size. It is found on reefs from 2 m to 30 m in depth, and can dominate rock fishing captures. It is a fair table fish.	Use strips of fish flesh, presented near or on the bottom. It is best targeted in shallow water by dropping baits close to natural rock walls and using minimum weight to enable the bait to sink slowly.

COOKING YOUR CATCH

Hook to Cook

The preparation stage is never as enjoyable as the act of fishing itself. However, the correct preparation will go some way towards making the eating as enjoyable as the sport. From hook to cook (spear to smear), the three most important steps are killing, cleaning and storing. Every fish killed deserves to be killed quickly and humanely, cleaned efficiently, stored responsibly, cooked thoughtfully and eaten slowly.

Most people have probably never been lucky enough to eat a fish that is really fresh. A fresh fish is one that has been caught, landed and killed quickly and without stress. It has been bled and gutted in clean water using a clean knife. Straight after the cleaning it has been laid in a slurry of ice and salt water (equal parts of each) in an esky or similar and cooked before the ice melts.

This is truly an experience worth trying because there's nothing quite like it, and once you have experienced the flavour, no other fish will taste the same. Fresh fish has the most wonderful taste, smell and texture, and is also very nutritious. If your fish is not fresh, all these other attributes are affected.

FISH FLESH

In cooking, the flesh is the part of the fish in which we are obviously most interested. In some fish, such as john dory, the flesh accounts for only 25 per cent of the whole fish. However, the fish carcass should not be wasted. Heads and bones, for instance, can be used to make fish stocks and soups.

Fish flesh is easily digested and is generally delicate in texture. It should never be overcooked or dried out. The muscles are fragile and the muscle fibres break down quickly when heated. It is a nutritious food, rich in protein and vitamins, low in carbohydrates and cholesterol. Because the essences, or the aromatic juices, are so subtle in fish, short simple cooking techniques are best. Fish rarely improves from long cooking or the addition of strong flavours.

Fish species vary in flavour, and generally the whiter-fleshed fish have milder flavours, while the darker-fleshed fish are richer in taste and require more technique in preparation and cooking. Fish quality is better out of the spawning season, during which time both texture and taste are adversely affected. Know your fish and learn about its habits, both in the water and in the pan.

John dory fillets account for only 25 per cent of the whole fish

SCALING

Start at the tail

Scrape, using short strokes toward the head

KILLING YOUR FISH

There has been much research done in this area, and yet nobody is sure whether fish suffer pain as we do. However, it is known that fish do experience stress, which in turn releases lactic acid to the blood supply and consequently has a detrimental effect on texture and taste. Apart from the undesirable affect on table quality, the fish does not deserve to suffer, and it is to everyone's advantage to kill quickly. How best to do it? The Japanese use the phrase 'ike jima' to describe the quick death experienced by all tuna for the sashimi market. A pointed instrument is used to pith (to deliver a quick blow to) the brain. However, the angler needs to be aware that the brain is not in the same place in all species of fish, and it takes practice to get it right every time.

Generally, one quick blow to the top of the head with a blunt instrument (often referred to as a 'priest' in fishing parlance) will kill the fish outright. A piece of hardwood, an old hammer, a cut-down axe or mattock handle will suffice – something that fits comfortably in your hand and can be accurately struck to the top of the fish's head. If you can't bring yourself to do this, cut its throat and bleed it, or throw it back while it is still alive. If you plan to return the fish to the water, handle it as little as possible because the slime coating on the fish protects it from exposure to various diseases. If you want to catch fish for the sport rather than for the eating, a good practice is to use flattened or barbless hooks, so that returning the fish to the water is simply a matter of releasing the pressure on the hook.

To remove head, slide serrated knife in behind gill

Cut through bone and repeat on other side

(Remove head.) Slip point of filleting knife in vent

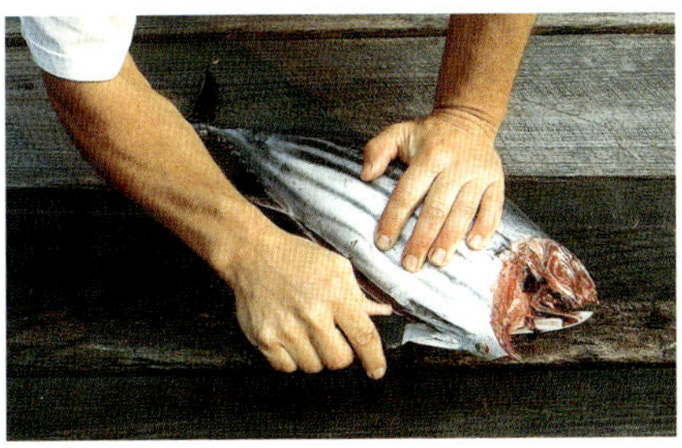

Push knife through to head end

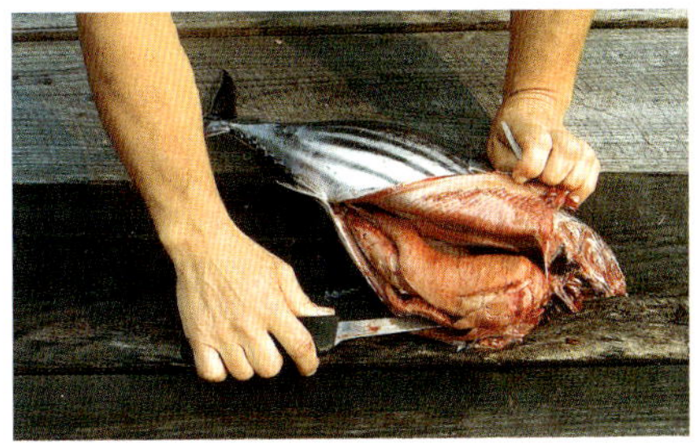

Open up to expose gut

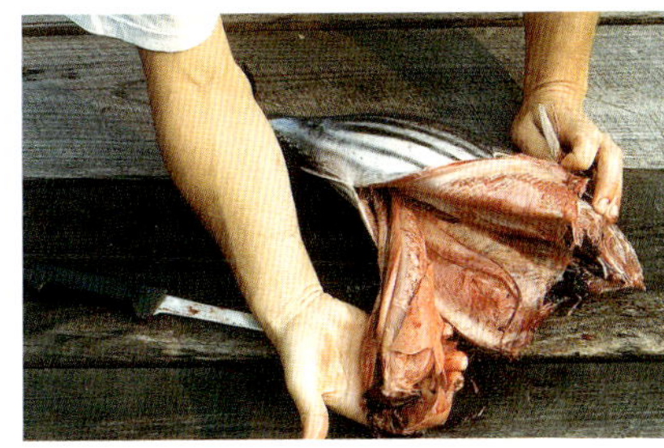

Grab what you can and remove

CLEANING YOUR FISH

All fish should be bled immediately after they have been killed, and then gutted and washed. Scaling and skinning the fish can be safely left until you are ready to prepare the fish for cooking. The skin and scales help extend the life of the flesh, and skin can be removed later in one swift action with a knife.

Bleeding To bleed most fish, cut the throat below the gills and bend the head back, which in turn breaks the spine. To remove the gut, lay the fish on its side, insert the point of the knife into the vent and slit the stomach open, turning the knife towards the centre of the gills. Using a knife, a spoon or your hand, forcefully pull out everything that is inside. Remove any blood vessels along the inside of the backbone and cut out any other red meat (in the case of white-fleshed fish), gills, etc. It is these red meats that speed up the decaying process if left in or on the fish. If you are at sea or upriver, throw the guts over the side. If you are onshore, keep the good bits of offal for bait and dispose of the rest thoughtfully; buried, they make great fertiliser for the garden.

Washing Once gutted, the flesh of the fish is exposed to attack by bacteria and it is very important to wash the fish thoroughly in clean water. If you are at sea or on a lake, up a river or on rocks, chances are that your water is clean. The worst place for fish cleaning is on or around slipways and loading ramps. These areas are alive with germs, spilt fuel, old bait, old fish guts, and other decomposing remains. Wash the insides of the fish out thoroughly and rinse the outside of the fish with clean water and leave the slime, scales and skin on the fish to help preserve the flesh.

If you leave cleaning and gutting your fish until returning to land, there is a chance that the gases emitted from the gut will begin to spoil and taint the flesh. It is for this reason that the cleaning and gutting is best done as soon as possible after killing your fish.

STORING YOUR FISH

Fish is best consumed as soon as possible after being caught. Fresh fish should never be put in any sort of a bag. Plastic, paper and even hessian speeds up the decaying process. Leave the scales and skin on and lay the fish flat in a slurry of ice and salt water (a ratio of 1:1). An ice slurry mixture is a quicker chilling medium than straight ice and therefore the best method of storing fish. If rigor mortis (stiffening) sets in, do not try to straighten the fish. This will only tear the flesh and speed up the decaying process. If the water is changed daily and the ice replaced, cleaned and gutted fish should keep in reasonable condition for up to 14 days. In a domestic refrigerator, with an average temperature of 4° C to 5° C, fish will keep fresh for 3 days. It will not be worth eating after 5 days.

If freezing your fish, they should be put into plastic bags prior to freezing. If storing in a domestic freezer (–18° C to –23° C), frozen fish should be eaten within 3 months. Temperatures ranging between –23° C and –30° C cause the water content in fish to change to ice crystals, rupturing the cells, and resulting in loss of flavour and nutrients.

Commercial freezers operate at temperatures below –30° C, which maintains flavour and nutrients. They can therefore provide a superior frozen product to the home-frozen fish. This is another reason to eat your fish fresh from the ocean. It follows that you should catch less fish and fish more often.

Remember, some fish species do not freeze well. Trevally, a delicious fish fresh, is almost inedible after freezing. Some fish that do freeze well are: those belonging to the Salmonidae family, such as trout, deepwater fish such as fingermark and orange roughy (sea perch); and firm, white-fleshed fish such as snapper.

It should also be noted that the warmer the climate, the quicker the degeneration of the fish flesh. In the tropical north of Australia it is mandatory to get your fish cleaned, gutted and onto ice within 5 to 15 minutes of capture. Further south, in the colder climates, the urgency is reduced somewhat, although as a general rule, 'the sooner the better'.

Fish can be stored in a slurry of ice and salt water

Cuts for Cooking

The size of the fish and the size of your cooking utensil will determine the method of preparing the fish. Generally, big fish can be cut into steaks and smaller fish are better suited to filleting. All fish can be cooked whole, but the size of the oven and pan will limit your options.

WHOLE FISH

Fish cooked whole are best if medium-sized, ranging up to about 3 kg. Whole fish are easy to cook, but they must be gutted and cleaned. The skin and scales can be retained during cooking; afterwards the skin will peel off, exposing the lovely moist flesh.

Leaving the head on during cooking is optional. The head does not improve the cooking. It is merely left on for appearance. Some people like the look of the whole fish; others savour the little pockets of flesh around the eyes. One thing to remember is that if the head is left on after killing, it will speed up the process of natural decomposition. If the head is removed, it is worth keeping to add to the other bones to make a wonderful fish stock, ideal for soups and sauces to complement fish dishes.

FISH STEAKS OR CUTLETS

Fish steaks or cutlets are best cut from larger fish of 3 to 10 kg in size. Use a knife with a serrated edge. Lay the fish on its side on a bench and start at the tail end. Cut off the tail by using a sawing action. Work your way along the fish, cutting steaks of about 30 mm thick. Cut thicker steaks at the tail end and thinner portions where the body gets larger. Steaks can be cooked by any of the suggested cooking methods on page 180. The fish most commonly cut into steaks include tuna, snapper, salmon and tailor.

FISH FILLETS

Smaller fish are better filleted. Some fillets like john dory and silver dory will keep their shape better if cooked with the skin on. However, a fish such as flathead is better with the skin removed. Fish such as bream, dory, whiting, trout and flathead are ideal for filleting. Bream is the easiest fish to fillet.

Filleting The fish must be gutted and cleaned before filleting, but scaling and skinning is easiest after the filleting process. Filleting of most fish can be done in the following way.

- Slip a very sharp knife in behind the gills (which are the side fins closest to the head).
- Cut through the bone. Turn the fish over and repeat this action on the other side. Remove the head.
- Cut flesh near the tail, down to the backbone. Lay the knife flat and slide it towards the head end, making sure the knife is working away from you.
- Turn the fish over and repeat the process.

Skinning fish fillets The majority of fish are easier to skin after filleting.

- Lay the fillet on a bench, skin side down.
- Grab the skin at the very tip of the tail end with your fingers or a pair of pliers and slip the knife in on the flesh.
- Cut down until you feel the skin.
- In one motion cut along the skin towards the wide end of the fillet.

Skinning whole fish There are some fish, such as leatherjacket, red morwong and flounder, that are easily skinned while still whole. If you are careful, you should end up with a fish with no skin and no torn flesh.

- With the point of a knife, cut the skin right around the perimeter of the body where it joins all fins, including a slit across the tail.
- Slip the knife in under the skin at the end of the tail and make a pocket big enough to get hold of the skin with either your fingers or a pair of pliers.
- Simply peel the skin gently back towards the head.

USEFUL TIP

Use a filleting knife to cut fish flesh and a serrated knife to saw through bone.

FILLETING A SMALL FISH

Slip knife in and down until stopped by bone

Change position and cut, keeping knife flat

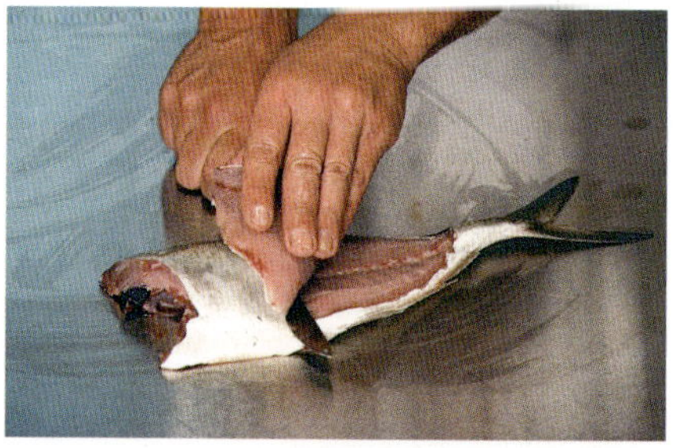

Continue to cut along the bone

SKINNING A SMALL FISH FILLET

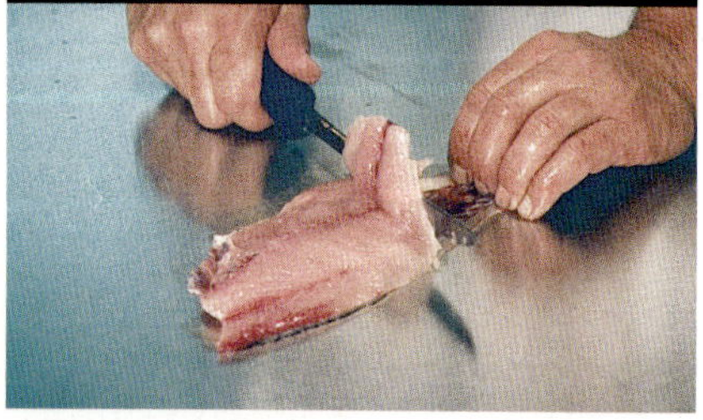

Place fillet skin side down

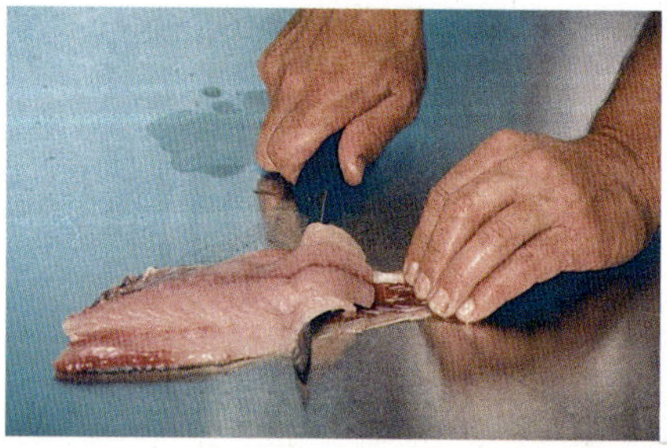

Cut through flesh to the skin

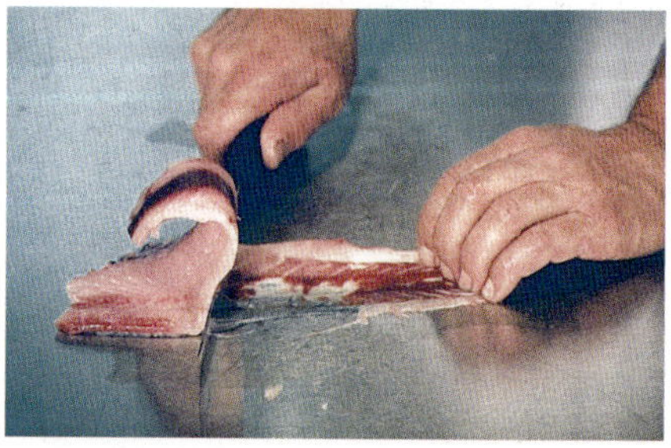

Flatten knife and slide along skin

FISH STEAKS

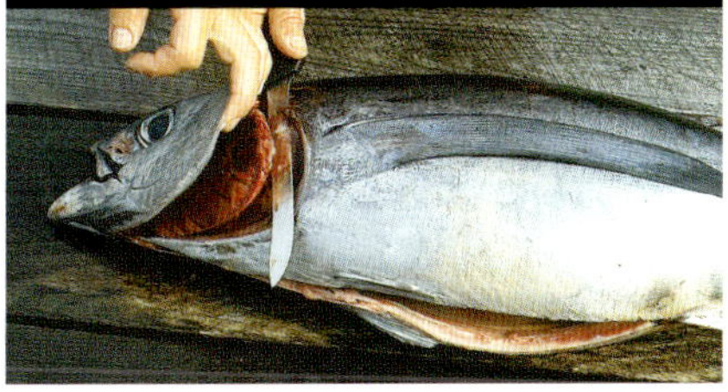

Remove gills

Remove any traces of red meat

Using serrated knife, start at tail

Saw through bone to other side

Cut steaks more thickly at tail end

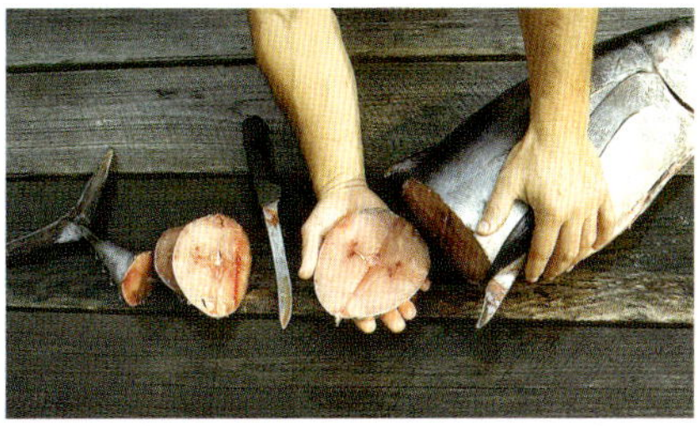

Cut steaks more thinly as body gets bigger

FILLETING A LARGE FISH

(Remove head.) Slip knife in and down to bone

Run knife along swiftly

Continue along bone

Slip fingers in to aid progress

Keep knife flat against backbone

Lift up fillet and finish cut

SKINNING A LARGE FISH FILLET

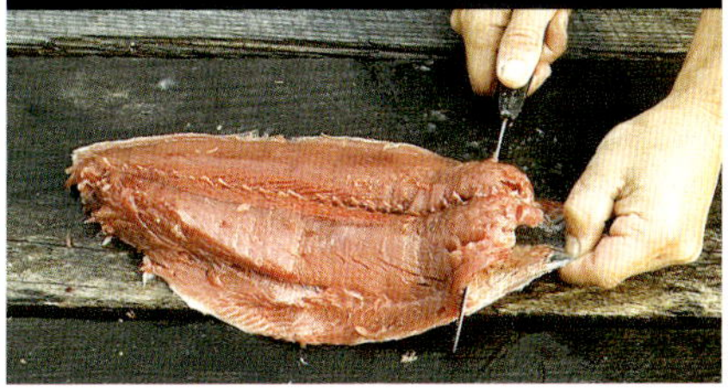

Fillet must be skin side down

Hold tail end and cut flesh to skin

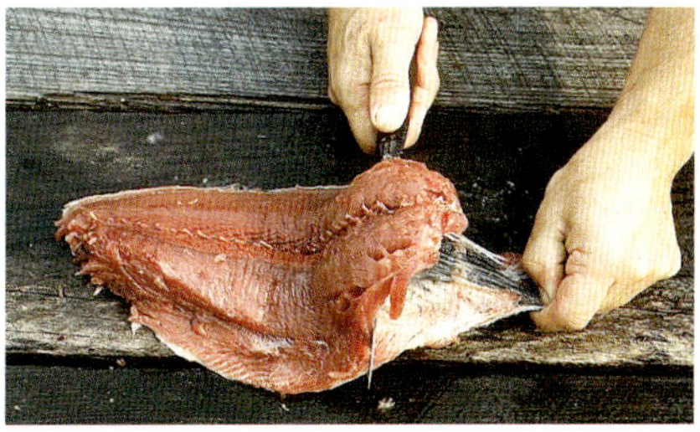

Run knife along flesh, keeping knife flat

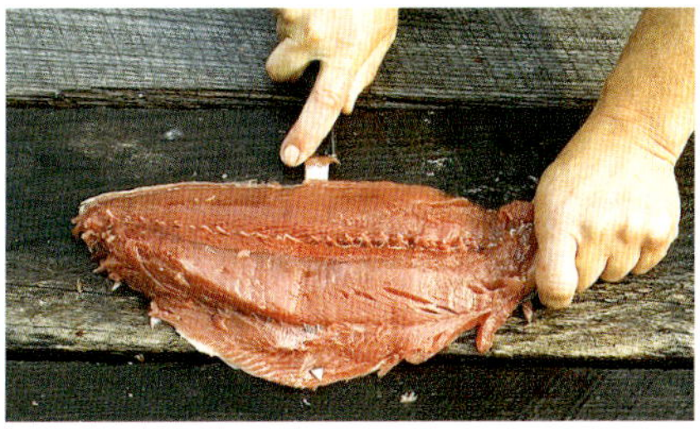

Keep firm grip on skin

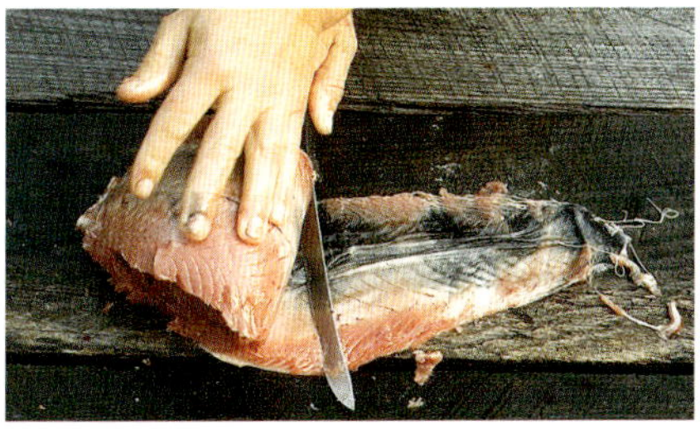

Fold back flesh

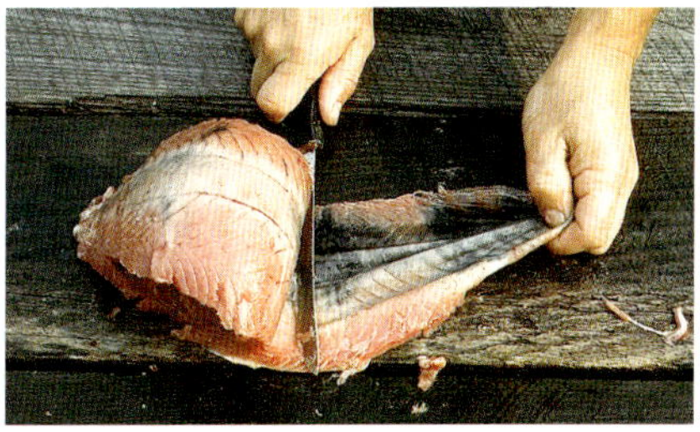

Pull skin against knife to finish off

Cooking Methods

Fish fall into several categories, each suiting particular cooking methods. The light white-fleshed fish, such as bream, flounder, whiting, john dory, mulloway and ling are all best suited to frying or gentle baking. The darker, oilier fish with a stronger flavour, including kingfish, mullet, tuna, gemfish and tailor, are better grilled, poached or braised.

Fresh fish flesh is reasonably translucent, becoming opaque or whitish when cooked. At this stage the flesh will flake along the muscle and release a clear juice. Once cooked the fish should be served immediately. Remember, the flesh will continue to cook a little when removed from the heat, so always serve fish firm and juicy, not firm and dry.

The following cooking methods and recipes are suggestions only. However, like the selection of a particular wine, anything goes. It is up to the individual palate. Why not experiment; you will discover that most fish can be cooked by any method. Just remember, it takes great chefs and even greater recipes to make something out of a second-rate fish. Really fresh fish only needs a simple recipe.

FRYING

Frying fish can be carried out by either of two methods: panfrying, also known as shallow frying; and deepfrying, which is the style used in fish and chip shops. Both frying techniques are suited to most fish species. However, in panfrying, the fish only needs a light dusting of flour before being placed gently into the hot cooking agent. In the case of deepfrying, the fish needs to be coated in batter or breadcrumbs to benefit from the oil saturation.

GRILLING

This is a method of cooking where the fish is either placed on a grill over a fire or placed under a griller. In the latter case, the heat source is above the food, and the heat is generally very severe. It is an ideal cooking method for people requiring a diet with no added fat. Alternatively, grilling can be done on a barbecue. Generally, the severe form of heat of the barbecue is ideal for all fish. Delicate-fleshed fish benefit from a little basting with butter or oil. Darker, fattier types of fish grill well without added fats, but a squeeze of lemon and some grated peppercorns will enhance the flavour.

When grilling fish, care must be taken not to overcook or dry out the fish and constant attention and basting with a little oil or butter will help. Leaving the skin on can also protect the flesh from drying out too quickly. The recipe on page 182 will work equally well with mullet, tailor, coral trout, estuary cod, threadfin salmon and pearl perch, to name but a few.

BAKING

This is one of the simplest ways to cook a whole fish, particularly a large specimen. The fish should be buttered on the outside, laid on a baking tray with a little liquid in the bottom, and moist baked.

POACHING

This is not a commonly used cooking method in Australia but it is suited to delicate-fleshed fish. In poaching, the cooking liquid is generally water, with an onion, bay-leaf and clove added. The water should only just simmer. Poaching is a great way to cook a whole fish, which can be served hot or cold. Served with a sauce, it is ideal for lunch.

STEAMING

This is the easiest method of cooking without the addition of any fats. The fish are laid out on a rack over water that must be boiled to maintain a constant temperature above 100° C. Bamboo steamers are ideal or a colander sitting over a saucepan of water will do. A tight-fitting lid is required or enough aluminium foil to seal in the steam. This method of cooking is quite quick, and a fillet takes only a few minutes.

BRAISING

Braising is a cooking method generally done in a large pot or casserole dish with a lid, or a baking tray, which is later covered with foil. The fish should be placed in the casserole, on a bed of vegetables, and barely covered with fish stock or wine, covered with a lid, and slowly simmered in the oven or over a very gentle heat on a stove, or on the hot coals of an open fire. In the oven, most fish will require slow cooking at 180° C for at least 1 hour. This method of cooking is best for fish that will improve with the addition of the subtle flavours of vegetables and wine.

The bed of vegetables is often referred to as a mirepoix, and comprises coarsely chopped vegetables and herbs cooked in butter. Shark and nannygai lend themselves to braised dishes with tomato and fennel. Large mulloway and eel (eel is becoming increasingly available live and chilled) can also be braised.

SMOKING

There are two forms of smoking: hot smoke and cold smoke. Recent research has shown that cold smoking can form perfect conditions for the incubation of harmful bacteria. Hot smoking, however, is safe, and the technique is described on page 184. This method was first employed to preserve fish, but the flavours imparted by the wood and smoke make fish cooked this way worth trying.

MARINATING

This is another form of preserving fish, but is also a way of imparting additional flavours to the flesh of what might normally be a fairly bland-tasting fish. You can use either a liquid marinade (a mixture of oil, acid – vinegar, wine or citrus juice – and spices), in which the fish will soak for several hours prior to cooking, or a dry marinade, made up of salts, sugar and spices. The dry marinade mix is sprinkled heavily over the fish flesh, which needs to be turned regularly over a period of 48 hours. The result will be a fish ready for eating, which has required no cooking. The Cajun style of marinating uses chilli, cumin and coriander, before cooking the fish over a very high heat. The 'blackened' result is attractive and particularly flavoursome.

STOCK, SOUP, PATTIES AND PIES

Good stock is made from good bones and fish offcuts, which must always be fresh. Pies and patties can be made from fresh uncooked fish pieces or from cooked leftovers. By adding herbs and spices, and eggs and flour, you can make crumbed patties or pastry-topped pies, all great hot or cold for picnics or that next fishing trip.

UNLESS OTHERWISE STATED, RECIPES SERVE 4.

Fried Fish

It is very important to control the temperature of the cooking agent when panfrying fish. It must be kept very hot but must not burn. For this reason oil is preferable to butter, but if care is taken, a little butter added to the oil just before cooking will provide the fish with that wonderful buttery flavour. Clarified butter (ghee) is also ideal. The oil should be almost smoking before adding the fish, which must be perfectly dry (wipe it with a paper towel). Dust the fish with flour and place it gently in the hot oil. Whole fish will take about 5 minutes on each side; fillets will take 2 or 3 minutes. Fish such as flathead, ling, whiting, barramundi, flounder, bream and leatherjacket can be cooked in this way.

PANFRIED TROUT WITH ALMONDS

1 CUP MILK
SALT
PEPPER
4 TROUT
4 TABLESPOONS FLOUR
3 TABLESPOONS OIL
150 G BUTTER
1 CUP FLAKED OR SLICED ALMONDS
1 TABLESPOON FRESHLY CHOPPED PARSLEY
2 LEMONS, CUT IN HALF TO SERVE

Panfried trout with almonds

Pour the milk into a shallow dish and season with salt and pepper. Dip each trout in the milk and then roll in the flour. Heat the oil in a pan and, when hot, add 50 g of butter. When the butter has melted, add the trout and cook until golden on each side. This will take about 5 minutes. Remove to serving plates. In a separate pan, heat the remaining butter. Add the almonds and carefully heat and stir until golden brown. Tip butter and almond mixture over the trout, add the chopped parsley and serve.

Panfried john dory

PANFRIED JOHN DORY

4 JOHN DORY FILLETS (SKIN ON)
50 G PLAIN FLOUR
60 G BUTTER, MELTED
OIL, FOR COOKING
PINCH OF PAPRIKA
SALT
WHITE PEPPERCORNS

Dry fillets with a paper towel and dust each one with flour. Holding the tip of the tail end, dip the floured fillet into the melted butter, making sure to coat both sides. Heat a little oil in a frying pan. When hot, gently lay fillets skin-side down in pan and sprinkle with paprika. Fry gently over a low heat until the flesh is just firm. This will take 2 to 3 minutes. Place a lid over the pan for the last minute to ensure even cooking. Season with a little salt and freshly ground white peppercorns.

Deepfried Fish

Deepfried fish should be coated with batter before cooking. It is important that the temperature of the oil should be kept constant at 180 °C to 190 °C. To check the temperature of the hot oil, simply drop a little batter into it. If the oil is hot enough, the batter will instantly come to the top of the oil and start bubbling and cooking. If the batter sinks, the oil is too cold. Some fish that are particularly suited to deepfrying include shark, snapper, blue grenadier, garfish, morwong, mulloway, red emperor, estuary cod, sweetlip, warehou and trevally.

BATTER FOR FISH

1 CUP WATER OR BEER
2 EGGS
1 TEASPOON OLIVE OIL
½ TEASPOON SALT
½ TEASPOON GROUND WHITE PEPPER
1 TABLESPOON CORNFLOUR
1 ½ CUPS PLAIN FLOUR

Beat the water and eggs and add the oil, salt and pepper. Gradually add the cornflour and plain flour, beating constantly as you do so. Let the batter sit for at least 1 hour before using. When ready, heat the oil to 180° C – 190° C, and check the temperature as discussed above. Dry your fish fillets completely, dust them with flour and then dip them into the batter. Wipe off any excess batter on the edge of the bowl. Gently and carefully slip the battered fish into the hot oil, taking care not to splash yourself. Cook for 5 to 10 minutes: 5 minutes for small fillets, 10 minutes for large, thicker fillets.

Grilled Fish

GRILLED TUNA

4 TUNA STEAKS
4 TABLESPOONS OLIVE OIL
1 LEMON, SLICED

Herb butter
150 G BUTTER, AT ROOM TEMPERATURE
1 TABLESPOON FRESHLY CHOPPED CHIVES
1 TABLESPOON FRESHLY CHOPPED PARSLEY
1 TABLESPOON WORCESTERSHIRE SAUCE
SALT
PEPPER

To make the herb butter, whisk the soft butter until creamy. Add all the other ingredients and mix until well blended. Roll like a sausage in foil and refrigerate until firm. When ready to use, slice off in 25-mm rounds and remove the foil. Brush the tuna with oil and place under a hot grill. Baste steaks with more oil as they begin to dry out. Turn over after 3 minutes, baste again and grill for 3 minutes more. Remove from the griller and place on a plate with a slice of herb butter. Serve with slices of lemon.

Grilled tuna

Baked Fish

Baking fish is a wonderful way of keeping a reasonably delicate piece of fish intact. Something as small and delicate as a whiting fillet can be dusted with flour, dipped in a bowl with a few tablespoons of melted butter, then laid on a tray and baked in an oven that has been preheated to 180° C. Bake for 5 minutes or until the flesh is firm to touch. Larger whole fish can be treated the same way (2 kg will take about 35 minutes, 3 kg about 45 minutes). Try baking albacore, whiting, dory, barramundi, trout, flounder, snapper, nannygai or Australian salmon.

FISH ON THE SPOT

All you need is a fire, a fish (cleaned) and some foil, and you do not really need the foil if you like that charcoal flavour.

Find a safe spot for lighting a fire. You need to establish a reasonable-sized log blaze in order to be left with good coals when the flames have died down. Wrap a whole fish in foil, place it gently in the coals and cover it with more coals. Allow it to cook until the flesh falls away from the bone when poked with a stick – 10 minutes or so should do it. If you are cooking without foil, simply put the whole fish on the coals and proceed in the same way.

For flavour variations when cooking the fish in foil, you can add butter, onion, garlic, lemon slices, tomato, bay-leaves, thyme and peppercorns – separately or in combinations, wrapped inside the foil. A few potatoes thrown into the coals and you will quite possibly end up with a fish dish that the great chefs dream about.

BAKED WHOLE FISH

1 WHOLE FISH, CLEANED
SALT
PEPPER
4 SHALLOTS, FINELY CHOPPED
1 CUP DRY WHITE WINE
2 TABLESPOONS FRESH BREADCRUMBS
2 TABLESPOONS FRESHLY CHOPPED PARSLEY
25 G BUTTER

Preheat the oven to 220° C. Make a few cuts across the fish flesh with a knife, place in an ovenproof dish and season with salt and pepper. Sprinkle the chopped shallots over the fish and add the wine. Sprinkle the breadcrumbs and parsley over the fish and dot with small pieces of butter. Bake for 25 to 30 minutes, with par-boiled vegetables.

FISH IN FOIL

4 SQUARES ALUMINIUM FOIL (LARGE ENOUGH
TO WRAP AROUND FISH)
2 TABLESPOONS OLIVE OIL
4 SMALL WHOLE FISH, CLEANED
3 CLOVES GARLIC, FINELY CHOPPED
3 MEDIUM-SIZED TOMATOES, DICED
1 TABLESPOON FINELY CHOPPED PARSLEY
SALT
PEPPER
4 BAY LEAVES

Preheat the oven to 180° C. Brush one side of the foil squares with some olive oil. Place one fish on each piece of foil. In a bowl, mix the garlic, tomato and parsley together and season with salt and pepper. Spoon an equal amount onto each fish. Place a bay leaf on each seasoning mound and dribble the remaining oil over the top. Wrap the foil so as to completely encase the fish and its seasonings. Place in the oven for 10 to 15 minutes or sit in the ashes of a fire for 5 to 10 minutes.

Baked fish in foil

RICE STUFFING FOR BAKED WHOLE FISH

½ CUP OLIVE OIL
1 ONION, FINELY CHOPPED
½ CUP WHITE WINE
2 TABLESPOONS FRESHLY CHOPPED PARSLEY
1 TABLESPOON TOMATO PASTE
SALT
PEPPER
1 CUP RICE
JUICE OF ½ LEMON

Tip half the oil into a pan and heat. Add the onion and sauté in the oil. Add the wine, parsley, tomato paste, salt and pepper to taste, and bring to the boil. Add the rice and cook until the liquid evaporates and the rice is partly cooked. Allow to cool a little, and then the add the lemon juice. The stuffing is now ready to put into the cavity of your fish before cooking it whole.

Steamed fish

Poached and Steamed

Poaching requires a constant and gentle simmering of liquid, which should only just cover the fish that is cooking in it. The poaching liquid should never boil and care must be taken in removing the fish after cooking as it will be very fragile. A bamboo skewer thrust through the tail and then in through the head can hold the fish in position while poaching and give a handle to remove it from the liquid after cooking. Trout, flathead, garfish, snapper, rosy Job-fish and john dory are ideal fish for poaching.

Steaming is the easiest method of cooking fish quickly without the addition of any fats. All that is needed is a little boiling water in the bottom of a saucepan, a colander or bamboo steamer sitting over the water and a tight-fitting lid or enough aluminium foil to seal in the steam. Fish suited to steaming include whiting, trout, golden perch, sweetlip, Westralian jewfish, red emperor and estuary cod.

STEAMED FISH WITH BABY VEGETABLES

4 X 100 G FISH FILLETS OR CUTLETS
300 ML FISH STOCK
150 ML CREAM
½ TEASPOON FRESHLY CHOPPED CHIVES
½ TEASPOON FRESHLY CHOPPED DILL
SELECTION OF BABY VEGETABLES

Quarter-fill a saucepan with water and bring to the boil. Place the fish fillets in a steamer or other perforated container, such as a colander, over the saucepan. Fit lid, or cover with foil, and steam for about 3 minutes for fillets, 4 to 5 minutes for cutlets and 5 minutes for a whole small fish.The fish will cook thoroughly without turning. When the fish is cooked the flesh should be firm to touch. Carefully remove from the steamer.

In a small saucepan bring the fish stock to the boil and cook the baby vegetables in the hot stock. This will take a few minutes. Remove the vegetables from the stock and keep warm. Continue to boil the stock for a few minutes to reduce slightly. Add the cream, chives and dill to the fish stock and stir. Place the fish on a plate, surround it with vegetables and spoon the sauce over the top.

Braised Fish

BRAISED LUDERICK

1 SMALL TO MEDIUM-SIZED FISH (½ – 2 KG)
1 LITRE WINE, WATER OR FISH STOCK (OR COMBINATION)

Mirepoix
1 TABLESPOON OLIVE OIL
1 CARROT, FINELY CHOPPED
1 STICK CELERY, FINELY SLICED
1 ONION, FINELY CHOPPED
1 BAY LEAF
2 SPRIGS THYME
2 SPRIGS PARSLEY

To make the mirepoix, heat the olive oil in a pan until smoking hot. Toss in all the ingredients, remove from the heat and stir until the sizzling stops. Spoon the cooked herbs and vegetables into the bottom of the dish being used to braise the fish.

Lay the fish on the bed of vegetables and add enough wine to almost cover the fish. Seal with a lid and simmer gently for 1 hour. The longer and slower the cooking, the more the vegetable flavours will enhance the flavour of the fish.

Smoked Fish

Hot smoked fish can have the most wonderful flavour, depending on the natural oils in the fish and the type of sawdust used during smoking. For seafood the best wood is apple. Next time you are near an apple orchard find out if you can buy some wood. Dry it out and run an electric planer over it. Gather the sawdust that results. You can experiment with different wood types until you find flavours you like. Sawdust or wood chips, in many flavours, can be obtained from your local tackle shop. Beware of some woods such as pine as they can give off undesirable chemicals that impart an unpleasant taste to the fish. In some cases the substances are even poisonous.

The following 'recipe' gives instructions on how to hot smoke a fish in a kitchen using the stove (gas or electric). Note that once fish is smoked it should still be kept refrigerated and treated as a perishable product. Some prized fish for smoking are Atlantic salmon, trevally, mullet, warehou, tailor, trout, snapper, tuna and eel.

2 BAKING TRAYS OF EQUAL SIZE
1 CAKE COOLING RACK
SAWDUST (OR WOOD CHIPS)
FISH
OIL FOR BASTING
HERBS AND SPICES (OPTIONAL)

Sprinkle a layer of sawdust over the bottom of a baking tray, sit the rack on the sawdust and lay the fish on the rack. Brush the fish with oil. Put the other baking tray upside down on top and place this little smoke house over a gentle flame or electric hotplate. To maintain a steady source of smoke, the heat needs to be 80° C to 90° C. The smoking process can take 30 to 60 minutes, depending on the size of the fish. Fish should feel firm to touch. Oil can be brushed on several times during the process to maintain moisture in a dry-fleshed fish. Herbs and spices in small quantities can be added to the smoking wood to impart flavour.

Braised luderick

SMOKED TROUT SALAD

SERVES 2
1 SMOKED TROUT
MIXED SALAD GREENS
½ RED CAPSICUM, SLICED
HANDFUL SNOWPEAS
FAVOURITE DRESSING

Smoked fish makes a wonderful addition to a salad. Simply place your choice of salad greens in a bowl with some sliced capsicum for colour and some snowpeas for crunch. Break the fish flesh into bite-sized pieces and add to the bowl. Toss with your favourite dressing.

Smoked trout salad

Marinated Fish

A marinade is a pickling liquid with aromatic flavours. Its use can tenderise the flesh and enhance the flavour by the addition of herbs, spices, fruits and wine. Fish suited to this process include Australian salmon, mackerel, mullet, trout, red emperor and tuna. Crustaceans such as rock lobster and bugs are also popular. The recipe below for gravlax is a Scandinavian speciality of raw salmon cured in a dill marinade.

Gravlax

GRAVLAX

1 TABLESPOON SEA SALT (OR OTHER SALT WITHOUT ADDED CHEMICALS)
3/4 TABLESPOON SUGAR
1/2 TEASPOON FRESHLY GROUND WHITE PEPPER
2 TABLESPOONS COARSELY CHOPPED FRESH DILL, WITH STEMS
500 G SALMON FILLET, WITH SKIN ON
1/2 TABLESPOON DILL SEED, COARSELY CHOPPED

Mix the salt, sugar and pepper and rub the fish flesh with the mixture. Place one salmon fillet flesh side up in a steel or plastic container and sprinkle dill over the top. Lay next fillet on top of the other and repeat. Place the fish in the refrigerator for two days. Turn at least twice a day and baste with juices that are formed. Cut salmon in very thin slices, down onto the skin, and serve with a coarse dark bread, like pumpernickel, and salad or pickled vegetables. An easy sauce of mustard-flavoured sour cream with mustard seeds is a good accompaniment.

Fish soup

Fish Stock and Soup

A good fish stock is a fairly simple thing to make, but the ingredients must be incredibly fresh and sweet to make a stock that will form the basis for your soups and sauces.

FISH STOCK

1.5 KG WHOLE FISH, CLEANED (GILLS AND GUTS REMOVED, BUT HEADS INTACT)
2.5 LITRES WATER
2 STICKS CELERY, SLICED
2 MEDIUM-SIZED ONIONS, SLICED
2 MEDIUM-SIZED CARROTS, SLICED
1 TEASPOON CRACKED PEPPERCORNS
1/2 BOTTLE DRY WHITE WINE

Bring all the ingredients to a rapid boil and remove any scum that appears on the surface. Boil for 15 minutes. Do not boil for longer than this because a bitterness will start to exude from the fish bones. Strain the stock, return the liquid to the pot and bring to a simmer.

When the reserved meat and bones have cooled enough to handle, separate the flesh from the bones and return the flesh to the liquid stock. Continue to simmer until the liquid has been reduced by half. Strain and refrigerate or freeze until required. Do not season with salt or pepper at this stage.

FISH SOUP

3 TABLESPOONS OLIVE OIL
2 CLOVES GARLIC, FINELY CHOPPED
1 LARGE ONION, FINELY CHOPPED
JUICE OF 1 LEMON
3 RIPE TOMATOES, PEELED AND CHOPPED
750 ML FISH STOCK (OR WATER)
1 KG ASSORTED FISH (INCLUDING SOME SHELLFISH
SUCH AS MUSSELS, PRAWNS, ETC.)
SALT
PEPPER

Heat the oil in a saucepan, toss in the garlic and onion and lightly sauté until clear, making sure not to brown. Add the lemon juice, tomato and water. Break the fish into bite-sized pieces and add to the saucepan. Do not add the shellfish at this stage. Simmer gently for 15 minutes.

Strain the liquid stock into a pot. Remove the flesh from the bones and skin and return it, with the vegetables, to the stock. Now add the shellfish, simmer for 5 minutes, season and serve. This soup is delicious with toasted bread that has been rubbed with a raw garlic clove prior to toasting.

Acknowledgements

Much of the material in this book originally appeared in *Fish Australia,* published by Penguin Books, 1995 and revised in 2002, where full acknowledgements for individual contributions appear.

The Publisher would also like to acknowledge the help of the following people in the production of this edition:

Editor
Steve Cooper

Specialist Consultants
Peter Horrobin (Inland fishing, North Coast and Sydney Harbour)
Jim Harnwell (Coastal fishing)
Geoff Wilson (Bait, tackle, knots and rigs)
Julian Pepperell (Fish species and common names)

Illustrations
iii RS; 5 JP; 13 RS; 28 & 29 Geoff Wilson; 66, 69 & 91 JP; 95 RS; 105, 132 & 142 JP; 158 (a) RS, (b–e) JP; 159 (a & b) RS, (c–e) JP; 160 (a & c) RS, (b, d & e) JP; 161 (a, b & d) JP, (c & e) RS; 162 (a) RS; (b–e) JP; 163 (a & c–e) RS, (b) JP; 164 (a–c) JP, (d & e) RS; 165 (a–c & e) JP, (d) RS; 166 (a, c & d) JP, (b & e) RS; 167 (a, b & d) JP, (c & e) RS; 168 (a, b & e) RS, (c & d) JP; 169 (a & c) JP, (b, c & e) RS; 170 (a & c–e) JP, (b) RS; 171 (a, d & e) JP, (b & c) RS; 172 (a & d) JP, (b, c & e) RS; 173 (a–c & e) RS, (d) JP; 174 (all) RS

Some fish illustrations by Roger Swainston previously published in *Sea Fishes of Southern Australia*, Roger Swainston and Barry Hutchins, Swainston Publishing, Perth, 1986. Other fish illustrations from Walter Stackpool, from the *Complete Illustrated Guide to Fish* by Jack Pollard (reprinted by permission of Bantam Books Australia © 1994). All rights reserved.

Photography
Cover: Brown trout in Kosciuszko National Park (Phillip Weigall)
Back cover: Fishing for Australian salmon (Paul Worsteling)
Title page: Catch of flathead and bream from Narooma inlet (Paul Worsteling)
ii Simon Griffiths; iii JM/APL; 1 BB/ANT Photo Library; 2 PL; 3 Gary Howard/MF; 4 (a) RB, (b) DM/R; 5 Owen Hughes/MF; 6 BB; 7 Bruce Peebles/MF; 8 Bob Walton/PL; 9 (a) RI, (b) DB; 10 RI; 11 Robert Gray/MF; 12 BB; 13 (a) WS, (b) BB; 14 TP; 15 & 16 WS; 17 (a) DR, (b) & 18 WS; 19 (all) SG; 20 (a) LT, (b) Alex Julius; 21 (all) & 22 (a) SG; 22 (b & c) BP, (d–g) & 23 (a) SG; 23 (b–e) BP; 24 (all) SG; 25 (swivels) BP, (traces) SG; 26 (jigs & skirted) BC, (flies, spinners & soft plastics) SG; 27 (Tassies, surfaces & flies) SG, (spoons & minnows) BC; 30 & 32 (all) SG; 34 & 35 WS; 36 Jack Atley; 37 Dennis Sarson/LT; 39 Peta Kowalski; 40 JB; 45 JB/APL; 47 (a) PH, (b) RSm; 48 (a) PH, (b) DM/R; 52 BC; 53 PH; 54 APL; 55 LN/MF; 56 KS/MF; 58 LN/MF; 59 AC; 60 LN/MF; 61 APL; 62 RSm; 63 JM/APL; 64 RB; 65 PH; 66 JC/APL; 67 JB/APL; 68 APL; 69 TD/MF; 70 KS; 71 Craig Lamotte/APL; 73 Fritz Prenzell/APL; 74 Don Skirrow; 77 PH; 78 JB/APL; 79 JC/APL; 82 & 84 KS; 86 PH; 87 JC/APL; 88 Noeline Kelly/MF; 89 JC/APL; 90 PH; 91 LM/APL; 92 RSm; 93 Douglass Baglin/APL; 94 PH; 95 Sean Davey; 96 LM/APL; 98 DM/R; 101 (a) APL, (b) JB/APL; 103 JM/APL; 106 AC; 107 DB; 108 Wayne Stead/APL; 109 JB/APL; 112 David Bassett/MF; 113 & 114 Australian Scenics; 115 JB/APL; 120 BC; 121 JC/APL; 122 & 127 BC; 129 (a) DR, (b) Rod Harrison; 130 PH; 131 BC; 132 PH; 133 TD/MF; 134 (a) BC, (b) PH; 135 TD/MF; 136 TP; 139 & 140 PH; 141, 143 & 144 BC; 145 PH; 146 & 147 BC; 148 & 149 Margot Seares; 151 & 153 Kaj Busch; 155 MF; 157 Shane Mensforth; 175–185 (all) SG

Abbreviations

AC	Andrew Chapman	LN	Lance Nelson
APL	Australian Picture Library	LT	Lochman Transparencies
BB	Bill Bachman		
BC	Bill Classon	MF	Masterfile
DB	David Buckley	PL	photolibrary.com
BP	Bruce Postle	RB	Ross Barnett
DR	David Roche	RI	Richard I'Anson
DM/R	Dale Mann/Retrospect	RS	Roger Swainston
JB	John Baker	RSm	Robin Smith
JC	John Carnemolla	SG	Simon Griffiths
JP	Jack Pollard	TD	Trevern Dawes
JM	Jonathan Marks	TP	Trevor Percival
KS	Ken Stepnell	WS	Warren Steptoe
LM	Leo Meier		

Explore Australia Publishing Pty Ltd
85 High Street
Prahran, Victoria 3181, Australia

10 9 8 7 6 5 4 3 2 1

The material in this book first appeared in *Fish Australia* published by Penguin Books in 1995 and revised in 2002.

ISBN 10 – 1 74117 222 5
ISBN 13 – 978 1 74117 222 5

Printed in China by SNP Leefung Printers Ltd

Publisher's Note: Every effort has been made to ensure that the information in this book is accurate at the time of going to press. The publisher welcomes information and suggestions for correction or improvement. Email explore@hardiegrant.com.au

Disclaimers: The publisher cannot accept responsibility for any errors or omissions. The representation on the maps of water features – depths, buoys, etc – is intended as a guide to fishing spots only. These maps should not be used as a navigational aid. The publisher recommends the Australian Admiralty Charts prepared by the Hydrographic Services of the Royal Australian Navy be used for navigational information. The representation on the maps of any road or track is not necessarily evidence of public right of way.